100

CHRISTIAN CLASSICS

A LITERARY BUCKET LIST FOR THE THOUGHTFUL CHRIST-FOLLOWER

ROBERT A. YOST

College&Clayton
Press

ATHENS, GEORGIA

College&Clayton
Press

ENDORSEMENTS

"Robert Yost has performed a valuable service for those who want to understand the riches so widely available to Christian readers today. If (like most of us) you can't read everything, this book is a great place to start prioritizing!"

William A. Brafford
Retired Assistant U.S. Attorney, Charlotte, NC
Co-chair, Synod Permanent Judicial Commission, ECO (A Covenant Order of Evangelical Presbyterians)

"When I first opened this book, I expected an annotated bibliography of 100 Christian books. Much to my surprise I found that and much more. It is a road map to the fundamentals of the Christian faith. Each chapter reviews one essential of the faith in such a way that challenges my understanding and provides an overview of pertinent historical writings. Collectively it guides the reader to some of the best books to grow one's biblical understanding and personal faith. I highly recommend this book not only to those new to the faith, but also seasoned veterans that could use a refresher course."

Phil Granger
Retired President, TMS Global mission organization
Former District Superintendent, United Methodist Church,
Kokomo, Indiana

"With so many quality Christian books and so little time, where should a serious reader begin? Thankfully, Yost has painstakingly distilled the substance of one hundred essential works into a readable format that whets one's appetite for diving more deeply into these classics. This is a book that you'll consult time and time again!"

Matthew Akers
Associate Dean of Doctoral Programs
Chairman of the Old Testament Department
Mid-America Baptist Theological Seminary

Dr. Robert Yost's newest book *100 Christian Classics*, is mostly what one would expect from a book with such a title. Chapter one is an essay in which he expounds on the joy of reading and is almost entirely experiential, as he writes about what he has gained from reading—and especially what he has gained from reading the Bible. Also, Dr. Yost strongly encourages his readers to allocate a portion of their time to daily Bible reading. When not reading the Bible, he goes on to recommend a hundred books to expand the Christian's understanding of the Holy Scriptures. Yost's list of his favorite one hundred classic works is essentially an annotated bibliography. I have no hesitation in recommending and endorsing Dr. Yost's *100 Christian Classics*, as it is an authoritative source that is soundly based on Scripture and Christian values.

Robert McInnes
Archives and Research Services Librarian
Westminster Theological Seminary

Christians are people of The Book, yes, but have also always been a people of books. Bob Yost cares too much for Christians to allow them to forget that, to be content with spiritual and intellectual superficiality, unaware of the deep wisdom bequeathed through books by many generations of Christians. Along with practical wisdom stemming from his own life of reading, he provides here introductions to authors and books that will – or should – motivate interest in important books.

Philip E. Thompson, Ph.D.
Professor of Systematic Theology and Church History
Kairos University/Sioux Falls Seminary

"If you feel a desire to grow in your Christian walk through reading good books that will help you then begin with this one. Dr. Yost has done a superb job in completing the difficult task of compiling all the great books that should go into a Christian's library. Take up and read!"

Jason Minter
Head Pastor
First Presbyterian Church of Haines City, FL.

This latest book by my friend Robert Yost is an excellent overview of best books every Christian should read—and while I agree wholeheartedly with his selections, I am put to shame by the realization that I have read only about half of these titles. Still, Robert has set before me the challenge of completing the task, and I think every reader of this book will be stimulated to do so. His insightful summaries of these books will be of great help for readers, as they whet the appetite to feast upon these great works of literature that will not only enrich the mind, but more importantly, will nourish the soul for a deeper knowledge of God.

Stephen O. Stout
Pastor, Shearer Presbyterian Church of Mooresville, NC
Adjunct professor, Charlotte Christian College & Theological Seminary and LAMP Charlotte

Contents

Brackets indicate combined entries

DEDICATION AND ACKNOWLEDGEMENTS

This book is dedicated to my companion, best friend, and wife for the past twenty-nine years, Tess. For the past eighteen months or so, she has been made to feel like a widow as I secluded myself in my study and wrote this book. She was long-suffering and basically cheerful throughout the entire process. I am so grateful to my dream girl for being so understanding.

Numerous individuals rendered assistance to me in the preparation and writing parts of this work and it is with deep gratitude that I make mention of each and every one. There were two long-time friends who were invaluable to me throughout the writing process: Sharon Williamson and Dennis LeRoy. Both of them read every section of the book and offered suggestions, helpful criticism, and encouragement. Without these two wonderful people, this book might never have been written. At least, it would have been a much poorer product. In 1988 when I began teaching English at the West Charlotte High School in Charlotte, NC, Sharon was my mentor and colleague. She helped me stay on the straight and narrow. Her grammatical insights were always spot on. Denny, a graduate of the Naval Academy in Annapolis, MD, has been a member of my Sunday school class and is a ruling elder at the First Presbyterian Church in Haines City, FL. His insights and suggested rewrites were extremely helpful. To Sharon and Denny: I love you both and am deeply grateful and indebted to you. Others read parts of my manuscript and offered comments. Dr. Andrea Coffey, a retired educator who lives in Wisconsin, my son Matthew, a Battalion Chief with the Charlotte Fire Department, and Jason Minter, my pastor at First Presbyterian Church.

A total of 388 books were suggested to me by the dozens of people I asked. The following pastors contributed lists of books: David Averill (UMC), Danny Bennett (UMC), Johnathon

Bush (Independent Baptist), Bill Cain (Baptist), Leslie Dibble (ECO), George Gasperson (Christ Community Church), Eric Grenier (ECO), Steven Harness (SBC), W. Anthony Lawson, Jr. (Jumping Run Church), Jason Minter (ECO), Jeff Winter (ECO, retired), Tom Osterhaus (PCA, retired), James O. Phillips, Jr. (North Hills Church), Jr., William N. Phillips (Baptist), Harry Reeder (PCA), Mackay Smith (AARP), Bruce Murray, (Independent Baptist), Steven Stinson (Redemption Church), Brian Walker, Steve Waterhouse (Westcliff Bible Church), Bob Burns (unknown), Kevin Kroiter (U.S. Alliance), John Terenyi (Baptist, retired), Stephen Johnson (unknown), Stephen Chapman (Clam River Chapel).

The following scholars and college/seminary professors contributed lists of books: Ryan Brandt (Grand Canyon University), Matthew Akers (Mid-American Baptist Theological Seminary), Bill Fleming (Charlotte Christian College & Theological Seminary), Donald Fortson (Reformed Theological Seminary, Charlotte, NC), Klaus Isslar (Talbot Theological Seminary, retired), Stephen Stout (PCA; Charlotte Christian College & Theological Seminary, Richard A. Taylor (Dallas Theological Seminary), Phillip Thompson (Sioux Falls Theological Seminary), Robert McInnes (Librarian, Westminster Theological Seminary), and Ray Ashmore (Charlotte Christian College & Theological Seminary).

The following missionaries or para-church workers contributed lists of books: Brad Beatty (Heart for Winter Haven), Dr. Steve Bailey (Encompass World Missions), Dr. F. Michael Grubbs (The Lyndon Center, Kansas City), Jack Kragt (Jack Kragt Academic Support Services), Dr. Christopher Matthews (Seminario Teologico De Sevilla), Bruce Sinclair (Presbyterian Church in America; Westminster Theological Seminary, Kampala, Uganda), Darrell DeHaven (Lighthouse Bible Studies Ministry).

The following from my adult Sunday school class at First Presbyterian Church in Haines City, FL: Judy Thompson, Dottie

Williamson, Dennis LeRoy, Donnie and Betsy Hussey, Roger Abbott, Lawrence Widener, Linda VanHook, and Rachel Minter and from my class at Westminster Presbyterian Church in Charlotte, NC my dear friend, William Brafford.

From the Winter Haven Horseshoe Club: Claudette Braswell, Scott Phillips

From my Monday morning Bible class at St. John's United Methodist Church in Winter Haven, FL: Sherman Shartzer, Bonnie Vorhees, Don Moore

From my neighborhood: Jeff and Eve Ridgeway, Myron Johnson

My State Farm Insurance agent and good friend: Dan Mann

To these and many others whose names have been inadvertently left out, I acknowledge my gratitude and indebtedness. I apologize profusely for anyone whose name has not been included.

FOREWORD

This book is about books, written by a lifetime book-lover and book-worm. Why trust Dr. Bob Yost? He's experienced at doing this kind of writing. After serving for decades in pastoral ministry and in Christian higher education as professor and dean, Bob recently published two books about books:

The Pastor's Library: An Annotated Bibliography of Biblical and Theological Resources for Ministry (2017) and

The Layperson's Library: Essential Bible Study Tools for the Man and Woman in the Pew (2020).

The first work mentioned above, Yost's *The Pastor's Library*, is an important resource and follow up to the legacy left behind by Dr. Cyril Barber (d. 2015) who was well-known for his valuable publication, *The Minister's Library*, Volumes 1 & 2 (1974, 1985). Earlier in my career, I had the privilege of knowing Cyril, from whom I gleaned much good counsel about books and library research. Now I have the privilege of knowing Bob Yost. With his wealth of background in books, he has gifted the body of Christ with another important resource, this time about Christian classics.

Such classics have touched many lives for many years in many ways. These books include such benefits as nurturing our relationship with and trust in God, growing in our maturity into Christlikeness, being encouraged and motivated in our own life journey through biographical accounts of great saints and imaginative Christian fiction, and gleaning insights from experienced and wise followers of Christ for daily Christian living and for loving and serving others. Dr. Yost believes these works can offer timeless wisdom for us today as well, so has taken the time and effort to provide notes from his readings of these 100 Christian classics.

This book offers a wide range of classics. Along with traditional classics—for example, Augustine's *Confessions*, and Bunyan's *Pilgrim's Progress*—Bob includes books on subjects such as apologetics, evangelism and missions; on Biblical studies and doctrine; on Christian living, prayer, and daily devotions, and also on Christian fiction and poetry. Each chapter includes an introduction to the importance of each subject. Then, for each book, Bob shares some historical background about the author and context in which the book was written, about key points of the book, and about how the book can be helpful for us. To help us appreciate a bit of the spirit and style of a book, he usually includes a sample of quotes and insightful gems. Bob's personal notes about how a book impacted his own life journey appear now and then.

Of course there are more than 100 Christian classics, so Bob includes an appendix with a second list of 100 to consider. We have a rich heritage of Christian books throughout church history. As you look over each entry, you'll likely be reminded of old friends, and become acquainted with new-to-you books. There's a wide-ranging assortment of classics from which you can develop your own reading plan. Enjoy the feast!

Klaus Issler
Emeritus Professor of Educational Studies and Theology
Talbot School of Theology, Biola University
Theological Consultant, EpikaStudios.com

PREFACE

The best way to describe the story of how this book came to be is that it constantly evolved from what it was originally intended to be. As best as I can recollect, the idea for this book germinated on the train from the Dallas Airport to Fort Worth in November, 2021. We were visiting Fort Worth for the annual meeting of the Evangelical Theological Society and as we rode on the slow-moving train, somehow the concept of a book about 100 books that every Christian should read in a lifetime popped into my head. The idea of 100 books was certainly not original with me. I had read Petersen and Petersen's interesting book, *100 Books that Changed the Christian Century*, and I thought that something similar would be a worthy project.

That is what it was at first—a project. I originally intended it to be a little side project for me to work on in my spare time while I researched and wrote on my main area of scholarly interest—Hebrew wisdom literature, particularly on the Book of Proverbs. I had a main project that I had already begun work on, that of wisdom, work, and wealth in Proverbs and how the teaching of that book refutes the popular prosperity gospel. However, my intentions and reality soon collided and my little side project took on a life of its own. It wasn't long before I began re-reading such classics as Augustine's *Confessions* and reading for the first-time numerous books that somehow escaped my notice such as Martin Luther's *Bondage of the Will*. I was soon up to my ears in reading and writing. My little side project would totally consume eighteen months of my life. The result is this book. It is a labor of much love. I hope you enjoy reading it as much as I did researching and writing it.

Robert A, Yost, Ph.D., D.Min.
June 1, 2023

CHAPTER I:
INTRODUCTION

The history of writing in general and of books in particular is a fascinating one that takes us back several thousands of years well before the time of Christ and even before the ancient Greeks. Before that, the transmission of knowledge and culture was accomplished orally or pictorially. The two cradles of writing were the Nile and Mesopotamia. The first writing as we know it was not done on stone, paper, animal skins, or papyrus, but on clay tablets. In fact, the oldest extant manuscript we have is a red clay tablet dating to around 3100 B.C. from the region now known as Iraq. It was written by a man named Kushim, an accountant, who apparently lived in the Sumerian city of Uruk and issued this receipt for a barley delivery in Mesopotamia. That type of writing, called cuneiform, a system of using wedge-shaped instruments to make marks in wet clay, was developed by the ancient Sumerians in Mesopotamia around 3,500 B.C. It became the most widespread and commonly-used system of writing in the ancient Middle East. It made it possible for ancient records to be portable. The Epic of Gilgamesh, to the chagrin of high school students everywhere, was preserved in this form on clay tablets.

The Sumerians, a non-Semitic people, would influence the Semitic peoples as their incursion would result in their adaptation of this system. Later literary innovations such as Hebrew were used as early as the time of Moses (1,500 B.C.) and were written with ink on scrolls, but its use was limited to the ancient Israelites. It was the people in Palestine who developed the first alphabet. Much later the ancient Greeks developed an alphabet around 400 B.C. which replaced pictographs as a form of writing visual communication.

In Egypt, possibly because they were influenced by Mesopotamia, writing began before 3,000 B.C. They used a pictographic form of writing called hieroglyphics. It was used mainly for religious purposes. This was a very cumbersome form of writing that never evolved into an alphabetic system

The meaning of hieroglyphics was a mystery until 1799 when one of Napoleon's soldiers discovered what is now known as the Rosetta Stone. It was an irregularly shaped stone of black granite 3 feet 9 inches long and 2 feet 4.5 inches wide. On it was an inscription composed by the priests of Memphis around 205-180 B.C. to commemorate the accession of Ptolemy V to the throne. It was written in three languages: hieroglyphic, demotic, and Greek. With the French surrender of Egypt in 1801, the Rosetta Stone passed into British hands where it was translated and proved to be the key to translating Egyptian hieroglyphics.

The earliest books, on whatever surface they were written, could only be reproduced by laborious copying of the manuscript. Hebrew manuscripts of Old Testament books, as well as later Greek manuscripts of the New Testament, were inscribed by a variety of materials including stylus, pen and ink, and chisel. The copying process, known as transmission, was a tedious and meticulous process that was done with a great reverence for the text.

The scribes had a specific set of rules to follow in the copying process and were so thorough they counted all the paragraphs, words, and even letters to ensure that it had been done perfectly. Please keep in mind that this was many centuries before the invention of the copy machine and the ubiquitous Kinko's (or FedEx) on seemingly every corner.

It was only after the invention of the moveable-type printing press and its introduction to Europe by a German named Johannes Gutenberg in the fifteenth century A.D. that books were able to be mass produced and available to the common person. Up until that time, books were all hand copied, extremely expensive, and available only to the very wealthy. In addition to making books and other written materials available to many, the printing press also helped to standardize language and increase literacy. All who love books are indebted to this invention which allows book lovers such as myself to own books cheaply and easily. This invention has truly revolutionized the world and all of us are the better for it.

WHY THIS BOOK?

This a book about books. The subject of books is something that has long been very near and dear to my heart ever since my childhood. I have been an unabashed bibliophile almost as long as I was able to read. As a youth I devoured the adventure and mystery stories of writers such as Robert Louis Stevenson, Daniel Defoe, Edgar Allan Poe, and Mark Twain. Through them I was able to explore worlds that were foreign to me. I also loved to read the stories of the great explorers such as Marco Polo, Magellan, and Christopher Columbus and how they discovered new lands and opened up the world to those who would follow. I read just about every biography I could put my hands on, particularly the biographies of explorers, Old West legends, and Major League Baseball stars. I became a world traveler without ever leaving my bedroom. In fact, my mother soon learned that it was futile to confine me to my room as punishment because I was able to escape into my own little world of books. It was like Brer Rabbit being cast into the briar patch in the familiar Uncle Remus story.

Alas, I lived in a foreign country during my formative years. It was a place called the past. Where I live now is almost unrecognizable from the residence of my youth. Reading has seemingly become less important to many people than it was in the past. Which leads to my question., why this book?

There was a time in the not-too-distant past when reading was perhaps the most important method for gaining information. It was also a major pastime for recreational purposes. For many people, it remains front and center in both areas. As Terry W. Glaspey, a confessed "biblioholic," writes in his delightful volume, *Great Books of the Christian Tradition*, "For me, reading is one of the most enjoyable ways to pass a rainy afternoon. I crave the knowledge and insights that truly great books bring into my life, and I can spend transported hours scouring book stores for volumes which 'I simply must have.' I love the smell and feel of well-loved books and the look of a bookcase full of books waiting to be taken down and read" (Glaspey, 9). There is also a well-known quotation attributed to Erasmus, "When I have little money, I buy books; and if I have any left, I buy food and clothes." Amen to that.

ARE BOOKS BECOMING OBSOLETE?

Had anyone asked me that question when I was a child or a half century ago when I was a university student, I would have thought him mad. It is true that the television had come into its own by the 1950s and 1960s rendering many who watched to excess "couch potatoes" or semi-gelatinous, inert globs rendered into semiconsciousness by watching endless reruns of *I Love Lucy* and *The Dick Van Dyke Show*, not to mention such mindless drivel as *The Beverly Hillbillies* and *Gilligan's Island*. How I survived my childhood with a functioning brain is anybody's guess. On the other hand, I grew up with the printed word and in addition to the many mindless hours I was parked in front of the television set in our home, I voraciously read books, magazines, and newspapers ever since my childhood.

Is reading becoming obsolete? When I was much younger, many people listed reading as a hobby or special area of interest. Is has been said that reading as a hobby is fast giving way to video games, listening to podcasts and iPods, and, of course, the ubiquitous television. The four television channels of my youth have given way to hundreds upon hundreds of channels so that people can watch twenty-four hours a day if so desired. With the advent of video technology and the long reach of computers and the Internet, it sometimes feels as if the days of print media such as books, magazines, and newspapers are about over. Anyone who remembers reading a newspaper a few decades ago and compares it to the ones today can see a huge difference both in terms of size and quality. From my perspective, I was crushed when my beloved weekly *Sports Illustrated* went to every other week and then to monthly. I could see the handwriting on the wall. From an anecdotal perspective, it appears that the number of readers of books becomes fewer and fewer with each passing year. Even though the number of readers appears to be decreasing, the number of books being published each year is increasing. Driving this is the self-publishing phenomena. But, still, by almost any estimate, the number of books being published each year is increasing. Furthermore, average book sales are falling, the book marketplace has become stagnant over the past two decades, and the publishing industry has changed dramatically and not for the better. This does not portend well for the future of printed books. In fact, some pundits have already pronounced funeral rites for printed books. One thing I do know about the future of books, whether in print form or Kindle, is that Christians will always be readers, a topic that will be explored in the next section.

WHY CHRISTIANS SHOULD BE READERS

How do Christians grow in the understanding and knowledge of God and our savior Jesus Christ? According to an eminent pastor and biblical scholar, the late John R. W. Stott in his classic work, *Basic Christianity*, "I would urge you not only to study the Bible but to read good Christian books. To neglect to grow in your understanding is to court disaster" (Stott, 137). According to one of my favorite childhood writers and the author of some of my favorite earliest reading treasures, Theodore Geisel (aka Dr. Seuss), "The more you read, the more things you will know. The more you learn, the more places you'll go." According to Gene Edward Veith, Jr., in his wonderful book *Reading Between the Lines*, "The habit of reading is absolutely critical today, particularly for Christians. As television turns our society into an increasingly image-dominated culture, Christians must continue to be people of the Word. When we read, we cultivate a sustained attention span, an active imagination, a capacity for logical analysis and critical thinking, and a rich inner life" (Veith, xiv).

Please keep in mind that we Christ-followers are people of "the Book," the Bible. When God gave us his revelation, he did so in the form of a book. The Hebrew people have revered the Masoretic text of the Old Testament for millennia and not only read and studied it, but committed many parts to memory. Christians, likewise, have done the same for the twenty-seven books of the New Testament, as well as the thirty-nine books of the Old. Christian children learn the stories of the Bible from a young age in Sunday school. They learn about Moses and the parting of the Red Sea, the falling of the walls of Jericho, and the story of Zacchaeus coming down from the sycamore tree to meet Jesus. These memorable stories and more are recorded in the books of Scripture.

But there is much more to Christian reading than the Bible. There is a treasure trove of great reading at the fingertips of many Christians that is underutilized. According to Veith, "Some Christians do not realize that they are heirs to a great literary tradition. From the beginnings of the church to the present day, Christian writers have explored their faith in books, and in doing so have nourished their fellow believers. Some of the best writers who have ever lived have been Christians, working explicitly out of the Christian worldview. To their loss, many contemporary Christians are unaware of Christian writers—both from past generations and those writing today" (Veith, xiv).

It is a well-established fact that many well-known Christians are influenced in their earthly pilgrimage by great books. The father of the Reformation, Martin Luther, was a young monk struggling with the concepts of sin, grace, forgiveness, and justification by faith. The writings of Augustine, in particular his *Confessions*, helped Luther gain clarity in his theological understanding. The slave trader, John Newton, was transformed through his reading of the timeless classic *Of the Imitation of Christ* by Thomas à Kempis. He went on to become an influential Anglican clergyman and hymn writer who gave us many wonderful hymns, including *Amazing Grace,* and *How Sweet the Sound.* Closer to our own time period, C. S. Lewis was greatly assisted in his journey from atheism to faith in Jesus Christ by his reading of G. K. Chesterton's *The Everlasting Man.* Finally, Charles Colson, the so-called "hatchet-man" of the Nixon White House, cites his eternal debt to the classic by C. S. Lewis, *Mere Christianity.* The incisive argumentation by Lewis was a deciding factor in moving Colson from atheism to faith in Christ. As Glaspey reminds us, "As believers we stand on the shoulders of the likes of Augustine, Aquinas, Luther, Calvin, and Jonathan Edwards. We can build on their insights and use their perspectives as a vantage point to critique our own time" (Glaspey, 19). Veith echoes that thought. He writes, "Some Christians do not realize that they are heirs to a great literary tradition. From the beginnings of the church to the present day, Christian writers have explored their faith in books, and in doing so have nourished their fellow believers. Some of the best writers who have ever lived have been Christians, working explicitly out of the Christian worldview. To their loss, many contemporary Christians are unaware of Christian writers—both those from past generations and those writing today" (Veith, xiv). One of the aims of this book is to remedy Veith's lament.

There are those who argue that we do not need to listen to the voices of Christians from the past, that we only need to hear God's voice today. Wiersbe laments in *Walking with the Giants,* "Is it any wonder that shallowness and pettiness characterize our ministries when we drink at the broken cisterns of the best-seller list and ignore the fresh waters that spring from the books of the ages" (Wiersbe, 233)? This book will give the reader no excuse for not exploring the literary treasures of our past and present.

A WORD OF EXPLANATION ABOUT THE TITLE

The title of this book has undergone countless revisions over the roughly nineteen months it took me to write it. It began with a tentative title of *100 Books that Every Christian Should Read in a Lifetime* and has been changed or modified at least a dozen time. I have often felt like Jacob who when he was working with Laban claimed that Laban had changed his wages a dozen times. I finally, after several helpful suggestions from a few trusted friends, came up with *100 Christian Classics: A Literary Bucket List for the Thoughtful Christ-follower*. Does that mean that every book included is a "classic?" Actually, I am using the term a bit loosely. There are some legitimate classics here such as Augustine's *Confessions*, Milton's *Paradise Lost*, and *The Pilgrim's Progress* by Bunyan to name just a very few. However, many such as Wood's *A Survey of Israel's History* and Hillenbrand's *Unbroken* would not really qualify as classics in the technical sense. They are just darn good books that deserve to be read. So, don't be put off by the word or hold my feet to the fire about the misuse of the word "classic."

HOW TO USE THIS BOOK

Reading 100 books may seem to be an overwhelming task for some people. We live in a world of sound bites where every piece of information is reduced to a ten-second snippet. It is a fact that some folks do not read as much as others, and some may read slower who devour books. I remember reading an article after I graduated from the University of Maryland in 1974 lamenting that the average college graduate never reads another hardcover book for the rest of his life. That article hit me like a sledgehammer. It did not seem true.

Since then, I set a goal of reading 100 books a year. I keep lists of every book I have read since then on a yearly basis. Sometimes I do not reach my goal. But at least I make the attempt. Someone once asked, "How do you eat an elephant?" Of course, the answer is "one bite at a time." Or "How do you begin a journey of 1,000 miles?" With the first step. Reading 100 books may seem to be a daunting task, but keep in mind that this is a lifetime reading plan. Keep in mind that the original title of this book was *100 Books that Every Christian Should Read in a Lifetime*. Most people will not complete the reading on this list in one year or two. Some may take ten years, and some may take longer.

Many people have decades of life ahead of them. If you read only ten books a year, in ten years, you can complete this list. Keep in mind that there are some books that you will read and reread repeatedly. I read an English Translation of the Bible cover to cover every calendar year beginning in Genesis 1 and ending in Revelation 22. Also, I read *My Utmost for His Highest* by Oswald Chambers every year, and Eugene Peterson's *Praying the Psalms* every other year. I have volumes of fiction in my personal library that are old friends that I have read several times. They delight me anew with each reading. The point is that reading multiple books is possible, but it requires a plan.

One way to complete reading all the books included in this volume is to read ten books per year. You could read two books from Chapter II: Classics such as the Bible and *Robinson Crusoe* by Daniel Defoe. Then choose one title from eight of the remaining ten chapters. Do the same thing the next year and the year after, and in ten years, you will have read all 100 books. If you are a faster reader, you can adjust the pace to your reading pace. The important thing is to read. Going back to the elephant for dinner, when you have a large goal, it is best to take small steps. But the important thing is to begin. Even if you do not feel you can read 100 books, you can certainly read one or two. You may then be challenged to read even more.

HOW DID I MAKE THE CHOICES TO INCLUDE AND EXCLUDE

My list of 100 books is a personal one and reflects the best judgment of one man. A lot of thought went into the list, and I had a lot of suggestions for inclusion which were carefully considered. Another person's list might be completely different, but I believe there would be huge areas of overlap. For example, what list of 100 Christian classics could fail to include *The Pilgrim's Progress* by John Bunyan or the Bible or *Of the Imitation of Christ* by Thomas a Kempis? Some will argue, and I cannot say that I totally disagree with them, that I should have included something by William Shakespeare or *Crime and Punishment* by Fyodor Dostoevsky or this book or that. Please keep in mind that the title is *100 Books*, not *101 Books* or *102 Books*. I had to make some difficult choices, and some truly excellent books were excluded. Frankly, I could probably make a good case for 200 books or 1,000 books. But where would it end? In the Appendix, I have listed another 100 books that were considered, but did not make my final cut. They are very worthy candidates for inclusion and excellent books. I just did not include them for some reason or other. In any case, the choices were mine and mine alone.

When I decided to write this book, I made a tentative list of "must read" books that came nowhere close to 100. I decided to poll a wide sampling of people for their opinions: pastors, scholars, and average church members. First, I asked pastors from a wide variety of church traditions to provide me with a list of from five to ten titles that they felt were important books for Christians to read. Then I asked the same of scholars from a variety of doctrinal backgrounds. The only commonality is that they needed to be evangelical. Finally, I asked laypersons from many different churches and backgrounds to provide me with the title of ONE book that should be read by every Christian. For this final step, I polled the good folks in my adult Sunday school class at First Presbyterian Church in Haines City, FL, as well as others in the church. I also asked believers from a good many churches and faith traditions with whom I have only a casual acquaintance. I wanted to get as wide a sampling of books as possible. From the roughly nineteen pages of data I compiled, I began to look for titles that showed up repeatedly. Although the final selections were mine alone, the recommendations of my "panel of experts" heavily influenced my decisions.

I then decided that my list of books needed to be well-balanced. For example, I did not want to include 100 books on discipleship alone or on apologetics. It was my hope to have numerous categories of books and to also include a chapter on biography and memoir as well as fiction and poetry in the interest of being well-rounded. It is my hope and prayer that my list reflects important books in many categories that would prove helpful to the thoughtful Christian.

I am excited about this book. In my judgment, as you read this book you are embarking on a great literary adventure. Happy reading!

CHAPTER II
CHRISTIAN CLASSICS

"A classic is something that everybody wants to have read and nobody wants to read." That quotation by Mark Twain really gets to the heart of the matter. People praise the classics. They extoll the classics. But they don't want to take the time to actually read the classics. One of the problems with reading the classics is that many were scared off because of their first exposure to them. They may have been forced to read *The Canterbury Tales* or *Paradise Lost* while in high school and they never recovered from that experience. They were introduced to the classics when they were least mature enough to appreciate them.

This is a problem not only in our society at large, but in the Christian Church. There is a tremendous ignorance of both the Bible itself and the formative Christian literature. As one lover of Christian literature put it so well, "In the church today there is an abysmal lack of awareness of both the historical rootedness and the creative richness of our faith. Reading the Christian classics is one of the surest ways to broaden and deepen our faith and commitment" (Glaspey, 27).

The late Warren W. Wiersbe, the well-known pastor, writer, and conference speaker, was a leading cheerleader for reading the Christian classics. In his wonderful book, *Walking With the Giants* (which by the way I have read at least a dozen times), he gives three reasons why they should be read. He writes, "For one thing, the classics have endured...the books that have lasted are usually the ones that really have something to say, we had better pay attention" (Wiersbe, 232). Wiersbe continues with his second reason, "It is a timeless, universal book that appeals to the reader in spite of time, place, or culture...It is rooted in something more substantial than the latest fads and fashions" (Ibid.) Finally, he gives his third reason. "It is an essential book, a seminal book, that so comes to grips with reality that anyone who later deals with this subject must take this book into consideration. It is a key that opens exciting new doors, or a seed that regularly produces a fresh harvest of thinking" (Ibid.)

Is it any wonder that so much of the church today is characterized by shallowness and superficiality? We flock to read the latest best-seller or mindless beach read when we could be drinking deeply at the wells of the books of the ages. Following are some that every believer should read at least once and have a familiarity. I suggest that you choose one of the books from the following (in addition to the Bible) and that you work your way through it until it is completed. It may not read like a James Patterson or Mary Higgins Clark novel, but it will be much more nourishing and satisfying. My guess is that you will wish you had read it long ago. Following are some absolute treasures that every believer should read and study at least once. Don't expect to speed read even one of twelve books in this chapter or any of the one hundred books in this volume.

1. THE BIBLE

The Bible towers above every one of the other ninety-nine books described in this book in that it is totally unique and special. It is the infallible Word of God, the only rule for faith and practice for the Christian. For the believer, the Scriptures are spiritual food. If people need to eat every day to sustain the body, how much more they need to read the Bible daily to sustain the soul. And yet, if the polls can be believed, the Bible is underread and often misunderstood—by Christians! According to a survey conducted by Statista from 2018 to 2021, eleven percent of Americans read the Bible daily along with about thirty-one percent who never ever read it. About twelve percent read it less than once a year and roughly ten percent read it only once a year. A 2021 poll conducted by the Cultural Research Center of Arizona Christian University found that nearly seventy percent of Americans claim to be Christian. That means that many professing Christians are not reading their Bibles. That also means that the old cliché about the father dusting off the family Bible before the preacher's visit is probably more true than apocryphal.

In 2003 Dan Brown published his blockbuster novel, *The Da Vinci Code*, that became a huge bestseller and was read by millions in the western world, including Christians. It spurred several sequels as well as a film by the same name. Many Christians were confused by the novel's message and shaken in their faith. The *Charlotte Observer* viewed the phenomenon with interest and wrote, "The debates over 'The Da Vinci Code book and movie have shown many curious Americans how ignorant they are about biblical history" (as cited by Meredith in *Tomorrow's World*). Many religious leaders and pastors have lamented the confusion that this novel has fomented. It is a sad and well-documented fact that most churchgoers do not read the Bible regularly and do not have a clue as to what it really teaches and thus are susceptible to "fiction" such as *The Da*

Vinci Code and any and every kind of religious idea someone is hawking. While most Christians do not read the Bible, fewer still study the Bible as one would history or mathematics. For Christians to receive the Bible as the Word of God and avoid reading or studying the text is alarming.

Dallas Willard, in his *The Spirit of the Disciplines* (see Chapter X), writes about the spiritual disciplines of prayer and Bible reading, "The 'open secret' of many 'Bible believing' churches is that a vanishingly small percentage of those talking about prayer and Bible reading are actually doing what they are talking about" (Willard, 186). The late J. I. Packer, an Anglican, in his 1973 classic *Knowing God* (see Chapter VII), cites Cranmer's Prayer Book lectionary which devout Anglicans follow, as a guide that will take its readers through the Old Testament once per year and the New Testament twice. He cites the late Archdeacon T. C. Hammond who used to read through the entire Bible each quarter of the year. Packer challenges believers, "How long is it since you read right through the Bible? Do you spend as much time with the Bible each day as you do even with the newspaper? What fools some of us are!—and we remain fools all our lives, simply because we will not take the trouble to do what has to be done to receive the wisdom which is God's free gift" (Packer, 91).

It is true that reading the Bible in its entirety is a daunting task. It is not like the average book that one can complete in a week or two. It will require planning and dedication. My suggestion is that you have a daily reading plan for the Bible and that you stick to it religiously. My personal plan is extremely uncomplicated and unsophisticated. I have been reading an English translation of the Bible through on a yearly basis for going on thirty years. I begin on January 1 every year in Genesis 1 and read book by book until I complete the Revelation of John usually on December 31. Every time I read it through, I gain new insights and learn new things that I did not realize previously. Usually, I read the *NIV* (*New International Version*), but I have deviated a few times and read the *ESV* (*English Standard Ver-*

sion) and the *NLT* (*New Living Translation*). Today's Bible reader has more choices than any other time in history. When I was growing up in the 1950s and 1960s, there were really only two options, the *King James Version* or the *Revised Standard Version*, or perhaps the *ASV* (*American Standard Version*). Today there are more than fifty English versions, so the problem is not a lack of choices. Your problem may be narrowing the many choices down to one or two translations that you feel comfortable with. For assistance in determining how to choose a Bible translation, see my 2020 book, *The Layperson's Library* (Yost, 22-27), or one of the many other fine books available on that subject.

Eugene Peterson contends in his book, *A Long Obedience in the Same Direction* (see Chapter X), that God uses Bible reading along with prayer to help us grow as Christians. He writes, "It is this fusion of God speaking to us (Scripture) and our speaking to him (prayer) that the Holy Spirit uses to form the life of Christ in us" (Peterson, 202). He argues that "the fusion is accomplished by reading these Scriptures slowly, imaginatively, prayerfully and obediently" (Ibid.). He claims that this is not how Christians today read the Bible, if indeed they even read it. He writes, "The reading style employed more often than not by contemporary Christians is fast, reductive information-gathering, and, above all, practical" (Peterson, 204). On the contrary, our reading of Scripture should be "slowly, imaginatively, prayerfully, and obediently" (Ibid.).

I cannot emphasize enough how important it is to read the Bible in its entirety. Unlike most of the other books suggested in this volume, you will want to read it over and over again. My suggestion is to read it through every year. There are many Bible reading plans available. My personal preference is to begin at Genesis and end in Revelation. However, whichever plan you use, read your Bible. I have several other suggestions that Christians have found useful over the centuries. These are not original with me, but they will help you. First of all, pray for a hunger for God's Word. Second, set a definite time of the day for reading. It helps to build your Bible reading into your schedule. Third, begin your reading with prayer. Fourth, guard against distractions. Many things in our lives distract us from the really important things. I suggest that you leave your cell phone elsewhere so that you are not distracted by incoming calls, texts, or the desire to check the Internet. Use a printed version of the Bible rather than an electronic one for obvious reasons. But most importantly, read your Bible.

2. CONFESSIONS

By Augustine of Hippo

For roughly 1,600 years since the days of Augustine of Hippo, it has been a proverbial saying that God has made the heart of man for himself, and that the heart of man finds no true rest until it finds itself in God. It has been observed that while the world of Islam today recognizes Augustine, the great theologian of late antiquity and Church Father, as Rami Kabir, "the Great Christian," many Christians today know him only as a name and nothing more. The Anglican scholar, Michael Marshall, writes, "It is perhaps ironic that while the world of Islam thus recognizes him while many folks in the pews of Christian churches scarcely know anything about him" (Marshall, 8). His *Confessions* portray a passionate and moving account of a soul in a quest for God. You, too, will be moved as you read and will be compelled to do some soul-searching of your own.

In *The Confessions*, Augustine tackled some of the timeless spiritual questions which thoughtful minds have addressed since the beginning of human history. Written around A.D. 397, it is an eloquent and passionate account of one man's spiritual walk and his struggle to overcome his sinful nature and achieve a life of grace. *The Confessions* consists of thirteen books. The first ten chronicle his spiritual pilgrimage from his childhood in Numidia, his troubled adolescence in Carthage, Rome, and Milan, and how he continually struggled with his passions. They relate his experimentation with Manichaeism and the Neoplatonists. Throughout his youth and early adulthood, his saintly mother Monica was untiring in her efforts to save young Augustine from self-destruction. Finally, it relates his conversion as age thirty-two to the Christian faith he had resisted for so long. The final three books act almost as an appendix in that they are seemingly unrelated to the first ten. They provide an allegorical explanation of Moses' account of the Creation.

Augustine of Hippo, also widely known as Saint Augustine, was the greatest of the Latin Church fathers, but his road to the Christian faith was a rocky one. He was born in 354 in North Africa. His mother, Monica, was a devout believer though domineering, while his father, Patricius, was a pagan until his conversion on his deathbed. Augustine was sent to school in Madaurus where he was well-schooled in Latin literature as well as its pagan beliefs and rituals, but showed a decided ineptitude in Greek, for which he was frequently beaten.

While a student at Madaura when Augustine was about sixteen years of age, he fell in with a group of wild, reckless youths. He writes, "With companions like these I roamed the streets of Babylon and wallowed in its filth as though basking amid cinnamon and precious ointments. My invisible enemy trampled on me and seduced me" (Boulding, 66). As a student at Madaura he possessed a facility for Latin, a skill which was not equaled because of his relative ineptitude in Greek. He was frequently beaten for his lack of progress in the latter. His only prayer in those days was the one that everyone knows—believers, agnostics, and atheists alike—the prayer of last resort, of desperation. Certainly, his godly mother, Monica, was a positive influence on the young man. But her influence and guidance were not enough to counterbalance his worldly ways.

Young Augustine was soon sent back to his hometown of Thagaste where he moved into his parents' home. His return was at an inopportune time. He was quickly growing into a young man with drives and passions. As Marshall observes, "Soured boredom soon turned to foolish and fruitless frivolities" (Marshall, 25) He became associated with some bad company of local youths "equally bored and vying with each other in lawlessness, vandalism, and vice" (Ibid.). Augustine describes one of his earliest forays into sin. "Close to our vineyard there was a pear tree laden with fruit. This fruit was not enticing, either in appearance or in flavor. We nasty lads went there to shake down the fruit and carry it off at dead of night. . . . We took enormous quantities, not to feast on ourselves but perhaps to throw to the pigs; we did eat a few, but that was not our motive. We derived pleasure from the deed simply because it was forbidden" (Boulding, 67-68).

Augustine's father, Patricius, a man of modest means, saved enough money to send his eighteen-year-old son to Carthage, which was farther away, to complete his education. Both parents were fully aware that he was wrestling with his sexual urges. Augustine writes, "So I arrived at Carthage, where the din of scandalous love-affairs raged cauldron-like around me. I was not yet in love, but I was enamored with the idea of love, and so deep within me was my need that I hated myself for the sluggishness of my desires" (Boulding, 75). He explains the effect all of this had on him. "I polluted the stream of friendship with my filthy desires and clouded its purity with hellish lusts" (Ibid.).

> "To Carthage then I came, Burning, burning, burning."

These famous lines written by T. S. Eliot in *The Wasteland* about a century ago (See Chapter XII) describe the sexual fires that burned in the young Augustine. His frequent battles with his youthful lusts almost always ended in defeat. Much has been made of his sexual peccadillos. It is possible that his struggles with sexual sin may have been overexaggerated. It is true that he did have a healthy libido, which is characteristic of eighteen-year-old young men, and a passionate desire for sexual relationships. It is also true that he often bragged of sexual conquests that had no basis in reality. What is known is that, while a student at Carthage, Augustine did have a lover with whom he lived in a relationship outside the bounds of marriage. They had a common-law relationship for about fourteen years which produced a son. Apparently, their sexual relationship was one of complete fidelity. Thus, he was not as profligate in his youth as often portrayed.

Augustine became a noted professor of rhetoric at the age of thirty in Milan. He had reached the pinnacle of his profession in that his position was the most enviable and visible in the Latin world of his day. He also developed a reputation as an orator. He soon met a man who would change his life, Bishop Ambrose. As Augustine wrestled with the truth of the Christian faith, he realized that his one great obstacle to embracing Christ in saving faith was his fear of a celibate life. He prayed for chastity and temperance, but not yet. He believed that a conversion to Christianity would mean that he could never marry.

Augustine was finally converted and baptized by Ambrose. He writes about his conversion: "How foolish are they who know not God! So many good things before their eyes, yet *Him Who Is* they fail to see. I was trapped in that foolishness no longer" (Boulding, 185). He became an ardent Bible student influenced greatly by Bishop Ambrose who schooled him in the allegorical method of biblical interpretation. This approach to Bible study has few adherents today and some of his interpretations might be off-putting to modern readers. However, Augustine became one of, if not the greatest, the most influential Christian writers and philosophers in the history of the Christian Church. He was one of the most prolific writers of the early Church and his writings have done much to influence Western philosophy as well as the Christian faith. His work on biblical anthropology, creation, ecclesiology, original sin, the human will, and predestination were important in the development of Church doctrine and practice. He saw human beings as enslaved in their sins and powerless to move in a Godward direction without the power of the Holy Spirit. Augustine was also actively engaged in the fight against the heretical Pelagians, who denied the doctrines of original sin and predestination. Pelagianism and Semi-Pelagianism have infected the Church for centuries.

His writings on sex and marriage have also greatly influenced the Roman Catholic Church's teachings on the subject. He felt that chastity was better than marriage, although he did not totally disparage the latter. Presumably, Augustine's understanding on sex and marriage were influenced by the Apostle Paul's writings. In any event, Augustine's writings have formed the foundation of much of the Catholic Church's doctrines in many areas, which of course means that Protestant teaching has been greatly influenced as well. There can be no denying the impact his writings have had, not only on all of Christendom, but on Western thought as well; it has been immeasurable.

My initial reading of *The Confessions* was of the 1961 Collier edition based on a nineteenth century translation by Edward B. Pusey. It kept many of the archaic linguistic conventions of Elizabethan English and therefore was a bit stilted in its phraseology. My second reading was much smoother. Sister Maria Boulding's wonderful translation is part of *The Works of Saint Augustine: A Translation for the 21st Century*. I highly recommend it. She makes Augustine's language come alive. All quotations in this review are from that edition.

"*The Confessions* are one long prayer, a poetic, passionate, intimate prayer" (Boulding, 9). Augustine gives his reasons for writing. "Why then am I relating all this to you at such length? Certainly not to inform you. I do it to arouse my own loving devotion toward you, and that of my readers, so that together we may declare, *Great is the Lord, and exceedingly worthy of praise.* . . . See, then, how long a tale I have told you, as best I could and as I truly wanted to, because you first willed that I should confess to you, my Lord and God, for you are good and your mercy endures forever" (XI, 1, 1). How sad that this great man of God has become almost forgotten today by most in the Christian church. I recently told a woman, who has been a member of a local church for many decades and who knows that I am writing this book, that I was writing a section on Augustine. She asked me who he was and informed me that she had never heard of him. How tragic this is! Augustine is a man who needs to be rediscovered by the average church member.

What better place to begin by a reading of his confessions? See if you don't agree.

Following are some gems from *The Confessions*:

Probably the best-known sayings from the writings of the church fathers is Augustine's "You made us and draw us to yourself, and our heart is unquiet until it rests in you" (Boulding, 39).

Childish sins:

> "I failed to recognize the whirlpool of disgraceful conduct into which I had been flung, out of your sight" (Boulding, 59).

Childish sins get worse:

> "These same sins grow worse as we grow: first it is offenses against pedagogues and teachers, or cheating over nuts and balls and sparrows; then later it is crimes against prefects and kings, and fraud in gold and estate slaves" (Boulding, 60).

On adolescence:

> "Look upon my heart, O God, look upon this heart of mine, on which you took pity in its abysmal depths. . . . The malice was loathsome, and I loved it. I was in love with my own ruin, in love with decay: not with the thing for which I was falling into decay but with decay itself, for I was depraved in soul" (Boulding, 68).

On His Indecision about Conversion:

> "I had grown used to pretending that the only reason why I had not yet turned my back on the

world to serve you was that my perception of the truth was uncertain, but that excuse was no longer available to me, for by now it was certain. But I was still entangled by the earth and refused to enlist in your service, for the prospect of being freed from all these encumbrances frightened me as much as the encumbrances themselves ought to have done" (Boulding, 193).

3. THE DIVINE COMEDY

By Dante Alighieri

The Divine Comedy is one of the major masterpieces of world literature, not just sacred literature. Dante occupies the rarified air of such notables as William Shakespeare and Geoffrey Chaucer. "Dante and Shakespeare divide the modern world between them; there is no third," is a widely-quoted tribute attributed to T. S. Eliot. James Joyce, one of the most important and influential writers of the twentieth century, called Dante "my spiritual food." It has been oft-said that reading Dante is "worth learning Italian for." The playwright and novelist Robert Weibezahl, in a review on a new book about Dante, wrote, "The influence of Dante and his *Divine Comedy* permeates Western history and literature—and, clearly, the consciousness of even the most modern writers" (Weibezahl, 6).

The Divine Comedy is an epic poem in three parts, or canticles, describing a mythical journey through the three realms of the Roman Catholic afterlife: *Inferno* (hell), *Purgatorio* (purgatory), and *Paradiso* (heaven). Dante wrote his masterpiece between 1308 and 1320 in Italian using a rhyme scheme, terza rima (aba, bcb, cdc, etc.), which he created for this very purpose. The best-known of the three parts of the poem is *Inferno*, which describes in great detail the horrors awaiting those who have the misfortune to wind up there to be punished for their sins. The famous words, "Abandon all hope ye who enter here" are inscribed just above the gates of hell. Dante begins his allegorical journey as a fictionalized character accompanied by the Roman poet Virgil as he descends into the nine circles of hell. He then ascends the seven-layered mountain of purgatory, where the saved purify themselves before they are allowed to enter into heaven. As he moves ever upward through purgatory, he is cleansed of such sins as avarice and incontinence. Finally, he meets his beloved Beatrice, who descends from heaven. She guides Dante through the ten levels of heaven ascending toward the abode of God.

Dante was born in 1265 in Florence, Italy, into a family that was moderately wealthy and was heavily involved in the political area of that city. His marriage was an arranged one by his family although his heart belonged to a mystery woman, Beatrice, whose true identity is unknown. He longed for her even after her sudden and tragic death in 1290. Dante's involvement in politics led to his eventual exile for life by the Black Guelphs, a political party in power in Florence at the time, which lasted until his death in 1321. During his exile, Dante wrote *The Divine Comedy*.

In *The Divine Comedy* those whom Dante meets are pilgrims and the Christian journey is a lifelong pilgrimage. Although the premise of *The Canterbury Tales* is that of a pilgrimage to the place where Thomas Beckett was assassinated, the pilgrimage in that story is a mere contrivance. In *The Divine Comedy*, the pilgrimage is the story itself. With the assistance of his muse, his beloved Beatrice, Dante learns how painful spiritual rehabilitation can be and that he must renounce the temporal world and its transitory allures.

Protestants may object to the portrayal of purgatory as an invention of medieval Roman Catholicism. Certainly, the idea of being purged for one's sins goes against the Reformed doctrine that the death of Jesus was an atonement for our sins. Martin Luther vehemently objected to the doctrine of purgatory as a clear violation of the doctrine of salvation as being *sola fide, sola gratia,* and *sola Christos.* It is impossible to purge oneself from one's sins. Luther called the doctrine an "unbiblical fiction." Although Dante did write about a place called purgatory, he was writing from the perspective of the popular church understanding of that time of purgatory as a place of purging/cleansing in preparation for heaven and hell as the inferno.

Dante was unflinching in his scathing critique of the church of his day, the political milieu of his time, and even the church hierarchy itself. He spared not even the popes of his day relegating most of them to the inferno. His denunciation of the Roman Catholic Church is no less bombastic than that of Luther himself. If you question how this could conceivably be called a "comedy," It is a comedy, because the ending is happy, as opposed to a tragedy whose ending is unhappy.

I highly recommend that you familiarize yourself with one of the greatest works of literature of all time. The reading itself is not difficult, but it would help to know something of the political and religious surroundings of Dante's time. For those who do not read Italian, there is a very fine translation by the late Dorothy L. Sayers, an English novelist and sometime guest of the Inklings at Oxford. There is also a very helpful annotated translation by John Ciardi. But by all means, read *The Divine Comedy*. It will be worth the journey.

4. THE CANTERBURY TALES

By Geoffrey Chaucer

This book is one of the acknowledged major masterpieces of English literature. Unfortunately, too many of us were first introduced to this classic of Middle English during our high school years when we were least able to appreciate its brilliance and profundity. Many an overzealous high school English teacher had his students memorize the first eighteen lines of the Prologue in Middle English thereby turning off a generation of young minds who might have benefited from its wisdom. This is most unfortunate in that Chaucer wrote with vigor and vividness and a profound understanding of human nature. He was considered to be the greatest English poet of the Middle Ages and has been called the "father of English literature."

Geoffrey Chaucer (c. 1343-1400) was born in London in the early 1340s. We know very little of his early life. He served in his adult life as civil servant in a variety of roles, but notably in the royal court of Edward III. He became an esquire and it is likely that he lived at court and performed royal duties. Although much of his adult life is shrouded in mystery and rumor, he apparently traveled to Spain, France, Flanders, and Italy because of his courtly duties. It has been suggested that during his Italian travels, he became acquainted with either Petrarch or Boccaccio who introduced him to medieval Italian poetry, which would explain his facility in the use of poetry and stories.

Some have questioned the Christian faith of Chaucer even suggesting that he was an agnostic. It is important that we do not confuse his attitudes towards the Church, which was notoriously corrupt and skewered in such tales as *The Pardoner's Tale*, with his attitudes towards the Christian faith itself. While he recognized that many in the Church were notoriously corrupt and greedy, he admired genuine Christians and even dedicated his writing and his life to God. It is obvious what my position is since I have included his masterwork in this book.

The Canterbury Tales is what is known as a frame story. In other words, there are stories within the frame of a larger story. The larger story is that of a group of pilgrims traveling to Canterbury to visit the shrine where Thomas Becket was martyred. Thomas Becket was the Archbishop of Canterbury until his martyrdom in 1170 supposedly at the behest of King Henry II. After his murder, he was venerated as a saint and martyr by both the Roman Catholic Church and the Anglican Church. Canterbury Cathedral became the third most visited site of Christian pilgrimage. The pilgrims mentioned are traveling from Southwark to Canterbury, a distance of some ninety miles. They decide to tell stories as they travel to while away the time. At its core, the book is simply a collection of twenty-four short stories held together by the larger premise (the frame) of a group of travelers on a pilgrimage each telling tales to pass the time. Each tale has a lesson or theme. It was Chaucer's intention to include over 100 stories, but his death in 1400 ended his writing. Each character was to tell four tales, two on the way to Canterbury and two more on the return home.

Two of Chaucer's favorite targets were religious hypocrisy and church corruption. His religious characters give us a vivid picture of the religious corruption and hypocrisy in the church at that time. His portraits of the nun, the monk, and the pardoner are particularly scathing. One of the fun things to do while reading *The Canterbury Tales* is to try to draw parallels between Chaucer's characters and modern religious figures. It is not difficult to see a direct parallel between the Pardoner, for example, and the religious hucksters of our day who preach the so-called prosperity gospel.

The nun, likewise, is pictured in a very unflattering light. Despite having taken vows of obedience, poverty, and chastity, she is pretentious and affectatious. She is quite unlike what we would expect a nun to be. The monk, too, is quite materialistic and overly concerned with his pleasure and the finer things of life. On the other hand, the simple parson was admired by Chaucer and portrayed in a most flattering light.

Why should the Christian read Chaucer today? The twenty-four tales in the book range from bawdy to inspirational to heroic to tragic. The social realism and the human personalities that Chaucer wrote about in the Middle Ages are just as much a part of us today in the twenty-first century. Clergy sex scandals are part and parcel of our daily existence in the United States as well as the desire for power and money. Great literature is never bounded by the sanctions of time. The characters of *The Canterbury Tales* live with us, work with us, and attend worship services with us and the tales they tell are timeless.

Only the bold and adventurous might venture to read *The Canterbury Tales* in the original Middle English. For the rest of us, a good modern translation such as the one by Peter Tuttle in the Barnes & Noble Classics series would be a good alternative. This timeless classic is not to be missed!

5. OF THE IMITATION OF CHRIST

By Thomas à Kempis

Thomas à Kempis begins his classic devotional work with the following words:

> "'He that followeth Me, walketh not in darkness,' saith the Lord. These are the words of Christ, by which we are admonished how we ought to imitate His life and manners, if we will be truly enlightened, and be delivered from all blindness of heart."

Thus, the monk Thomas Haemerken, also known as Thomas à Kempis (so called because he was from Kempen), began this beloved collection of meditations which have lighted the way for believers for over a half a millennium. It is the most popular Christian devotional book ever published and the greatest religious best seller with the exception of the Bible. It has been translated into over fifty languages and there are too many editions to tabulate. One estimate is that that were already 1,800 editions by 1779.

Little is known about Thomas Haemerken, who was born in 1379 in Germany. More is known about the tumultuous Roman Catholic Church of his day which was the center of corruption and dissension and questions about the papacy. In little over a hundred years, the Protestant Reformation would forever change the Church of Jesus Christ. We also know a great deal about the social and political events which shaped Haemerken's life and view of the world. The Hundred Years' War, perhaps a the most significant armed conflict of the Middle Ages, was in full swing and the Black Death, the most fatal pandemic recorded in human history, was not that far away in the recent past. In addition, there were peasant revolts in response to rising taxes.

When he was twelve years old, Haemerken followed his brother, Johann to the Netherlands to attend the Latin school in Deventer. His parents were of the opinion that this would be a positive step for the boy with the world in the state it was. While a student, he became acquainted with the Brethren of the Common Life. They perceived themselves to be true Christ-followers and exemplars and custodians of the Apostolic tradition. It was during his time with the Brotherhood that he learned that salvation does not come from doing good works, but rather by trusting in Christ alone. He later entered a monastery called Mount St. Agnes at Zwolle where he lived as a monk. He received Holy Orders almost a decade later and served as sub-prior of the monastery beginning in 1432.

While at Mount St. Agnes, his duties as sub-prior included engaging in devotional exercises and copying manuscripts. Keep in mind that this was well before the printing press that was invented by Johannes Gutenberg around 1450. It has been reported that he copied the entire Bible at least four times. One of those copies has been preserved at Darmstadt, Germany. One of his other duties was that of instructing novices and out of this came four booklets written between 1420 and 1427. It was these booklets that were later collected and then named after the title of the first chapter of the first booklet, *Of the Imitation of Christ, and Contempt of all the Vanities of the World.*

I own two personal copies of the book. One is a beautiful, but fragile, 1878 edition published by Chapman and Hall in London, which I pull from the shelves from time to time only to admire, but not to actually read. I also have a little paperback edition published by Baker Book House that I use for daily reading. It has been said that *Of the Imitation of Christ* is the most widely-read Christian devotional book after, of course, the Bible. It is also the most influential book in Christian literature. It is one of the few books that boasts a following from both Protestants and Roman Catholics. It is easy to read and infused with Scripture in almost every line. It begs to be read and re-read. If any book deserves to be called a classic, this one does.

Of the Imitation of Christ is a devotional feast that is best taken in small bites and chewed slowly. Do not expect a buffet table where you pile your plate high. It should be read slowly and meditated upon and prayed over. When I first read it, I did it one chapter every day along with my daily Scripture reading and my daily dose of Oswald Chambers (*My Utmost for His Highest*. See Chapter VIII). I would suggest that you read this book once very slowly and meditatively and then repeat the process over and over again. You will benefit from repeated readings.

Consider some of the following nuggets from the book:

> "What are all temporal things, but seducing snares?" (The Third Book, Chapter I)

> "Let nothing seem great, nothing precious and wonderful, nothing truly commendable and to be desired, but that alone which is eternal." (The Third Book, Chapter IV)

> "Learn to be content with a little, and to be pleased with plain and simple things, nor to murmur against any inconvenience." (The Third Book, Chapter XI)

> "Thou oughtest therefore to call to mind the more heavy sufferings of others, that so thou mayest the easier bear thy own very small trouble" (The Third Book, Chapter XIX).

"Choose always to have less rather than more. Seek always the lowest place, and to be inferior to every one" (The Third Book, Chapter XXIII).

"Follow thou me: I AM the Way, the Truth, and the Life. Without the Way, there is no going; without the Truth, there is no knowing; without the Life, there is no living" (The Third Book, Chapter LVI).

6. GOLDEN BOOKLET OF THE TRUE CHRISTIAN LIFE

By John Calvin

During the Protestant Reformation, no figure loomed larger than John Calvin, with the possible exception of Martin Luther. He was a French theologian, pastor, and reformer who left a trail of controversy in his wake. His system of Christian theology, later called Calvinism for its chief proponent and formulator, included the doctrines of predestination and God's sovereignty in salvation. Calvinism has been codified, for better or for worse, into a system of five main points using the acrostic, TULIP, which stand for total depravity, unconditional election, limited atonement, irresistible grace, and perseverance of the saints. His teachings were largely influenced by the church father, Augustine, and gave birth to the various Reformed and Presbyterian churches, who look to Calvin as their father. His was a remarkable intellect; he published his seminal magnum opus, *The Institutes of the Christian Religion*, when he was only twenty-six years of age. The *Institutes* and the other writings of Calvin were hugely influential in the life of multitudes over the centuries, including the nineteenth century English preacher, Charles Haddon Spurgeon.

As a great devotional classic, *Golden Booklet of the True Christian Life* stands alongside and in the spirit of other great works such as Augustine's *Confessions*, Thomas à Kempis' *Of the Imitation of Christ*, and Bunyan's *Pilgrim's Progress*. However, as a work that is brief, succinct, and facile, it is virtually unmatched in the Christian literature. It is quite unique and unlike anything else ever written.

First published in 1550 in both Latin and French, the *Golden Book of the True Christian Life* was originally not a separate volume, but part of Calvin's monumental *Institutes of the Christian Religion*. On my original listing of 100 books for this volume, I had perhaps unwisely and optimistically included the *Institutes*, but then thought better of it after much reflection and substituted this little booklet instead. The *Golden Book* was expressly written in a simpler style than the other sections of the *Institutes*, which made it much more accessible to the lay reader with a much wider appeal. I have read the *Institutes* in its entirety and it is undeniably a challenge for the average reader. It is not for the faint of heart.

Calvin was one of the great systematizers of the Christian faith. But he was also one of the great distillers of its complex doctrines. Calvin believed that there was no better scriptural principle to follow than that expressed in God's own affirmation, "Be thou holy, for I am holy." Thus, he believed that Scripture was the rule of life and holiness its key principle. According to Calvin, a profession of faith in Christ is not enough. He writes, "Let us ask those who possess nothing but church membership, and yet want to be called Christians, how can they glory in the sacred name of Christ (Calvin, 16)?" He calls a profession of faith in Christ "a false and dangerous make-believe, however eloquently and freely lips servants make talk about the gospel" (Calvin, 16-17). He believed that nominal Christians were an insult to God and said that such religion does not "change our heart, pervade our manners, and transform us into new creatures" (Calvin, 17).

Reading the *Golden Booklet* is almost like reading the Old Testament Book of Proverbs or Thomas à Kempis' *Of the Imitation of Christ*. It is full of pithy statements that are usually spot on and resonate with the reader and are memorable. Calvin arranged his brief book into five compact chapters titled (1) *Humble Obedience: The True Imitation of Christ*, (2) *Self-denial*, (3) *Patience in Crossbearing*, (4) *Hopefulness in the Next World*, and (5) *The Right Use of the Present Life*.

Calvin's comments on cross-bearing are most instructive and helpful. He made it quite clear that the Christian life is no bed of roses. He wrote, "For all whom the Lord has chosen and received into the society of his saints, ought to prepare themselves for a life that is hard, difficult, laborious, and full of countless griefs" (Calvin, 45). He particularly viewed cross-bearing as an antidote to arrogance. "Therefore, that we may not become haughty when we acquire wealth; that we may not become proud when we receive honors; that we may not become insolent when we are blessed with prosperity and health, the Lord himself, as he deems fit, uses the cross to oppose, restrain, and subdue the arrogance of our flesh" (Calvin, 53).

Calvin was scathing in his comments about pride in his chapter on self-denial. He wrote, "Everyone flatters himself and carries a kingdom in his breast" (Calvin, 28). He believed that true humility meant respect for others. "If the same talents which we admire in ourselves appear in others, or even our betters, we depreciate and diminish them with the utmost malignity, in order that we may not have to acknowledge the superiority of others" (Calvin, 28). He also believed that having humility meant putting others above oneself. "Let us rather seek the profit of others, and even voluntarily give up our rights for the sake of others" (Calvin, 30). He gave no quarter when it came to the subject of generosity and its counterpart, stinginess. "There are people who are known to be very liberal, yet they never give without scolding, or pride, or even insolence" (Calvin, 35).

I found Calvin's chapter on death and the life to come most helpful. It is a sad reality that there are some Christians who fear death. Calvin wrote, "It is terrible that many who boast themselves to be Christians, instead of longing for death, are so filled with fear of it that they tremble whenever the word is mentioned, as if it were the greatest calamity that could befall them" (Calvin, 77). "But this we may positively state that nobody has made any progress in the school of Christ, unless he cheerfully looks forward towards the day of his death, and towards the day of his final resurrection" (Calvin, 79).

At times, I felt as if I were reading Brother Lawrence's *The Practice of the Presence of God* instead of Calvin's *Golden Booklet*. See if you agree. "Indeed, a Christian ought to be disposed and prepared to keep in mind that he has to reckon with God every moment of his life" (Calvin, 23). "For why were we delivered from the quagmire of iniquity and pollution of this world, if we want to wallow in it as long as we live" (Calvin, 14)?

Calvin's *Golden Booklet of the True Christian Life* is the kind of book that you will want to read slowly and meditatively. It is so brief that the temptation would be to hurry through it, but I suggest that you take your time. It is also the kind of book that you can read on an annual basis as a spiritual inventory. But please do yourself a favor and read it for the experience. If you are in the mood for a nice, juicy spiritual steak, then Calvin's *Golden Booklet* is just right for you. But if you feel you have the appetite and inclination to eat the entire cow, read his *Institutes*.

7. THE PILGRIM'S PROGRESS

By John Bunyan

Next to the Bible, *The Pilgrim's Progress* is the most read book in the English language. At least that was true just over half a century ago. Over the centuries since its publication in the seventeenth century, it has become one of the most beloved books of all time. Everyone today, it seems, has heard of the book, but fewer and fewer Christians have ever read it. Warren Wiersbe laments that even many pastors have never read it. He writes, "*Pilgrim's Progress* is a book Christians talk about but do not read" (Wiersbe, 234). And yet, it is a book that is crying out to be read today. Its spiritual themes are just as fresh and relevant as when Bunyan first put them to pen.

The story of how *The Pilgrim's Progress* was written is a tale in itself. Its author, John Bunyan (1628-1688), was an uneducated tinker who likely learned how to read the English language through his acquaintance with the Bible. He did attend grammar school as a lad, but left early to pursue the family trade. As a boy, he was doubtless influenced, along with the Bible, by the popular tales of adventure that were found in chapbooks and sold at fairs such as the one at Stourbridge near Cambridge. It likely provided the inspiration for Vanity Fair, a perpetual fair in the city of Vanity.[1] It symbolizes in *The Pilgrim's Progress* worldly frivolity and ostentation. It was created by demons to sidetrack heavenly-minded pilgrims on the way to the Celestial City. It contains everything the world has to offer and proves to be a temptation to the unwary.

---

[1] Vanity Fair is a perpetual fair within the city of Vanity, which is over 5,000 years old and founded by Beelzebub. It symbolizes worldly ostentation and frivolity.

Bunyan was a dissenter who was arrested for preaching, which was an offense prohibited by the Conventicle Act of 1593, an English law which prohibited the conducting of religious services that were held outside the Church of England and requiring separatists to convert to Anglicanism. He was imprisoned intermittently from 1660 to 1672. It was in prison that Bunyan was able to produce his masterwork as well as other writings. Theologically Bunyan was a Puritan in that he held Calvinistic views of grace, but as a separatist he held different views on baptism and the church.

Today, Bunyan is mainly known for his three major works, *The Pilgrim's Progress, The Holy War* (1682), and *Grace Abounding to the Chief of Sinners* (1666). The first, along with *Foxes Book of Martyrs* (See Chapter VI), were mainstays in the Victorian homes in England, read by children and adults alike. It has fueled the imaginations of numberless readers over the centuries including C. S. Lewis, Herman Melville, Charles Dickens, Nathaniel Hawthorne, Louisa May Alcott, George Bernard Shaw, William Thackeray (*Vanity Fair*), Charlotte Bronte, Mark Twain, and John Steinbeck. It has been translated into more than 200 languages including Fijian, Cree, Esperanto, and Pitman shorthand. As Rosalie De Rosset writes in her introduction to the Moody Classics edition of the book, "At one time it was the book most read by Christians with the exception of the Bible. Even up until about seventy-five years ago, it was part of the common stock of our culture, one of the handful of books that bound generation to generation, a book alluded to everywhere in sermons, advertising, and as the title of a prominent and very secular magazine. Sadly, today it is more well known than well read; in fact, it is now one of the world's least-read books" (DeRosset, 6).

The full title of Bunyan's book is *The Pilgrim's Progress from This World to That Which Is to Come*. Bunyan's twofold reason for writing is expressed in his poetic "The Author's Apology" for his book. He writes that he wanted to stir the minds of the listless, those who had grown lazy and bored in their faith and to present the gospel with urgency. Bunyan chose an unusual approach in which the Christian life is portrayed as a journey, a pilgrimage, if you will, throughout life with a beginning and a destination. In doing so, he utilizes a dream sequence in which an omniscient narrator relates the action. Bunyan felt that his approach was so original that he explained his reasons in his apology. He wanted not only to entertain, but to move his reader's heart by dramatizing the Christian pilgrimage using scriptural principles as men and women live and move throughout the world until they pass into their eternal home. As J. I. Packer reminds us in his classic book *Knowing God* (See Chapter VII), "You are called to go through this world as a pilgrim, a mere temporary resident, travelling light" (Packer, 244).

The Pilgrim's Progress is an allegory whose protagonist, Christian, functions as an "everyman," who goes on a spiritual pilgrimage from the City of Destruction, his place of residence, to the Celestial City. Along the way, he encounters numerous trials and temptations common to every Christian no matter in which age he lives. It is important to note that all fiction that is meaningful utilizes some kind of conflict, whether it is internal or external. Thematic conflict is also used very effectively in many stories. For example, *The Pilgrim's Progress* explores in concrete, rather than abstract, forms the battle between ideas and values as well as good and evil. Christian's dilemma lies in the myriad monsters, giants, and deceivers he encounters on his journey. These adversaries represent in theological and psychological terminology the temptations that are representative of what all believers must face on their own personal spiritual pilgrimage. One helpful feature of Bunyan's book is that although the storyline is presented in allegory form, the reader is not left guessing. His rich and imaginative symbolism is explained every step of the way.

The story is told in two parts. The first relates Christian's pilgrimage and the second that of his wife, Christiana, and their sons, along with the maiden Mercy. Of course, the first part about Christian is the most familiar.

Foundational to an understanding of the narrative is the beginning of the book and the commencement of Christian's journey. As Christian leaves the City of Destruction, alone without his family who refuse to accompany him, he realizes that he is weighed down by a great burden, the realization that he is a sinner. When he first meets Evangelist, he tells him, "Sir, I perceive by the Book [the Bible] in my hand, that I am condemned to die, and after that to come to judgment, and I find that I am not willing to do the first, nor able to do the second" (Bunyan, 15). He explains, "Because I fear this burden that is upon my back will sink me lower than the grave, and I shall fall into Tophet [probably means "the place of burning"]" (Ibid.). Obstinate and Pliable go after Christian to try to convince him to return. He refuses and attempts to convince them to accompany him. Obstinate replies, "What! And leave our friends and our comforts behind us" (Bunyan, 17)! Only Pliable is persuaded to go with Christian, but they soon fall into the Slough of Despond, a bog where "they wallowed for a time, being grievously bedaubed with dirt, and Christian, because of the burden that was on his back, began to sink in the mire" (Bunyan, 21). Pliable is able to extricate himself and abandons Christian. It is only after Help, who had heard Christian's cries, rescues him.

As you read *The Pilgrim's Progress*, you will encounter numerous people, creatures, and visit many places. Early in the story you will meet Pliable who questions Christian's judgment over and over again and Obstinate who always seems to have an excuse. You will meet Mr. Worldly Wiseman as well as Mr. Legality and his son, Civility. Evangelist exposes them as frauds. You will meet Goodwill, a not-so-thinly disguised Jesus figure. Goodwill rescues Christian from Beelzebub's archers and shows him the way to deliverance. Along the way, you will also meet characters named Simple, Sloth, Presumption, Formality, Hypocrisy, Mistrust, Timorous, Demas, Hopeful, Faithful, and Little Faith, among numerous others. It doesn't require the reader to be an Einstein to understand the symbolism behind these names. As you read, you will also visit many places, good and ill, such as the Valley of the Shadow of Death, the Wicket Gate, a city named Morality, the Hill of Difficulty, the "straight and narrow" King's Highway, Beelzebub's castle, the House of the Interpreter, the House of the Palace Beautiful, the Valley of Humiliation, a hill named Lucre, the Giant's Doubting castle, the Hill Error, the Mountain Caution, the Lake of Fire, and Vanity Fair*. You will meet creatures along the way such as Giant Despair and his wife, Diffidence, Beelzebub, Shining Ones (angels), demons, Apollyon, Pope and Pagan, and Giant Maul among many others. All of this is presented in unforgettable, down-to-earth prose that even a child can understand astonishing in its spiritual insight.

If the great nineteenth century English preacher Charles H. Spurgeon can be trusted as a reference, he claimed in his autobiography that he had read *The Pilgrim's Progress* over a hundred times. Since he died at the age of fifty-eight, he must have read it at least twice a year since his childhood. Quite a recommendation in my estimation! As you read the book, you will see yourself as if looking into a mirror. You will also see other believers you have known over the years as well as many unbelievers. Along with yourself, you will see members of your own local church congregation. Reading *The Pilgrim's Progress* is like shining a light onto your soul.

You might be wondering whether you should read *The Pilgrim's Progress* in Bunyan's original English or a more modern paraphrase. There are two sides to this question. On the one hand, we wouldn't dream of reading Shakespeare in anything but the original. Such thought would be anathema to purists such as myself. Admittedly, such an accommodation might shed light on the meaning of the Shakespearean text, but it would "light fools the way to dusty death." On the other hand, most people today don't read the Bible in the King James Version since so many good, readable modern translation of the Bible are available. If you read in the original, you may miss some nuances because of your unfamiliarity with the seventeenth century language. A modern translation or paraphrase will help you overcome that deficiency. You will need to weigh the pros and cons and make that determination yourself. A perfectly fine example of this is James H. Thomas' *Pilgrim's Progress in Today's English*. Another recommended version is by Cheryl Ford although she leaves some of the material out. One of my own personal copies is a lovely undated edition with woodcut illustrations published by The Peter Pauper Press in Mount Vernon, New York. All quotations in this review will be from the Moody Classics version edited by Rosalie De Rosset, which has the added value of including Scripture references in parentheses to show where Bunyan gleaned his material. The reader will soon learn that Bunyan's writing is saturated with Scripture.

The great Scottish preacher, Alexander Whyte (See Chapters IV and VIII.), loved Bunyan's writings so much that he preached a series of sermons on the characters from *The Pilgrim's Progress*. I highly recommend his wonderful little book, *The Characters in Pilgrim's Progress*. But by all means, read *The Pilgrim's Progress*. It is an investment of time that you will not regret. You will likely find yourself coming back to it again and again.

8. THE BONDAGE OF THE WILL

By Martin Luther

The Bondage of the Will, literally *On the Bondage of the Will* (On Un-free Will) from the Latin *De Servo Arbitrio*, is one of the true classics of the Christian faith. It was published in 1525 as Luther's response to Desiderius Erasmus' 1524 publication of *On Free Will* (Latin: *De Libero Arbitrio Diatribe Sive Collatio*), a work in which the author "held that matters of doctrine were all comparatively unimportant, and that the issue as to whether a man's will was or was not free was more unimportant than most" (Luther, 42). Luther, on the other hand, believed that doctrine was of utmost importance. It is most interesting that Luther was once an admirer of Erasmus, a brilliant New Testament Greek scholar who lectured at Cambridge, England, but left because the food, drink, and climate did not agree with him and finally landed in Basil, Switzerland, after numerous stops along the way including Ghent, Antwerp, Liege, Mainz, and Strasburg. Translators Packer and Johnston write in their excellent "Historical and Theological Introduction" to the Baker Academic edition that "his journey across Europe was something like a triumphal progress" (Packer and Johnston, 17).

Erasmus was a man of singular achievement and reputation. According to Packer and Johnston's excellent "Historical and Theological Introduction" to their translation, "Erasmus was now a man of unsurpassed learning. No man in Europe could rival him in reading and writing the classical tongues. No man had such mastery of the treasures of ancient literature, both secular and patristic. No man commanded the ear of the Pope, cardinal and king as did Erasmus" (Packer and Johnston, 17). His edition of the Greek New Testament was a groundbreaking and monumental work in the area of biblical textual criticism. Unfortunately, he was not a professional theologian and theo-

46

logical doctrines held little interest for him. He was the leading Christian humanist of his day. His hope for the Roman Church was to reform it through scholarship and instruction in Christ's teachings and a return to primitive Christianity. It is difficult to assess Erasmus even today after so many centuries. Some have said that he was an anti-Reformer, some a Lutheran at heart who was afraid of the power of the Church, and some the forerunner of Luther. It has been said that "Erasmus laid the eggs that Luther hatched."

Luther's style of writing is polemical, satirical, and bombastic. For the modern reader more accustomed to a level of civility in public discourse, his tone may seem a bit over the top. He pulls no punches in his attack on Erasmus. For example, he begins with an opening salvo, "Your book struck me as so worthless and poor that my heart went out to you for having defiled your lovely, brilliant flow of language with such vile stuff. I thought it outrageous to convey material of so low a quality in the trappings of such rare eloquence; it is like using gold or silver dishes to carry garden rubbish or dung" (Luther, 63). He continues adding insult to injury, "So, you see, what kept me from rushing in with an answer to you was not the difficulty of so doing, nor pressure of other work, nor the grandeur of your eloquence, nor fear of you, but simply disgust, disinclination, and distaste—which, if I may say so, express my judgment of your diatribe" (Luther, 64). He further informs him that "in your usual way, you have taken vast pains throughout to be slippery and evasive" (Luther, 64). The reader is not left wondering where Luther stands. Luther concludes his Introduction, "For though what you think and write about 'free-will' is wrong, I owe you no small debt of thanks for making me far surer of my own view; as I have been since I saw the case for 'free-will' argued with all the resources that your brilliant gifts afford you—and to such little purpose that it is now in a worse state than before" (Luther, 65).

Erasmus had his own criticisms of the contemporary Roman Catholic Church, but unlike Luther, he believed that such reformation was best accomplished from within and that Luther was being excessive. He believed that all persons possessed free will and rejected the doctrine of predestination as unbiblical. On the other hand, Luther affirmed that man is unable to will to turn to God and that he is thus unable to play any part in the process leading to his salvation. God is the one who initiates in the salvation process. God is the great enabler. He writes about the doctrine of grace. "So, either it is false that we receive our grace for the grace of another, or else it is apparent that 'free-will' is nothing; for these two positions cannot stand together, that the grace of God is *both* so cheap that it may be gained anywhere, and everywhere by a little endeavor on the part of any man, *and* so dear that it is given to us only in and through the grace of this one great man" (Luther, 304)!

Luther then discusses the comfort that comes from knowing that salvation doesn't depend on free will.

> "I frankly confess that, for myself, even if it could be, I should not want 'free-will' to be given me, nor anything to be left in my own hands to enable me to endeavor after salvation; not merely because in the face of so many danger, and adversities, and assaults of devils, I could not stand my ground and hold fast my 'free-will' (for one devil is stronger than all men, and on these terms no man could be saved); but because, even were there no dangers, adversities, or devils, I should still be forced to labor with no guarantee of success, and to beat my fists at the air. If I lived and worked for all eternity, my conscience would never reach comfortable certainty as to how much it must do to satisfy God. Whatever work I had done, there would still be a nagging doubt as to whether it pleased God, or whether he required more. The experience of all who seek righteousness by works proves that; and I learned it well enough

myself over a period of many years, to my own great hurt. But now that God has taken salvation out of the control of my own will, and put it under the control of His, and promised to save me, not according to my working or running, but according to his own grace and mercy, I have the comfortable certainty that he is faithful" (Luther, 314).

In *The Bondage of the Will*, Luther brilliantly demolishes the concept of free will as set forth by Erasmus. In doing so, he explicates the doctrine of man's complete inability to save himself or cooperate in his salvation, affirming God's sovereignty and grace in our salvation. This book is foundational in understanding one of the key doctrines of the Reformation. Luther believed this to be at the heart of the gospel.

Martin Luther's literary output was substantial in his lifetime. He translated the Bible into German in addition to writing a substantial commentary on the Epistle to the Galatians as well as *On the Freedom of a Christian* and *Table Talk*. I also have in my library a very fine eight volume set of his sermons. But it is this seminal work, *The Bondage of the Will*, that is Luther's magnum opus. It is a true classic of the Christian faith. It has been said that John Bunyan's *The Pilgrim's Progress* owes a debt of gratitude to his reading of Luther's commentary on Galatians. For more on the life of Martin Luther, see my review of *Here I Stand* by Roland Bainton in Chapter V.

Unless you plan to read *The Bondage of the Will* in its original Latin, my suggestion is that you obtain the excellent translation by J. I. Packer and O. R. Johnston published by Baker Academic. It captures the vitality of Luther's language and thought and includes a fine Historical and Theological Introduction. All quotations in this review come from that publication. Do not be put off by the fact that this is a weighty book in its theology. It is one of the masterworks coming out of the Reformation and deserves to be read, even today. You probably won't run out and convert to Lutheranism, but you will be greatly blessed.

9. THE PRACTICE OF THE PRESENCE OF GOD

By Brother Lawrence

What was most remarkable about Brother Lawrence, the author of *The Practice of the Presence of God*, is that he was so utterly unremarkable. During his lifetime, he apparently never accomplished anything great or out of the ordinary. He never preached a great evangelistic crusade or led tens of thousands to faith in Jesus Christ, or was never spiritual counsel to presidents as Billy Graham was. He was never regarded as the greatest poet of his age as both Dante and Geoffrey Chaucer were. He was never awarded a Nobel Prize for Literature as Aleksandr Solzhenitsyn was. In fact, everything about his life here on earth screamed the word "unremarkable." The truth be told, unremarkable is probably too charitable a word. "Marginal" might be a better word to describe him.

From the viewpoint of the world, Brother Lawrence's life was a wholly unremarkable one. But from the viewpoint of heaven's balcony, he was most remarkable and his spiritual influence has been incalculable. This Christian classic, which bears his name, has made a profound impact upon generations of Christians who have learned valuable spiritual lessons from this simple monk, who learned to live moment by moment in the presence of God. *The Practice of the Presence of God* is a true Christian classic, beloved by millions, Protestant, Roman Catholic, and Orthodox alike, which has left its mark on countless Christian leaders and clergy, as well as laity.

The Practice of the Presence of God, published posthumously, is a very brief collection of conversations and letters with Brother Lawrence. It is so brief and the style of writing so simple, humble, and direct, that it could probably be read within an hour.

51

But that is not the way to read this book. It should be read slowly and meditatively.

What is it about this unremarkable man that has made such a life-changing difference upon so many Christians for roughly the past 300 years? After all, he is as unlikely a hero of the faith as there could possibly be. Brother Lawrence (1614-1691) was a monk who lived in France in the seventeenth century. He served first as a lay brother in a Carmelite monastery in Paris. He didn't have one of the more glamorous positions in the monastery such as preaching or translating the Bible. Rather, he was assigned to the monastery kitchen where he cooked and washed dishes. He had no delusions of grandeur or an in-flated opinion of himself as some believers do. He wrote, "I consider myself as the most wretched of men" (Lawrence, 25, Second Letter).

Brother Lawrence began life in Lorraine, France, as Nicholas Herman, the son of peasants who lived in abject poverty. He joined the army as a young man to escape his penurious exis-tence. During his time in the army, he had two experiences which pointed him in a particular spiritual direction. The first was a spiritual vision or what he called an awakening to God's purpose for his life. The second was being wounded in the Thirty Years War which left him lame and led to his discharge from the army. He was left with an abhorrence of the horrors of war and a renewed passion for his religious faith.

Herman decided to seek spiritual fulfillment as a hermit, and at the age of twenty-six entered the Order of the Discalced Carmelites in Paris, first as a lay brother before ultimately tak-ing his vows and taking the name "Lawrence of the Resurrec-tion." He wrote, "I took a resolution to give myself to God as the best return I could make for his love, and for the love of Him, to renounce all besides" (Lawrence, 23, Second Letter))

Brother Lawrence was a simple monk with a lowly position in life and the priory. Despite this, many were attracted to his character, which led many to seek spiritual guidance from him. He passed this wisdom on to them in the form of conversations and letters which comprise the substance of this book. His approach to the Christian life was very simple. He wrote, "I walk before God simply, in faith, with humility and with love; and I apply myself diligently to do nothing and think nothing which may displease Him" (Lawrence, 24, Second Letter). He saw himself as always being in the presence of God, which was a constant reality in his consciousness. Thus, what he did on a daily basis "applying my mind carefully the rest of the day, and even in the midst of my business, to the presence of God, whom I considered always with me, often as in me" (Lawrence, 23, Second Letter).

Brother Lawrence believed that spirituality was a slow process. He wrote, "One does not become holy all at once" (Lawrence, 28, Ninth Letter). Spiritual progress was a constant pressing forward because (not to advance in the spiritual life is to go back" (Lawrence, 29, Fourth Letter). Lawrence also believed that he needed to continually walk in the presence of God and continually converse with him. "There is not in the world a kind of life more sweet and delightful than that of a continual conversation with God. Those only can comprehend it who practice and experience it" (Lawrence, 31, Fifth Letter). He advised, "You should keep it strictly in the presence of God; and being accustomed to think of him often, you will find it easy to keep your mind calm in the time of prayer, or at least to recall it from its wanderings" (Lawrence, 36, Eighth Letter). "But think on Him often, adore Him continually" (Lawrence, 40, Tenth Letter).

What can we who live in the twenty-first learn from this simple seventeenth century monk whose life was seemingly so unremarkable? With our lives seemingly always in a hurry, it seems we have not yet learned his simple lesson that the Christian life can be lived moment by moment in the presence of God. God can be known intimately and that we can be aware of his presence in our daily lives. That is why this Christian classic should still be read and why it continues to challenge lives hundreds of years after its writing. See for yourself!

> "It is not necessary for being with GOD to be always at church: we may make an oratory of our heart wherein to retire from time to time to converse with Him in meekness, humility and love. Everyone is capable of such familiar conversation with GOD" (Lawrence, 35, Seventh Letter).

> "Accustom yourself, then, by degrees thus to worship Him, to beg His grace, to offer Him your heart from time to time in the midst of your business, even every moment if you can. Do not always scrupulously confine yourself to certain rules, or particular forms of devotion, but act with a general confidence in GOD, with love and humility" (Ibid.).

10. PARADISE LOST

By John Milton

Paradise Lost has long been regarded as one of the masterworks of English literature. It is universally acknowledged as the greatest epic poem in the English language that soars to literary heights and grandeur. One writer describes Milton, "He plays with the English language like Bach playing the organ" (Veith, 165). The poem has inspired and influenced multitudes of great writers including William Blake and is considered to be Milton's masterpiece solidifying his reputation as one of the English language's greatest poets. It has been instrumental in shaping some of the misconceptions of popular culture about God and the devil. It is unfortunate that the poem is little read these days and that, if read at all, is usually encountered in small samples in a high school or college English class at a time in life when it is least likely to be appreciated.

Paradise Lost is an epic poem written in blank verse. The original version published in 1667 consisted of ten books with over 10,000 lines of verse. In 1674, a second edition followed with a twelve-book arrangement after the example of Virgil's *Aeneid*. The book chronicles the Genesis story of the fall of man including the temptation of Adam and Eve by the serpent Satan and their subsequent expulsion from the Garden of Eden. The entire poem is a masterful apology to justify the ways of God to men. It is also the dramatic story of a cosmic struggle between good and evil.

It has been conjectured that *Paradise Lost* was first conceived as a tragedy and not an epic biblical poem. Initially, it was intended to be based on a legendary Saxon or British king since epics were usually written about the heroic ventures of kings. He began writing the poem in 1658 and it was completed in 1663. Since Milton became blind in 1652, the work was com-

posed totally through dictation with the assistance of amanu-
enses during a period when he was often ill from gout and
suffering from depression after the premature deaths of his
wife and infant daughter. Considering that backstory, it is incredible that the poem ever saw the light of day.

Paradise Lost is an example of epic poetry in the Greek tradition, but unlike anything ever attempted by Homer or Hesiod
of the Greeks or Virgil of the Romans. Milton redefined the
epic of old substituting Christian, as opposed to pagan, values
and themes. It is a tragedy of Shakespearean proportions in its
complexity and the power of its emotions. There are actually
two story arcs, two different perspectives in the poem, one of
Satan and his fall and the other of Adam and Eve and their expulsion from the Garden of Eden. Milton's stated purpose is to
"justify the ways of God to men" (Milton, Book I, 26).

Epic poetry historically has utilized the literary convention of
the muse, a "goddess of artistic inspiration." Milton also invokes the assistance of a heavenly Muse to help him in his
quest to describe man's fall. His only deviation from the convention is that his muse was the Holy Spirit.

The poem opens shortly after Satan's expulsion, along with his
army of angels, from Heaven and banishment to Hell (or Tartus
as it is also called in the poem). Milton begins with these
words:

> "Of man's first disobedience, and the fruit
> Of that forbidden tree, whose mortal taste
> Brought death into the world, and all our woe,
> With loss of Eden, till one greater Man
> Restore us, and regain the blissful seat" (Milton, Book I, 1-
> 5).

Anyone who has ever sinned can identify with Satan's defiance
when he states, "Better to reign in Hell, than serve in Heaven"
(Milton, Book I, 263). His pride and rebelliousness burn

through the pages of the text. After the fall, Milton portrays Satan and his fellow dissenters chained to a lake of fire in Hell. After freeing themselves, they fly away to a land that has minerals where they construct their place of meeting, which is called Pandemonium. They, the angels now being called devils, debate the wisdom of another war with God and decide on a different plan, to seduce the human race away from God. Thus, after the fall of Satan and his renegade angels, we have the fall of mankind through the agency of Adam and Eve. There are, then, two tragedies in this storyline.

This is the story of the fall of mankind into sin and the loss of paradise. As you read, you will encounter a celestial cast of characters that begins with Satan, Adam, and Eve, and moves on to the Son of God, God the Father, and the two archangels, Raphael and Michael. Before he leaves the Garden of Eden, Adam receives a glimpse of the future of mankind by Michael including snippets from both the Old and New Testaments.

Why should readers read *Paradise Lost* today? Sir Walter Raleigh's oft-noted description of the poem as a "monument to dead ideas" is most assuredly off the mark and most unkind, at least to me. According to Veith, "Christians need theologians to explain the Biblical text and to apply its truths, but Christians also need poets such as Milton who can help us imagine and contemplate those truths more fully" (Veith, 166). I will admit that reading Milton is not for the faint of heart. His writing is challenging, but eminently rewarding. He wasn't, as he himself admits, writing for just anyone. He saw himself as a prophet and a visionary speaking truths beyond comprehension to most people. He was writing for a "fit audience find, though few" (Milton, Book VII, 31-33). He wanted readers of value and worth, not those who yearned for literary "fast food." Milton was always a critic of "reading promiscuously." But for those who are mature and willing to persevere, the rewards are great. Diamonds must be mined; they are rarely picked up off the ground. Such it is with Milton. See for yourself and experience one of the great literary treasures of the English language. You will, I think, surrender to its enchantment as I did.

Essential quotations from *Paradise Lost*:

"Th'infernal serpent, he it was, whose guile
Stirr'd up with envy and revenge, deceiv'd
The mother of mankind." (Milton, Book I, 34-36)
"The mind is its own place, and in itself
Can make a heaven of hell, a hell of heaven." (Milton,
Book I, 254-55)

"Who overcomes
By force, hath overcome, but half his foe." (Milton, Book I,
648-49)

"From morn
To noon he fell, from noon to dewy eve,
A summer's day; and with the setting sun
Dropp'd from the zenith like a falling star." (Milton, Book
I, 742-45)

O progeny of heaven, empyreal thrones;
With reason hath deep silence, and demur,
Seiz'd us, though undismay'd: Long is the way
And hard, that out of hell leads up to light." (Milton, Book
II, 430-33)

"So farewell hope, and with hope farewell fear,
Farewell remorse: all good to me is lost;
Evil be thou my good." (Milton, Book IV, 108-110)

"What if earth
Be but the shadow of heaven and things therein,
Each to other like, more than on earth is thought?"
(Milton, Book V, 574-76)

"Her rash hand in evil hour
Forth reaching to the fruit, she pluck'd, she ate;
Earth felt the wound, and Nature from her seat,
Sighing through all her works, gave signs of woe
That all was lost." (Milton, Book IX, 780-84)

"The world was all before them, where to choose
Their place of rest, and Providence their guide.
They, hand in hand, with wand'ring steps and slow
Through Eden took their solitary way." (Milton, Book XII,
646-49)

11. ROBINSON CRUSOE

By Daniel Defoe

The name, Robinson Crusoe, is familiar with most people in the English-speaking world whether or not they have actually read the novel of the same name. Most people know that there was a novel by the same name and that it was about a castaway on a desert island after a shipwreck. But from that starting point, facts begin to get a bit fuzzy and one learns that most people do not know much at all about the novel.

In fact, many do not even consider *Robinson Crusoe* to be a novel at all. They see it more as kind of a mythology such as *Don Juan, Don Quixote,* or *Faust.* When the novel was first published in 1719, it credited the story's protagonist, Robinson Crusoe, as the author, leading many to believe that the work was a true account of actual events, a realistic travelogue. It depicts in journal form the account of a castaway who is shipwrecked and the lone survivor on a remote desert island probably near the coasts of Venezuela and Trinidad. The book chronicles Crusoe's adventures as he encounters cannibals and mutineers along the way as he tries to survive using only what he could salvage from the ship, the bounty of the land, and his own cunning and ingenuity.

Defoe's novel is often regarded to be the first English novel and the first example of a new literary genre called realistic fiction. The novel was well-received in the literary world and spawned many imitators. It has been adapted several times by film makers including the movie version from the 1812 German novel, *Der Schweizerische Robinson* (English: *Swiss Family Robinson*) by Johann David Wyss. There can be no denying *Robinson Crusoe's* literary influence. By the end of the nineteenth century, there had been at least 700 editions, translations, and imitations. There would likely been no *Gulliver's Travels* by

Jonathan Swift published seven years later, had Defoe not written his novel first. Although Swift's novel can be read on many levels, it has been suggested that it is a rebuttal of Defoe's optimism in humanity. Robert Louis Stevenson also seemingly parodies Crusoe in his character from *Treasure Island*, Ben Gunn, a man who had been marooned on Treasure Island for three years by his crewmates.

It has been commonly supposed that Defoe's novel derived from the true-to-life account of Alexander Selkirk, a Scottish sailor and Royal Navy officer, who survived in the Juan Fernandez Islands for over four years after being marooned by his captain. During his time on the island before his rescue in 1709, he survived by learning the art of hunting and utilizing the resources available to him on the island. Although many details of Defoe's account of Robinson Crusoe are inconsistent with Selkirk's experience, this is not the place to debate how much he was influenced by it.

Daniel Defoe may seem to be a dubious choice to write a novel, which has been so influential and is perhaps second only to the Bible in its number of translations. Although he was a prolific writer, his over 300 works span a variety of topics, religion being only one. He is most famous for *Robinson Crusoe, Moll Flanders*, and *A Journal of a Plague Year*, but it was his writing of political tracts that inflamed the authorities of his day and even led to his imprisonment on one occasion. He is credited, along with others, as being an early architect of the English novel, a literary form that would later take on a life of its own. Defoe's father had hoped that he would become a minister, but such a career choice interested Defoe very little. His family and he were considered Dissenters, a derisive term used to describe those who were not members of the Church of England. Defoe himself was a Presbyterian, and his understanding of God's providence permeates *Robinson Crusoe*. The novel can also be seen to be a bit autobiographical as Defoe's own person struggles with religion and morality can be seen depicted in the title character. Robinson Crusoe chooses a career at sea against the wishes of his father. Early in his sojourn on the island, Crusoe writes, *"Why has God done this to me? What have I done to be thus us'd?* My conscience presently check'd me in that Enquiry, as if I had blasphem'd, and methought it spoke like a voice; WRETCH! *dost thou ask what thou hast done! Ask,* Why is it *that thou was not long ago destroy'd?* (Defoe, 68). As a Dissenter, in direct opposition to the teachings of the Anglican Church of his day and the Roman Catholic Church, Defoe understood salvation to be a matter of individual faith and having a person relationship with God through Jesus Christ. This concept can be seen over and over again in his novel.

The plot of *Robinson Crusoe* is quite straightforward. Defoe uses a simple narrative style to tell his tale. Crusoe sets sail on a sea voyage against the wishes of his parents who wished for him a career in the law. He has numerous adventures and misadventures on his sailing ventures, including a shipwreck, before finally several years later joining an expedition to purchase slaves, which ends in disaster. The boat is shipwrecked forty miles out to sea on an island near the Venezuelan coast. He, along with a dog and two cats, are the only survivors of the mishap. Before the ship breaks apart and sinks, Crusoe is able to rescue tools, arms, and supplies, which he uses for survival. Before going to sea for his fateful voyage, Crusoe had been counseled by an older, wiser shipmate to take the first shipwreck as a warning and not to go to sea anymore. He says, *"You see what a taste Heaven has given you of what you are to expect if you persist; perhaps this has all befallen us on your account, like Jonah in the Ship of Tarshish"* (Defoe, 12).

The years pass as Crusoe learns how to survive off the fat of the land. He builds an enclosure near a cave which he excavates, grows barley and rice, dries grapes to make raisins, shoots mammals and birds for meat, learns how to make a crude form of pottery, raises goats, creates a primitive calendar which he uses to mark his days, and adopts a parrot, which he teaches to say words. Most importantly, he begins to read a rescued Bible and begins to develop a relationship with God.

After some years, Crusoe discovers cannibals who sometime visit the island to kill and devour prisoners. He does not disturb them, but he does dream of someday freeing one or two prisoners to use as his servants. Finally, one escapes the cannibals and he assists him and names him "Friday" after the day of the week on which he met Crusoe. He teaches Friday how to speak English and leads him to a saving faith in Jesus Christ. This leads to further encounters with the cannibals. He and Friday kill some of them and rescue two prisoners, one of whom is Friday's father and the other a Spaniard, who tells Crusoe about other Spaniards who are shipwrecked on the mainland. The devise a plan in which the two rescued prisoners would return to the mainland, inform the others, and then build a ship whereby they would all return to Spain.

Before the Spaniards arrive, an English ship which has been commandeered by mutineers arrives at the island. Their intention is to maroon the captain. Crusoe helps the captain retake his ship, the ringleader of the mutineers is hanged, and Crusoe returns to England arriving in 1687. The rest of the narrative is somewhat anticlimactic.

The first time I read *Robinson Crusoe*, I did so as a wee lad about ten years old. The reason I can remember it so vividly is because *Moon River* by Andy Williams was popular then. Over the past six decades, I cannot hear Williams sing *Moon River* but that it conjures up in my mind thoughts of one of the first novels I ever read. However, I didn't read the novel as a story with strong religious elements, but as a pure adventure story along the lines of Rudyard Kipling's *Gunga Din* or Robert Louis Stevenson's *Treasure Island*. It wasn't until several decades later that I realized that there was more to the story than meets the eye. Biblical allusions are prevalent throughout the book and the providence of God can be seen everywhere.

Robinson Crusoe is, if nothing else, a spiritual journey; it describes the spiritual pilgrimage of a man from selfish indifference to God to a mature, strong faith in Jesus Christ. Crusoe's pilgrimage begins when as a youth he repeatedly disregarded his parental guidance to go his own way. His father often quoted Bible verses such as Proverbs 30:9 about seeking neither poverty nor riches. When Crusoe became stranded on the island, he began to see his condition as the worst punishment imaginable. He writes, "No sooner was the first Fright over, but the Impression it made went off also. I had no more Sense of God or his Judgments, much less of the present Affliction of my Circumstances being from his Hand, than if I had been in the most prosperous Condition of Life" (Defoe, 66). He describes himself as "miserable" and the island the "island of Despair." Rather than giving thanks that he of all the mariners on board was spared, he began to feel sorry for himself.

He gradually begins to see the beneficent hand of God in his circumstances. Perhaps the first weakening in his defensive wall of unbelief comes when he sees barley growing where, by all rights, it should not be growing. He writes, "But after I saw Barley grow there, in a Climate which I know was not proper for Corn, and especially that I knew not how it came there, it startl'd me strangely, and I began to suggest that God had miraculously caus'd this Grain to grow without any Help of Seed sown, and that it was directed purely for my Sustenance on that wild miserable Place" (Defoe, 58). Later, when he found a logical explanation for the phenomenon, he again denounced the providence of God.

Another weakening in his defensive wall of unbelief came not long after the barley incident when Crusoe became extremely ill from the ague, a condition that lasted over a week and left him extremely weak and lightheaded and fearful of death. He writes, "I was so ignorant, that I knew what not to say; only I lay and cry'd, *Lord look upon me, Lord pity me, Lord have Mercy upon me*" (Defoe, 64). He had a dream or a vision in his feverous delirium in which he "saw a Man descend from a great black Cloud, in a bright Flame of Fire" (Ibid.). He is told that since he has not been brought to repentance, he will die. Crusoe writes, "At which Word, I thought he lifted up the Spear that was in his

Hand to kill me" (Defoe, 65). It is at this point that he begins to examine himself and realize his need for Jesus Christ as a sinner.

That trial led Crusoe to a renewed faith in his Lord and he began the very next day to read the Bible and seek God. His view of his circumstances had changed as well. Whereas formerly he saw the island as someplace that was a punishment for him; now he viewed it as a blessing. He writes, "And now I saw how easy it was for the Providence of God to make the most miserable Condition Mankind could be in *worse*. Now I look'd back upon my desolate solitary Island as the most pleasant Place in the World, and all the Happiness my Heart could wish for" (Defoe, 101). What a metamorphosis had taken place in Crusoe's outlook! He had now learned what the apostle Paul had so many centuries ago. "I have learned the secret of being content in any and every situation" (Phil. 4:12). In fact, Crusoe realized that he was actually happier on the desert island that he had been while living in human society. He no longer longed for a ship to rescue him. He began to make a home on the island. This was the will of God.

Robinson Crusoe is an important novel to read on many levels. For children, it is a rousing adventure story. For adults, it is important because it was a forerunner of the English novel and one of the earliest examples of realistic fiction. But more important, for the Christian it is a simple tale of one man's journey to faith in Jesus Christ. It also just happens to be one of the classics of English literature and one of the greatest treasures of Christian fiction. You already have a nodding acquaintance with the basic storyline; you should read it for yourself and be magically transported to a desert island where you live with your Bible, your God, and your wits as you struggle to survive. You will enjoy the journey.

12. OUT OF THE DEPTHS

By John Newton

Most folks, it seems, are unfamiliar with the name of the author of *Out of the Depths*. If the name John Newton is known at all by Christians today, it is usually as the hymn writer who gave us those wonderful hymns, *Amazing Grace* and *Glorious Things of Thee are Spoken*. Personally, I am partial to his lovely *How Sweet the Name of Jesus Sounds*. Little is known by the average person of this remarkable man who had a road to Damascus experience much like the apostle Paul and who was once a vile and despicable man who ended up as an Anglican minister and famous hymn writer. However, John Newton knew fully of the depths from which he was rescued by God. He was a ship captain and slave trader whose life was turned topsy turvy by an encounter with Jesus Christ. He was redeemed and became an Anglican clergyman and famous hymn writer.

Newton was the son of an English merchant sea captain. Having a father who was away at sea for long periods, Newton's childhood was unsettled and his adolescence very turbulent. His mother was a godly woman who immersed young John in the Scriptures, but she died when he was only seven years of age. His father took him to sea when he was eleven years old. At this time, he alternated between intense religious experiences and gross sin. He writes, "These struggles between sin and conscience were often repeated, and every relapse sank me into still greater depths of wickedness" (Newton, 14). His experiences mirror those of many believers who continually struggle with sin. Newton explains his rationale, "I saw the necessity of religion as a means of escaping hell, but I loved sin, and was unwilling to forsake it" (Newton, 15).

Newton joined the Royal Navy under duress and attempted to escape. He was arrested in West Africa and became the slave of a white slave trader and his vindictive black wife. He was humiliated and systematically starved by that woman and her husband. He describes his treatment in slavery. "From that time, he likewise used me very hardly. Whenever he left the vessel, I was locked upon deck, with a pint of rice for my day's allowance, and if he stayed longer, I had no relief till his return. Indeed, I believe I should have been nearly starved" (Newton, 41). While virtually a slave, he was also involved in the slave trade. However, in reflection after his conversion, he writes, "What a comfortable thought is this to be a believer, to know that amid all the various interfering designs of men, the Lord has one constant design, which He cannot, will not miss, namely, His own glory in the complete salvation of His people; and that He is wise and strong, and faithful, to make even those things which seem contrary to this design, subservient to promote it" (Newton, 51).

After two years of that kind of treatment, in 1747 Newton boarded a ship bound for England, but the ship nearly sank during a violent storm. It was at this time that he had a spiritual awakening and he turned to the Lord Jesus Christ. The ship limped into a port in Lough Swilly, Ireland, just two hours before a violent storm arose which would surely have sunk the ship. Newton writes, "*About this time I began to know there is a God who hears and answers prayer.* How many times has He appeared for me since this great deliverance! Yet, alas! how distrustful and ungrateful is my heart unto this hour" (Newton, 65)! Newton could not understand why he, of all people, had been singled out by God for salvation. He writes, "I was the most unlikely person in the ship to receive an impression, having been often before quite stupid and hardened in the very face of great dangers, and having always before hardened my neck more and more after every reproof. I can see no reason why the Lord singled me out for mercy" (Newton, 66). The echoes of Newton's great hymn, *Amazing Grace! How Sweet the Sound*, can be seen in his words here. He wrote, "through many dangers, toils, and snares, I have already come." He doesn't explicitly mention shipwreck, but it certainly couldn't have been far from his mind.

Newton described his conversion experience. "The Lord had wrought a marvelous thing: I was no longer an infidel. I heartily renounced my former profaneness; was seriously disposed, and sincerely touched with a sense of undeserved mercy in being brought safe through so many dangers; I was sorry for my past misspent life and purposed an immediate reformation; I was freed from the habit of swearing which seemed to have been deeply rooted in me as a second nature. To all appearance, I was a new man" (Newton, 68). It is an interesting fact and disappointing, at least to me, that Newton continued his slave trading even after his conversion. His feelings about his vocation were conflicted to say the least. He wrote, "During the time I was engaged in the slave trade, I never had the least scruple as to its lawfulness. I was upon the whole satisfied with it as the appointment providence had marked out for me. It was, indeed, accounted a genteel employment, usually very profitable, though to me it did not prove so, the Lord seeing that a large increase in wealth would not be good for me" (Newton, 96). He explains his apprehension. "However, I considered myself as a sort of jailer and I was sometimes shocked with an employment that was perpetually connected with chains, bolts, and shackles. In this view I had often prayed that the Lord in His own time would be pleased to place me in a more humane calling" (Ibid.).

This prayer was answered by God. Within two days of sailing on another slave trading voyage, Newton suffered a "seizure which deprived me of sense and motion, and left me no sign of life but of breathing" (Newton, 97). When he had recovered, Newton decided that "it would not be safe or prudent for me to proceed on the voyage" (Ibid.). He resigned his command the day before the ship sailed. He writes, "Thus I was unexpectedly called from that service, and freed from the consequences of that voyage" (Ibid.). He then began to study Scripture seriously and was "called" into a new vocation.

Newton tells us why he wrote this memoir. He explains that it is "addressed to all who are passing through the wilderness of this world to a heavenly Canaan; who by faith in the promises and power of God, are seeking an eternal rest in that kingdom which cannot be shaken" (Newton, 5). His early maternal influences and his reading of Thomas à Kempis's classic Christian devotional, *Of the Imitation of Christ*, made deep impressions upon him. Upon his rejection of the seafaring life, Newton was benefited greatly by his association with the Wesley brothers, John and Charles. He also had a long and fruitful friendship with William Cowper, the Anglican poet and hymn writer, with whom he co-wrote the famous *Olney Hymns*, and from whose pen gave us the wonderful hymn *There Is a Fountain Filled with Blood*. Newton was ordained in the Anglican Church and was appointed Rector of St. Mary Church in London in 1780. He became a friend to William Wilberforce and was a positive influence in his fight to abolish slavery in the British Empire.

Out of the Depths is a remarkable book by a remarkable man whose life and literary legacy continues to impact Christians over 200 years after his death. This book is surely one of the true classics of the Christian faith and should be read at least once by every believer. His epitaph, which Newton wrote himself, can be seen near the pulpit at the St. Mary Woolnoth Church in London. It tells the story of his life. It reads in part:

JOHN NEWTON, Clerk
Once an infidel and libertine
A servant of slaves in Africa,
Was, by the rich mercy of our Lord and Saviour
JESUS CHRIST,
restored, pardoned, and appointed to preach
the Gospel he had long laboured to destroy

CHAPTER III:
APOLOGETICS, EVANGELISM, AND MISSIONS

APOLOGETICS

The assault on the gospel has, for centuries, been a favorite pastime for Satan and his minions. The recent onslaught of secular humanism has been painfully effective in turning the hearts of men and women from God toward a life that satisfies self and opposes the truth of God's Word. Sincere Christians must do everything possible to embrace Ephesians 6:13; "Therefore, take unto you the whole armor of God, that you may be able to withstand in the evil day and, having done all, to stand." The books in this first section on apologetics provide the academic and the practical tools for believers to stand firm and defend the gospel.

The term "apologetics" may be an unfamiliar one to many Christians, but it is an important subdivision of Christian theology. The word itself comes from the Greek *apologia*, which was the legal defense one made in a court of law. It is used in Paul's second letter to young Timothy. "At my first defense, no one came to my support, but everyone deserted me. May it not be held against them" (2 Timothy 4:16). Literally in Classical Greek, the word meant "to speak in defense; defend oneself." The Apostle Peter wrote, "But in your hearts set apart Christ as Lord. Always be prepared to give an answer for the hope that you have" (1 Peter 3:15). In a certain sense, apologetics is a necessary component of evangelism, at least pre-evangelism. Therefore, since God commands that we practice apologetics, it behooves us to know something about what it means.

In purely theological terms, apologetics is the academic discipline that deals with the rational defense of the Christian faith. But you don't have to be a theologian to practice apologetics. As Peter commanded, every Christian should. The reason for this is that the Christian faith makes certain claims that are audacious on the face of it. First of all, there is a God. There are many in the world who deny this simple assertion. They are called atheists. What do you, as a Christian, say when your atheist neighbor or co-worker says that there is no God? Another claim the Christian faith makes is that God has inserted himself into human history and revealed himself to mankind. That is quite a stretch for many people in today's world who do not have a Christian worldview. Another claim, one that is foundational to our Christian faith, is that God became a man, died on a Roman cross, and rose from the dead. We take these claims for granted, but there are some who think that Christians are crazy for believing such nonsense. So, what do you say to your unbelieving skeptic?

The books that I have included in this section were carefully chosen because they will help you to think through some of the big issues in apologetics. They have been extremely helpful to me as I, a young university student and doubter, worked through some of these very questions that I have raised so many decades ago. We should, as the Apostle Paul said it so well, "Demolish arguments and every pretension that sets itself up against the knowledge of God, and we take captive every thought to make it obedient to Christ" (2 Corinthians 10:5).

13. THE EVERLASTING MAN

By G. K. Chesterton

A century ago, the fundamentalist/modernist controversy, which originated in the Presbyterian Church USA and soon affected just about every denomination in the United States, was in full swing. J. Gresham Machen of the Princeton Theological Seminary, the standard bearer for the fundamentalist side of the conflict, was bringing his formidable intellect into play and wielding it as a club against the theological liberals. At that time, it was fashionable to question the orthodox tenets of the Christian faith as well as many of its cherished beliefs. By this time, the writings of Karl Marx and Charles Darwin had infiltrated the church and what had begun initially in the Presbyterian Church in the USA soon spread to other denominations and had a widespread effect.

Christians, already blindsided by Darwin's 1859 publication of *On the Origin of Species*, were also reeling from the effects of the science fiction writer H. G. Wells' publication in 1920 of *The Outline of History*. The work was subtitled *The Whole Story of Man* or *Being a Plain History of Life and Mankind*. To many, it was more another work of fiction from the fertile mind of Wells rather than a historical account. Wells envisioned mankind as the seamless progression from animal life and Jesus Christ as simply a charismatic teacher, nothing more. It was at this point, that G. K. Chesterton jumped into the fray and gave us his delightful rebuttal, *The Everlasting Man*. This book is one of Chesterton's three great apologies: *Heretics*, *Orthodoxy*, and *The Everlasting Man*. In fact, these three books are collected together into one compilation titled *The Three Apologies of G. K. Chesterton*. All of my quotations in this review are taken from it. In his classic work, Chesterton asks and answers some of the most compelling questions that a person can ponder. What do you believe about Jesus Christ? Was he just another man albeit an extremely charismatic figure? What do you believe about mankind? Do you believe that human life and civilization are simply the logical and inevitable result of evolution? Is man just another animal, albeit somewhat more intellectually advanced than say, a monkey?

Gilbert Keith Chesterton wore many hats in his sixty-two years (1874-1936). He was a philosopher, journalist, literary and art critic, Christian apologist, and writer, but it was primarily as an apologist and writer that he is known today. The truth be told, many modern Christians do not even recognize his name and this is tragic. His three great apologies are classics and his enduring fictional character, the priest-detective, has delighted generations of readers. Chesterton was a brilliant and witty writer who has been called "the prince of paradox" as well as "the Shakespeare of the aphorism." His masterwork, *The Everlasting Man*, gave voice to a generation of Christians who were reeling in the face of the numerous attacks against their faith. C. S. Lewis acknowledged his reading of this book as one of most importance in his pilgrimage towards the Christian faith. One can certainly see the fingerprints of Chesterton throughout the great apologetic by Lewis, *Mere Christianity.*

Chesterton, who was born in London and lived his entire life in England, was baptized in the Church of England though his family were sometimes practicing Unitarians. His marriage in 1901 to Frances Blogg lasted his entire life and led him back to the Anglican faith. However, he became a Roman Catholic in 1922 and later was critical of the Church of England. Whether Anglican or Roman Catholic, his understanding of the Christian faith permeated his writings. Christian themes and symbolism appear over and over again in his writings which were prolific. Veith writes of him, "G. K. Chesterton persuades his readers of the truth of Christianity by first helping them to notice the marvels inherent in ordinary life" (Veith, 140).

Chesterton's literary output was substantial. In addition to his roughly eighty books which included his wonderful novel, *The Man Who Was Thursday*, he wrote hundreds of poems, about 200 short stories, several plays, and some 4,000 essays most of which appeared as newspaper columns. One of his many books was *Charles Dickens: A Critical Study*, a work of nonfiction which was well-reviewed. Chesterton seems to me to have been a real "Renaissance Man," writing with a sense of authority, wit, and humor on a staggering array of topics. Glaspey writes of him that he "had the ability to pack more paradox and more truth into a single sentence than possibly any writer in history" (Glaspey, 82).

Chesterton divides his book into two parts. The first is "a sketch of the main adventure of the human race in so far as it remained heathen," and the second "a summary of the real difference that was made by it becoming Christian" (Chesterton, 228). He lets loose an opening salvo against Wells. He writes that "this brilliant and versatile author simply forgot for a moment that he was supposed to be writing a history and dreamed he was writing one of his own wonderful and imaginative romances" (Chesterton, 258).

Chesterton writes of mankind in comparison with animals that walk on four legs that "the queerest creature of all walks about on two" (Chesterton, 236). He dismisses the theory of evolution as an explanation for man. He writes of its proponents, "It has the fatal quality of leaving on many minds the impression that they do understand it and everything else; just as many of them live under a sort of illusion that they have read the *Origin of Species*" (Chesterton, 235). He also writes of the qualitative difference between mankind and other animals. "It is the simple truth that man does differ from the brutes in kind and not degree; and the proof of it is here; that it sounds like a truism to say that the most primitive man drew a picture of a monkey and that it sounds like a joke to say that the most intelligent monkey drew a picture of a man. Something of division and disproportion has appeared; and it is unique. Art is the signature of man" (Chesterton, 241). He further explains, "All we can say of this notion of reproducing things in shadow or representative shape is that it exists nowhere in nature except in man; and that we cannot even talk about it without treating man as something separate from nature" (Chesterton, 242). He concludes that history, then, "must begin with man as man, a thing standing absolute and alone. How he came there, or indeed how anything else came there, is a thing for theologians and philosophers and scientists and not for historians" (Chesterton, 242). Chesterton further ponders, "His body may have been evolved from the brutes; but we know nothing of any such transition that throws the smallest light upon his soul as it has shown itself in history" (Chesterton, 247). In his delightful chapter, "The Man in the Cave," Chesterton writes about evolution, "There is something slow and soothing, and gradual about the word and even about the idea" (Chesterton, 235). He explains some of the limitations of the theory and its adherents. But he never warms to the theory.

Chesterton discusses the limitations of science in diagnosing the problem of mankind. He writes that it "cannot experiment in making men; or even watching to see what the first men make" (Chesterton, 246). He tellingly deduces, "Sometimes the professor with his bone becomes almost as dangerous as a dog with his bone. And the dog at least does not deduce a theory from it, proving that mankind is going to the dogs—or that it came from them" (Chesterton, 246-47). Whatever you think of the science of paleontology, you must appreciate the brilliance of Chesterton's rapier wit. His point is that science is clueless in dealing with matters of the soul and of sin. He concludes with respect to man's soul, "Whatever else men have believed, they have all believed that there is something the matter with mankind" (Chesterton, 254).

Chesterton begins his discussion of mankind with a chapter appropriately titled "On the Creature Called Man," and he talks about evolution right off the bat. He muses that nobody could possibly "imagine how a world was created any more than he could create one" (Chesterton, 235). He surmises that however God created the world and mankind, it was still a miracle. One of Chesterton's best shots at Wells is, "Mr. H. G. Wells has confessed to being a prophet, and in this matter he was a prophet at his own expense" (Chesterton, 235).

Chesterton concludes that if man is just another animal, he is really a rather bizarre one. He writes, "The queerest of all walks about on two" (Chesterton, 236). He concludes, "It is not seeing straight to see him as an animal. It is not sane. It sins against the light; against that broad daylight of proportion which is the principle of all reality" (Chesterton, 243). Chesterton rails against those brilliant university professors who devise their theories. "Sometimes the professor with his bone becomes almost as dangerous as a dog with his bone. And the dog does not deduce a theory from it, proving that mankind is going to the dogs—or that it came from them" (Chesterton, 247). He wonders how the soul supposedly "evolved." If the theory of evolution is indeed true, then the formation of the soul in man is unexplained.

With respect to who Jesus was, Chesterton concludes that if Jesus was just another human leader and Christianity just another human religion, then both Jesus and his followers are basically lunatics. He writes of this delusion, "It can be found, not among prophets and sages and founders of religions, but only among a low set of lunatics" (Chesterton, 355). Chesterton concludes about Jesus. "For nobody supposes that Jesus of Nazareth was that sort of person. No modern critic in his five wits thinks that the preacher of the Sermon on the Mount was a horrible half-witted imbecile that might be scrawling stars on the walls of a cell. No atheist or blasphemer believes that the author of the Parable of the Prodigal Son was a monster with one mad idea like a cyclops with one eye" (Chesterton, 355). One can easily discern echoes of Chesterton's reasoning in *Mere Christianity* by C. S. Lewis.

A word of caution is in order here. It is well-known that Chesterton's use of racial stereotypes and, to the twenty-first century mind, insensitive racial terminology will be deemed offensive to many. Keep in mind that Chesterton was very much a product of his age and that we should not judge a book written a century ago by our modern standards and sensibilities. Mark Twain's classic *Huckleberry Finn* has likewise become the target for today's politically correct censors and book- burners. From my perspective, when Chesterton writes of the "Red Indian" in comparison with the terminal treaty breakers white men, it is sometimes difficult to draw the line between who is the savage and who is not. I would encourage the reader to not throw the baby out with the bath. Do not dismiss him because of his era in history. My judgment is that you will be taken in by Chesterton's whimsical style of writing.

In *The Everlasting Man*, Chesterton takes us on a spiritual journey, that of Western civilization. The pivotal figure of the history of Western civilization, indeed of the world, is Jesus Christ. He writes, "For it was the soul of Christendom that came forth from the incredible Christ; and the soul of it was common sense. Though we dared not look on His face we could look on His fruits; and by His fruits we should know Him" (Chesterton, 400). With verve and wit, Chesterton demonstrates that Jesus was not just another charismatic figure or religious crackpot. He was the very Son of God, God Incarnate. You owe it to yourself to see why C. S. Lewis was so enamored by the writings of this man. It will be quite the experience!

14. MERE CHRISTIANITY

By C. S. Lewis

C. S. Lewis is perhaps the towering figure in twentieth century Christian literature and an intellectual giant. This book is arguably the most influential Christian book of that century. His books have influenced millions of believers and are considered, both fiction and non-fiction, to be modern classics by children and adults alike. His books have been embraced by evangelicals and theological liberals alike.

But Lewis was something of an enigma to many. He certainly was not a classic evangelical and surely not a fundamentalist. In the first place, he smoked cigarettes and a pipe. Both were considered big "no-no's" around the middle of the twentieth century in conservative Christian circles. He was also known to visit English pubs and drink beer on regular occasions. These practices were strictly forbidden in many churches particularly in the United States.

His theology was also suspect. He was an Oxford professor and had all of the academic qualifications, but some of his theological beliefs were a wee bit suspect. For example, he didn't believe in biblical inerrancy, a twentieth century hot-button issue, nor did he subscribe to penal substitution and his view of the atonement was considered deficient. He also believed in purgatory and baptismal regeneration, two views certain to earn demerits among evangelicals, and was also suspected of being a universalist. How could such a man become so revered to so many in the evangelical world?

Charles W. Colson, in his excellent memoir *Born Again*, credits the influence of *Mere Christianity* as the book that helped to nudge him into the Kingdom of God. Colson, the former "hatchet man" for the president in the Nixon White House, was not an easy conversion. However, Lewis (and the Holy Spirit of course) won him over with his brilliant appeal. Colson wrote, "I opened *Mere Christianity* and found myself face-to-face with an intellect so disciplined, so lucid, so relentlessly logical that I could only be grateful I had never faced him in a court of law" (Colson, 121).

Another well-known figure who was mightily influenced by this book is Francis Collins, the head of the Human Genome Project and one of the world's leading scientists. Collins encountered *Mere Christianity* as a young medical doctor wrestling with atheism. As he reflects on his initial reading of Lewis's book in his own wonderful work *The Language of God*, he writes that he struggled "to absorb the breadth and depth of the intellectual arguments laid down by this legendary Oxford scholar." He wondered at the insights of Lewis. "Lewis seemed to know all of my objections, sometimes even before I had quite formulated them." He claims that the impact of the book and Lewis's arguments about moral law "rocked my ideas about science and spirit down to their foundation." Only eternity will reveal how many people credit an encounter with this book or any of Lewis's classic writings to their exposure to the Christian faith.

This book began as a series of radio messages delivered over the BBC from 1942 to 1944 during the height of the uncertainty over the outcome of World War II. Its contents were previously published in three separate parts as *The Case for Christianity* (1943), *Christian Behavior* (1943), and *Beyond Personality* (1945) before being gathered into the book that we know as *Mere Christianity*. It was not intended to be a polished literary work, but is rather a work of oral literature basically written down the exact way the words were spoken on the airwaves without editing. Thus, it is more a series of fireside chats utilizing a whimsical style addressed to a nation engaged in a bitter war. Try to imagine a country still reeling from the effects of German bombing and the daily reports of the death toll of British soldiers. They tune into the radio and hear a genial Oxford don talking about decent and humane behavior, fair play, and right and wrong. One can only wonder how Lewis's talks resonated with his original audience and how many were converted to faith in Jesus Christ as a result of them. In his Preface, Lewis utilizes a metaphor of Christianity as a great hall with different doors leading to rooms which have "fires, and chairs, and meals." His listeners are making their way each to their own room (or Christian denomination). He concludes his Preface with the following gracious words. "When you have reached your own room, be kind to those who have chosen different doors and to those who are still in the hall. If they are wrong they need your prayers all the more; and if they are your enemies, then you are under orders to pray for them. That is one of the rules common to the whole house."

Lewis was attempting to set forth a set of basic common Christian beliefs. Many were deriding Christianity as a relic from the distant past and irrelevant to the threat that England was facing from the Axis powers. Others were bickering over denominational differences and were unable to see the forest for the trees. Lewis welcomed all to enter into the hall. There are four sections, or books, each dealing with a different area of Christian belief. Book I is titled "Right and Wrong as a Clue to the Meaning of the Universe;" Book II is "What Christians Believe;" "Book III is "Christian Behaviour;" and Book IV "Beyond Personality: Or First Steps in the Doctrine of the Trinity."

Interestingly, Lewis begins his book about mere Christianity not with a barrage of Bible quotes, but with everyday observations about human nature. His opening salvo is quite innocuous. "Every one has heard people quarreling." (Lewis, 17). He proceeds to demonstrate in a delightful fashion that all quarrels derive from competing notions of right and wrong, "some kind of Law or Rule of fair play and decent behavior or morality or whatever you like to call it, about which they really agreed" (Ibid.). He explains exactly what morality is. "In reality, moral rules are directions for running the human machine. Every moral rule is there to prevent a breakdown, or a strain, or a friction, in the running of that machine. That is why these rules at first seem to be constantly interfering with our natural inclinations" (Lewis, 69).

On almost every page you will encounter simple but sublime observations by Lewis. For example, he writes about fornication in his chapter on Christian marriage. "The monstrosity of sexual intercourse outside marriage is that those who indulge in it are trying to isolate one kind of union (the sexual) from all other kinds of union which were intended to go along with it and make up the total union" (Lewis, 96). About "the great sin" which he identifies as pride, he writes that we "are strutting about like the little idiots we are" (Lewis, 114). I was greatly moved by Lewis's little chapter on hope. He writes, "The Apostles themselves, who set on foot the conversion of the Roman Empire, the great men who built up the Middle Ages, the English Evangelicals who abolished the Slave Trade, all left their mark on Earth, precisely because their minds were occupied with Heaven. It is since Christians have largely ceased to think of the other world that they have become so ineffective in this. Aim at Heaven and you will get earth 'thrown in': aim at earth and you will get neither" (Lewis, 118). Also, "If I find in myself a desire which no experience in this world can satisfy, the most probable explanation is that I was made for another world" (Lewis, 120).

Of course, his famous chapter titled "The Shocking Alternative" is absolutely priceless. He makes our purpose on this earth very clear. "A car is made to run on gasoline, and it would not run properly on anything else. Now God designed the human machine to run on Himself" (Lewis, 54). His discussion about Jesus as a great moral teacher in that same chapter is brilliant. He says about Christ's claim to be able to forgive sins, "Now unless the speaker is God, this is really so preposterous as to be comic" (Lewis, 55). He concludes, "A man who was merely a man and said the sort of things Jesus said would not be a great moral teacher. He would either be a lunatic—on a level with the man who says he is a poached egg . . . You must make your choice. Either this man was, and is, the Son of God: or else a madman or something worse" (Lewis, 56).

Today, eighty years after Lewis began his radio addresses over the BBC that became the basis for this book, *Mere Christianity* is still hugely influential. It is still widely read and Lewis is still widely quoted. In fact, his writing is as fresh today as it was so many decades ago. Like his contemporary, Dietrich Bonhoeffer, Lewis still speaks loudly today. You owe it to yourself to discover C. S. Lewis.

15. BASIC CHRISTIANITY

By John R. W. Stott

When this book was published in 1958, many people were, as John Stott so ably put it, "hostile to the church, friendly to Jesus Christ." This was particularly true of younger people. They were opposed to a religion which smacked of institutionalism. Although the antiestablishment movement would not be in full swing until the late 1960's, there was a decided mood that abhorred the established church and along with its "entrenched privileges." Many rejected the contemporary church because of what they perceived as a cognitive dissonance, a contradiction between who Jesus, the founder of the movement which bears his name, was and what he taught and how it is often practiced by his followers. This apparent hypocrisy, whether grounded in truth or not, was a definite turn off to large numbers of people in the 1950's and succeeding decades.

To John Stott, basic Christianity was more than "the belief that Jesus is the Son of God who came to be the Saviour of the world." For its adherents, it went far beyond acknowledgement of those facts, an intellectual assent to the basic historical facts about Jesus. He wrote, "Our intellectual belief may be beyond criticism, but we have to translate our beliefs into deeds." Thus, as Stott argues passionately in this book, basic Christianity is a religion of action. The religion of the hypocrites and pew warmers of the institutional church needed to re-examine not only their religious beliefs, but their practices as well.

The late John Stott was the right man in God's perfect timing to address these issues. I have to confess right off the bat that Stott has been one of my personal heroes of the faith ever since I was introduced to his writings during my seminary years almost a half century ago. Several of his books have been extremely influential in my life including *The Preacher's Portrait*

(1960), *Between Two Worlds: The Art of Preaching in the Twenti-eth Century*, and his two-volume work, *Involvement: Being a Responsible Christian in a Non-Christian Society*. His was a re-markable life of service to the Lord Jesus Christ. He studied theology at the University of Cambridge and became curate of All Souls, Langham Place, in London, his boyhood church where he served from 1945-1950 in that position before becom-ing rector from 1950 to 1975. The church was strategically lo-cated near London University, the BBC, and several hospitals and attracted many educated young adults. While serving at All Souls, Stott became increasingly influential, not only in the Church of England, but internationally. He founded the Church of England Evangelical Council in 1960 to consolidate the different conservative factions within the church. He also was instrumental in the founding of the Lausanne Committee for World Evangelization in the 1974, and his fingerprints are all over the Lausanne Covenant, its founding constitution, which has been called one of the most significant documents in mod-ern church history. Through his work with Lausanne, it was demonstrated that it was possible to be an evangelical and still show concern for the poor and underprivileged. It was also possible for evangelicals of the many varying theological tradi-tions to work together towards that end and to meld the gospel together with their efforts. Stott believed in ministering to the whole man by meeting his physical, emotional and spiritual needs. There was a time when that was not a given in the evan-gelical world.

How does a man do so much for Christ's kingdom while also serving as a rector of a church for twenty-five years? In the first place, he was a dedicated scholar as well as a pastor. He was the model for the pastor-theologian that is so much dis-cussed today. As a university student, Stott worked with and was greatly influenced by the Christian Union leader, John Bridger Nash, who portrayed the ideal clergyman as one who would give his entire life to the service of his Lord without the distractions of a wife and children. Christopher Catherwood, the maternal grandson of D. Martyn Lloyd-Jones, writes of this decision, "There is little doubt that he would not have been able to do many of the things that he has done had he been married with a wife and family to look after" (Catherwood, 20). This decision to remain a lifelong bachelor, while not the path most clergy would choose, certainly worked for Stott, allowing him the freedom to do research and write extensively as well as travel widely, often to the Third World.

Stott begins his book with the words, "In the beginning God," which he says "supply the key which opens our understanding to the Bible as a whole. They tell us that the religion of the Bible is a religion of the initiative of God" (Stott, 11). However, he doesn't simply assume that the inquiring reader already believes that, so at the end of the first chapter he concludes with a simple prayer, "God, if you exist (and I don't know if you do), and if you can hear this prayer (and I don't know if you can), I want to tell you that I am an honest seeker after the truth. Show me if Jesus is your Son and Saviour of the World" (Stott, 19).

Stott then proceeds to begin with the person, Jesus Christ. As already stated, he believed that people were "hostile to the church, friendly to Jesus Christ." So, he begins on common ground. He begins with Christ's person, the claims that he made for himself and his character, and then moves to the central fact of the Christian faith, the resurrection of Jesus Christ. On this, all else hinges. He carefully lays out the evidence for its occurrence and then concludes that "Perhaps the transformation of the disciples of Jesus is the greatest evidence of all for the resurrection, because it is entirely artless" (Stott, 58). After laying out all of the evidence, Stott writes, "There is no adequate explanation of these phenomena other than the great Christian affirmation, 'The Lord is risen indeed'" (Stott, 59).

Having established that Jesus Christ is deity incarnate, he proceeds to Man's Need in Part Two. He lays out in convincing fashion the fact and nature of sin and its consequences. But Stott does not leave the reader hanging. He writes, "Christianity is a rescue religion. It declares that God has taken the initiative to deliver us from our sins" (Stott, 81). He then lays out just what Christ's death on the cross accomplished and the centrality of that in the Christian faith. He then proceeds convincingly to write about man's need, how Christ meets that need, and man's response. Finally, he concludes by discussing duty to God, the church, and the world. He challenges the reader to count the cost. "Jesus never concealed the fact that his religion included a demand as well as an offer. Indeed, the demand was as total as the offer was free" (Stott, 107). He ruminates on the countless so-called Christians who did not count the cost and who have strayed from the faith. Using the well-known question that Jesus posed about a man undertaking the building of a tower, Stott writes, "The Christian landscape is strewn with the wreckage of derelict, half-built towers—the ruins of those who began to build and were unable to finish." He continues, "The result is the great scandal of Christendom today, so-called 'nominal Christianity'" (Stott, 108). His depiction of such a religion is scathing. "Their religion is a great, soft cushion. It protects them from the hard unpleasantness of life, while changing its place and shape to suit their convenience. No wonder the cynics speak of hypocrites in the church and dismiss religion as escapism" (Ibid.). Stott says that the call to Christian discipleship is a call to not only renounce sin, but to renounce self.

Stott's book is a call to the uncommitted as well as to the committed. Many are seeking and this book is a wonderful apologetic for the Christian faith. However, Stott has a warning for them. He writes, "if then, you suffer from moral anemia, take my advice and steer clear of Christianity. If you want to live a life of easy-going self-indulgence, whatever you do, do not become a Christian" (Stott, 119). On the other hand, many have made a nominal commitment to Jesus Christ. He believes that such a condition is tragic. "Everybody loves children, but nobody in his right mind wants them to stay in the nursery. The tragedy, however, is that many Christians, born again in Christ, never grow up. Others even suffer from spiritual regression" (Stott, 136).

Basic Christianity is a great book to give to a nonbeliever who wants to consider the claims of Christ. It is also a great book for a mature believer to read to confirm the reality of one's faith. I am a huge fan of Stott, a man who has been greatly influential in my life. This book is a great place to begin discovering the treasure trove of riches written by this great man of God.

16. WHO MOVED THE STONE?

By Frank Morison

The story behind the writing of this book is a fascinating one. In the first place, the name, Frank Morison, is a pseudonym for Albert Henry Ross. Ross was an English journalist who was determined to write a book debunking the resurrection of Jesus Christ. He relates how, as a very young man, he began studying the life of Christ and came to the conclusion that "His history rested upon very insecure foundations" (Morison, 9). He wrote that the "prevailing intellectual attitude" of the late 1890s influenced his thinking. It is important to remember that German Higher Criticism was in its heyday and it was actually taught in universities and seminaries that the source materials for the narrative of Christ's life and death (the Gospels) were, in truth, "unreliable." At that time, Ross writes, "The fact that almost every word of the Gospels was just then the subject of high wrangling and dispute did largely colour the thought of the time, and I suppose I could hardly escape its influence" (Morison, 10). He concluded that Huxley was correct in his assertion that "miracles do not happen."

Ross conceived the idea of writing a brief monograph about the last seven days of the life of Jesus. His goal in writing about this period was "to strip it of its overgrowth of primitive beliefs and dogmatic suppositions," (Morison, 11) and see Jesus as he really was sans the miraculous element. He had a great admiration for Jesus, the man. But he believed as any skeptic would that Jesus was only that . . . a man. Unfortunately for Ross, his work on the book was sidetracked by other commitments and he did not have time to complete it until years later. By then he was a full-fledged investigative journalist and he used the tools of his trade to investigate first the biblical account of Christ's trial and crucifixion as well as the resurrection. He found the accounts of the trial and crucifixion plausible, but not the resurrection. He saw the resurrection of Jesus as the linchpin of the Christian faith. If he could disprove it with certainty, the Christian faith would no longer be viable. That was the book Ross intended to write.

Ross began his book with a chapter titled *The Book That Refused to Be Written.* In that chapter he detailed his reasons for writing the book and how he would go about to prove his basic thesis. He began by investigating the trials of Jesus before the Roman and Jewish authorities. Ross went far beyond a study of the gospel sources by referencing the works of the Jewish historian, Josephus, as well as other early extra-biblical historical sources. He proved to be a particularly adept researcher combining his scientific mind with his writing skills to untangle the cobweb of mythology and historical accounts, all in the cause of disproving that Jesus actually rose from the dead.

Ross structured the evidences in his book as if he were an attorney proving a case in a court of law. His second chapter is titled *The Real Case Against the Prisoner.* Then he painstakingly calls each of his characters to the witness stand to present evidence. The final witness in his legal case is not a person, but it speaks loudly and without equivocation. That chapter is titled *The Witness of the Great Stone.* Who moved the stone? is his main argument that the resurrection did indeed occur, and it is a powerful one indeed.

Ross examines in turn six of the most "plausible" lines of critical approach for the empty tomb. These hypotheses range from the implausible ("That Joseph of Arimathea secretly removed the body to a more suitable resting-place.") to the utterly absurd ("That the grave was not visited at all and that the story about the women was a later accretion."). Did the Romans steal the body? Did the Jewish leaders? Did the disciples? Ross demolishes all of these hypotheses in turn and demonstrates the incredulity of each one.

Ross concludes, "Personally, I am convinced that no body of men or women could persistently and successfully have preached in Jerusalem a doctrine involving the vacancy of that tomb, without the grave itself being physically vacant. The facts were too recent; the tomb too close to that seething centre of oriental life. Not all the make-believe in the world could have purchased the utter silence of antiquity or given the records their impressive unanimity. Only the truth itself, in all its unavoidable simplicity, could have achieved that" (Morison, 175). What we are left with is that Jesus was miraculously raised from the dead. There is no other reasonable explanation.

On a personal note, when I was a young graduate student at the University of Maryland almost fifty years ago, I was bordering on agnosticism. I had been raised in a conservative, fundamentalist Bible church, but four years of college had left that shipwrecked. Three books were recommended to me: *The God Who Is There* by Francis Schaeffer, *Evidence That Demands a Verdict* by Josh McDowell, and this one *Who Moved the Stone?* It is difficult today, even many decades after the fact, to relate how profoundly this book changed my life. It is compelling and a must-read. Even after its publication nearly a century ago, its message thunders loud and clear.

17. KNOW WHY YOU BELIEVE

By Paul E. Little

Paul Little is a figure who loomed large in my early years as a Christian. When in high school and in college, I struggled with my faith as many of that age do, and often did not know where to turn. The books by Paul Little were an oasis to me because they were written in a way that I could actually understand. They were not ponderous tomes impenetrable to all but the most scholarly or learned. Here was somebody who wrote at my level. He was a writer who wrote as if he were writing directly to me. Little worked for twenty-five years with InterVarsity Christian Fellowship and was also associate professor of evangelism at Trinity Evangelical Divinity School in Deerfield, IL and was an expert at reaching young minds.

Little immediately engages us in a humorous fashion and sets the entire tone of the book in with his first paragraph. "'What is faith?' asked the Sunday School teacher. A young boy answered in a flash, 'Believing something you know isn't true'" (Little, 11). When I first read this book as a high school student, I was so relieved to learn that I could be a Christian and not have to "kiss my brains goodbye" as Little so graphically states it.

According to Little, many reject the Gospel because it has never been presented in a cogent fashion. They equate faith with superstitious nonsense and therefore summarily reject it. However, Little concludes that such rejections are not intellectual in nature, but rather moral. He writes, "Alleged intellectual problems are often a smoke screen covering moral rebellion" (Little, 16). He sees it as unlikely in the extreme that a new objection to the Christian faith will arise after centuries of consideration. He writes, "It is improbable that anyone thought up, last week, the one question that will bring Christianity crashing down. Brilliant minds have thought through the profound questions of every age and have ably answered them" (Little, 18).

Little then goes on in just over 150 pages to examine some of the most important questions that both Christians and atheists have been asking for centuries. The first question: "Is there a God?" He sees both sides of the coin, theism and atheism, as acts of faith. He writes, "Believing there is *no* God is also very clearly an act of faith. It is pure presupposition, as much as faith *in* God is a presupposition for belief" (Little, 29). He then concludes that three pieces of evidence point to the existence of God: creation, history, and contemporary life, and that this God can be known through personal experience.

The next question that Little entertains is whether Christ is God. Here he covers much of the same ground as other writers such as C. S. Lewis and John Stott do in their excellent books. He concludes that Christ's supreme credential authenticating his claim to deity was his resurrection from the dead, which leads to his next question: "Did Christ rise from the dead?" He argues, "If Christ did *not* rise from the dead, Christianity is an interesting museum piece—nothing more. It has no objective validity or reality" (Little, 42-43). In this chapter, Little also covers ground that other writers have covered previously examining some of the numerous theories that have been postulated to account for the empty tomb. He concludes that only a supernatural event could change "a band of frightened, cowardly disciples into men of courage and conviction" (Little, 57).

Little then proceeds to ask two questions in the next two chapters: "Is the Bible God's Word?" and "Are the Bible documents reliable?" He first lays out the biblical view of inspiration and then the view of Jesus regarding Scripture before proceeding to the role of the Holy Spirit in influencing the writers of Scripture. His discussion of the reliability of the biblical manuscripts is particularly helpful. He examines the role of the Dead Sea Scrolls, then the Septuagint, the three different text types of the

Hebrew Old Testament manuscripts, as well as a brief discussion of the New Testament Greek manuscripts. Some of this data might appear on the surface to be beyond what would interest the average reader, but Little approaches it in such a way that it is both easy to grasp and fascinating.

Chapter 8 is an examination of the possibility of miracles in Scripture. The stories of Jonah being swallowed by a great fish and Jesus feeding the 5,000 are often marshaled forth as evidence of events that strain the credulity of skeptics. Little cuts right to the chase. He hits the nail right on the head. He writes, "With many questions, it is more important to discern the root problem than to become involved in discussing a twig on a branch. This is especially true of questions about miracles. The questioner's problem is generally not with a particular miracle, but with a whole principle" (89). He sees the solution as being very simple. "Once we assume the existence of God, there is no problem with miracles, because God is by definition all-powerful" (Little, 90).

The next chapter is titled "Do science and Scripture conflict?" Little discusses largely the theory of evolution as compared with the biblical teaching about creation. He writes, "Many think that either a person believes in total fiat creation or he is an agnostic or atheistic evolutionist" (Little, 107). He then explains three different strands or theories that have been advanced: naturalistic theory of evolution, emergent evolution, and theistic evolution. He warns that two extremes must be avoided. "First is the assumption that evolution has been proved without doubt and that anyone with a brain must accept it. The second is the notion that evolution is 'only a theory,' with little evidence for it" (Little, 109). He concludes that "there is no fundamental conflict between science and Scripture" (Little, 116).

Little considers several other questions in an interesting, engaging, and convincing fashion. Many consider this book to be a classic in the field of apologetics. It was written for the average person and is a must read for anyone searching for answers or knows someone who is searching. As a teenager over a half century ago, I read it and was enthralled. I recently reread the book and was immediately struck by how well the book has held up and how contemporary and relevant it still is today. For such a short little book, it still packs a powerful punch. Read it for yourself and see if you agree.

18. EVIDENCE THAT DEMANDS A VERDICT

By Josh McDowell

This book was one of the first that I read while a university student searching for answers. Along with *Who Moved the Stone* by Frank Morison and the writings of Francis Schaeffer, *Evidence That Demands a Verdict* was clearly one of the most influential in my life. As an undergraduate student, I took a class titled "The Old Testament" in which I was taught that much of the Bible was based on mythology and legends and that the miracles of the Bible could not be believed. McDowell's book was one of the shining lights that helped me move out of the darkness.

The subtitle of the book tells exactly what it is about, *Historical Evidences for the Christian Faith*. That was exactly what I needed when it was published in 1972 while I was a college sophomore searching for answers. Over the years, I have reread the book several times and each time it has bolstered my faith in Jesus Christ. It covers much of the same ground as another recommended book, *Know Why You Believe*, by Paul Little. McDowell's work has been revised several times, the latest in 2017 by McDowell himself with assistance from his son, Sean, with the new title *Evidence That Demands a Verdict: Life-Changing Truth for a Skeptical World*. This revised and expanded work won the 2018 ECPA Christian Book award for Bible Reference Works. Although the Bible itself is unchanging, the attacks of its critics change with each generation. The latest edition includes the basic core of the original, but updates some of the material for a new generation. I will write more about the changes between the 1972 and 2017 editions later in this review.

Although Josh McDowell has published dozens of books during his lifetime, none have made such an impact as *Evidence* has. In 2006, the book was listed by *Christianity Today* as among the most influential evangelical books published after World War II. It has proven to be a life-changing book for many. McDowell's spiritual journey was much like my own. He was an agnostic in college when he set out, much like Frank Morison did, to write a paper debunking the historical evidences for the Christian faith. That led to his conversion and subsequent enrollment at Wheaton College and after graduation at Talbot Theological Seminary. He became a traveling representative of Campus Crusade for Christ International in 1964 and has continued his affiliation ever since. His work as a campus speaker and his interactions with numerous skeptics, including Marxist and Fascist student groups, led to the writing of this book.

Since the publication of *Evidence That Demands a Verdict*, Mc-Dowell has become well-known as a Christian apologist. His writings have concentrated on answering the questions many honest seekers have posed such as doubts about faith, the credibility of the Bible, the divinity of Jesus, other religions, and the like. His books have attempted and succeeded in distilling the essence of some of the higher critical attacks on the Bible's credibility and presenting them to a general audience. The 2017 revised edition includes a response to the claims of atheist New Testament scholar Bart Ehrman. Ehrman, a former Moody Bible Institute student who along the way lost his faith, has disturbed many evangelical Christians with his volatile attacks on the Christian faith.

Evidence That Demands a Verdict provides an expansive defense of Christianity's core truths, rebuttals to some recent and popular forms of skepticism, and insightful responses to the Bible's most difficult and misused passages. It invites readers to bring their doubts and doesn't shy away from the tough questions.

The 1972 edition had three major sections: Evidence for the Bible, Evidence for Jesus, and God at Work in History and Human Lives. The latest edition rearranges some of the material and has four major sections: Evidence for the Bible, Evidence for Jesus, Evidence for the Old Testament, and Evidence for Truth. I will discuss the book's original arrangement of topics.

Section I is titled The Bible—I trust it. In this section, McDowell deals with the uniqueness of the Bible and why anyone would want to read it. He also discusses the canon of Scripture and why the Protestant Bible has a total of sixty-six books and does not include the Apocrypha as well as other epistles and gospels. He is detailed and thorough in his presentation, and convincing. The final chapter of this section explains why the Bible is reliable. Here he lays out the argument that the Bible's reliability is confirmed first by the historical text itself and then secondly by archaeological findings.

Section II is titled "The Academy Awards—If Jesus were not God, then he deserves an Oscar." In this section, McDowell argues for the historicity of Jesus Christ, the man of history. Then he presents the case for Jesus being God's Son. He explains the great trilemma that C. S. Lewis first proposed. Was Jesus actually Lord, or was he a liar or lunatic? One chapter that has really stuck with me over the decades is his wonderful explanation of the Messianic prophecies of the Old Testament and how they are fulfilled in Christ. McDowell lists 332 distinct predictions which were fulfilled literally by Jesus Christ. This chapter has always fascinated me. His discussion of the probability that Jesus would fulfill just eight of the sixty major prophecies about Jesus has always amazed me. For example, he cites Peter Stoner's book *Science Speaks* to conclude that the statistical probability that Jesus would fulfill just eight prophecies would be one in 100,000,000,000,000,000 or ten to the seventeenth power, a number that just staggers the mind. Finally, this section deals with the resurrection and whether it is actual history or an elaborate hoax. The resurrection of Jesus Christ is the linchpin of the Christian faith. The entire religion rises or falls on this one question. Did Jesus really rise from the dead? McDowell argues convincingly that he did.

Section III is titled "God at Work in History and Human Lives." Although McDowell includes a lot of useful information, this section is almost anticlimactic after his engaging and compelling examination of who Jesus is. He concludes with two chapters titled "Prophecy Fulfilled in History" and "The Uniqueness of the Christian Experience." Finally, the author gives his own personal testimony about how his relationship with Jesus Christ transformed his life.

McDowell covers the same ground that many authors did earlier and makes a wonderful case for Jesus Christ. But he does this more thoroughly than anyone else ever had and builds a convincing case for the Christian faith. He deals with some of the tough questions believers face particularly on college campuses. His arguments for the Christian faith provide a huge arsenal for the believer who faces skeptics or who is questioning his own faith. You owe it to yourself to read this book.

19. THE CASE FOR CHRIST

By Lee Strobel

Is there credible evidence that Jesus Christ was, in fact, the Messiah, the Son of God? This book is an absolutely fascinating and absorbing examination of that question by a skeptic who was also an investigative journalist. It is an example of investigative journalism at its best that reads more like a novel than a work of non-fiction. It grabs you by the throat on the first page and never lets you go.

Lee Strobel was once a spiritual skeptic with a law degree from Yale and an award-winning journalist at the Chicago Tribune. In this compelling book, he traces his personal spiritual journey from atheism to faith in Jesus Christ. Strobel was formerly the legal editor of the *Chicago Tribune* which influences how he attacks his subject. He interviews—actually cross-examines might be a better word—a dozen authorities in different fields with doctoral degrees from such eminent institutions as Cambridge, Princeton, Durham, Oxford, Aberdeen, and Brandeis, all recognized authorities in their fields, several of whom are colleagues of mine. He challenges them with probing questions such as *Can the biographies of Jesus be trusted? Is there credible evidence for Jesus outside his biographies? Was Jesus really convinced that he was the Son of God? Was Jesus' death a sham and his resurrection a hoax?* Strobel goes for the jugular and pulls no punches in his rapid-fire journalistic questioning style. It will keep you turning the pages in anticipation.

The book begins with a brief Introduction: Reopening the Investigation of a Lifetime and ends with a conclusion: The Verdict of History. The body of the book is divided into three major sections:

- Part I: Examining the Record
  - (1) The Eyewitness Evidence
  - (2) Testing the Eyewitness Evidence
  - (3) The Documentary Evidence
  - (4) The Corroborating Evidence
  - (5) The Scientific Evidence
  - (6) The Rebuttal Evidence
- Part II: Analyzing Jesus
  - (7) The Identity Evidence
  - (8) The Psychological Evidence
  - (9) The Profile Evidence
  - (10) The Fingerprint Evidence
- Part III Researching the Resurrection
  - (11) The Medical Evidence
  - (12) The Evidence of the Missing Body
  - (13) The Evidence of Appearances
  - (14) The Circumstantial Evidence

Each chapter concludes with a section titled "Deliberations" with Questions for Reflection or Group Study.

Each chapter begins with the absorbing investigation of an infamous crime and how the evidence pointed one way, but ended up in another place. For example, Strobel begins Chapter 13, "The Evidence of Appearances," with the true story of the 1963 Birmingham church bombing and the body of fourteen-year-old Addie Mae Collins, whose body was discovered missing in 1998 when the family decided to "disinter the deceased for reburial at another cemetery." He makes the point that just because her body was missing from the grave, nobody was suggesting that she had been resurrected. The solution, Strobel explains, is that her tombstone was placed at the wrong gravesite.

I found the first section of the book in which he examines the eyewitness evidence absolutely riveting. In the first two chapters, Strobel interviews Craig Blomberg, a leading authority on the New Testament in general and the Gospels in particular.

The credibility of the gospel writers has been called into question for well over a century and Strobel wanted to know if they could be trusted and could stand up to scrutiny. Strobel then hit Blomberg with both barrels blasting in his interview with him. He asked him about eight different tests about the gospel writers. One was, for example, the bias test. As Strobel explains, "This test analyzes whether the gospel writers had any biases that would have colored their work. Did they have any vested interested in skewing the material they were reporting on" (Strobel 61)? Blomberg's reply is masterful and compelling. He said, "Besides these disciples had nothing to gain except criticism, ostracism, and martyrdom. They certainly had nothing to gain financially. If anything, this would have provided pressure to keep quiet, to deny Jesus, to downplay him, even to forget they ever met him—yet because of their integrity, they proclaimed what they saw, even when it meant suffering and death" (Strobel, 62).

Strobel then interviewed Bruce Metzger of Princeton Theological Seminary, perhaps the world's leading expert on the New Testament documents and text. Since this is one of my areas of scholarly interest, I paid attention to what he had to say. Metzger waxed eloquently on the authenticity of the New Testament manuscripts and the reliability of the text. He concluded that the New Testament is well attested with a grand total of 5,664 Greek manuscripts extant, and if you include 8,000 to 10,000 of the Latin Vulgate plus 8,000 or so in Ethiopic, Slavic, and Armenian, "There are about 24,000 manuscripts in existence." Since I once studied Old English and taught *Beowulf* for many years, this kind of blew me away. The epic poem survives in a single copy in the manuscript known as the Nowell Codex dating from around 975-1025. Nobody disputes that we have an accurate copy of *Beowulf*. Strobel was impressed by Metzger's arguments as well. He concludes, "Metzger had been persuasive. No serious doubts lingered concerning whether the New Testament text has been reliably preserved for us through the centuries" (Strobel, 91).

Strobel's fifth chapter, "The Scientific Evidence," is one of my favorites and makes for interesting reading. He begins with a discussion of the infamous Jeffery MacDonald murder case in North Carolina. MacDonald, a former Green Beret and a practicing physician, was found guilty of stabbing to death his wife and two daughters. Strobel rightly concludes, "In MacDonald's case it was serology (blood evidence) and trace evidence that dispatched him to the penitentiary" (Strobel, 123).

In this chapter, Strobel interviews John McRay, a noted professor of New Testament and archaeology at Wheaton College who explains the scientific, archaeological evidence for the accuracy of the Markan, Lukan, and Johannine gospel accounts. In doing so, he explicates three "long-standing riddles" that have long vexed biblical archaeologists: the census, the existence of Nazareth, and the slaughter at Bethlehem. He also refutes some of the bizarre claims surrounding the Dead Sea Scrolls, such as John Marco Allegro's fantasy "in which he theorized that Christianity emerged from a fertility cult in which adherents tripped out on a hallucinogenic mushroom" (141). Wow! What an imagination! Strobel concludes, "Archaeology's repeated affirmation of the New Testament's accuracy provides important corroboration for its reliability" (Strobel, 143).

Chapter 6 titled "The Rebuttal Evidence" tackles the dubious claims of the Jesus Seminar, which Time magazine featured on the cover of its April 8, 1996, issue under the title, "The Search for Jesus: Some scholars are debunking the Gospels. Now traditionalists are fighting back. What are Christians to believe?" Scholars of the Jesus Seminar have concluded that Jesus categorically did not say eighty-two percent of what the gospels say he did with sixteen of the remaining eighteen percent doubtful. Only two percent of Christ's sayings were deemed to be authentic. Gregory Boyd, Strobel's expert with a doctorate from Princeton Theological Seminary, has clashed on more than one occasion with those who are skeptical of Christ's credentials. He offers his assessment of the Jesus Seminar: "The Jesus Seminar represents an extremely small number of radical-fringe scholars who are on the far, far left wing of New Testament thinking. It does not represent mainstream scholarship" (Strobel, 152). Members of the Jesus Seminar believe that there is a huge chasm between the Jesus of history and the Jesus of faith, whereas evangelicals believe them to be the very same. In the view of the Jesus Seminar, "Jesus was a bright, witty, countercultural man who never claimed to be the Son of god, while the Jesus of faith is a cluster of feel-good ideas that help people live right but are ultimately based on wishful thinking" (Strobel, 166). Both conceptions are wrong in the minds of Bible-believing Christians. Boyd concludes his discussion with Strobel by saying, "The evidence for Jesus being who the disciples said he was—for having done the miracles that he did, for rising from the dead, for making the claims that he did—is just light-years beyond my reasons for thinking that the left-wing scholarship of the Jesus Seminar is correct" (Strobel, 169). Strobel concludes this chapter with two final quotes from distinguished scholars who call the Jesus Seminar "a self-indulgent charade" and "an academic disgrace." This is a very entertaining chapter.

One fascinating chapter from Part 2, Analyzing Jesus, is titled "The Psychological Evidence: Was Jesus Crazy When He Claimed to Be the Son of God?" I had read numerous books that covered much of the same ground as this chapter did such as *Evidence That Demands a Verdict* by Josh McDowell, *Mere Christianity* by C. S. Lewis, and *Basic Christianity* by John R. W. Stott. However, this is the first book that included an interview with an expert with a Ph.D. in clinical psychology who was able to interact with the evidence for and against. Gary R. Collins, the expert who is also a professor of psychology at Trinity Evangelical Divinity School in Deerfield, IL, discusses the claims of British skeptic, Ian Wilson, who has suggested that Christ's miracles, such as turning of water into wine and the raising of Lazarus were instances of hypnosis, the former mass hypnosis. Collins methodically shoots down the argument and concludes, "It doesn't stand up to analysis. It's full of holes" (Strobel, 201). He argues first of all that not everyone is "equally susceptible" to hypnosis and that in a large group, such as the feeding of the 5,000, there would have been many who would have been resistant. Second, he points out that "skeptics and doubters" usually cannot be hypnotized. Third, citing the elephant in the room, he notes that the empty tomb of Jesus was just as empty to the followers of Christ as it was to the doubters such as the Romans and the Pharisees.

In addition to concluding that Jesus was not a master hypnotist, Collins believes that he actually did perform exorcisms and that he did not have a preposterous imagination. Strobel was challenged by his interview with Collins. He writes that it "prompted me to spend time that night carefully rereading the discourses of Jesus. I could detect no sign of dementia, delusions, or paranoia. On the contrary, I was moved once more by his profound wisdom, his uncanny insights, his poetic eloquence, and his deep compassion" (Strobel, 206).

A highlight of "Part 3, Researching the Resurrection," is Chapter 11 titled "The Medical Evidence: Was Jesus' Death a Sham and His Resurrection a Hoax?" In this chapter, Strobel interviews Alexander Metherell, a former research scientist with two doctoral degrees including an M.D. from the University of Miami. Metherell interacts with adherents of the swoon theory that claims that Jesus never actually died on the cross, but that he merely passed out and then was revived in the coolness of the tomb. This is a theory that is resurrected (pardon the joke) from time to time and was popularized in such books as the 1965 best-seller *The Passover Plot*, the 1972 book *The Jesus Scroll*, the 1982 *Holy Blood, Holy Grail*, and the 1992 *Jesus and the Riddle of the Dead Sea Scrolls*. What these books have in common is that they are pure poppycock. Metherell makes a more than convincing case that it would have been impossible for Jesus to have survived what he went through before, during, and after the crucifixion. Strobel concludes, "Appealing to history and medicine, to archaeology and even Roman military rules, Metherell had closed every loophole: Jesus could not have come down from the cross alive" (Strobel, 269). Metherell reviews his main points, "He was already in hypovolemic shock from the massive blood loss even before the crucifixion started. He couldn't possibly have faked his death, because you can't fake the inability to breathe for long. Besides, the spear thrust into his heart would have settled the issue once and for all. And the Romans weren't about to risk their own death by allowing him to walk away alive" (Strobel, 270).

The final three chapters of Part 3 all deal with the resurrection of Jesus looking at it through different lenses with interviews with three top scholars in religious and philosophical fields: William Lane Craig, Gary Habermas, and J. P. Moreland. Strobel then ends with a very helpful chapter titled "Conclusion: The Verdict of History." He asks and answers the question, "What does the evidence establish—and what does it mean today?" Strobel then asks again the fourteen questions that opened each chapter and answers them in one succinct paragraph. Very helpful summary!

Lee Strobel has written an intriguing book that will sink its hooks into you. You will find it, as I did, difficult to put it down. For better or for worse, Jesus has been in the news and his life and work have been questioned. A cloud has surrounded his deity. It certainly behooves the Christian to be familiar with the questions and to know some of the answers. This book provides them in spades. And you will have fun reading it!

EVANGELISM

"Therefore go and make disciples of all nations, baptizing them in the name of the Father and of the Son and of the Holy Spirit, and teaching them to obey everything I have commanded you" (Matt. 28:19-20). Ever since Jesus spoke those immortal words to his disciples almost 2,000 years ago, the Church has considered them to be their marching orders. For many centuries, there were true believers who accepted the commission and went forth to evangelize. More recently it has been referred to as the "Great Commission." But in reality, it has been more like the "Great Omission." The sad truth is that many Christians do not share their faith with others. There may be many reasons why this is so. They may be afraid. They may be indifferent. Or they just might not know how. In any event, the three books in this short chapter will help you to know why you must be engaged in evangelism and how to do it. They will also help to eliminate the fear factor.

It is regrettable that we Christians have done a very poor job of reaching the world with the message of Jesus Christ. The evangelistic efforts of the average Christian in North America have been abysmal. Many believers have never shared their faith in Jesus Christ with an unbeliever and most have never led one to a saving faith in our Savior.

It is unfortunate that many Christians have missed the joy of sharing the Good News and seeing the changed lives of those who respond. Your heart will be thrilled when you pray with a new believer, whether it be a friend, neighbor, or beloved family member. It is no less a pleasure when you learn of God's Word taking root halfway around the world where you have invested in missionary outreach. Hopefully, reading the three books reviewed in this section will ignite a spark and beyond that, show you how to do it. You will be richly rewarded as you learn to set aside your fears and give away your faith.

20. THE MASTER PLAN OF EVANGELISM

By Robert E. Coleman

How do we transition from our twenty-first century misconceptions about evangelism and discipleship to how the early church understood them? Robert E. Coleman was the McCreless Professor of Evangelism at Asbury Theological Seminary in Asbury, KY. He also taught for many years at Gordon-Conwell Theological Seminary and the Trinity Evangelical Divinity School. He is best known for his outstanding little book that was published in 1963 titled *The Master Plan of Evangelism*. Of course, the Master is a reference to Christ. He argues that we need to follow Christ's example in this entire matter of evangelism and discipleship. As we have already done, Coleman also questions today's methodologies. He writes, "That we are busy in the church trying to work one program of evangelism after another cannot be denied. But are we accomplishing our objective" (Coleman, 11-12)? Obviously, he did not believe that we are accomplishing our objective. He felt that the Church of his day, and of today has lost sight of its goal.

Coleman proposed that we follow the methodology of Jesus who modelled how evangelism should be done. He saw the evangelism method of Jesus as an eight-part process. This may appear perfectly logical to us, but in 1963 when Coleman published his book, it was revolutionary. Churches were trying one desperate evangelism program after another, many of them relying on "canned" presentations of the gospel, in trying to reverse trend overnight.

Jesus began the principle of selection. Jesus called a few men to follow him. As Coleman put it, "His concern was not with programs to reach the multitudes, but with men whom the multitudes would follow" (Coleman, 21). He continues, "The initial objective of Jesus' plan was to enlist men who could bear witness to His life and carry on His work after He returned to the Father" (Coleman, 21). Coleman saw the church of his day's attempts to do evangelism as "flabby" and ineffective. He muses, "It is ironic when one stops to think about it. In an age when facilities for rapid communication of the Gospel are available to the Church as never before, we are actually accomplishing less in winning the world for God than before the invention of the horseless carriage. Yet in appraising the tragic condition of affairs today, we must not become frantic in trying to reverse the trend overnight. Perhaps that has been our problem. In our concern to stem the tide, we have launched one crash program after another to reach the multitudes with the saving Word of God" (Coleman, 36).

The second plank of Christ's plan was that of association. "Having called his men, Jesus made it his practice to be with them" (Coleman, 38). Twelve men spent three years in intimate association with Jesus and their lives and the world were revolutionized as a result. This process cannot be shortchanged. It requires spending time with people. Coleman again, "There is a lot of talk in the church about evangelism and Christian nurture, but little concern for personal association when it becomes evident that such work involves the sacrifice of personal indulgence" (Coleman, 47). Coleman is very clear about this. "When will the church learn this lesson? Preaching to the masses, although necessary, will never suffice in the work of preparing leaders for evangelism . . . Building men is not that easy. It requires constant personal attention, much like a father gives to his children" (Coleman, 47).

The next step was that of consecration. Coleman writes, "Jesus expected the men He was with to obey Him. They were not expected to be smart, but they had to be loyal" (50). There could be no compromise. Jesus said, "No servant can serve two masters." We are told that when Jesus began to talk about the true spiritual quality of the kingdom of God and the sacrifice necessary to achieve it, many of his disciples went back and walked no more with him. They said, "This is a hard saying; who can hear it?" Coleman asks the question, "Why are so many professed Christians today stunted in their growth and ineffectual in their witness? Or to put the question in its larger context, why is the contemporary church so frustrated in its witness to the world? Is it not because among the clergy and laity alike, there is a general indifference to the commands of God, or at least, a kind of contented complacency with mediocrity?"

Where is the obedience of the cross? Why do churches water down the requirements for church membership and not stress the need for consecration and obedience?

The fourth and fifth principles that Christ utilized were impartation and demonstration. Christ's life was one of giving and when he ascended to the Father in Heaven, he gave us the Holy Spirit. That is why Coleman writes, "Love is like that. It is always giving itself away" (Coleman, 61). Jesus also used demonstration. Howard Hendricks of the Dallas Theological Seminary once said that if teaching were telling, his children would all be geniuses. My mother used to tell me, "Do as I say, not as I do." That is not the way to teach. Teaching is best done by modeling what you want to teach. The life of Jesus was a living demonstration of Kingdom principles. He allowed his life to speak for itself. As Coleman observes, "Jesus was so much the Master in his teaching that he did not let his method obscure his lesson. He let his truth call attention to itself" (Coleman, 78). He didn't use professional techniques of communication or sure-fire gimmicks. He allowed his disciples to simply observe his behavior. When they were with Jesus, class was always in session.

The sixth and seventh elements of Christ's evangelism method are also vital components of good leadership. They are delegation and supervision. Jesus assigned his disciples work to do. He was always building up to the time when they would take over the work. In raising children, a parent who does not prepare children to be able to live in the world is doing them a disservice. Jesus sent his disciples out to do ministry (Matt. 10:1, 11). He did not go with them. He delegated some of the work. That was the Apostle Paul's strategy in planting churches. Sometimes he would send an apostolic delegate such as Timothy to Ephesus or Titus to Crete to work with a fledgling congregation. Paul knew that he couldn't be everywhere at once and he learned to delegate. He also learned to supervise the work. He didn't just assume that it would get done. No matter how gifted a person may appear or how much potential he shows, supervision is still needed.

The final principle that Jesus used was reproduction. He intended his disciples to reproduce other disciples in the likeness and image of Jesus Christ. Dawson Trotman, the founder of the Navigators, many years ago wrote a little pamphlet titled *Born to Reproduce*. It is based on Paul's words to young Timothy in 2 Tim. 2:2: "And the things you have heard me say in the presence of many witnesses entrust to reliable men who will also be qualified to teach others." This was the *modus operandi* of Christ—begin with a small group and grow through reproduction. It didn't matter how small the group was initially as long as they reproduced and then taught their disciples to reproduce. That is called spiritual multiplication. Should the Church practice spiritual addition, as has been her plan for most of her existence, or spiritual multiplication. Take this simple test. Would you rather be paid $10,000 per day for a month or one penny which would double each of the thirty-one days? If you choose to take the $10,000 a day, you will net a total of $310,000 at the end of the month. If you choose the other way, on your final day, you will receive a grand total of $10,737,417.00 on the thirty-first day not including what you received for days one through thirty. It is obvious that the practice of spiritual multiplication, Christ's methodology, is the superior plan.

That, in a nutshell, is the Master's plan of evangelism. This is a very short book, only 124 pages, but it packs a wallop. There is nothing groundbreaking here, simply foundational principles that have largely been ignored by generations of believers. I urge you to read this book and forever revolutionize the way you view the practice of evangelism.

21. HOW TO GIVE AWAY YOUR FAITH

By Paul E. Little

This little book by Paul Little may well be the first Christian book, other than the Bible, that I ever read as a teenager. It was published in 1966 and it took a lot of the mystery out of evangelism. Growing up in a fundamentalist church as I did, we were weekly bombarded by the pastor and the Sunday school teacher with the message that we needed to witness. I must confess that to a teenage lad, that was a terrifying prospect. The main problem, apart from the usual teenage insecurities, is that nobody ever took the time to tell us how to do it. As Little states, "Many want to witness, but are frustrated because they don't know how" (Little, 5).

Paul Little is an able guide to the world of personal evangelism. He was certainly no armchair evangelist having served with InterVarsity Christian Fellowship for twenty-five years as well as teaching evangelism at Trinity Evangelical Divinity School in Deerfield, IL. He has the rare ability to connect with young minds and communicate complex ideas in a simple way. After all, I was not very sophisticated as a teenager and it immediately resonated with me. I couldn't put the book down.

Little begins his book with "The Essential Foundation." He begins by admitting, "So you want to witness! I did too, but I didn't have a clue about how to do it without stubbing my toe in the process" (Little, 9). He then asks the reader, "How about you? Do you know how to make the good news relevant? Do you know how to communicate to people to whom the gospel seems alien" (Ibid.)? When he wrote those words, he was speaking directly to me. Little sets out some basic points of agreement among most Christians. He writes, "We've agreed

(1) that a genuine, personal relationship with Jesus Christ is a prerequisite to being a Christian witness; (2) that Christian witness involves our whole life; (3) that involvement in evangelism is an essential vitamin for a growing experience with the Lord and a vital Christian life. But we've also admitted a basic problem: we don't know how to witness verbally. More specifically we don't know how to communicate the gospel graciously on a person-to-person basis" (Little, 25). He concludes with the statement, "Every Christian is a missionary" (Ibid.)).

Little's next chapter is titled "How to Witness." He examines the Lord's interview with the Samaritan woman at a well near Sychar and extracts seven basic evangelistic principles of action. They are: "(1) Contact others socially. (2) Establish a common interest. (3) Arouse interest. (4) Don't go too far. (5) Don't condemn. (6) Stick with the main issue. (7) Confront him directly" (Little, 26-45). Little believes that if we follow the model for evangelism that Christ demonstrated for us, we will discover ample opportunities to bear witness in our daily encounters with people.

Little then deals with "Hurdling Social Barriers." Now that we are ready to witness, what then? Little writes, "Anyone who moves out of his safety zone and gets involved in the real world is sure to run into ticklish situations" (Little, 47). He then offers some practical advice on how to navigate those treacherous waters. For example, how should we respond to profanity in a witnessing situation. He observes that some Christians become "huffy" and adopt a "holier-than-thou" attitude, which is precisely what should not be done. Little suggests a little casual humor to ease such a situation. Some Christians are ready to stone the perpetrator on the spot, which may be a bit too extreme. Little explains, "By the grace of God we can, without compromising ourselves or condoning his words, respond with love to the one who swears or tells off-color stories" (Little, 48).

In his next two chapters, Little urges the reader to be certain just what the message of the gospel is and why we should believe it. Some Christians are a bit fuzzy as to what exactly the good news is. If a person is uncertain of his message, he will never be an effective ambassador for Christ. In explaining why we should believe our message, Little covers some of the same ground he explicates in greater detail in his later book, *Know Why You Believe*. All of this is extremely important information and he conveys it in an interesting and straightforward manner.

This little book (no pun intended) is hands down the very best introduction to personal evangelism that I have ever seen. It is practical and easy to read. It captivated me at a very young age and it has not lost its appeal. You owe it to yourself to read it. And then read it again in five years.

22. EVANGELISM EXPLOSION

By D. James Kennedy

How did a man go from being an Arthur Murray Dancing School instructor to a Presbyterian pastor to the writer of one of the best-selling books on evangelism in history? It is the fascinating story of D. James Kennedy and how he took a church of forty-five people and watched it grow using spiritual principles of evangelism and discipleship to a church membership in the thousands. For fifteen years, the Coral Ridge Presbyterian Church was the fasted-growing Presbyterian church in the United States.

The story began when Kennedy decided to make a career change. He was a very successful dance instructor who was one day employed by Arthur Murray in Tampa and the next day a Presbyterian pastor. In 1959 the Coral Ridge Presbyterian Church was a presbytery mission church and Kennedy was fresh out of seminary. There was an average attendance of about forty-five each Sunday, which under Kennedy's preaching grew after six months... to seventeen. Something obviously was not working. He was asked to preach a series of evangelistic messages at the church of an older ministerial colleague in Decatur, GA. That man was Kennedy Smartt and he was to play an influential part of Kennedy's life. He taught the younger Kennedy how to lead people into a saving relationship with Jesus Christ. James Kennedy took home the lessons he learned from Kennedy Smartt and he began utilizing those principles at his Coral Ridge Church. By 1968 the church had 1,366 members and was continuing a fast rate of growth.

Evangelism Explosion is the book he wrote outlining the methodology he used to build his church. His program emphasizes the training of laypeople to do the task of evangelism as they visit in homes and encounter people in the community. It also focuses on the principle of spiritual multiplication, instead of spiritual addition, to increase membership in the church. In 1970 the film *Like a Mighty Army* starring Chris Robinson as Kennedy dramatized the evangelism explosion story at Coral Ridge Presbyterian Church. Also in 1970, *The Kennedy Explosion* was published documenting this amazing story.

Evangelism Explosion is best known for the two questions that are used to ask non-Christians as a spiritual diagnostic tool. They are, "Have you come to a place in your spiritual life where you can say you know for certain that if you were to die today you would go to heaven?" and "Suppose you were to die today and stand before God and he were to say to you, 'Why should I let you into my heaven?' what would you say?" The book includes a chapter titled "A Presentation of the Gospel," in which Kennedy outlines the elements of a gospel presentation and then provides an example. It is astonishing how many Christians do not know what the gospel is and how to share it with another person. Other chapters include "An Analysis of the Presentation," "The Proper Use of Testimony," "Handling Objections," "Dos and Don'ts," and "Witnessing As a Way of Life." The book ignited an "evangelism explosion" upon its initial publication over a half century ago. Billy Graham, no stranger to evangelism himself, wrote the "Foreward" and related how he had invited Kennedy to come regularly to address the many thousands of students, pastors, and the like at his Crusade School of Evangelism.

The fourth edition is an expanded version that includes a section on friendship evangelism. Published in 1996, it also includes how to build a vision for worldwide discipleship. The book, along with its accompanying training materials, has been translated into over seventy languages worldwide. It has been credibly suggested that it is the most widely-used evangelistic training program in the history of the church.

In 1972, Evangelism Explosion became an incorporated organization It is estimated that almost a half million people have been trained in the program and that Christian converts using it can be numbered in the millions. In 1977 Evangelism Explosion changed its approach to focus more on relationship-building and the discipleship of new believers. This "friendship evangelism" approach was deemed to be less confrontational than the traditional one. The organization is now called Evangelism International. Its purpose statement is "Equipping believers to multiply in and through local churches worldwide."

In 1942 Roland Leavell published a book titled *The Romance of Evangelism* in which he listed in round percentages the status of the church. He included statistics about prayer, church attendance, Bible reading, contributing to missions, but his most telling finding was that he estimated that ninety-five percent never win a soul to Christ. In the roughly eight decades since the book's publication, it would amaze me if that figure had changed significantly. The main issue with presenting the gospel is that most Christians simply do not know how to do it. *Evangelism Explosion* tells believers how to share their faith with unbelievers. It is a skill that every Christian should have. After all, Jesus himself commanded us to do so. Isn't that reason enough to learn how to do it?

MISSIONS

Throughout the entire history of the Christian church, missionary outreach has been a priority. From the earliest efforts of the Apostle Paul and his companions Barnabas, Timothy, Luke, and many others to the sophisticated efforts of twenty-first centuries missionaries, the one commonality has been the mandate to "make disciples of all nations." The Great Commission of Matthew 28 has provided the marching orders for the countless millions of missionaries who have preached the gospel in foreign countries as well as those who have done the same in their own. The names Hudson Taylor, William Carey, David Livingstone, and Count von Zinzendorf, to name just a few, have become very familiar to Christians particularly in the Western world.

With such a glorious history, it is sad that the very idea of missions has been called obsolete. It has been said that the missionary era has come to an end and that modern missionaries would do well to get out of the way and allow churches in the Third World to evangelize on their own. After all, church growth in the continent of Africa has been exponential as it has in other places. Most of this church expansion has been accomplished without the help of foreign interlopers. This has led many would-be missionaries to rethink their calling and wonder whether a missionary career is even viable in the modern world in which we live. However, I remind the reader that missionary endeavor is firmly rooted in Scripture as is its mandate to evangelize the lost souls of which there are still billions who have never heard the gospel of Jesus Christ.

The brevity of this section is in no way reflective of the importance of missions in the life of the church. Had I not limited myself to 100 books in this volume, there is no doubt that there might have been at least a dozen worthy titles covered here. Thousands upon thousands of books have been written about the subject. However, because of the self-imposed limitations, I have included two books, but they are absolute bombshells. Hudson Taylor revolutionized how missionary work is carried out with his wide vision and systematic plan for evangelizing China. Jim Elliott, on the other hand, along with his four missionary companions, made international headlines after their deaths at the hands of the Auca (Waorani) Indians of Ecuador. Both books make for thrilling reading and should be read by the thoughtful believer. I would also suggest a prayerful study of the book of Acts, particularly chapters thirteen to twenty-eight. The story of the first Christian missionaries makes for thrilling reading.

23. HUDSON TAYLOR'S SPIRITUAL SECRET

By Dr. and Mrs. Howard Taylor

Hudson Taylor is one of the most remarkable figures in the field of Christian missions. When I was a wee lad, I always heard his name mentioned with regard to missions in hushed tones approaching awe. Warren Wiersbe, in *Walking with the Giants*, includes a chapter about him and his remarkable work in China. However, Taylor never saw himself as a great man. He considered himself to be a little man of no particular talents. However, he believed that he had two things going for him. He had great faith and he had a great God. This book is one of the classic must-read missionary biographies of all time. My reaction after reading this book was twofold. First, I felt very small after reading about this spiritual giant. Second, I felt shame at my selfishness and pettiness. Reading this book was not only informative and challenging, it was like a slap in the face to me.

Taylor was born in 1832 in Barnsley, Yorkshire, England, the son of James Taylor, a pharmacist who was also a Methodist lay preacher, and his wife, Amelia. He rebelled against his parents' Christian beliefs as an adolescent, but finally professed faith in Christ in 1849 at the age of fifteen after reading an evangelistic tract that he had found in his father's library. He came into contact with Edward Cronin of Kensington, a Plymouth Brethren missionary to Baghdad and apparently learned his faith mission principles from him. He began teaching himself Mandarin, Greek, Hebrew, and Latin in preparation for future ministry.

In 1851 he moved to Hull to work as a medical assistant and began his preparation for a life of faith and service to God. It was during these days as a student that he learned to trust God for his financial needs. It was his firm belief that if he had not been able to prove God's faithfulness at home in England, he would not be able to trust him on a foreign mission field. While studying medicine in Hull, Taylor was paid a meager salary of which one tenth went to the work of God. During this time, he was conducting evangelism in a part of the city that had urgent temporal needs as well as spiritual help. He asked himself this question: "Why should he not spend less for himself and have the joy of giving more to others?" He then worked out a way to live on fewer luxuries such as milk and butter, which we might consider to be necessities. He found that by eating essentially an oatmeal and rice diet, he was able to live on one third of his salary and give the other two thirds to others. The author's write, "In these days of easy-going Christianity, it is well to remind ourselves that it really does 'cost' to be a man or woman whom God can use. One cannot obtain a Christlike character for nothing; one cannot do a Christlike work save at great price" (Taylor, 27).

In 1852 Taylor began studying medicine at the Royal London Hospital in Whitechapel as part of his preparation for mission work in China. During this time of preparation for missionary work, China was prominent in the news because of the Taiping Rebellion. Hopes for the evangelization of China sparked and waned in others, but not with Hudson Taylor. In a letter to his mother, he wrote, "Missionary work is indeed the noblest any mortal can engage in" (Taylor, 32). He also said, "I feel as if I could not live if something is not done for China" (32). The hope of doing missionary work in China became Taylor's great obsession. His big break came in 1853 when he was chosen to go to China as a missionary representing the Chinese Evangelization Society. Although he was a member of a mission society, Taylor always preferred to work independently, which would lead eventually to the formation of the China Inland Mission.

While still working with the Chinese Evangelization Society, Taylor made a decision that greatly influenced the evangelization of inland China. He always felt that he needed to follow God's leading without consulting others and this decision ostracized him from the small foreign community in the Ports. He decided to alter his appearance to fit in with the Chinese people he was attempting to win for Christ. Non-Chinese people tended to stick out like a sore thumb and Taylor felt that was a hindrance to effective ministry. He shaved much of his head and wore a long black braid and adopted native dress. In doing so, he sacrificed approval from his own people. But for Taylor after his physical transformation, "everything opened up . . . in a new way" (Taylor, 67). He was no longer recognized as a foreigner. "While missing some of the prestige attached to Europeans, he found it more than made up for the freedom his changed appearance gave him in moving among the people" (Ibid.). It was this kind of departure from traditional missionary methods that finally led to his parting of the ways with the Chinese Evangelization Society.

His resignation from the Chinese Evangelization Society in 1857 was a matter of scriptural principle for Taylor. He realized that the Society had been in debt for some time and that his salary was being paid from borrowed money. He wrote, "To me it seemed that the teaching of God's Word was unmistakably clear: 'Owe no man anything.' To borrow money implied to my mind a contradiction of Scripture—a confession that God had withheld some good thing, and a determination to get for ourselves what He had not given. Could that which was wrong for one Christian be right for an association of Christians? Or could any amount of precedents make a wrong course justified? If the Word taught me anything, it taught me to have no connection with debt" (Taylor, 82-83). He received a letter of support from George Müller, which led to his resignation. Eight years later in 1865, the China Inland Mission (now OMF International) was officially founded by Taylor together with William Thomas Berger.

From the very beginning, the China Inland Mission was a work of faith. This was one of the core values of the mission. He refrained, unlike so many missionaries of that time and today, from asking for support. He believed that a begging ministry was not a faith ministry and so he deplored it. He said that when the mission becomes a begging work, it dies. His founding principle for financial support was that the work should be entirely supported by the free-will offerings of God's people. The needs of the work were to be laid before God in prayer. There were to be no personal solicitations or collections taken. There was also to be no debt incurred as that would be inconsistent with being entirely dependent upon God. An oft-quoted statement has been generally attributed to Taylor: "God's work done in God's way will never lack for God's supplies." You may not agree with all of Taylor's principles of ministry, but it must be admitted that he lived out his faith and his principles throughout his entire adult lifetime and they worked for him.

In 1866, after Taylor launched the China Inland Mission, he left England again for China with his wife, Maria, and their children and sixteen missionaries. By the late nineteenth century, the mission had sent out hundreds of missionaries to China with the message of the gospel of Jesus Christ. Taylor died in 1905 after serving for fifty years in China. By 1939, the China Inland Mission had more than 1,300 missionaries and almost 200,000 Chinese and minority people were baptized.

Hudson Taylor's life was one of the most remarkable in missions' history rivaling that of the Apostle Paul. He is a person that every believer should get to know. I heartily recommend your first exposure to this man of faith be *Hudson Taylor's Spiritual Secret*, written by his son and daughter-in-law, Howard and Mary Taylor. You may also want to read John Pollock's wonderful biography, *Hudson Taylor and Maria*. Pollock was the official biographer for Billy Graham as well as the biographer for William Wilberforce, John Wesley, George Whitefield, John Newton, and D. L. Moody. Dr. and Mrs. Howard Taylor published two other books that are worth reading: *Hudson Taylor and the China Inland Mission: The Growth of a Work of God* and *Hudson Taylor in Early Years: The Growth of a Soul*. All are worth reading to learn how God worked in an ordinary man to move him to do extraordinary things for a great God.

24. THROUGH GATES OF SPLENDOR

By Elisabeth Elliot

My favorite quotation that is not a verse right out of the Bible was recorded by Jim Elliot on October 28, 1949, in his personal journal soon after his graduation from Wheaton College that same year. He wrote these immortal words: "He is no fool who gives what he cannot keep to gain what he cannot lose." Jim Elliot was one of five young missionaries who had landed on a small strip of land in the Ecuadoran jungle. The young men had planned and waited for this opportunity for years and finally their plans and hopes were coming to fruition. They were at last going to make contact with the Auca (Waorani) Indians with the gospel of Jesus Christ.[1]

The Aucas were a warlike and dangerous tribe who had had no contact previously with the outside world. For months the missionaries had flown over the area dropping gifts and shouting greetings in their native language. When they completed their dangerous landing, they built a hut and waited for the Aucas to find them. The men knew the danger and the fierce reputation of the Aucas. Their wives waited nearby in a village around a radio receiver listening for the news of their historic meeting. The news that they received was not what the women had hoped. Instead, the news coming out of Ecuador in 1956 shocked the world.

This book relates the powerful story of Operation Auca, a venture by five missionaries to reach the Huaorani tribe of South

------

[1] The name Auca is no longer used. It is a Quichua word which means "savage" or "naked." The people now call themselves Waorani.

America. The five, Jim Elliot (the author's husband), Pete Flemming, Ed McCully, Nate Saint, and Roger Youderian were martyred soon after they established contact with the tribe. This book tells the horrific story and its aftermath. The book is largely taken from the diaries and journals of the five men with judicious comments by Elliot interspersed. The well-known American preacher and pastor, Chuck Swindoll, wrote that "God used this book to change my life."

The title of the book comes from a favorite hymn of the five men, "We Rest on Thee." The last verse declares:

"We rest on Thee, our Shield and our Defender,
Thine is the battle, Thine shall be the praise
When passing through the gates of pearly splendor
Victors, we rest with Thee through endless days."

Elliot wrote the book while a missionary in Ecuador and with the friendly cooperation from the families of the other four men. The original edition of the book came out in 1957, a year before peaceful contact with the Auca was made.

One of the main characters in this story was not a human being at all, but rather a bright yellow Piper airplane of the Missionary Aviation Fellowship. It was piloted by Nate Saint who is described by Elliot as "the man whose vision had changed missionary life in the jungle" (Elliot, 49). Operation Auca was a visionary plan to reach the Auca Indians, a tribe that up until then had not had contact with the outside world. The airplane was a major factor in that first contact was made through air drops of gifts such as clothing and pots before personal contact could be attempted. The chapter titles tell the story better than I ever could as they trace the progression of the missionary endeavor. Chapter I is titled "I Dare Not Stay Home," followed by "Destination: Shandia," "All Things to All Men," "Infinite Adaptability," "Expendable for God," "Missionary to the Head-Shrinking Jivaros," "Breaking Jungle Barriers," "The Aucas," "Operation Auca Begins," "A Line from Plane to Ground," "The

Savages Respond," "Why Did the Men Go?" "We Go Not Forth Alone," and "Silence" to give you a sampling.

Elliot demonstrates great pathos in her description of the recruitment of Roger Youderian to join Operation Auca. At the time of this recruitment, only Nate, Jim, and Ed were definitely committed, but they wanted a team of five men. Nate was the only one on the team who really knew Roger, but he judged him to be "a soldier of Christ." He wrote of Roger in his diary that he was "a man capable of great effort, trained and disciplined. He knows the importance of unswerving conformity to the will of his Captain. Obedience is not a momentary option; it is a diecast decision made beforehand. He was a disciplined paratrooper. He gave Uncle Sam his best in that battle and now he is determined that the Lord Jesus Christ shall not get less than his best. Everything that made him a good soldier has been consecrated to Christ, his new Captain" (Elliot, 116). What none of the men who made up Operation Auca knew was that at that time, Roger was fighting terrible discouragement. He wrote in his diary at about that time, "About ready to call it quits. The reason: Failure to measure up as a missionary and get next to the people" (Elliot, 147). He and his family had been working among the Jivaria Indians at a place called Macuma station. He wrote out of his anguish, "If I couldn't make the grade here in Macuma I'm not foolish enough to expect a change of setting would change me. This is my personal 'Waterloo' as a missionary" (Elliot, 148). He was undergoing his "dark night of the soul" when he was approached by Nate Saint about joining the missionary party. He wrote in his diary, "I will die to self. I will begin to ask God to put me in a service of constant circumstance where to live Christ I must die to self. I will be alive unto God. That I may learn to love Him with my heart, mind, soul, and body" (Elliot, 149-50).

The five missionaries went to their deaths. Their fates were not immediately known. First there was radio silence and long hours and days of uncertainty. When the bodies were finally discovered by the military and the news broken to the widows,

Eliot wrote, "Their news had been met with serenity. No tears could rise from the depth of trust which supported the wives" (Elliot, 231). Barbara Youderian, the widow of Roger, wrote in her diary: "Tonight the Captain told us of his finding four bodies in the river. One had tee-shirt and blue-jeans. Roj was the only one who wore them. . . . God gave me this verse two days ago, Psalm 48:14, 'For this God is our God for ever and ever; He will be our Guide even unto death.' As I came face to face with the news of Roj's death, my heart was filled with praise. He was worthy of his home-going" (Elliot, 231). Olive Fleming, the widow of Pete, "recalled the verses that God had impressed on her mind that morning: 'For we know that if our earthly house of this tabernacle were dissolved, we have a building of God, an house not made with hands, eternal in the heavens'" (Elliot, 236). Such were the reactions of the martyr's widows. Elliot wrote, "To the world at large this was a sad waste of five young lives. But God had his plan and purpose in all things" (Elliot, 247).

The aftermath of the story is really the beginning. In the Epilogue dated November 1958, almost three years have passed since the martyrdom of the five brave missionaries who gave their lives for the sake of the gospel of Jesus Christ. The author is writing from a leaf house with her daughter who is now three and a half years old, not very far from where the deaths occurred. Sitting nearby are two of the seven men who killed her husband. They had killed the missionaries, it was later learned, because they thought they were cannibals. Fear had led to the deaths of Jim Elliot and his four companions. Now these formerly savage and warlike Auca Indians were brothers in Christ. Elliot writes, "How did this come to be? Only God who made the iron swim, who caused the sun to stand still, in whose hand is the breath of every living thing—only *this* God forever and ever, could have done it" (Elliot, 253). This book tells that amazing and inspiring story. It behooves every believer to read it. It will change your life.

CHAPTER IV:
BIBLICAL STUDIES AND
BIBLICAL AUTHORITY

BIBLICAL STUDIES

The Apostle Paul, in writing to the Roman Christians, tells them, and us, that they are no longer to be conformed to this world, but to be totally transformed, a metamorphosis, and that the key to this transformation is the renewing of your mind (Rom. 12:2). Years later Paul wrote to his young protege, Timothy, who was managing the affairs of the church at Ephesus as Paul's representative, "Study to show thyself approved" (2 Tim. 2:15, King James Version). We may be involved in the study of many different subjects such as physics, pedagogy, medicine, history, and chemistry, but the study of which the Apostle Paul was speaking was the Word of God. No matter what other field of endeavor you may find to be of interest, there is no area of study more important than the study of the Word of God.

During the Middle Ages, people were limited in their ability to engage in Bible study. In the first place, the printing press had not yet been invented and the only books available were manuscripts that were copies of other manuscripts. These manuscripts were rare commodities indeed. The only Bibles that existed were confined to churches. Second, most people, at least in Europe, were illiterate and would not have been able to read anyway had books been available.

Such is not the case in today's modern world. Literacy rates in
the Western world are at an all- time high and there is a proliferation of Bible versions available. The only excuse most people have to not study the Word of God is apathy. Christians can
study the Bible in the *New International Version*, the *King James
Version*, the *New King James Version*, the *Revised Standard Version*, the *New Revised Standard Version*, the *English Standard
Version*, the *New Living Translation*, and dozens of others. In
addition, there are literally dozens of study Bibles available in
most of those translations. The problem is no longer a lack of
Bibles, but how to choose from among the many.

The purpose of this book is not to help you choose a Bible
translation. It will also not assist the reader in finding the best
commentaries.[1] What the five books included in the first section of this chapter will help you to do is study the Bible. From
how to actually study the Bible to the characters of the Bible to
the Sermon on the Mount and the Parable of the Prodigal Son,
there is much of interest here from some real giants of the faith.

---

[1] See the author's book, *The Layperson's Library: Essential Bible
Study Tools for the Man and Woman in the Pew* (Eugene, OR:
Wipf & Stock, 2021).

25. HOW TO READ THE BIBLE FOR ALL ITS WORTH

By Gordon D. Fee and Douglas Stuart

Many Christians don't study the Bible because it is a mystery to them. Apart from the gospels and Acts and perhaps a few Old Testament books such as the Proverbs and Psalms, most of the Bible's contents is incomprehensible and stultifying them. They feel that much of the Bible is best left for the few such as scholars or the more academically inclined. The authors would beg to differ with them. They believe that the Bible is meant to be read and understood by everyone "from armchair readers to seminary students" (from the back cover).

There have been many books written on the topic of how to understand the Bible. Some are excellent and some not so good. In the Preface to the first edition, the authors joke about how they almost called their book, *Not Just Another Book on How to Understand the Bible.* However, they explained that "wisdom prevailed" and they found another title. The technical name for the science of biblical interpretation is hermeneutics and there are some excellent books available on the subject. The only problem is that they were written for people with seminary or college training and not the average lay person sitting in the pew. *How to Read the Bible for All Its Worth* is not that kind of book. It was written for the average person in mind and can be understood by anyone willing to invest some time to read it carefully.

Now in its fourth edition, this book was originally published in 1982. The authors were, at that time, both professors at Gordon-Conwell Theological Seminary. Gordon Fee's specialty area is New Testament and Douglas Stuart's is Old Testament. Fee is currently retired and Professor Emeritus of New Testament of New Testament Studies at Regent College, Vancouver, British Columbia. In addition to being an internationally renowned New Testament scholar, he is also an ordained minister in the Assemblies of God (USA) denomination and the author of dozens of books in the area of biblical studies. Stuart has served as Professor of Old Testament and Biblical Languages at Gordon-Conwell since 1971 and has pastored several churches over the years, mainly Baptist and Congregational. He has written numerous books in the area of Old Testament studies. They are both experts in their respective areas of biblical studies, but have the wonderful gift of making complex subjects easy to understand.

This book is hands down the very best book I have ever read on making the science of hermeneutics understandable to the common person. I have used it for years as a college-level textbook and it is excellent. Although written by two seminary professors, it is far from dry and stodgy. The authors believe that understanding the different types of literature (genres) is key to understanding the Bible. The Bible is comprised of different genres such as history, poetry, epistles, and prophecy. It is sheer lunacy to attempt to interpret them the same way. And yet, that is the way that many approach the study of the Bible.

The great concern of the authors that gave rise to the writing of this book was the question of hermeneutics and how to apply the teachings of Scripture. They write, "Many of the urgent problems in the church today are basically struggles with bridging the hermeneutical gap, that has to do with moving from the 'then and there' of the original text to the 'here and now' of our own life settings" (Fee and Stuart, 12). Unfortunately, however, some today read the Bible with only application in mind and not what it originally meant. Their rallying cry is, "I don't care what it meant back then; I only care about what it means for me today." The authors believe that such an approach leads to "a great deal of nonsense" and "every kind of imaginable error" (Fee and Stuart, 13). They insist that the per-

son who studies the Bible must understand it in two dimensions: what it meant then. This is called *exegesis*. The second
dimension is what is means for us today. That is called
hermeneutics. But you must have both in Bible study. You can't
have one without the other or the Bible will not make any
sense. The authors guide the reader in their task to do both.

Fee and Stuart engagingly walk the reader through how to understand the Bible beginning with the basics such as the need
to interpret and the basic tool, which is a good translation.
They provide the reader with a basic primer on how to choose
a translation. They then discuss the different genres in biblical
literature and how each one needs to be approached differently.
For example, one who attempts to study the Bible must not approach the New Testament epistles in the same way that he
would approach the Old Testament narratives or the parables.
They are particularly helpful in their discussion of Old Testament prophetic literature. The neophyte attempting to read one
of the major prophetic books such as Isaiah or Jeremiah
chronologically is soon going to become hopelessly confused.
They write, "When one comes to the actual study or exegeti-
cally-informed reading of the prophetical books, the first thing
one must learn to do is to THINK ORACLES (as one must learn
to think paragraphs in the epistles)." They then explain the
different forms that oracles take in the prophetic literature
such as the lawsuit, the woe, and the promise. I shudder to
think that some attempt to read the prophets without having
any kind of basic understanding just what kind of literature it
is.

There are extremely helpful chapters on the Psalms, wisdom
literature (Proverbs, Job), New Testament history (Acts), the
parables, the Old Testament narratives, the Law (covenant stipulations for Israel), the New Testament epistles, gospels, and
New Testament apocalyptic literature (Revelation). There has
been more confusion spouted by the uninformed about the
book of Revelation than any other book in the Bible. Some of
the teachings that I have heard are just plain wild. As Fee and

Stuart explain, "Most of the problems stem from the symbols, plus the fact that the book deals with future events, but at the same time is set in a recognizable first-century context" (Fee and Stuart, 205). They also point out that the Revelation is "a unique, finely blended combination of three distinct literary types: apocalypse, prophecy, and letter. No wonder so many people are hopelessly confused when trying to read the book.

How To Read the Bible for All Its Worth is a book that every Christian not only should read, but should read every five or ten years to reinforce its concepts. It treats Scripture for what it is, the inerrant Word of God, and provides a sane, balanced approach on how to study the Bible. If there was ever an idiot's guide to Bible study, this is it! It is by far the best book available on how to do basic Bible study. I used it in the classroom for years. I cannot recommend it highly enough. "Now go and do likewise."

26. WHAT THE BIBLE IS ALL ABOUT

By Henrietta Mears

Henrietta Mears is a name that is unfamiliar to the average Christian. Many are familiar with Billy Graham, Bill Bright (Campus Crusade for Christ), Jim Rayburn (Young Life), Richard Halverson (Fourth Presbyterian Church, Bethesda, MD and U.S. Senate Chaplain), and Louis H. Evans (National Presbyterian Church in Washington, D.C.). However, these men would not have had the wide influence that they had were it not for their association with Mears. Henrietta Mears was not a pastor as were Louis Evans and Richard Halverson, nor was she an evangelist preaching to tens of thousands of people as was Billy Graham, and she was not the founder of a parachurch organization such as Bill Bright and Jim Rayburn. What she was is perhaps even more incredible. She was the nearly blind co-founder of the National Sunday School Association, but was perhaps best known as the innovative and energetic Director of Christian Education at the First Presbyterian Church of Hollywood, CA, a tireless advocate for Sunday school programs for all age groups from small children to adults.

During the mid-1900s, she trained and discipled a dedicated and enthusiastic staff and implemented a graded, age-appropriate curriculum from the cradle to adulthood. Within two years, her Sunday school attendance at Hollywood Presbyterian Church was averaging more than 4,200 per week. Under her tireless leadership, the Sunday school program grew from about 400 to 6,000. She taught the college-age class herself.

Although Mears is a virtual unknown to many believers, she is widely considered to be one of the most influential Christian leaders of the twentieth century. She was the founder of Gospel

Light, which even today continues to be a leader in publishing Sunday school and other training materials and now is under the banner of the David C. Cook Family. She profoundly influenced Billy Graham, Bill Bright, Jim Rayburn, Richard Halverson, and Louis Evans, Jr. the founding pastor of the Bel Air Presbyterian Church, where Ronald Reagan and numerous stars in the film industry attended. It is said that her fingerprints are all over Bill Bright's evangelistic tract, *Four Spiritual Laws*, which more or less defined evangelism in the latter half of the twentieth century. It has been estimated that hundreds of men and women used her Sunday school program as a springboard to full-time vocational Christian service.

Mears was not only a gifted educator and mentor to influential Christians, her legacy lives on today in her most enduring work, *What the Bible is All About*. This is a book that belongs on every believer's bookshelf. It is quite simply the best one-volume Bible handbook/survey available even after almost seventy years since its initial publication. Billy Graham, in the Preface to the Special Edition for the Billy Graham Evangelistic Association published in 1953, wrote, "One of the greatest tragedies today is that, although the Bible is an available, open book, it is a closed book to millions, either because they leave it unread or because they read it without applying its teachings to themselves." This book will be invaluable to the Christian wanting to read Scripture and make it interesting, understandable, and practical. It is not simply a handbook, but also a survey that illuminates in a user-friendly format the treasures of the Bible. The 1999 edition I have from Regal also has more than 500 full-color photos, illustrations, maps, and charts. There are also selected Scripture readings for each day of the week making this book extremely useful for both individual as well as group Bible study.

That *What the Bible is All About* was ever published at all is almost a miracle in itself. In her childhood, Mears was plagued by poor health, having contracted muscular rheumatism at age twelve, as well as having chronically poor eyesight. She was healed from her rheumatism after numerous prayers on her behalf, but her childhood nearsightedness was exacerbated by a severe eye injury at age sixteen. She had planned to enroll at the University of Minnesota, but her doctors informed her that she would be blind by age thirty if she continued her studies. She enrolled anyway and she was still able to see by graduation. However, her eyesight never improved and her older sister, Margaret, dedicated her life to being her "eyes" and her companion. This allowed Henrietta to fulfill what God had called her to do and to influence the thousands that she did.

I have used this book as a tool for teaching my adult Bible studies and its simplicity, clarity, and ease of use never ceases to amaze me. I cannot recommend it highly enough. My suggestion is that as you read the Bible, keep your copy of *What the Bible is All About* next to you and consult it often. It will prove to be a life saver.

27. BIBLE CHARACTERS

By Alexander Whyte

I am deeply indebted to Warren Wiersbe who first introduced me to Alexander Whyte in his 1976 book, *Walking with the Giants*. Whyte (1836-1921) was a Scottish pastor who worked with and succeeded the famous Robert S. Candlish, whose exposition of 1 John is one of the treasures of my personal library. Upon Candlish's death, Whyte began what would turn out to be forty-seven years remarkable and fruitful years of ministry at St. George's Free Church in Edinburgh. He had a well-deserved reputation as one of the greatest English-speaking preachers of the nineteenth century. The pulpit was his throne. Wiersbe describes Whyte's preaching as surgical. He writes, "he felt his sermon was not a success if he did not sting the conscience and expose the heart" (Wiersbe, 92). However, if preaching at Free St. Georges was all that Whyte ever did, his memory might be lost to us forever. What lives on is his prolific literary legacy. He left us a treasure trove of golden literary nuggets that can be mined by the curious seeker. Whyte was steeped in the writings of the Puritans, particularly Thomas Goodwin, which shows in the depth of his writings.

Whyte was born in Kirriemuir, Scotland, in 1836 to an unmarried girl named Janet Thompson. The boy's father, John Whyte, wanted to marry the pregnant girl, but she refused. He thereafter left behind his paternal responsibilities by going to the United States leaving only his surname for the child. Whyte was raised in poverty, but received much spiritual guidance from his mother who joined the Free Church of Scotland and encouraged him in his academic pursuits. In 1848 while still a bit of a wee lad, he was apprenticed to a cobbler. He never abandoned his studies, however, and was tutored by a local pastor who taught him Latin and Greek. Despite his inauspicious beginnings, Whyte eventually was able to study divinity first at the University of Edinburgh and then at New College, Edinburgh. He became a minister in the Free Church of Scotland and served a church in Glasgow before moving to Edinburgh and beginning his remarkable ministry at first under the able tutelage of the legendary Robert S. Candlish. For over a century his writings have been a source of inspiration for pastors and laypersons alike.

An interesting side note is that Dr. Joseph Bell was Whyte's physician for many years and a trusted friend and elder at St. George's Free Church. Bell taught at the University of Edinburgh where he tutored a young medical student by the name of Arthur Conan Doyle. Doyle would often escort patients into Bell's lectures where the physician would then reveal different facts about the patient without a single word passing between the two or any prior knowledge. It was Dr. Bell who became the model for Doyle's endearing character, Sherlock Holmes.

Whyte's magnum opus was his *Bible Characters*, which was first published in six volumes from 1898-1902. He had a particular gift for making the people of the Bible come alive. My own personal copy of the book was first published by Zondervan in a one-volume edition in 1967. It has had numerous reprintings since. In the Old Testament in his First Series, Whyte explores the characters from Adam to Achan, in his Second Series from Gideon to Absalom, and in his Third Series from Ahithophel to Nehemiah. Along the way, you will meet well-known Old Testament figures such as Abraham and Lot, Moses and Joshua, Samson, David and Jonathan, Solomon, Elijah and Elisha, Job, Daniel, and Esther. But you will also meet such lessor known saints and scoundrels as Lot, Enoch, Abel, Balaam, Nabaal, and Achan. The New Testament characters are similarly divided with three series respectively covering Joseph and Mary to James, the Lord's brother; Stephen to Timothy; and The Sower Who Went Forth to Sow to the Angel of the Church of the Laodiceans. You will in like fashion meet some of the major players in the New Testament such as Paul, John the Baptist, Peter, Mary Magdalene, and John the apostle. But you will also meet some of the lesser-known characters such as Nicodemas, Ananias and Saphira, Cornelius, Eutychus (the patron saint for all who have ever fallen asleep during a church service), King Agrippa, and Onesiphorus. One thing is certain as you read about well-known characters as well as the more minor ones, they will come alive in such a way that you will never forget them. Whyte's unique gift was that he could portray biblical characters in such a vivid way that they almost seem to leap off the pages of his book. What a gift! I suggest that you read about one Bible character each day as a supplement to your daily devotions. The chapters are brief and most can be read in about five minutes. If you are disciplined in your reading, you will complete the entire book within six months. And then you will likely want to read it again, and again. I can guarantee you that you will wonder at the variety of human personality and you will never again see these characters in the same light again.

I suspect that *Bible Characters* will only serve to whet your appetite for the writings of Alexander Whyte. If that is true, you will also want to read some of his other writings. Some of my favorites are *The Walk, Conversation, and Character of Jesus Christ Our Lord, Lord, Teach Us to Pray* (See Chapter VIII), and *The Characters in Pilgrim's Progress*. The latter is an exposition of John Bunyan's classic allegory tale. It is the perfect companion to *The Pilgrim's Progress*.

Here are a few gems from Whyte's portrayals:

> "Shimei was a reptile of the royal house of Saul. When Shimei saw David escaping for his life out of Jerusalem, Satan entered into Shimei, and he came forth and cursed at David as he passed by" (XLV, Shimei).

> "Hophni and Phinehas were the only children in all Israel who saw the temple every day and paid no attention to it" (XXXII, Eli).

"Joab was a stern, haughty, imperious, revengeful man. His only virtue was a certain proud patronising loyalty to his king" (XLVI, Joab).

"But as long as Esau lives, as long as that man or that woman lives whom our son supplanted so long ago, he will build his house over a volcano, and will travel home to it with a trembling heart" (XVII, Jacob).

"Abraham was the father of the faithful. And Lot, his nephew, was the father of all such as are scarcely saved" (XII, Lot).

28. STUDIES IN THE SERMON ON THE MOUNT

By D. Martyn Lloyd-Jones

Let me begin by saying that D. Martyn Lloyd-Jones has been one of my spiritual heroes for almost fifty years. I was introduced to the man when I first read Warren Wiersbe's *Walking with the Giants*, when it came out in 1976. In the book, which by the way bears reading and re-reading, he includes a chapter about Lloyd-Jones and his magnificent preaching and writing ministry. Please allow me to tell you about his remarkable ministry before getting to the book itself.

Lloyd-Jones was best-known as the pastor of Westminster Chapel in London for almost thirty years. He was certainly one of the most influential preachers and evangelical leaders of the twentieth century. Wiersbe called him "a staunch Calvinist of the Puritan school" (Wiersbe, 181). He was called in 1939 to serve as associate to the legendary G. Campbell Morgan, who was by then well into his seventies. He succeeded Morgan in 1943 upon the latter's retirement and began one of the greatest preaching ministries in the history of the church. At Westminster, Lloyd-Jones become known for his style of expository preaching which attracted thousands of listeners at his Sunday morning and evening services as well as his Friday night Bible studies. He would usually preach for fifty minutes to an hour. Most modern congregants begin looking at their watches after twenty-five minutes. He spent decades preaching through the epistles to the Ephesians and Romans. In my library for example, I have eight volumes from his preaching series on Ephesians. He could preach for an hour on a single verse. Christopher Catherwood wrote about him, "His great strength was that he made Puritan, Reformed doctrine relevant to the twentieth century and in such straightforward, contemporary language that everyone listening to it could understand" (Cather-wood, 83).

One of the most interesting things about Lloyd-Jones is that his academic training did not prepare him to be a preacher at all. He received an M.D. degree from the University of London and studied bacterial endocarditis, though he never did become a cardiologist. Although he was progressing rapidly in his chosen profession of medicine, God apparently had other plans for him and he felt the tug towards the ministry in 1925. The rest is history, and we in the evangelical world have been the better for it.

Studies in the Sermon on the Mount began as a series of some sixty sermons preached at Westminster Chapel. It was originally published in two volumes in 1959. My copy has the two volumes bound as one book consisting of some 650 pages. Do not let the number of pages scare you. Reading it was one of the most enriching experiences of my life. I guarantee you that you will be enthralled. The sermons were taken down in shorthand as there was no way to record the sermons. Lloyd-Jones wrote in 1959 in the Preface to his first volume, "I am profoundly convinced that the greatest need of the Church today is a return to expository preaching." And that he did with a flourish. In explaining why he decided to preach on the Sermon on the Mount, he writes, "I do not think it is a harsh judgment to say that the most obvious feature of the life of the Christian Church today is, alas, its superficiality" (Lloyd-Jones, Vol. 1, 9). Since he wrote those words over sixty years ago, one wonders what he would think of the twenty-first century church. He would likely recoil in horror.

Lloyd-Jones was one of the main leaders of the evangelical movement against liberal theology in the churches. He believed that "one main cause is our attitude to the Bible, our failure to take it seriously, our failure to take it as it is and allow it to speak to us" (Lloyd-Jones, Vol. 1, 10). He was one of the first to advocate conservative, Bible-believing churches leave their liberal denominations, which was quite controversial at the time. Lloyd-Jones felt that the Sermon on the Mount exemplified what Kingdom living was supposed to be. He writes, "The Sermon on the Mount is nothing but a great and grand and perfect elaboration of what our Lord called His 'new commandment'" (Vol. 1, 15). He believed that it provided a blueprint for the Christian life. He argues, "This is how Christians ought to live; this is how Christians are meant to live" (Lloyd-Jones, Vol. 1, 17). "The world today is looking for, and desperately needs, true Christians" (Lloyd-Jones, Vol. 1, 18). He concludes his introduction with a fiery statement, "Do not say that it has nothing to do with us. Why, it has everything to do with us! If only all of us were living the Sermon on the Mount, men would know that there is a dynamic in the Christian gospel; they would know that this is a live thing; they would not go looking for anything else" (Lloyd-Jones, Vol. 1, 20).

Reading *Studies in the Sermon on the Mount* was one of the most transformative experiences of my life. In my opinion, it is the very best work he has ever done, and that is saying a lot. I recommend that you read a sermon a day, slowly, reflectively highlighting as you read, as I do. The Holy Spirit will use Lloyd-Jones' powerful words to challenge you and change you.

Following are some samples to give you a taste of Lloyd-Jones:

On the Beatitudes:

> "Meekness is essentially a true view of oneself, expressing itself in attitude and conduct with respect to others" (Lloyd-Jones, Vol. 1, 68).

> "Whenever you put happiness before righteousness, you will be doomed to misery. That is the message of the Bible from beginning to end" (Lloyd-Jones, Vol. 1, 75).

"I can never make myself like Jesus Christ, but I can stop walking in the gutters of life" (Lloyd-Jones, Vol. 1, 90).

"He looked at his band of ordinary, insignificant people and said, 'You and you alone are the light of the world'" (Lloyd-Jones, Vol. 1, 163).

On the Righteousness of the Scribes and Pharisees:

"We can all rationalize our own sins and explain them away. That was typical of the Pharisees" (Lloyd-Jones, Vol. 1, 205).

On the Mortification of Sin:

"Do we all realize that the most important thing we have to do in this world is to prepare ourselves for eternity" (Lloyd-Jones, Vol. 1, 246).

On Denying Self:

"Self is the main cause of unhappiness in life" (Lloyd-Jones, Vol. 1, 295).

On What is Special about You:

"If God is your Father, somewhere or another, in some form or other, the family likeness will be there, the traces of your Parentage will inevitably appear" (Lloyd-Jones, Vol. 1, 320).

On Living the Righteous Life:

"There is no reward from God for those who seek it from men" (Lloyd-Jones, Vol. 2, 17).

On Prayer:

> "Prayer is beyond any question the highest
> activity of the human soul. Man is at his greatest
> and highest when, upon his knees, he comes
> face to face with God" (Lloyd-Jones, Vol. 2, 45).

On Treasures on Earth and in Heaven:

> "It is not what a man may have, but what he
> thinks of his wealth, what his attitude is towards
> it" (Lloyd-Jones, Vol. 2, 81).

On God or Mammon:

> "Earthly treasures are so powerful that they grip
> the entire personality. They grip a man's heart,
> his mind and his will; they tend to affect his
> spirit, his soul, and his whole being" (Lloyd-
> Jones, Vol. 2, 94).

29. THE CRISES OF THE CHRIST

By G. Campbell Morgan

As a preacher, G. Campbell Morgan's name is spoken in the same breath alongside some of the other great English-speaking pulpit luminaries of the past several hundred years such as Jonathan Edwards, George Whitefield, Charles H. Spurgeon, Alexander Whyte, and D. Martyn Lloyd-Jones. The British-born-Morgan, a contemporary of Rodney "Gipsy" Smith, was an itinerant preacher and Bible teacher who preached his first sermon at the age of thirteen and visited America fifty-four times during his ministry. The first time was in 1896 at the invitation of D. L. Moody to lecture to the students at the Moody Bible Institute. His longest pastorate was at the prestigious Westminster Chapel in London from 1904 until 1917. He returned to the United States for seven years of ministry before returning to Westminster Chapel from 1933 until 1943 where he mentored the esteemed D. Martyn Lloyd-Jones, who succeeded him in his final year. If all he had ever accomplished in his ministry was to mentor Lloyd-Jones, his service to the church would have been inestimable.

Morgan was about as unlikely a person to achieve international fame as there could be. Born in 1863 on a farm in the little village of Tetbury, England, he was frail as a child but had a passion to preach. He faced early rejection for the Methodist ministry, but that did not deter him. When he was twenty-seven, a rather advanced age for ordination in those days, he became a pastor of a tiny Congregational church in Staffordshire, England, which launched his career. By all earthly standards, it is difficult to explain his success. He didn't study in a college or seminary, yet his books have been used in those schools and many of his more than sixty books were on the desks of many a twentieth century pastor as he prepared his weekly sermon. He taught as a faculty member at three institutions and was the president of Cheshunt College, Cambridge. That is not bad for an itinerant preacher from such inauspicious beginnings.

Morgan was the reputed master of the four Gospels. He was a great devotional preacher, not a doctrinal one as Lloyd-Jones was, and he made his home in the Gospels and the Acts of the Apostles. In my opinion, *The Crises of the Christ* is his *magnum opus* and ought to be read by every Christ-follower. It is a masterful exposition on the seven pivotal events of our Savior's life: his birth, baptism, temptation, transfiguration, crucifixion, resurrection, and ascension of Jesus and how they accomplished God's eternal plan. He writes of these events, "Each of them ushered in a new order of things in the work of Christ, crowning that of the past, and creating the force for that which was to come" (Morgan, 17). Morgan's analyses are exceptional! Although most of Morgan's works are expositional in nature, this book is his most doctrinal and what a gem it is!

Morgan begins with a three-chapter introduction in which he discusses man's fall into sin. He first discusses the problem of man distanced from God by sin and then man's ignorance. He writes, "As a bird cannot fly except in air, and a fish cannot swim save in water, so man cannot exercise the necessary functions of his life save in relation to God" (Morgan, 42). He then argues how unlike God man is because of his fall into sin. He talks of man's total alienation from God. He argues convincingly. "No man can know himself who does not know God. Just as man, having lost the vision of God, creates a false deity upon the basis of his own distorted intelligence, so thereafter, he attempts to bring himself into conformity with the false deity, and thus perpetuates the ruin, and ensures the final degradation" (Morgan, 52).

Morgan's discussion of man's predicament because of sin is masterful. He states plainly, "It is hardly a popular doctrine. It cuts underneath the feet all ground for human boasting. God is not bound to do anything for man. Man has forfeited his whole claim upon God by sin. There is absolutely no reason why the distorted and ruined image should be redeemed or reconstructed" (Morgan, 61).

Morgan begins his discussion of the birth of Christ talking about the mystery of the Incarnation. He writes of the Johannine phrase, "In the beginning was the Word," "By it man is borne back into the infinite and unfathomable reaches of the unmeasurable" (Morgan, 72-73). Of John's declaration, "The Word became flesh," Morgan writes "The statement is appalling, overwhelming. Out of the infinite distances, into the finite nearness; from the unknowable, to the knowable; from the method of self-expression appreciable by Deity alone, to a method of self-expression understandable of the human" (Morgan, 73).

According to Morgan, Christ's baptism was the door he passed through from private to public life. Prior to that, he lived roughly thirty years in relative obscurity. Morgan explains, "His being baptized was an act by which he consented to take His place among sinners. John's baptism was that of repentance. There was no room for repentance in Jesus, and yet because of His devotion to their redemption, He took His place with them" (Morgan, 120). Morgan is poetic in his description of the baptism. He writes, "He left the seclusion and the privacy, and standing on the threshold of public work, with the waters of a death baptism, which He had shared in the grace of His heart with man, still clinging about Him, the silent heavens broke into the language of a great music, as the Almighty Father declared, 'This is My beloved Son in Whom I am well pleased'" (Morgan, 136).

The temptation of Christ, which is recorded in the three Synoptic Gospels, is examined by Morgan in three parts as three different temptations. The temptation takes place immediately after God the Father's declaration about Jesus at his baptism.

Morgan writes, "Now evil appears before Him in all its tremendous strength and naked horror in the personality of the devil. In all likelihood never had there been such an attack before and certain it is that it never occurred again" (Morgan, 154). Of particular value to us facing temptation today is not only how Jesus faced it, but how Satan operates. "One of the chief values of this account of the temptation lies in the fact that Jesus here dragged Satan into the light, and revealed to all His followers the fact of his personality, and the method of his operations" (Morgan, 158).

How does Satan try to appeal to the weakness of mankind? Morgan points outs, "Wealth, fame, position, and power are all in the gift of the devil. He holds them, and actually dispenses them, in order to attain ends upon which his malice is set. What these gifts are worth, in the last analysis, is another question" (Morgan, 190). Jesus certainly knew what they were worth, according to Morgan. "He knew, too, that the glory was the glory of tinsel, rather than of gold. It was passing, fading, tarnished, even as He looked upon it. The splendour was undoubtedly great, but it was not lasting" (Morgan, 196). Morgan's prose rises to heights of eloquence. "The glorious consciousness of coming victory was the joy that was set before Him, and that joy made hell's offer paltry, mean, blasphemous, and impertinent; and with stern and magnificent authority He commanded Satan to depart, and announced the fact of His abiding in the will of God, to Whom alone He would render worship, and Whom alone He was prepared to serve" (Morgan, 198). Morgan's summation of the three temptations is compelling. "Looking back on that threefold process, in the wilderness, on the wing of the temple, and on the high mountain, there is seen a Man, on each occasion occupying an impregnable position, standing in a fortress that hell is utterly unable to capture, replying to each attack in one brief sentence. The silence of the enemy after the reply of the Lord was a clear confession of his defeat, and a remarkable proof that he is unable to gain any advantage over those who are content to abide, at whatever cost, in the will of God" (Morgan, 202).

Morgan's description of the transfiguration and what Peter, James, and John observed is both eloquent and compelling. "They beheld no longer the Man of sorrows, upon Whose face was the mark of perpetual pain, but a Man shining in all the splendours of His own perfect character, as it transformed and transfigured the veil of His flesh" (Morgan, 216). He points out that "the transfiguration of Jesus was the consummation of His human life, the natural issue of all that preceded it" (Morgan, 229).

About the reaction of his three companions, Morgan titles that chapter "The Dazed Disciples." He writes, "He was Master of death. On the mount of transfiguration He stood superior to death, transfigured, and yet conversing of death to be accomplished" so that these three men "might see the Master's connection with death" (Morgan, 249). One of them was afraid and the other two opportunistic. They wanted to make tents and live there in the moment. Morgan writes, "The mistake is by no means an obsolete one. Men are still attempting to make tabernacles, one for Christ, one for Confucius, one for Buddha" (Morgan, 252). Powerful! But what was the permanent effect on them? Morgan argues, "They never could think of Him again as they had thought of Him before. For once they had been permitted to look at Him changed, altered, transfigured, shining with all the splendour of that indwelling glory; and even though He had come back to the old form, and the voice of their Friend and Teacher, and the touch of the Man Jesus, they knew that underneath the veil of that humanity there was hidden a radiant splendour" (Morgan, 258-59).

Morgan argues that it was not just Jesus who was changed on that mount. He argues, "Peter and James and John were taken to the mount of transfiguration for a set purpose, in order that their conception of death might be changed and altered" (Morgan, 261). John would later write, "We beheld His glory." Peter likewise would write that "we were eyewitnesses of His majesty." Although these three disciples of Jesus might have wanted to remain at that place permanently, it was not possible for them to stay. Morgan writes, "Men must leave the mountain for the valley, but they can carry the mountain with them into the valley. They who visit the mount may pass back into the commonplaces of life in new power, taking with them the truth, that behind the commonplace lies the light that flashed upon the mount of transfiguration" (Morgan, 266).

Morgan examines the crucifixion of Christ from different angles providing a panoramic view of his sufferings. I believe that to understand fully the depth of man's sin, we must comprehend the enormity of Christ's sufferings. Morgan begins with Christ's three years of public ministry as the prelude to his crucifixion and how he was ever aware of the cup he would have to drink. "The pathway of the three years was a pathway ever resolutely trodden towards the Cross" (Morgan, 287). He then proceeds with an eloquent discussion of Christ's sufferings particularly when he cried out that God had forsaken him. He explains, "There is no agony for the human soul like that of silence" (Morgan, 301). He also wonders at the mystery of what transpired. He writes, "How in the depth of the darkness the mighty work was accomplished, men will never perfectly understand" (Morgan, 302).

Morgan's discussion of the those who viewed this spectacle is masterful. He writes, "All sorts of conditions of men are gathered to the Cross, representative crowds, the whole scene being a picture and a prophecy of how, through the centuries, every sort and condition would be gathered to the uplifted Cross of the Son of man" (Morgan, 332). He explains, "Sorrow was supremely represented by the presence of the women. Worldly government by the centurion, the soldiers, and the malefactors. Religious failure by the chief priests and the Sanhedrim. The great shepherdless crowd over which Christ had so often mourned, and in the presence of which His heart had ever been moved with compassion was largely represented in the great multitude of which Luke speaks. Familiarity with Jesus had its representation in the presence before the Cross of His kinfolk and acquaintance. Discipleship was there, in the person of His own, and particularly that of John" (Morgan, 333).

I appreciated Morgan's careful discussion of what led Christ to his crucifixion. Why did Christ have to suffer on the cross? His analysis of the human condition is priceless. "That is the supreme and overwhelming degradation of human life. It is, moreover, the whole story of man. Yielded to sin, he is the slave of sin, bound hand and foot, bruised and ruined in the whole fact of his life (Morgan, 323). Morgan continues, "Man is the slave of sin, is paralyzed in all the highest powers of his being, in the whole of which the poison operates with ever increasing and terrific power. These problems are solved in the mystery of the King's passion" (Morgan, 324).

Morgan concludes his treatment of the crises of the Christ with discussions of the resurrection and his ascension. It is my judgment that the bodily resurrection of Jesus Christ from the dead is the most important historical event in the history of the world. Upon its truth the Christian faith stands or falls. Morgan's chapter headings say it all: "Perfect Victory," "The Divine Seal," and "Faith's Anchor." He writes, "Having thus gained a victory over every conceivable form of sin, covering the whole territory of its domain, death cannot hold Him" (Morgan, 359). Morgan calls it "the unanswerable argument for the accomplishment by Jesus Christ, of God's purpose for destroying the works of the devil" (Ibid.)). He further writes, "Upon the fact of the historic resurrection stands or falls the whole fabric of Christianity" (Morgan, 373). Amen!

As for the ascension, Morgan explains that it is a necessary link between His resurrection from among the dead, and reappearance amid His disciples; and the coming of God the Holy Spirit on the day of Pentecost" (Morgan, 389). He informs us that the gospel accounts of this event are brief because of our inability to comprehend it. He explains, "Very little is said because little can be said which could be understood by those dwelling still

within the limitations of the material, and having consciousness of the spiritual world only by faith" (Ibid.).

I confess to being an unabashed fan of Morgan's writings and
sermons. In my personal library among the dozens of volumes
I own that were authored by him, I have his complete works on
the four gospels as well as his ten-volume *The Westminster Pulpit*, a collection of his sermons preached at the Westminster
Chapel in London during his roughly quarter century of pastoral ministry there. I have spent many a happy hour reading
his sermons totally enraptured. By all means, I encourage you
to introduce yourself to the writings of this extraordinary man
of God and there is no better place to begin than with *The Crises
of the Christ*.

BIBLICAL AUTHORITY

The Bible has played a central role in shaping the thought and
history of the world, particularly in the West. Its authority was
basically unquestioned by Christians for centuries because it
originates in the nature of its author, God himself. The doctrine
of biblical infallibility was pretty much assumed by the church
at least until about the nineteenth century.

Although the accuracy and authority of the Bible has been
questioned for about 300 years, a byproduct of the Enlightenment, the situation reached a crisis level during the twentieth
and twenty-first centuries. This crisis exists both outside and
inside the church. As the world outside changes at warp speed
and the foundations of society appear to be collapsing, the
church itself slowly begins to reflect those changes too. In
many churches, the Bible is seldom read and often questioned.
Certainly, the attacks against the infallibility of Scripture came
from within and without the church. Christians and church
leaders began to question the reliability of the Bible which
their doctrines and creeds say is the Word of God.

The authority of Scripture means that in all matters of faith and practice, the Word of God is the only rule and guide for Christians. It is the final arbiter in these matters. Historically, the authority of the Bible has resided in its authorship. The church, both Protestant and Roman Catholic, has always believed that it is God's Word, inspired by God, literally "God-breathed" (2 Timothy 3:16). Two terms usually arise when we talk about the inspiration of Scripture, inerrant and infallible. Is the Bible inerrant? Or is it full of errors? Is the Bible infallible? Is it our supreme authority? Today, the questions about the inerrancy and infallibility of Scripture are being answered more and more in the negative thus drawing the battle lines for Christians. That is what the fight for biblical authority is all about.

The twentieth century has seen the widespread abandonment of the doctrine of inerrancy in the mainline Protestant denominations. The publication of J. Gresham Machen's *Christianity and Liberalism* (See Chapter VII) was a landmark event in 1923 in the heat of the Fundamentalist/Modernist controversy, but it was Harold Lindsell's 1976 *The Battle for the Bible* that drew the battle lines for a new generation. This led to the formation of the International Council on Biblical Inerrancy which met in 1978, 1982, and 1986 and produced the seminal Chicago Statement on Biblical Inerrancy. Craig L. Blomberg's 2014 *Can We Still Believe the Bible?* is one of several excellent books dealing with the topic.

30. THE BATTLE FOR THE BIBLE

By Harold Lindsell

When Harold Lindsell published this book in 1976, it was like a bombshell. He was concerned about two issues in evangelical Christianity: the inerrancy and authority of Scripture and the growing fragmentation of the evangelical camp. He rightly saw that two opposing camps were emerging. Harold Ockenga ably sums up the two prevailing positions in his Foreword. He writes, "The first view considers all of Scripture to be inspired and true, including the historical, geographical, and scientific teaching. The second view holds that only the Bible teaching on salvation-history and doctrine is true." Lindsell saw the issue as a watershed in the evangelical world. Just as in a watershed, waters on each side flow to different rivers, basins, or seas, the doctrine of inerrancy marks a turning point which leads to very different places theologically.

Lindsell wasn't the first to sound the alarm, but he sounded it louder than anyone else. He sounded the battle cry for the evangelical movement and drew the battle lines. He certainly wasn't the first, but his voice was the loudest. The opening salvo came in 1881 when B. B. Warfield of Princeton Theological Seminary published *The Inspiration and Authority of the Bible* and defined just what the conflict was. J. Gresham Machen touched on the issue as early as 1923 when his *Christianity and Liberalism* was published. J. I. Packer crystallized the problem in his 1958 book *Fundamentalism and the Word of God*, as did other evangelicals such as Francis Schaeffer, R. C. Sproul, and James Montgomery Boice. But it was Lindsell who best declared war and identified the enemy.

At the time of the book's publication, Lindsell was the editor of *Christianity Today*, the highly-respected publication begun by Billy Graham, and a former professor at Fuller Theological Seminary. In other words, he was a theological insider. He named names, knew where the bodies were buried, and took no prisoners. He wrote in his Preface, "I regard the subject of this book, biblical inerrancy, to be the most important theological topic of this age."

After defining the terminology and giving a historical overview, he begins by documenting three egregious doctrinal departures devoting a chapter each to the Missouri Synod Lutheran Church, the Southern Baptist Convention, and Fuller Theological Seminary, his former institution. He then documents the erosion of biblical inerrancy in other smaller denominations and smaller parachurch groups. Finally, Lindsell discusses deviations from the doctrine in the recent history of the church. He spares nobody skewering among others the Anglican Church, Lutherans in the U.S. my own former denomination, the United Presbyterian Church USA, the United Church of Christ, and the United Methodist Church. Of the latter, he writes, "One of the signs of the times in Methodism is how far to the left some of its seminaries have gone" (Lindsell, 153). He then documents the strange situation in which a professor at the denomination's Candler School of Theology would begin each class by stating, "Ladies and Gentlemen, I am an atheist." He concludes, "All of this is quite different from what historic Methodism has stood for, and John Wesley would be dismayed at what has transpired in the church he founded and the institutions that rose from the church. He would be astounded at the attitude of all too many clergymen and teachers toward the Bible he believed in and held to be without error" (Lindsell, 154).

Some believed that Lindsell was too black and white in drawing his battle lines and too bombastic in his approach. For example, his definition of evangelical included the notion of biblical inerrancy. This was seen as divisive and he took a lot of criticism for his stand. Lindsell actually preempted his detractors when he wrote, "For me to so define 'evangelical' may appear divisive, and it may seem to present a threat to the unity of faith. We are always confronted with the dilemma of having to choose between truth and unity. Where truth is not at stake and there is disunity, it is not only unfortunate, it is also wrong. But where unity must be foregone because of adherence to truth it is a different matter" (Lindsell, 139).

Lindsell includes a helpful chapter on alleged discrepancies in Scripture and how they may be resolved. He does not lightly dismiss them. He writes, "I can say, however, that a multitude of what formerly were difficulties have been solved, so that the detractors have had to back water again and again. But as each apparent discrepancy is resolved, another objection is raised. Although in hundreds of cases criticisms of Scripture have shown to be unfounded, those who refuse to believe in inerrancy never seem to be satisfied. Why is this so? Does it not constitute a frame of mind that *wants* to disbelieve? Does it reflect a viewpoint that says in effect, 'I will not believe what the Scripture teaches about itself until *every* objection has been answered to my satisfaction'? Does this not tell us something about the nature of man who, though he may be regenerated, yet retains strong characteristics of the old nature so that unbelief crops up again and again? May not the real difficulty be a want of biblical faith rather than a want of evidence" (Lindsell, 161)?

Lindsell wraps up his argument by giving several examples of what happened in the past when the doctrine of inerrancy was abandoned. This chapter is titled "How Infection Spreads" and resonated with me because it hit very close to home. My own denomination, the Presbyterian Church USA, had been infected to the point that biblical authority had been entirely abandoned which led me to be a part of three exoduses over the decades when churches left the denomination for greener pastures, or at least more biblically sound ones. The heartache one feels when being involved in such a divorce is real and enduring. It still makes me want to weep.

The controversy surrounding the doctrine of biblical inerrancy is not going away and has been analyzed and defended by numerous well-qualified biblical scholars. The International Council on Biblical Inerrancy (ICBI) was founded in 1977, an outgrowth of this book, to clarify and defend the doctrine. There are also several helpful books that are very accessible to a general audience. I highly recommend Craig L. Blomberg's excellent *Can We Still Believe the Bible?* But please read *The Battle for the Bible*. It is imperative that we understand just what the issues are and their implications for those of us who call ourselves Evangelical Christians.

31. CAN WE STILL BELIEVE THE BIBLE?

By Craig L. Blomberg

I recently went with my wife to a drop-in get together at a local taproom. While she socialized, I tried to make small talk with a man sitting at the same table as I and our discussion invariably came around to what I do and then the Bible. He asked me how I could believe the Bible, a book that is full of myths and inaccuracies. He cited as evidence the pericope from the gospels about Jesus walking on the water. He insinuated that only an idiot could actually believe that Jesus did it. This exchange, I think, summarizes many people's attitudes toward the Bible today.

The title of Blomberg's book says it all. *Can We Still Believe the Bible?* Is belief in an authoritative Bible outdated and hopelessly misguided? Is it full of contradictions and outright falsehoods? Did the miracles actually happen? These questions obviously lead to ancillary ones concerning the history of Bible transmission and the reliability of the biblical manuscripts, the accuracy of our translations, and the historicity of the biblical narratives. Blomberg begins his book with the statement, "Questions about the Bible have flourished since its inception" (Blomberg, 1). He concludes, "Our liberal American love affair with the newest and the novel seems to condemn each new generation to rehearse the same debates as in the past, making some of the same mistakes all over again, even if minor variations and changes of nomenclature intrude" (Blomberg, 6).

Craig Blomberg is certainly an able guide to walk the reader through these issues. Recently retired, he was Distinguished Professor of New Testament at Denver Seminary having joined the faculty there in 1986. He completed his Ph.D. in New Testa ment at the esteemed Aberdeen University in Scotland and was formerly a research fellow in Cambridge, England, at Tyndale House. He has written or edited at least twenty books and has contributed numerous articles in professional journals, multi-author works, and dictionaries or encyclopedias. He is certainly widely considered a top-flight biblical scholar and an authority in that field. On a personal note, I had the opportunity to interact with Dr. Blomberg on both a formal and informal level back in 2015 when we participated together in the New Testament and Economics Colloquium at Southwestern Baptist Theological Seminary in Fort Worth, TX.

The book is organized into six chapters not including the Introduction and Conclusion. The first chapter asks the questions, "Aren't the copies of the Bible hopelessly corrupt? Consider, for example, that there are roughly 400,000 textual variants among the ancient New Testament manuscripts alone, not even including the ones from the Hebrew Old Testament. Blomberg writes, "Certain skeptics conclude that it is ridiculous to imagine ever reconstructing the original text of Scripture, much less being able to affirm its trustworthiness" (Blomberg, 13). He laments that so many, believers and unbelievers alike, consider such figures daunting "and ask no further questions" (Ibid.). Countless skeptics and seekers have read the self-proclaimed agnostic Bart Ehrman's 2005 book *Misquoting Jesus: The Story behind Who Changed the Bible and Why* and have astonishingly accepted it as "gospel truth." Blomberg meets the arguments of Ehrman and many others head on and concludes that they are overblown and baseless. He writes, "For every practical purpose for which Christians use the Bible, the modern editions of the Hebrew Old Testament and Greek New Testament, like all the standard modern-language translations in use around the world today, can more than adequately function as remarkably close approximations of God's inerrant autographs and can guide us theologically and ethically in every walk of life" (Blomberg, 40-41).

The second question that Blomberg entertains is "wasn't the selection of books for the canon just political?" This leads obviously to why the canon of the Roman Catholic Church is different from that of Protestants. Blomberg adeptly walks the reader through the major issues. For example, he discusses the Old Testament canon and its development as well as the Apocrypha and the Pseudepigrapha. He concludes, "No *Jews* ever seriously supported the canonization of any of the Apocrypha" (Blomberg, 51). He then moves on to a discussion of the New Testament canon and its criteria for inclusion. He lays out the issues for why some books were included as well as why others were excluded. Of particular interest is his interaction with the claims of Dan Brown, whose blockbuster novel, *The Da Vinci Code*, weirdly mixed together fiction and fantasy and has incredibly received serious scholarly attention as if his version of what happened at the Council of Nicea (AD 315) was actually the true interpretation of facts. Blomberg concludes that the sixty-six books of the Protestant canon were "well chosen" and the councils did not err in rejecting the Apocryphal books that the Roman Catholic Church accepted.

The third question that Blomberg entertains is "can we trust any of our translations of the Bible?" He explains the three predominant theories of Bible translation and then informs the reader that some Westerners have argued loudly for an "essentially literal" translation of the Bible. He writes, "But in modern Bible translations worldwide, the dominant approach is to prioritize translation that is the clearest or easiest to understand for a broad cross-section of the speakers of the language into which the Scriptures are being rendered" (Blomberg, 83). He provides reasons for why the issue is so important today and why the average Christian needs to be informed. He elucidates, "The writers who have engaged in the most-heated translation wars rarely seem to think about the damage they have done among unbelievers and skeptics who have little understanding of what is being debated" (Blomberg, 84). He believes the issue of Bible translations has been a bit overblown. He concludes, "We cannot emphasize our main point strongly enough. All the major, nonsectarian Bible translations are more than adequate for teaching God's people everything God wants them to know that really matters" (Blomberg, 117).

Blomberg then moves to his fourth question: "Don't these issues rule out biblical inerrancy?" Evangelicals in the twentieth and twenty-first centuries have defended the doctrine of inerrancy with particular fervor. It has been attacked and ridiculed with equal fervor by those of other theological camps. It is not facile to suggest that this issue has been the biggest theological battleground over the past century. Blomberg discusses two different approaches to the doctrine of inerrancy, the inductive approach and the deductive, and then provides a working definition. "Inerrancy means that when all facts are known, the Scriptures in their original autographs and properly interpreted will be shown to be wholly true in everything that they affirm, whether that has to do with doctrine or morality or with the social, physical, or life sciences" (from Paul Feinberg at Trinity Evangelical Divinity School). He then handles some of the objections that have been raised and concludes that the Bible is trustworthy and can be believed in all that it affirms.

Chapter 5 deals with the question, "Aren't several narrative genres of the Bible unhistorical? Blomberg then discusses several examples ranging from the Torah, to the wisdom literature, to the prophets of the Old Testament before turning to the New Testament. His examples from the newer testament range from the Gospel of Matthew to Revelation and apocalyptic literature. He includes a helpful discussion of pseudonymous epistles. He includes a helpful suggestion and caution. "Not all writings of a narrative genre intend to record history; we need to treat each on a case-by-case basis" (Blomberg, 176). His conclusion is telling. *"The truth claims of the Bible, appropriately cherished by inerrantist, can never be determined apart from our best assessment of the literary forms and genres involved"* (Blomberg, 177-78).

The final chapter deals with the question "Don't all the miracles make the Bible mythical?" Many reject the Bible out of hand because they do not believe that miracles are possible. After all, they attest, it is a scientific impossibility for a man to rise from the dead. Or walk on water. Or heal the blind. And on and on. They simply pontificate on what modern science has proven or disproven. Blomberg argues that miracles lie outside the realm of science because they 'cannot be tested or experimentally reproduced in a laboratory" (Blomberg, 179). Thus, he concludes that they "should not be defined as the violation of the normal laws of nature or of the universe but as involving their temporary suspension or transcendence" (Ibid.). What follows is a brief examination of miracles in the Old Testament, Gospels, and Acts of the Apostles. He concludes that they are not arbitrary "sprinkled throughout an ordinary narrative to give it an extraordinary quality. They are part and parcel of the biblical revelation from start to finish" (Blomberg, 207). He writes, "People can choose not to believe that they could have happened, but in light of the massive amount of documented parallels in today's world, this would be a leap of faith in spite of the evidence, not the logical outgrowth of scientific or philosophical reasoning" (Ibid.). Of course, he considers the resurrection of Jesus Christ to be "the central fact of Christian history on which the credibility of our faith depends" (Ibid.).

Blomberg is a firm believer in the authority of the Bible. This book is an important one for Christians to read in that it exposes the reader to some of the attacks on its veracity. How does a Christian respond when told that it is silly to believe the Bible? Blomberg provides a reasoned and balanced examination of the issues and is a trustworthy guide to the many issues being discussed today. I think you will agree.

Dr. Craig Blomberg joined the faculty of Denver Seminary in 1986. He is currently a distinguished professor of New Testament.

Dr. Blomberg completed his PhD in New Testament, specializing in the parables and the writings of Luke-Acts, at Aberdeen University in Scotland. He received an MA from Trinity Evangelical Divinity School, and a BA from Augustana College. Before joining the faculty of Denver Seminary, he taught at Palm Beach Atlantic College and was a research fellow in Cambridge, England with Tyndale House.

In addition to writing numerous articles in professional journals, multi-author works and dictionaries or encyclopedias, he has authored or edited 20 books, including *The Historical Reliability of the Gospels*, *Interpreting the Parables*, commentaries on Matthew, 1 Corinthians and James, *Jesus and the Gospels: An Introduction and Survey*, *From Pentecost to Patmos: An Introduction to Acts through Revelation*, *Christians in an Age of Wealth: A Biblical Theology of Stewardship*, *Neither Poverty nor Riches: A Biblical Theology of Possessions*, *Making Sense of the New Testament: Three Crucial Questions*, *Preaching the Parables*, *Contagious Holiness: Jesus' Meals with Sinners*, and *Handbook of New Testament Exegesis*.

32. THE PRODIGAL GOD

By Timothy Keller

The name Tim Keller is one that is very familiar to evangelicals. He is a *New York Times* bestselling author who has been called by *Newsweek* the "C. S. Lewis for the twenty-first century." Retired since 2017, Keller was the founding pastor of the megachurch Redeemer Presbyterian Church in Manhattan. Today Redeemer has roughly 6,000 regular attendees and a host of daughter churches. Keller has written roughly three dozen books and has been widely influential through his writing ministry and his organization, Redeemer City to City, which trains pastors for service around the world.

Keller's intention in this brief book—and at 133 pages of easy text it is a brief book—is to "lay out the essentials of the Christian message, the gospel" (Keller, xi). He believes that the Parable of the Prodigal Son does just that. It encapsulates the message of the gospel in a brief, readable format that anyone can understand. It is a primer of the Christian faith using perhaps the most familiar parable that Jesus taught. The title of the book may be off-putting to some. In this parable, we are familiar with the younger son being the prodigal, the wayward son who squanders his inheritance in a distant land and is reduced to feeding pigs. What was a nice Jewish boy doing feeding these unclean animals is the question Jesus never asks, but certainly implies. Is it possible for God to be "prodigal?" Keller defines "prodigal" as "recklessly spendthrift." He believes that "it means to spend until you have nothing left" (Keller, xiv), which is appropriate for describing the father's behavior towards his wayward son. The response of the father in the story was "reckless" in that he did not count the younger son's sin against him. This response offended the older brother much as the gospel offends countless multitudes.

Keller begins his exposition of the parable by describing the people around Jesus, the original listeners. He claims that we sentimentalize the story if we imagine the first hearers of the parable shedding a tear as they hear the story of the gospel and how God will welcome them no matter what they have done. Keller writes, "The targets of this story are not 'wayward sinners' but religious people who do everything the Bible requires" (Keller, 10). "No," Keller continues, "the original listeners were not melted into tears by this story but rather they were thunderstruck, offended, and infuriated. Jesus's purpose is not to warm our hearts but to shatter our categories" (Ibid.).

Keller believes that churches are not attracting the sinners like Jesus did. He argues, "Jesus's teaching consistently attracted the irreligious while offending the Bible-believing, religious people of his day. However, in the main, our churches do not have this effect" (Keller, 15). Keller then skewers many of our preachers and modern-day church members. "If the preaching of our ministers and the practice of our parishioners do not have the same effect on people that Jesus had, then we must not be declaring the same message that Jesus did. If our churches aren't appealing to younger brothers, they must be more full of elder brothers than we'd like to think" (Keller, 15-16).

Keller believes that the Parable of the Prodigal Son might better be named the "Parable of the Two Lost Sons" (Keller, 17). He first discusses the younger brother's request and the effect it must have had on the father. "The father patiently endures a tremendous loss of honor as well as the pain of rejected love" (Keller, 20). Keller sees the parable as a play in several acts. Act 1 deals with the younger son, who by the way is never named, and sets the stage for Act 2 by challenging "the mind set of elder brothers with a startling message: God's love and forgiveness can pardon and restore any and every kind of sin or wrongdoing" (Keller, 24).

Keller then discusses the elder brother, the one who always did what his father required. He is furious when he hears that his father has welcomed his brother home and is throwing a feast for him. Keller argues that the elder brother's response to his father is insulting and disrespectful. He writes, "In a culture where respect and deference to elders was all important, such behavior is outrageous" (Keller, 27). He gives a modern-day equivalent of a son who writes a "tell-all" memoir that "destroys his father's reputation and career" (Ibid.). Keller concludes his chapter about the two lost sons by concluding. "In short, Jesus is redefining everything we thought we knew about connecting to God. He is redefining sin, what it means to be lost, and what it means to be saved" (Keller, 28).

Chapter Three is titled "Redefining Sin." He describes two ways that people attempt to find happiness and fulfillment: "the way of *moral conformity* and the way of *self-discovery*" (Keller, 29). He writes, "The younger brother in the parable illustrates the way of self-discovery. In ancient patriarchal cultures some took this route, but there are far more who do so today" (Keller, 30). An example might be the son or daughter who decides to take a year off between high school and college to backpack across Europe. Of course, most return home, but some do not. Keller describes the unforeseen twist in this parable. "But Act 2 comes to an unthinkable conclusion. Jesus the storyteller deliberately leaves the elder brother in his alienated state. The bad son enters the father's feast but the good son will not. The lover of prostitutes is saved, but the man of moral rectitude is still lost. We can almost hear the Pharisees gasp as the story ends. It is the complete reversal of everything they had ever been taught" (Keller, 34).

As Keller redefines sin, he sees the two sons as very similar in that they were both rebellious, but in different ways. They both resented the father's authority. He comments, "Do you realize, then, what Jesus is teaching? Neither son loved the father for himself. They both were using the father for their own self-centered ends rather than loving, enjoying, and serving him for his own sake. This means you can rebel against God and be alienated from him by either breaking his rules *or* by keeping all of them diligently. It's a shocking message: Careful obedience to God's law may serve as a strategy for rebelling against God" (Keller, 36-37). Thus, according to Keller, Christ's redefinition of sin shakes us at the core of our being. He explains, "Here, then, is Jesus's radical redefinition of what is wrong with us. Nearly everyone defines sin as a breaking a list of rules. Jesus, though, shows us that a man who has violated virtually nothing on the list of moral misbehaviors can be every bit as spiritually lost as the most profligate, immoral person. Why? Because sin is not just breaking the rules, it is putting yourself in the place of God as Savior, Lord, and Judge just as each son sought to displace the authority of the father in his own life" (Keller, 43).

In Chapter Four, having redefined what sin is, Keller goes on to redefine what it means to be lost. He informs us that the parable teaches "another, more subtle, but no less devastating form of lostness" (Keller, 49). He differentiates between elder brothers and genuine gospel-believing Christians, but warns against the latter who are "elder brother*ish*." He describes in graphic detail the mindset and sorry plight of the elder brother. "Elder brothers have an undercurrent of anger toward life circumstances, hold grudges long and bitterly, look down at people of other races, religions, and lifestyles, experience life as a joyless, crushing drudgery, have little intimacy and joy in their prayer lives, and have a deep insecurity that makes them overly sensitive to criticism and rejection yet fierce and merciless in condemning others. What a terrible picture! And yet the rebellious path of the younger brother is not a better alternative" (Keller, 70-71).

Why are churches and religious institutions often such unpleasant institutions with which to associate? It is because, as Keller explains, they are filled with elder brothers. In his penultimate chapter, he does not leave us without hope, but rather redefines just what hope is. Keller understands the Parable of the Prodigal Son to be nothing less than the gospel story in miniature. He writes, "If we read the narrative in light of the Bible's sweeping theme of exile and homecoming we will understand that Jesus has given us more than a moving account of individual redemption. He has retold the story of the whole human race, and promised nothing less than hope for the world" (90). He continues his application. "The message of the Bible is that the human race is a band of exiles trying to come home. The parable of the prodigal son is about every one of us" (Keller, 97-98).

In his final chapter, Keller utilizes the metaphor of salvation as a feast. He titles this chapter "The Feast of the Father." He then cites Isak Dinesen's delightful story, "Babette's Feast," and how it "also teaches us about two common ways to live that are inadequate, and the reality of another path" (Keller, 128). Keller believes that some who claim to be Christians have not really understood the gospel message. He writes, "If we say 'I believe in Jesus' but it doesn't affect the way we live, the answer is not that now we need to add hard work to our faith so much as that we haven't truly understood or believed Jesus at all" (Keller, 124). We are all invited to the feast of the Father.

Keller has given us a fresh look at a familiar parable of Jesus and, in doing so, has exposed the elder brother in all of us. He reiterates the grace of God which is offered freely to all, but especially to the irreligious and the moralistic. Keller has done a service to the church in helping us to see the familiar in an entirely different way. It is a book for skeptics; it is a book for the devout. But it will challenge you and shape your thinking.

CHAPTER V:
BIOGRAPHY AND MEMOIR

That wise king of antiquity, Solomon, once wrote in his collection of writings titled the Proverbs, "He who walks with the wise grows wise" (Prov. 13:20). It is not possible to actually walk with the wise people from bygone eras, but we can do the next best thing. We can read biographies, autobiographies, and memoirs and thus benefit from their lives.

I wrote the following in my 2021 book, *The Layperson's Library: Essential Bible Study Tools for the Man and Woman in the Pew*, "The genre of biography is a very early form of literature in the church. Accounts of the early martyrs of the church were common reading material and served to both instruct and inspire believers" (Yost, 155). Phillips Brooks, the beloved nineteenth century preacher who gave us the wonderful hymn, *O Little Town of Bethlehem*, addressed an assembly of students of Phillips Exeter Academy in New Hampshire in 1886. In his address, he succinctly gave the purpose of reading about the lives of others. He said, "The object of reading biography, it cannot be said too earnestly or too often said, is not imitation, but inspiration." Thus, we read Christian biography and memoir for the spiritual lessons that they can provide and the inspiration they can give to us for our Christian walk.

To bolster my case, Kevin Eikenberry, a leadership consultant who is the head of the Kevin Eikenberry Group, in his Blog *Leadership and Learning*, gives five compelling reasons to read more biographies. First, "they allow you to stand on the shoulders of giants." That certainly is the idea behind the title of one of my favorite books, *Walking With the Giants*, by Warren Wiersbe. Second, "they remind you that history repeats itself." Third, they promote self-discovery." Fourth, "They allow you to see the world in new ways." Finally, "They give you mentors at a distance" (https://blog.kevineikenberry.com).

I have loved to read biographies and memoirs ever since I was able to read beyond about the third-grade level. I read about explorers and generals and scouts such as Kit Carson, Buffalo Bill Cody and Henry Stanley. I loved every minute that I was able to read and I consumed the books like someone who was starving. I was able to enter into different worlds and it was almost as if I was walking in their very steps. My tastes in reading are a bit more sophisticated now than they were in my elementary school days, but I still love to read a good biography or memoir. In addition, my tastes lean towards Christian books and so I love to read about some of the "giants" of the faith. It is exciting to read about someone like Hudson Taylor or George Whitfield or Billy Graham. But I don't limit myself to Christian biography and memoir. I have recently read biographies of Theodore Roosevelt and Mark Twain. Nobody has ever accused the latter of being an evangelical Christian. But I have learned much even from people with whom I may disagree.

In any event, I challenge you to read the following books by and about Billy Graham, Charles Colson, Martin Luther, George Whitefield, John Wesley, Alexander Solzhenitsyn, Louis Zamperini, Corrie Ten Boom, George Müller, Thomas Merton, and C. S. Lewis. Read them prayerfully and ask God to teach you lessons from their lives. It will not be time wasted. You are embarking on a grand adventure.

33. HERE I STAND: A LIFE OF MARTIN LUTHER

By Roland H. Bainton

Martin Luther is one of the best-known figures in world history, not just Church history. His story is well-known how his religious convictions led him to voice his disagreement with the Roman Catholic Church risking his life and his soul in the process. He was accused of heresy, threatened with excommunication and death, and he refused to yield when he spoke those fateful words in 1517 before the Diet of Worms, "I cannot recant. I will not recant! Here I stand." That famous declaration provides the title for Roland Bainton's remarkable biography of one of the most pivotal people in Western history.

Bainton introduces the young Martin Luther on the very first page of this book. He writes, "On a sultry day in July of the year 1505 a lonely traveler was trudging over a parched road on the outskirts of the Saxon village of Stotternehim. He was a young man, short but sturdy, and wore the dress of a university student" (Bainton, 15). As he came near to the village, a violent storm quickly arose and a bolt of lightning knocked Martin Luther to the ground. In terror he cried out, "St. Anne help me! I will become a monk" (Ibid.). This singular man is described by Bainton, "The man who thus called upon a saint was later to repudiate the cult of the saints. He who vowed to become a monk was later to renounce monasticism. A loyal son of the Catholic Church, he was later to shatter the structure of medieval Catholicism. A devoted servant of the pope, he was later to identify the popes with Antichrist. For this young man was Martin Luther" (Ibid.). The Protestant Reformation, which would shatter and shape the world for centuries to come, was begun by this seemingly unremarkable young man.

The Reformation itself was much more than a religious movement affecting only the church. It was a vast and complicated affair involving kings and peasants, the pope, cardinals and the lowest country priests, monks and merchants and it spread like wildfire throughout the Europe of the sixteenth century. However, to understand the Reformation in all its complexity, one must begin with one man, Martin Luther. He is the towering historical figure of his day and pivotal if we are to understand both Church history and Western history.

Here I Stand: A Life of Martin Luther set the standard for Luther biographies when it was published in 1950. *Time* magazine called it "The most readable Luther biography in English." The *Chicago Tribune* described it as "A sound and well-rounded picture of the man and his role in history." Although Luther has been the subject of numerous biographers before and after this seminal work, Bainton's treatment of Luther's life remains the standard as well as the most readable. It is authoritative, well-researched, and a compelling read that will have you turning page after page even though you know how it ends. If you begin reading this amazing biography expecting the dry and dull tome of a Yale professor, you will be disappointed. This is a biography that lives and springs right off the page.

Roland Bainton, born in Derbyshire, England, in 1894, came to the United States with his family in 1902. He received a Ph.D. from Yale and became a specialist in Reformation history. He served for forty-two years as the Titus Street Professor of ecclesiastical history at Yale. Although he was a top scholar in his field, it is said that he wore his scholarship lightly and that his writing was much more readable than most academic writing. This is particularly true of *Here I Stand*, perhaps his greatest work. It stands alone as the classic work on a classic subject.

Luther's relationship with God was a complicated affair. He was consumed by guilt, a guilt that was fueled by the Roman Catholic Church of his day. He felt that he could never live up to God's standards. Bainton writes, "Luther's tremor was augmented by the recognition of unworthiness. 'I am dust and ashes and full of sin.' Creatureliness and imperfection alike oppressed him. Toward God he was at once attracted and repelled" (Bainton, 31). It is well-documented that Luther would spend hours in the confessional trying to cover every possible sin he may have committed. R. C. Sproul once preached a brilliant sermon on this subject which he titled *The Insanity of Luther*. Sproul went into great detail about how Luther would obsess over every little shortcoming in his life. It is quite possible that the guilt he felt drove him to the brink of insanity. Modern psychoanalysts would likely diagnose him as neurotic.

In addition to his obsession in confessing his sins, Luther was obsessive in his fasting and penance. Bainton writes, "He fasted, sometimes three days on end without a crumb. The seasons of fasting were more consoling to him than those of feasting. Lent was more comforting than Easter. He laid upon himself vigils and prayers in excess of those stipulated by the rule. He cast off blankets permitted him and well-nigh froze himself to death. At times he was proud of his sanctity and would say, 'I have done nothing wrong today.' Then misgivings would arise. 'Have you fasted enough? Are you poor enough? He would then strip himself of all save which decency required. He believed in later life that his austerities had done permanent damage to his digestion" (Bainton, 34). It was later Luther's opinion that had he keep up this pace of vigils, prayer, reading, and other works that these activities would have been fatal to him. These ascetic practices usually ended in abuse.

Bainton brilliantly sets the scene for the famous Diet of Worms confrontation fully capturing the drama. "The scene lends itself to dramatic portrayal. Here was Charles, heir of a long line of Catholic sovereigns—of Maximilian the romantic, of Ferdinand the Catholic, of Isabella the orthodox . . . ruling over a vaster domain than any save Charlemagne, symbol of the medieval unities, incarnation of a glorious, if vanishing heritage; and here before him a simple monk, a miner's son, with nothing to sustain him save his own faith in the Word of God" (Bainton,

141). Bainton's analysis of the scene is riveting. He writes, "Here the past and the future were met. Some would see at this point the beginning of modern times. The contrast is real enough. Luther himself was sensible of it in a measure. He was well aware that he had not been reared as the son of Pharaoh's daughter, but what overpowered him was not so much that he stood in the presence of the emperor as this, that he and the emperor alike were called upon to answer before Almighty God" (Ibid.). Wow! Such powerful writing!

But the life of Martin Luther does not end at the Diet of Worms. In a very real sense, it is only the beginning. Of course, we know that Luther was declared an outlaw by his actions, his denunciation of indulgences and other abuses of the Roman Catholic Church and was excommunicated by Pope Leo X in 1521. Later he married Katherine of Bora, a former nun, a union which produced five children. His actions led to the founding of the Lutheran Church as well as the production of the Augsburg Confession, the Lutheran confession of faith. Luther translated the Bible into German, a major literary achievement. He also wrote the monumental hymn, *A Mighty Fortress Is Our God*, certainly one of the greatest hymns in the depository of the Church. He influenced the other great reformers such as John Calvin and Zwingli. Bainton captures all of this and tells many amusing anecdotes along the way.

Luther also wrote his *magnum opus, The Bondage of the Will* (See Chapter II), a brilliant treatise that was a refutation to Desiderius Erasmus' teachings on free will that argued that salvation can only be achieved by the initiative of God, and not the free will of man. It is one of the true classics of the Christian faith and should be read by every believer. For many Christians, the name Martin Luther is just that, a name. They may know that he has a vague connection to the Reformation and that he wrote *A Mighty Fortress*, which is sung every Reformation Sunday in October. But beyond that, they know very little. This book will cure that and will give every Christian a greater appreciation for this great, and deeply flawed, hero of the Christian faith.

34. GEORGE WHITEFIELD

By Arnold Dallimore

&

35. SERIOUS JOY: JOHN WESLEY'S JOURNAL

Edited by Robert H. Morris

George Whitefield and John Wesley are two of the towering figures in the history of the Christian church. They burst upon the scene like two whirlwinds at a time when England's spiritual and moral condition was at its nadir. They were primary figures in the Great Awakening. My initial plan was to deal with these two works separately, but because the lives of these two men were so intimately intertwined, I decided to combine them into one longer section.

When Whitefield matriculated at Pembroke College, Oxford, in 1732, he entered that great university as the lowest of the low, a servitor, who, "in exchange for free tuition, served as a lackey" to several other students. He was a rather unsophisticated youth, raw and provincial with a pronounced West Country twang, which he apparently never lost during a lifetime of preaching. He was introduced to the Wesleys through the Holy Club at Oxford and quickly joined their fellowship after being invited by John's brother, Charles. Both of the brothers were older than he and served as spiritual mentors, although the more emotionally accessible Charles was his chief influence. Whitefield had the utmost respect and deference for both John and Charles and even referred to the former as his "spiritual father in Christ."

After the death of his father in 1735, Wesley, along with his brother Charles, was persuaded by Col. James Oglethorpe, the governor of Georgia in North America, and John Burton, an Oxford colleague, to oversee the spiritual lives of the colonists and to evangelize the Native Americans as an emissary for the Society for the Propagation of the Gospel. He entrusted Whitefield with the spiritual care of the Oxford methodists while he was away. Things in Georgia did not go well as Wesley's high church mannerisms offended his rough-hewn frontier flock and he was unsuccessful in his attempts to convert the heathen. As Wesley was returning to England in 1738 after what he considered an unsuccessful mission trip to Georgia, he wrote the following, "I went to America to convert the Indians; but, oh, who will convert me! Who will deliver me from this evil heart of unbelief? I have a fine summertime religion; I can talk well, and even believe my own words when no danger is near; but just let death look me in the face, and my spirit is troubled" (Morris, 34). The one positive that he took back home to England was his exposure to some Moravian Christians who seemed to possess the spiritual peace that had so long eluded him.

Back in England, Wesley came under the influence of Peter Boehler, who hammered home to him the doctrine of salvation through faith alone. Boehler, he said, "affirmed that the one true faith in Christ was always accompanied by two fruits: power over sin and constant peace in knowing we're forgiven" (Morris, 45). He wrote the following in his journal, "I couldn't understand how this faith could be given in a moment—how a man could be instantly changed from darkness to light, from sin and misery to righteousness and joy in the Holy Spirit" (Morris, 38). His understanding of the truth of the gospel was rather murky at this point in his life. He wrote, "At this point I hoped to be saved by: 1. Not being as bad as other people; 2. Still having a religious inclination; and 3. Reading the Bible, going to church, and saying my prayers" (Morris, 42).

Perhaps the best-known event and most oft-repeated from the life of John Wesley is the account of his conversion at Aldersgate. He wrote, "That evening, against my will, I went to a fellowship meeting in Aldersgate Street, where someone was reading Luther's preface to the book of Romans. About a quarter of nine, while he was describing the change God works in the heart through faith in Christ, I felt my heart strangely warmed. I felt I did trust in Christ, Christ alone for salvation, and I received an assurance that he had taken away my sins—even mine—and had saved me from the law of sin and death" (Morris, 45-46).

Shortly after his conversion, Wesley visited the Moravian settlement at Herrhut in Saxony where he met Count Ludwig von Zinzendorf. It has been said that if the apostle Paul had his Arabia for preparation for his ministry, then Wesley had Saxony. Upon his return to England he commenced his missionary endeavors with a zeal to reform both England and the Church of England, and to spread scriptural holiness. He turned to open-air preaching as a vehicle for spreading the gospel at the instigation of George Whitefield in 1739. His unorthodox message was to encounter much resistance in the face of the rigidity and spiritual declension of the Church of England and he was forced to take his message to the fields and to the masses. Wesley's ministry was soon to spread including Scotland and Ireland. Although he never did return there, he sent preachers to North America.

Opposition to Wesley's message also often came in the form of angry crowds which, upon occasion, were a threat to the evangelist's life. However, he had a winsome way with people and often was able to swing the mob leader over to his side. Later in his life opposition was largely to cease as pulpits which were previously closed to him welcomed him with open arms. By the time of his death in 1791, Methodism was well-organized and on its way to the great numerical gains which were to come in the nineteenth century.

Although Wesley remained a Church of England man until his dying day, he never allowed it to stand in the way of expediency. He made two major decisions with respect to his methodology which violated the norms of that august body. The first was to preach in the open air and the second was his approval of lay preaching. The latter practice was even more scandalous than the former in the eyes of the Church of England, yet Methodism would never have assumed its stature without this deviation from normalcy.

Another factor in the ascendency of Methodism was the excellent organizational skills of Wesley. He first decided to organize his converts in order for them to receive biblical instruction. He was concerned for the spiritual growth of his converts. Thus, he organized them into small societies patterned after the Oxford Holy Club where they could meet under the auspices of a leader for Bible study and mutual edification. Then he made the decision to house his societies. As the societies multiplied, they were knit together into an inclusive organization. By this means, Methodism was provided with a framework which has remained essentially unchanged. It was only by degrees that Methodism separated from the Church of England, but without the organizational structure which Wesley provided the movement likely would have sputtered and the flame die out. Even though separation was not initially on his mind, he inadvertently adopted an organizational policy which later facilitated the inevitable.

Not to be overlooked is Wesley's emphasis on education. This may seem dichotomous when we consider that early Methodism was primarily a lay movement of uneducated preachers to uneducated masses comprised of the lower classes of society. Yet Wesley himself stressed education in every way and it is hardly surprising that Methodist schools are nearly as old as the movement itself. Education was needful for ministry in a changing world and Wesley acutely perceived this need.

Whitefield, on the other hand, used his early association with the Wesleys as a springboard to success and greatness. He enjoyed astonishing evangelistic success as in 1739 he took the revolutionary step of preaching outdoors. He preached to coalminers around Bristol and then to the poor on the streets of London. Everywhere he preached, Whitefield attracted huge crowds and transformed the Methodist movement from respectable Anglicanism to the masses. He pushed a reluctant Wesley to follow him in this way of preaching and it reaped huge dividends. Although Whitefield regarded Wesley as his mentor, he eclipsed the latter as a preacher and influential figure of the Great Awakening in almost every way. They complemented one another in that Whitefield's brilliant oratory was the vehicle the Holy Spirit used to bring untold multitudes to faith in Christ, but it was Wesley's organizational genius that took them beyond that.

As we evaluate the lives of John Wesley and George Whitefield, it is interesting to note that Wesley is the best-known today. However, as Dallimore observes about Whitefield, "Throughout much of his adult life (he) was as famous as any man in the English-speaking world. From the age of twenty-two till his death he was the foremost figure of the immense religious movement that held the attention of multitudes on both sides of the Atlantic" (Dallimore, 5). Yet, it is John Wesley, the founder of the Methodist Church, who is best-known today along with his brother Charles, the composer of dozens of beloved and memorable hymns such as "Hark, the Herald Angels Sing," "O For a Thousand Tongues," "Soldiers of Christ, Arise," "Love Divine, All Loves Excelling," "Jesus Christ is Risen Today," and "Rejoice, the Lord is King" to name just a very few. Today the name George Whitefield is almost an afterthought. His fame among the average modern Christian has long been eclipsed by that of the Wesley brothers. However, as Dallimore argues, "As contemporary documents show, during the eighteenth century Whitefield was the foremost figure and Wesley the secondary one, but such has been the neglect of Whitefield and the emphasis on Wesley that these positions are now entirely reversed" (Dallimore, 12).

Both Whitefield and Wesley were key figures in the eighteenth-century revival known as the Great Awakening. It has been regarded as the greatest revival in history since that of the Apostles, a great moving of the Holy Spirit of God. As Dallimore observes, "This is the movement which, in overlooking Whitefield, mankind has also largely overlooked. Whitefield's ministry was the one human factor which bound this work together in all the lands it reached" (Dallimore, 14). Yet as early as 1740, Wesley and Whitefield were at a doctrinal impasse which split the fledgling Methodist movement in two. It was the issue of predestination which divided Wesley from Whitefield. The Wesleys were Arminians, a position which denied predestination, while Whitefield was moving in a decidedly Calvinistic direction.

It is difficult to overestimate the impact of George Whitefield. He became an international sensation wherever he preached whether it was England, Scotland, or the American colonies. He was the most prolific and prominent preacher of his era and changed people's perceptions of the church. It has been estimated that eighty percent of the colonists in the New World heard Whitefield preach. The result of this was a unification of theological orthodoxy and political ideas leading to the Revolutionary War. It has been argued that his was the most influential voice in the Great Awakening though Jonathan Edwards and Wesley are mentioned in the same breath. While in Savannah, Georgia, at the behest of John Wesley, he also founded the Bethesda Orphanage. Charles H. Spurgeon, the English-speaking world's greatest preacher of the nineteenth century, considered Whitefield to be his preaching hero.

Wesley, unlike John Calvin, never developed an organized, comprehensive theological system, but today his theological outlook is well-known. He had a practical concern for holiness which he felt was negated by the Calvinistic doctrine of predestination. He saw sanctification as the goal of justification and as something that a Christian could attain in this life. On the other hand, he resisted the extremist position that some took that one could attain sinless perfection on earth. His mind apparently wrestled with the concepts of sanctification and perfection and ultimately, he assumed a mediating position. Whitefield took a polar opposite position on predestination from that of Wesley and this was their major point of clash. The core of his theology can be found in the conversation between Jesus and Nicodemus in John 3. He focused on the New Birth or regeneration in his preaching ministry.

It is helpful to our understanding of their controversy over pre-destination to understand that the moral force of Calvinism had declined by the eighteenth century and there was a mood of fatalism which at least indirectly contributed to the moral degeneracy of the day. This was entirely due to a misunder-standing of the theological system itself and was not at all in-dicative of its true teachings. In any event, the masses simply saw themselves as puppets of the divine will who could do nothing about their spiritual estate. It was to this prevailing de-spair that Wesley and Whitefield proclaimed their message of salvation available to all men. The masses responded mightily to this message as beggars starving for the bread of life.

John Wesley and George Whitefield are two of the towering figures in church history and their stories should be known to Christians of all ages. Although Wesley's name is familiar to most nowadays, the name of George Whitefield gets mostly blank looks. That is such a shame because their roles were re-versed during their lifetimes. The best way to become ac-quainted with the life of Whitefield is through this excellent biography by Arnold Dallimore. The great British preacher, M. Martyn Lloyd-Jones (See Chapter IV) who wrote the Foreword said this, "This volume is something for which I have been waiting for over forty years." Although Lloyd-Jones has to be on anyone's short list of candidates for greatest preacher of the twentieth century, this is his assessment of Whitefield. "Above all he was the greatest preacher—indeed one can say that he was the greatest preacher that England has ever produced" (ix). The great evangelists who came later—D. L. Moody, Billy Sunday, Billy Graham—all stand upon his shoulders.

The best way to learn about the life and ministry of John Wesley is through his journal. As for which version of Wesley's journal to read, please keep in mind that the standard published edition, which is an abridgment of his diary is roughly 2,000 pages and the language is rather archaic being almost 300 years old. Wesley's diaries have never been published in full. My recommendation is that the modern reader use a condensed version in contemporary English. I also recommend *Serious Joy: John Wesley's Journal (Condensed and Gently Paraphrased)* as being better than most, but keep in mind that there are several other excellent ones from which to choose. One word of warning: Some versions edit out some of Wesley's doctrines that are unpopular today among theological liberals. These may include Wesley's beliefs in Satan and his demons as well as a literal hell. Those versions attempt to make Wesley into a kinder, gentler man with twenty-first sensibilities and beliefs. Avoid them!

But by all means, get to know these two giants of the faith. Both were great men of God whose hearts were set aflame by the penetrating love of Christ and their ministries changed the world. The gospel calls us to be like them, men and women of action. Their examples cry out to Christians of every age.

36. GEORGE MÜLLER OF BRISTOL: HIS LIFE OF PRAYER AND FAITH

By A. T. Pierson

Have you ever wondered why it seems that sometimes our prayers go no farther than the ceiling? Have you ever wondered why it seems that our prayers are met with God's silence? Have you ever wondered why it seems that God does not answer our prayers? It is indeed unfortunate that for many Christians prayer appears to be an exercise in futility and is not a vibrant part of their lives. Such was not true of George Müller of Bristol. He was known as a great man of faith and prayer. His life of prayer and faith is one with which every believer should be familiar and emulate.

Müller was a pastor, evangelist, and the director of the Ashley Down orphanage in Bristol, England. He was hugely influential in these roles. He and his friend, Henry Craik, pastored the Bethesda Chapel where he preached and ministered from 1832 until his death in 1898 at the age of ninety-two. He continued in this ministry while he was involved in other ministries. In 1834, he founded the Scriptural Knowledge Institution for Home and Abroad, which was established for the express purpose of aiding Christian schools, and missionaries along with other varied ministries. It is estimated that he established over 100 Christian schools, which offered Christian education to over 100,000 and cared for over 10,000 orphans in his lifetime. He accomplished this with the Lord's help by never asking people for financial support or going into debt. His ministries were truly faith-based. His method was to ask God alone for assistance. In his later years beginning at the age of seventy-one, he began a seventeen-year period of itinerant missionary travel visiting numerous countries such as Switzerland, France, Spain, Italy, Germany, Canada, the United States, Australia, New Zealand, Russia, India, China, and Japan. That was quite a feat for a man of his advanced years. In addition to all of the above, Müller was one of the founding members of the Plymouth Brethren movement.

A. T. Pierson, the author of this biography of Müller's life, was a remarkable man in his own right. He was a prominent preacher serving churches in the United States and Great Britain, the best-known being the famous Metropolitan Tabernacle in London following the death of the esteemed Charles H. Spurgeon. His lectureships included the Moody Bible Institute in Chicago and the Pierson Bible Institute in Seoul, Korea. He was also a consulting editor to the Scofield Reference Bible. Pierson's biography of this great man of prayer and faith is the consummate work on him, written by a man who knew him, and approved by Müller's son-in-law.

George Müller was an unlikely candidate for sainthood. His beginnings were inauspicious at best. He had no proper parental training. Pierson tells us that in his youth he "was a flagrant sinner against common honesty and decency, and his whole early career was a revolt, not against God only, but against his own moral sense" (Pierson. 9). At an age when today's adolescents are looking to acquire a driver's license and go on their first date, we're told of Müller, "This boy of sixteen was already a liar and thief, swindler and drunkard, accomplished only in crime, companion of convicted felons and himself in a felon's cell" (Pierson, 11). His "wasted years of a sinful and profligate youth" lasted until he was twenty years of age. Pierson lays out in detail the sin and misery of those years "to make the more clear that his conversion was a supernatural work, in explicable without God" (Pierson, 13).

What led to Müller's conversion was his providential attendance some might say chance encounter—at a meeting of believers where they gathered "to sing, to pray, and to read the

Word of God and a printed sermon" (Pierson, 14). Not the place a felonious juvenile delinquent might want to be seen! Why he felt compelled to attend this meeting was a mystery to him. Pierson writes, "There was no doubt a conscious void within him never yet filled, and some instinctive inner voice whispered that he might find food for his soul-hunger—a, satisfying something after which he had all his life been unconsciously and blindly groping" (Pierson, 14-15). He was most impressed by a man, who later went to Africa for the London Missionary Society, who knelt and prayed for God's blessing. "That kneeling before God in prayer made upon Müller an impression he never lost" (Pierson, 15). This encounter left an indelible mark that influenced him for the rest of his life. Pierson writes, "Prayer on the knees; both in secret and in such companion of believers, was henceforth to be the one great central secret of his holy living and holy serving. Upon this cornerstone of prayer all his life-work was to be built" (Pierson, 17).

One cannot help but be impressed with how George Müller ordered his financial dealings in all of his ministerial work. Many, including Billy Graham, have been influenced by Müller's financial structuring of his ministry. Keep in mind that his ministry experienced "frequent and at times prolonged financial straits." The money in hand that was available for daily expenses was "often reduced to a single pound, or even a penny, and sometimes to nothing" (Pierson, 41). Müller claimed in his journal that this was the case thousands of times. There was not even enough for even one more meal at the orphanage, but God never failed them and the orphans never went hungry. On one occasion at the orphanage, the table was set and the children were seated around the breakfast table even though there was no food. Thanks was given for the food they were about to eat, even though the plates were empty, when a knock on the door came. A baker came in with enough fresh bread to feed the entire orphanage. Then a milkman's truck broke down outside the orphanage and he donated his supply of fresh milk lest it spoil. This story and hundreds of others illustrate Müller's answers to prayer. Such was the daily life of the remarkable George Müller, man of prayer and faith.

Two things that have always impressed me about Müller is that he never asked people for money and he never publicized the ministry's needs. He also made it a practice to only ask God for funds. Pierson makes this very clear. "Nothing was ever to be revealed to outsiders of existing need, lest it be construed into an appeal for help; but the only resort must be to the living God" (Pierson, 79). He was very careful about receiving donations, too. Pierson informs us, "If there was any evidence or suspicion that the donation was given grudgingly, reluctantly, or for self-glory, it was promptly declined and returned" (Pierson, 42). His was a faith ministry. This led to boldness in asking God to supply their needs and trusting him for great things. "As faith was exercised, it was energized, so that it became as easy and natural to ask confidently for a hundred, a thousand, or even ten thousand pounds, as once it had been for a pound or a penny" (43). He adopted the Old Testament prophet Habakkuk's message, "The just shall live by his faith." With so many 'begging ministries" today, I think they and we could learn a lesson from George Müller. Pierson summarizes Müller's credo, "George Müller believed, and because he believed, prayed; and praying, expected; and expecting, received" (Pierson, 46).

It was interesting to read about the major influences in Müller's life. Two of them, John Newton and George Whitefield, are the subjects of sections in this book. Müller read Newton's autobiography and then the Whitefield biography by Robert Philip. Pierson writes about Whitefield's influence, "The life story of the converted blasphemer had suggested his narrative of the Lord's dealings; and now the life-story of the great evangelist was blessed of God to shape his general character and give new power to his preaching and wider ministry to souls" (Pierson, 70). Whitefield's example was particularly inspiring to young Müller that of his "unusual prayerfulness, and his habit of reading the Bible on his knees" (Ibid.). Pierson also reminds us about the preaching of George Whitefield that "there was about his preaching, moreover, a nameless charm which held thirty thousand hearers half-breathless on Boston Common and made tears our down the sooty faces of the colliers at Kingswood" (Ibid.). Müller was also a friend of Hudson Taylor, the founder of the China Inland Mission. With respect to financing their ministries, he and Taylor were two peas in a pod.

George Müller is a man with whom every Christian should become acquainted. His life of prayer and faith has been an inspiration to multitudes of believers. After Müller's death, his work continued to thrive through The George Müller Foundation, renamed The George Müller Charitable Trust in 2009. The trust honors Müller's faith principles and seeks donations solely by petitioning God in prayer. It engages in no fund-raising activities. Having seen so many "begging ministries" in action over the years and some of the scandals involving well-known televangelists, Müller has something to teach all of us. Read this inspiriting biography. Or better yet, read his original journals. It will change your life of faith.

37. THE HIDING PLACE

By Corrie ten Boom with John and Elizabeth Sherrill

Heroes sometime emerge from the unlikeliest of places during times of extreme crisis. Out of the crucible of World War II emerged a middle-aged Dutch woman who never toted a rifle and never shot an enemy, but she saved countless lives from the clutches of the Nazis who occupied her country. Corrie ten Boom was that woman. She was a spinster living with her watchmaker father and sister during the Nazi occupation. This is a book about many things. It is about courage, resilience, compassion. But I believe that the triumph of Christian faith is the predominant theme.

Since the release of the 1975 film of the same name by World Wide Pictures, many people have become familiar with the basic story behind *The Hiding Place*, but have never actually read the book. On one level, the book is the heartwarming story of a Christian family living in Holland during the years just preceding and including World War II. It is a simple story of a loving family attempting to live out their Christian values during a very difficult time. On another level, it is a heroic story of ordinary people forced by circumstances to do extraordinary things. Corrie ten Boom was a rather ordinary woman living what might have appeared to outsiders to be a drab existence in the Dutch town of Haarlem. But as the book reveals, she was anything but ordinary.

The 1994 Stephen Spielberg film *Schindler's List* invited comparisons of Corrie ten Boom's heroism with that of Otto Schindler. I loved the film and I was inspired by the story of Schindler, but Corrie has won a special place in my heart for her courage and Christian faith under fire.

The book begins in an idyllic fashion with a birthday party. Corrie lived in the Dutch town of Haarlem with her father and Betsy, her sister. The Dutch prime minister has assured the citizens of neutral Holland that they were safe from invasion by Hitler's Nazis. "Holland's neutrality would be respected" (ten Boom, 61). Unfortunately, he underestimated the viciousness of Adolf Hitler. Germany soon attacked and almost overnight the streets were filled with Nazi soldiers. The result was immediate. As one result of the German mindset is explained to the ten Boom family. "The old have no value to the State. They're also harder to train in the new ways of thinking. Germany is systematically teaching disrespect for old age. . . . It is the old and weak who are to be eliminated" (ten Boom, 59). The ten Boom family was aghast. Corrie writes, "We rode the train home in stunned silence" (Ibid.). The clubs for girls and the mentally handicapped that Corrie had operated for twenty years were forced to close.

After the invasion, things changed, but slowly. The German soldiers spent money and that was good for the watchmaking business. But the occupation soon brought hardships. There was a curfew and identity cards were issued and then ration cards. Radios were then confiscated and finally Jews were being attacked. As Corrie writes, "The true horror of occupation came over us only slowly" (ten Boom, 67). Jews could not be served in places of business and they were banned from public parks. Then a synagogue mysteriously burned down and the disappearances of Jews began. German soldiers ransacked the shop across the street that belonged to a Jewish shopkeeper. The ten Booms took him into their home, which soon led to other Jews seeking refuge. The ten Booms eventually built a secret room, "a hiding place," to accommodate their growing extended family. The ten Boom family became heavily involved in the Dutch underground resistance movement that involved smuggling Jews to places where they were safe. It has been estimated that the lives of least 800 Jews were saved as a result of her work.

The book deals in a very touching and sympathetic way with the ethical issues of lying and dishonesty. These issues go back thousands of years at least to the time of Rahab, the harlot, who befriended the Israelites of Joshua's day as they prepared for their crossing of the Jordan River. After hearing rumors of an active underground following the invasion of the Nazis, Corrie wrote, "The rumors tended to get more spectacular with each repetition. But always they featured things we believed were wrong in the sight of God. Stealing, lying, murder. Was this what God wanted in times like these? How should a Christian act when evil was in power?" (ten Boom, 71). The ethical dilemma was very real in their minds. Should a Christian acquiesce to evil and follow the law, or disobey the state to save lives? There was disagreement even among the ten Booms. Nollie, Corrie's sister, who was married and lived elsewhere, believed that God would provide if his commandments were honored. Corrie's father, her sister Betsie, and Corrie herself believed as the Apostle Peter said in the Book of Acts that "we should obey God rather than men."

The little refuge in the ten Boom home could not be sustained forever and eventually Corrie was arrested by the Nazis, along with her father and sister, Betsie, and taken to Scheveningen Prison after stolen ration cards and resistance materials were found in their home. Her father, who was elderly, died ten days later, as did Betsie sometime later in the Ravensbruck concentration camp, which was the temporary home of some 35,000 women. After being confronted by a prison official after receiving a letter informing her of her father's death, she was told, "Whatever happens, you brought it on by breaking the law" (ten Boom, 145).

One feature about this book that is so beautiful is how Corrie and Betsy made the most of a very unpleasant experience in prison and finally the concentration camp. Corrie had ample opportunities for Christian witness in her prison camp home. She always attempted to live for Christ no matter the circumstances. For example, as she was summoned to a hearing after three months in prison, she prayed, "Lord Jesus, you were called to a hearing too. Show me what to do" (ten Boom, 146).

The irony is that although Corrie was in a prison camp, she was not in prison, but some of her captors were. Her interactions with Lieutenant Rahms were particularly instructive and inspiring. She asked him, "Is there darkness in your life, Lieutenant?" He replied, "There is great darkness. I cannot bear the work I do here" (ten Boom, 149). When Corrie attempted to get Lieutenant Rahms to allow her to see Betsie when they were separated, he said that he was unable. "He lifted his eyes from the desk and I saw anguish in them. 'Miss ten Boom, it is possible that I appear to you a powerful person. I wear a uniform, I have a certain authority over those under me. But I am in prison, dear lady from Haarlem, a prison stronger than this one'" (ten Boom, 150). She also had to wrestle with one of the oldest questions known to mankind; Why do the righteous suffer? She writes, "The hardest thing for him seemed to be that Christians should suffer. 'How can you believe in God now?' He'd ask. 'What kind of God would have let that old man die here in Scheveningen'" (Ibid.)?

A concentration camp became the ten Boom's mission field and they were tireless in telling others, both inmates and guards, of God's goodness and salvation through Jesus Christ. On New Year's Day 1945, Corrie was finally released. And during the second week in May 1945, the allied forces retook Holland. After the war, ten Boom returned to the Netherlands and set up a rehabilitation home in Bloemendaal for refugees. She returned to Germany in 1946. During her visit, she met with two of the Germans who had been working at Ravensbruck and forgave them. She traveled the world and became an ambassador of God's grace and forgiveness. During her travels as a public speaker, she visited more than sixty countries and wrote numerous other books. *The Hiding Place* was made into a 1975 World Wide Pictures film starring Jeanette Clift as Corrie and Julie Harris as Betsie. She died in 1983 at the age of ninety-one.

The Hiding Place is beautiful and riveting at the same time and ought to be read by every Christian. The lessons it teaches are priceless and all-the-more real because the events actually happened. You will learn as did the ten Boom family that "the center of his will is our only safety." It is terrific book that will haunt and inspire you long after you finish reading it.

38. UNBROKEN

By Laura Hillenbrand

As the book cover states, this book tells a story of "survival, resilience, and redemption." It is the story of a man who is taken to the brink of desperation and death time and time again who survives against all odds. It is a remarkable story, almost unbelievable. But it is all true. It is "a testament to the resilience of the human mind, body, and spirit" (inside cover). But the most important thing about this story is that it is the story of a man who is eternally changed through an encounter with Jesus Christ. It is the story of salvation. That is the reason for its inclusion in this book.

I must confess that I had never heard the name, Louis Zamperini, even though many years ago I had been a middle-distance runner and he had been a world class runner. My repertoire of track icons essentially began and ended with my hero, Jim Ryun, from the 1960s. Although I was familiar with Jim Thorpe who also ran and perhaps one or two others, I was basically ignorant of the great runners from previous decades. Louis Zamperini was not even on my radar screen. But I know all about him now. And I admire him for his courage and his spirit and his unabashed Christian faith.

Louis Zamperini is one of World War II's forgotten heroes. Everyone, it seems, has heard of Audie Murphy and Oskar Schindler and Winston Churchill, but I had never heard the name Louis Zamperini until I heard the literary buzz back in 2010 about a new book with the title *Unbroken*. I purchased the book, couldn't wait to read it, and was completely enthralled, totally mesmerized by the story it told.

Zamperini was a middle-distance runner who wound up representing the U.S. in the 1936 Olympic Games which were held in

Berlin. He ran the 5,000-meter distance event and finished eighth. However, his final lap was run in fifty-six seconds, fast enough to capture the attention of Adolf Hitler who requested a meeting with him to shake his hand. Little did he know then that he would be fighting in a world-wide conflict a few short years later begun by the madman whose hand he shook. Zamperini enlisted in the U.S. Army in 1941 and served in the Army Air Corps and was commissioned a second lieutenant. His posting was to the Pacific where he served as a bombardier on the Consolidated Aircraft's B-24 Liberator bomber named *Super Man*.

As a young man, Zamperini had been something of an incorrigible delinquent. As he began high school, he looked less like an impish teenage and "more like a dangerous young man." He was angry and defiant and appeared headed to a life of crime and prison. However, with the help and guidance of his older brother, he learned to channel that defiance into running and his talent and hard work made him into a world-class athlete. That and World War II led him to the vast Pacific Ocean where his plane was attacked by three Japanese Zeros after a successful bombing raid against the Japanese-held island of Nauru. His plane was disabled and wound up crashing into the Pacific Ocean in May 1943. Five of the six-man crew were wounded with one dying. Zamperini administered first aid to his wounded comrades. He would eventually be awarded the Distinguished Flying Cross, which is awarded to individuals who "distinguish themselves by singular acts of heroism or extraordinary achievement while participating in aerial flight."

Zamperini and his comrades would be driven to the ends of endurance while spending forty-seven days drifting in a raft in the Pacific Ocean with little food or water. During his ordeal, four more of his crewmates would die. On the forty-seventh day adrift, Zamperini along with his lone surviving comrade, the pilot, Russell Allen Phillips, reached the Marshall Islands and were taken prisoner by the Japanese. Their real ordeal was just beginning.

Zamperini and his fellow captives suffered almost unbelievable deprivation, beatings, and torture. The captives were systematically starved, particularly those who were suspected of withholding vital intelligence from the enemy. His "food was infested with rat droppings, maggots, and so much sand and grit" that his "teeth were soon pitted, chipped, and cracked" (Hillenbrand, 197). Deaths among the inmates were common. It was concluded that some of the guards and prison officials were psychopaths. One particularly deranged guard "beat POWs every day, fracturing their windpipes, rupturing their eardrums, shattering their teeth, tearing one man's ear half off, leaving men unconscious" (Hillenbrand, 236-37). Zamperini lived at two different prison camps in Japan and was selected for special treatment due to his status as a famous Olympic runner. He suffered more than the typical prisoner because of his "special" status and had one particularly sadistic guard, Mutsuhiro "The Bird" Watanabe, who was on General Douglas MacArthur's list of the forty most wanted war criminals in Japan. Zamperini's captivity lasted more than two years. He was officially pronounced dead by the U.S. military.

Zamperini survived the prison camps and was eventually liberated. He received a well-deserved hero's welcome. However, after the war, he understandably suffered from post-traumatic stress and struggled to overcome the trauma from his ordeal. He married Cynthia, but his demons kept coming back to haunt him. He suffered from alcoholism and he and Cynthia came close to getting a divorce. Hillenbrand writes, "He had become someone he didn't recognize" (Hillenbrand, 363). What changed his life in the providence of God was his reluctant attendance at a Billy Graham evangelistic rally in Los Angeles in 1949. After wrestling with God much as the patriarch Jacob did in the book of Genesis, Zamperini surrendered his heart to Jesus Christ. The change was instantaneous. After he and his wife arrived home after an evangelistic meeting, Hillenbrand writes, "When they entered the apartment, Louis went straight to his cache of liquor. It was the time of night when the need usually took hold of him, but for the first time in years, Louis had no desire to drink. He carried the bottles to the kitchen sink, opened them, and poured their contents into the drain. Then he hurried through the apartment, gathering packs of cigarettes, a secret stash of girlie magazines, everything that was part of his ruined years. He heaved it all down the trash chute" (Hillenbrand, 376). "Resting in the shade and stillness, Louis felt profound peace. When he thought of his history, what resonated with him now was not all that he had suffered but the divine love that he believed had intervened to save him. He was not the worthless, broken, forsaken man that the Bird had striven to make of him. In a single, silent moment, his rage, his fear, his humiliation and helplessness, had fallen away. That morning, he believed, he was a new creation" (Ibid.).

Louis Zamperini was indeed transformed. He was undeniably, as the Apostle Paul described it, a "new creation." He forgave his Japanese guards and torturers. He returned to Japan on at least two occasions. He visited a Tokyo prison in 1950 where he met personally with those serving sentences for war crimes and again in 1998 when he returned to carry the torch at the Nagano Winter Olympic Games. He attempted to meet with Mutsuhiro Watanabe through CBS, but he refused to meet with Zamperini. He founded the Victory Boys Camp in 1952, a camp for troubled youth, which lasted until 2014. Now the Louis Zamperini Foundation continues the legacy of the camp partnering with camps, foster-care programs, inner city outreach, military schools, and youth correctional facilities to help at-risk youth. He later became a Christian evangelist continuing the work that Billy Graham began.

I highly recommend that you read *Unbroken*. It is one of the most inspiring nonfiction books that I have ever read. I was totally mesmerized. But more importantly, it reminded me again of the matchless grace of God and his power to change a human being. Zamperini's life has been the subject of three films: *Unbroken* (2014) directed by Angelina Jolie; the sequel *Unbroken: Path to Redemption* (2018), and *Captured by Grace* (2015). I absolutely loved the movie adaptation even though it ends before his conversion, but the book is better. See for yourself.

39. THE SEVEN STOREY MOUNTAIN

By Thomas Merton

This book is the 1948 autobiography of Thomas Merton, a Trappist monk whose work has been compared favorably to the account of Augustine's conversion as related in his *Confessions*. It is widely considered one of the most influential and beloved religious books of the twentieth century. The timing of its publication was almost perfect coming as it did in the aftermath of World War II and the widespread disillusionment it engendered. It struck a chord with readers particularly in the United States, but also throughout the world, for its honest portrayal of a young man's search for meaning which ended well. The book's admirers range far and wide including both Protestants and Roman Catholics and was revered by acclaimed British novelists Graham Greene (See Chapter XII) and Evelyn Waugh. Over the course of his lifetime, Merton published more than fifty books mostly on topics related to spirituality, pacifism, and social justice. He was born in Prades, France, in 1915 and died in 1968 in Bangkok, Thailand.

The Seven Storey Mountain chronicles Merton's early years and his quest for a living faith in God and conversion despite many obstacles along the way. He describes grippingly the circumstances of his birth. "I came into the world. Free by nature, in the image of God, I was nevertheless the prisoner of my own violence and my own selfishness, in the image of the world into which I was born. That world was the picture of Hell, full of men like myself, loving God, and yet hating Him; born to love Him, living instead in fear and hopeless self-contradictory hungers" (Merton, 3). The title of the book comes from the mountain of purgatory from Dante's *The Divine Comedy*. It tells the story of Merton's search for meaning and peace in a world in which there was little. The author's restlessness in his search for faith reminds the reader of the young Augustine. Finally, at the age of twenty-six, after numerous fits and starts, this passionate young seeker takes vows in the Trappist order, one of the most demanding in the Roman Catholic Church, and enters the Abbey of Gethsemani where he finally finds the faith and freedom he has craved. It was there that he wrote this book, one of the most amazing religious biographies of all time.

Merton's account of his childhood is entertaining, at times quite funny, and at other times heartbreaking. After the death of his American mother from cancer in New York City when he was a young child, his father, a New Zealand artist and lapsed Anglican, moved him back and forth between France and England, with brief forays into Switzerland. When he was ten years old, he was enrolled in a French boarding school by his father where his talent for writing was first recognized. His father died when Merton was fifteen years old as a result of a brain tumor and he became the ward of Dr. Thomas Bennett, a friend of his father. Merton describes his parents, "My father and mother were captives in that world, knowing they did not belong with it or in it, and yet unable to get away from it" (Ibid.). He describes the convoluted values of that world. "If what most people take for granted were really true—if all you needed to be happy was to grab everything and see everything and investigate every experience and then talk about it, I should have been a very happy person, a spiritual millionaire, from the cradle even until now" (Merton, 4). He mentions his baptism at Prades in France, curiously instigated by his non-religious father, as pretty much worthless. He writes, "But I don't think there was much power, in the waters of baptism I got in Prades, to untwist the warping of my essential freedom, or loose me from the devils that hung like vampires on my soul" (6).

Merton writes about his first unpleasant feelings about Catholicism. He admits that he didn't really understand the meaning of the word, but that it "conveyed a kind of cold and unpleasant feeling" (Merton, 29). He further writes, "The devil is no fool. He can get people feeling about heaven the way they ought to feel about hell. He can make them fear the means of grace the way they do not fear sin. And he does so, not by light but by obscurity, not by realities but by shadows, not by clarity and substance, but by dreams and the creatures of psychosis. And men are so poor in intellect that a few cold chills down their spine will be enough to keep them from ever finding out the truth about anything" (Merton, 29-30).

When Merton learned that his father was unwell, in fact seemingly dying, he was "profoundly affected" and fearful. He reflects that even atheists in time of profound need may be led instinctively to pray. He muses on this mystery. "The need to worship and acknowledge Him is something deeply ingrained in our dependent natures, and simply inseparable from our essence" (Merton, 31). He also discusses the "religious" upbringing he received from his decidedly unreligious no-longer-Anglican father. He writes, "The only really valuable religious and moral training I ever got as a child came to me from my father, not systematically, but here and there and more or less spontaneously, in the course of ordinary conversations. Father never applied himself, of set purpose, to teach me religion. But if something spiritual was on his mind, it came out more or less naturally. And this is the kind of religious teaching, or any other kind of teaching, that has the most effect" (Merton, 39).

When Merton was eleven years old, his father enrolled him in a male boarding school in Montauban. He was most unhappy there and rejoiced when his father gave him the news in 1928 that they were moving to England. He writes of his delight at the news. "I looked around me like a man that has had chains struck from his hands. How the light sang on the brick walls of the prison whose gates had just burst open before me, sprung by some invisible and beneficent power" (Merton, 66). He considered his escape from his "prison" as most providential.

Merton describes his life as having been lived in phases. He describes a two-year period as a teenager in England as his "religious phase." He writes, "If the impulse to worship God and to adore Him in truth by the goodness and order of our own lives is nothing more than a transitory and emotional thing, that is our own fault. It is so only because we make it so, and because we take what is substantially a deep and powerful and lasting moral impetus, supernatural in its origin and in its direction, and reduce it to the level of our own weak and unstable and futile fancies and desires" (Merton, 72). He describes this period of his life as a time when he was incapable of reasoning and was influenced mainly by his emotions and feelings.

Unfortunately for Merton, England proved not to be an improvement over France. He was placed in a boarding school in Oakham. He describes this period of his life by the chapter title, "The Harrowing of Hell." When he learned that his father was ill and had to go to London for treatment, he describes his isolation, "I sat there in the dark, unhappy room, unable to think, unable to move, with all the innumerable elements of my isolation crowding in upon me from every side: without a home, without a family, without a country, without a father, apparently without any friends, without any interior peace or confidence or light or understanding of my own—without God, too, without God, without heaven, without grace, without anything" (Merton, 79).

The illness and death of Merton's father profoundly affected him. After many visits and endless hours of sitting in a hospital room with his father unable to talk, he tells his readers of how this impacted his father. "Behind the walls of his isolation, his intelligence and his will, unimpaired, and not hampered in any essential way by the partial obstruction of some of his senses, were turned to God, and communed with God Who was with him and in him, and Who gave him, as I believe, light to understand and to make use of his suffering for his own good, and to perfect his soul. It was a great soul, large, full of natural charity. He was a man of exceptional intellectual honesty and sincerity and purity of understanding. And this affliction, this terrible and frightening illness which was relentlessly pressing him down even into the jaws of the tomb, was not destroying him at all" (Merton, 91-92). He admired his father's courage in the face of this enemy. He writes, "And my father was in a fight with this tumor, and none of us understood the battle. We thought he was done for, but it was making him great" (Merton, 92).

The aftermath of his father's death led Merton to reject God totally. He writes, "The death of my father left me sad and depressed for a couple of months. But that eventually wore away. And when it did, I found myself completely stripped of everything that impeded the movement of my own will to do as it pleased. I imagined that I was free. And it would take me five or six years to discover what a frightful captivity I had got myself into. It was in this year, too, that the hard crust of my dry soul finally squeezed out all the last traces of religion that had ever been in it.. There was no room for any God in that empty temple full of dust and rubbish which I was now so jealously to guard against all intruders, in order to devote it to the worship of my own stupid will" (Merton, 94).

At the age of seventeen, Merton's understanding of philosophy and theology were colored by the arrogance of youth. He writes about the former, "I was just turning seventeen, and thought I knew all about philosophy without having learned any" (Merton, 104). I absolutely love his sense of humor as he considers the study of metaphysics. He writes, "Even in the purely natural order, a certain amount of purity of heart is required before an intellect can get sufficiently detached and clear to work out the problems of metaphysics. . . . No one needs to be a saint to be a clever metaphysician. I dare say there are plenty of metaphysicians in hell" (Ibid.). On theology: "I used to keep my lips tight shut, with full deliberation and of set purpose, by way of declaring my own creed which was: 'I believe in nothing.' Or at least I thought I believed in nothing. Actually, I had only exchanged a certain faith, faith in God,

Who is Truth, for a vague and uncertain faith in the opinions and authority of men and pamphlets and newspapers—wavering and varying and contradictory opinions which I did not even clearly understand" (Merton, 108).

Merton's descriptions of his early struggles as he is in the world and very much of it are often profound and moving beyond belief. For example, "In that flash, instantly I was overwhelmed with a sudden and profound insight into the misery and corruption of my own soul and I was pierced deeply with a light that made me realize something of the condition I was in, and I was filled with horror at what I saw, and my whole being rose up in revolt against what was in me, and my soul desired escape and liberation from all this with an intensity and an urgency unlike anything I had ever known before" (Merton, 123). He minces no words in his abhorrence of the morass of sin in which he was mired. "With every nerve and fibre of my being I was laboring to enslave myself in the bonds of my own intolerable disgust" (Merton, 133).

While a student at Clare College, University of Cambridge, Merton was providentially introduced to the writings of Dante. At the time, he could not accept all of the doctrines espoused such as Purgatory and Hell, but the seed was sown. He writes of his time there. "I myself had turned out to be an extremely unpleasant sort of a person—vain, self-centered, dissolute, weak, irresolute, undisciplined, sensual, obscene, and proud. I was a mess. Even the sight of my own face in a mirror was enough to disgust me" (Merton, 146). It often takes a person to reach rock bottom before he can begin to climb. So it was with Thomas Merton. He writes, "I had come very far, to find myself in this blind-alley: but the very anguish and helplessness of my position was something to which I rapidly succumbed. And it was my defeat that was to be the occasion of my rescue" (Merton, 182). He left Cambridge and entered Columbia University at age twenty and graduated in 1938 with a B.A. in English. It was while at Columbia that Merton decided to study Catholicism further. During his time living in New York, he was introduced to and read both *The Confessions of Augustine* and *Of the Imitation of Christ*. His inquiries and reading led him to undergo the rite of baptism at Corpus Christi Church in 1938. The next year he received his M.A. in English from Columbia and decided to pursue a Ph.D. at the same institution.

Merton has the rare gift of being able to wax profoundly and poetically on the human condition. That is certainly one reason that this book has inspired millions throughout the ensuing decades including World War II veterans, students, and teenagers to seek monastic life. He writes, "There is a paradox that lies in the very heart of human existence. It must be apprehended before any lasting happiness is possible in the soul of man. The paradox is this: man's nature, by itself, can do little or nothing to settle his most important problems. If we follow nothing but our natures, our own philosophies, our own level of ethics, we will end up in hell" (Merton, 185). He writes beautifully on the human condition. "The intellect is only theoretically independent of desire and appetite in ordinary, actual practice. It is constantly being blinded and perverted by the ends and aims of passion, and the evidence it presents to us with such a show of impartiality and objectivity is fraught with interest and propaganda. We have become marvelous at self-delusion; all the more so. Because we have gone to such trouble to convince ourselves of our own absolute infallibility" (Merton, 225).

Merton's conversion and subsequent baptism proved to mark only a beginning of a new stage in his spiritual pilgrimage. He writes, "The essential thing was to begin the climb. Baptism was that beginning, and a most generous one, on the part of God. For, although I was baptized conditionally, I hope that His mercy swallowed up all the guilt and temporal punishment of my twenty-three black years of sin in the waters of the font, and allowed me a new start. But my human nature, my weakness, and the cast of my evil habits still remained to be fought and overcome" (Merton, 242). He also muses, "How beautiful and how terrible are the words with which God speaks to the soul of those He has called to Himself. They are words lovely

to those who hear and obey them: but what are they to those
who hear them without understanding or response" (Merton,
247)? Merton relates how at the beginning of his walk with
Christ, he had "backslid" as the Baptists are wont to say. He
admits, "I simply slipped into the ranks of the millions of tepid
and dull and sluggish and indifferent Christians who live a life
that is still half animal, and who barely put up a struggle to
keep the breath of grace alive in their souls" (Merton, 250-51).
Merton explains the problem, "but the conversion of the intellect is not enough. And as long as the will, the *domina voluntas*,
did not belong completely to God, even the intellectual conversion was bound to remain precarious and indefinite" (Merton,
253).

Soon after his conversion, Merton began to become enamored
with the prospect of entering a religious order. He explains his
process of winnowing his choices, "No matter what religious
Order a man enters, whether its Rule be easy or strict in itself
does not much matter, if his vocation is to be really fruitful it
must cost him something, and it must be a real sacrifice. It must
be a cross, a true renunciation of natural goods, even of the
highest natural goods" (Merton, 319). He relates how God led
him. "I had to be led by a way that I could not understand, and
I had to follow a path that was beyond my own choosing. God
did not want anything of my natural tastes and fancies and selections until they had been more completely divorced from
their old track, their old habits, and directed to Himself, by His
own working" (Ibid.).

As Merton began to gravitate towards the Trappists, he explains the attraction of this religious order. "They were free
from the burden of the flesh's tyranny, and their clear vision,
clean of the world's smoke and of its bitter sting, were raised
to heaven and penetrated into the deeps of heaven's infinite
and healing light. They were poor, they had nothing, and therefore they were free and possessed everything, and everything
they touched struck off something of the fire of divinity" (Merton, 346). He describes his moment of decision as heart-rend-

ing. "The thought of those monasteries, those remote choirs, those cells, those hermitages, those men in their cowls, the poor monks, the men who had become nothing shattered my heart" (Merton, 348). He made his decision after many bumps on the road and numerous doubts. He describes his elation. "I was free. I had recovered my liberty. I belonged to God, not to myself: and to belong to Him is to be free, free of all the anxieties and worries and sorrows that belong to this earth, and the love of things that are in it" (Merton, 406).

Please be forewarned: Merton lived life in the Trappist monastery on his own terms. He became a somewhat controversial figure later in life as he dabbled in the mysticism of the East. But he always remained anchored to his steadfast faith in Christ. Also, most Protestants who have drunk deeply from the pure waters of the Reformation will be put off by some of the beliefs of Roman Catholics. For example, the idea that sin can be alleviated by our own good works is repugnant to most Protestants. Merton, however, writes, "As I left the church, there was no lack of beggars to give me the opportunity of almsgiving, which is an easy and simple way of wiping out sin" (306). Merton also believes per Roman Catholic teaching that Mary was the mother of God, a theological position to which Protestants do not adhere" (Merton, 307). As always, readers need to separate the wheat from the chaff.

The Seven Story Mountain is not only a Christian classic; it is one of the finest and most-influential books written in the twentieth century. Sadly, Merton was accidently electrocuted at the age of fifty-five while attending an international monasticism conference in Bangkok, Thailand. However, his life inspired the formation of The International Thomas Merton Society and The Thomas Merton Center at Bellarmine University. The Society's mission statement is "To encourage exploration of Thomas Merton's life and thought to build knowledge, cultivate community, foster contemplative awareness, encourage interfaith encounters, and inspire just living." That sounds like something we Protestants need to do more.

40. THE GULAG ARCHIPELAGO, VOLUME 1

By Aleksandr Solzhenitsyn

Aleksandr Solzhenitsyn is one of the most recognizable figures of the twentieth century. Born in 1918, he served as a decorated captain in the Soviet Army during World War II. However, in 1945, while still serving in the Red Army, he was arrested by SMERSH and sentenced to prison for eight years for his criticism of Joseph Stalin in his private correspondence. Solzhenitsyn's upbringing was Christian. His parents, members of the Russian Orthodox Church, defied the Soviet Union's anti-religious campaign in the 1920s, but young Aleksandr went his own way religiously, drifted away from his familial Christian faith, and became an atheist. He became an ardent Marxist-Leninist. His experiences in the prison camps of the Soviet Union changed him and he became a follower of the Eastern Orthodox faith.

Beginning in the mid-1950s, Nikita Khrushchev, First Secretary of the Communist Party of the Soviet Union, denounced Stalin's policies and began what is today known as the "Khrushchev Thaw," a period of de-Stalinization during which censorship and repression were relaxed and peaceful coexistence with other countries was sought. Leonid Brezhnev succeeded Khrushchev in 1964 ending the "thaw." However, during Khrushchev's time in power, Solzhenitsyn was released from prison and exonerated.

Solzhenitsyn began to write novels about Soviet repression primarily based on his own experiences and those with whom he was imprisoned. In 1962 he published his first novel, *One Day in the Life of Ivan Denisovich*, a fictional account of Stalinist repressions, with Khrushchev's approval. This catapulted Solzhenitsyn from unknown school-teacher to international fame. This was followed by *Matryona's Place*, a novella that was published in 1963 and became Solzhenitsyn's last work published in the Soviet Union. After Khrushchev's removal from power, Solzhenitsyn was discouraged in his writing endeavors by the state. However, he continued to write powerful books including *Cancer Ward* in 1966, *In the First Circle* in 1968, *August 1914* in 1971, *The Gulag Archipelago* in 1973, all of which were published outside the Soviet Union. The last book mentioned did not go over well and led to his loss of citizenship in 1974 and his exile from the Soviet Union. In 1970 Solzhenitsyn was awarded the Nobel Prize in Literature "for the ethical force with which he has pursued the indispensable traditions of Russian literature."

The Gulag Archipelago is a nationwide prison camp system in the former Soviet Union, hence the title of this book. The residents of this archipelago were people who were arrested for crimes against the state, whether real or trumped up. They were arrested primarily at night, half-dressed, confused, not understanding the charges. Solzhenitsyn describes what that experience actually was for so many. "Arrest is an instantaneous, shattering thrust, expulsion, somersault from one state into another" (Solzhenitsyn, 4). Such was the fate of the tens of thousands who were cast into the nightmare meat grinder prison system called the Gulag Archipelago. This horrific system began in 1917 under Lenin with his declared "Red Terror." It not only destroyed the lives of those arrested, it forever changed the lives of their families. Solzhenitsyn writes, "For those left behind after the arrest there is the long tail end of a wrecked and devastated life" (Solzhenitsyn, 6).

Solzhenitsyn's arrest experience was different from that of most. He was arrested in 1945 in an army tent about 200 yards away from where German bombs were exploding at the front of the battle. But it was none the less shattering for him. He had no idea what he could possibly have done to merit this. He writes, "For several decades political arrests were distinguished in our country precisely by the fact that people were arrested who were guilty of nothing and were therefore unprepared to put up any resistance whatsoever. There was a general feeling of being destined for destruction, a sense of having nowhere to escape from the GPU-NKVD" (Solzhenitsyn, 11). Authors note: The NKVD was the People's Commissariat for Internal Affairs, the interior ministry of the U.S.S.R.).

Solzhenitsyn describes his trip from the German front back for his trial in the first chapter of Part I. What haunted him as he traveled and came into contact with other Russians is that he kept silent about what was being done to him. He asks himself, "Why, in my last minute out in the open, did I not attempt to enlighten the hoodwinked crowd" (Solzhenitsyn, 17)? Back in Moscow he says, "They kept coming in an endless ribbon from down there, from the depths of ignorance—on and on beneath the gleaming dome, reaching toward me for at least one word of truth—so why did I keep silent" (Ibid.)? A powerful argument that Solzhenitsyn makes is that this silence and brutality of the gulag system made it possible for the Soviet government to exert almost total control over its citizens. People were afraid to speak out. He had a premonition perhaps of his writing career. He writes, "Vaguely, unclearly, I had a vision that someday I would cry out to the 200 million. But for the time being I did not open my mouth, and the escalator dragged me implacably down into the nether world" (Solzhenitsyn, 18).

It is telling that Solzhenitsyn titled his second chapter of Part I, which traces the beginnings of the gulag system, "The History of Our Sewage Disposal System." That dissidents and other undesirables could be described as "sewage" speaks volumes about the Soviet system and ideology. In comparing the flow of people into the prison camps to the flow of sewage, what he meant is that sometimes the flow was strong and sometimes not so strong, but the pipeline was always there. People were simply sewage to be disposed. This is the longest chapter in the book and it is heartbreaking to read. In this chapter, Solzhenitsyn destroys the mythology the Soviet Union was promulgating that arrests and imprisonments were mainly occurring in

1937 and 1938. He estimates that there were millions of prisoners in the Gulag during the 1930s and 1940s. These were not
just peasants, but educated people, artists, and religious people.
He relates how one woman received a ten-year sentence for
simply writing.

> "You can pray freely
> But just so God alone can hear."

Solzhenitsyn writes, "In the twenties the religious education
was classified as a political crime" (Solzhenitsyn, 37-38). In
fact, most people had no idea just what constituted a crime and
so they were always paranoid. The mood was such that everyone who lived in the Soviet Union was in a constant state of
fear of being arrested.

The third chapter of Part I is titled "The Interrogation" and details how they were conducted and their effects. He begins the
chapter by musing about, of all people, Anton Chekov. He
writes, "If the intellectuals in the plays of Chekov who spent all
their time guessing what would happen in twenty, thirty, or
forty years had been told that in forty years interrogation by
torture would be practice in Russia; that prisoners would have
their skulls squeezed within iron rings; that a human being
would be lowered into an acid bath, that they would be trussed
up naked to be bitten by ants and bedbugs; that a ramrod
heated over a primus stove would be thrust up their anal canal;
that a man's genitals would be slowly crushed beneath the toe
of a jackboot; and that, in the luckiest possible circumstances,
prisoners would be tortured by being kept from sleeping for a
week, by thirst, and being beaten to a bloody pulp, not one of
Chekov's plays would have gotten to its end because all the heroes would have gone off to insane asylums" (Solzhenitsyn,
93). What would have astonished and horrified Chekov became
commonplace in the post-revolution U.S.S.R. As Solzhenitsyn
concludes, "Given the fact that the cases were always fabri-
cated, violence and torture had to accompany them" (Solzhenitsyn, 98-99). He explains, "The time allotted for investigation

was not used to unravel the crime but, in ninety-five cases out of a hundred, to exhaust, wear down, and render helpless the defendant, so that he would want it to end at any cost" (Solzhenitsyn, 97).

Although physical torture was commonly utilized, Solzhenitsyn explains that it was not always needed. "Indeed, the actual boundaries of human equilibrium are very narrow, and it is not really necessary to use a rack or hot coals to drive the average human being out of his mind" (Solzhenitsyn, 103). He then lists thirty-one methods of psychological torture which have proven to be most effective. These include humiliation, confusion, intimidation, light and sound effects, sleep deprivation, the bedbug-infested box, and punishment cells. Physical methods of torture included beatings, starvation, and fingernail or teeth removal. All of this was done to get prisoners to confess to crimes that they and their interrogators both knew that they had not committed. Solzhenitsyn makes it clear that all of this was part of the dysfunction of the Soviet system of justice. Anyone could be arrested at any time for no reason.

Solzhenitsyn relates how his arrival at his first prison cell was almost anticlimactic, a relief, after ninety-six hours of interrogation. However, internment in the Gulag was hardly a picnic. Prisoners were exposed to the harsh Russian weather, the inhumane conditions, and sadistic guards. They were often stripped of their clothes as well as their humanity. Life in a Gulag, he soon learned, was a microcosm of Soviet society. Every prisoner was under the constant threat of punishment for breaking one of a myriad of senseless rules. Toilet facilities were primitive and disgusting. Everything in the Gulag system was meant to dehumanize the prisoners. In the end, Solzhenitsyn came to the conclusion that the Soviet political system was even worse than that of the Nazis.

Today the word "gulag" is used figuratively or loosely, but in the Soviet Union of Solzhenitsyn's day it was a daily nightmarish reality for millions. There were many "gulags," camps scattered over the entire country, the worst of which were in the Kolyma region in northeastern Siberia. Temperatures there reached fifty, sixty, and seventy degrees below zero in those "islands" where prisoners worked poorly clad and fed. As reports filtered out of the gulags, they were disbelieved and even ridiculed until Solzhenitsyn's account was smuggled out. The reports could no longer be discarded as figments of overactive imaginations.

Solzhenitsyn's writing has invited criticism over the years. The scale and population of the gulags, in his estimation, was perhaps exaggerated. While Solzhenitsyn implies that between twelve and fifteen million were imprisoned between 1917 and 1953, the actual figure is probably much smaller. However one crunches the numbers, it is undisputed that millions of lives were destroyed in the gulags and the conditions of these camps with their brutality, abuse, theft, sexual violence, and random executions and the parallels he drew with the death camps run by the Nazis during World War II. This has never been questioned or contradicted.

The Gulag Archipelago is without a doubt one of the most important works of literature of the twentieth century. *Time* magazine called it the "best Nonfiction Book of the Twentieth Century." There is a reason why it was banned in the Soviet Union and why Solzhenitsyn was persecuted and imprisoned by his own government for his writings. It shined a spotlight to the world the brutality and abuses of the Soviet prison labor camps known as gulags from 1917 onward. He hoped that the world would take notice of the horrors committed under Lenin and Stalin and other Soviet leaders thereby putting enough pressure on the country and ending its systemic violence, which he believed was part and parcel of the Soviet state. His writing places him in the rare stratosphere of Russian writers inhabited by Tolstoy and Dostoevsky who portrayed human beings in the worst of situations buttressed by their unshakeable faith in God. Solzhenitsyn stands as a giant among modern writers. *The Gulag Archipelago* is a rare literary treat. You will never be the same after reading it.

41. JUST AS I AM

By Billy Graham

Billy Graham (1918-2018) is a name that hardly needs an introduction to almost anyone in the United States, whether believer or unbeliever, living over the roughly past seventy years. His worldwide evangelistic crusades have brought him international fame and a well-deserved reputation as the most successful Christian evangelist in history. It is estimated that he has preached the gospel of Jesus Christ to more people, whether in person or on television, than anyone ever has. He has also wielded wide influence as the confidante of numerous sitting presidents from Harry S. Truman to Barack Obama. He was particularly close to Presidents Eisenhower, Johnson, and Nixon.

Graham had very humble beginnings. He was born on November 7, 1918, and raised on a farm just outside Charlotte, N.C. His parents were active church members, but little Billy was not so committed and had a bit of a wild side. In the fall of 1934, Graham's life changed radically after hearing the fiery evangelist, Mordecai Ham, who was preaching a crusade in Charlotte. Near the end of the crusade, he committed his life to Jesus Christ as his Lord and savior. He would never be the same again.

After attending Bob Jones College in Tennessee for a brief time and then the Florida Bible Institute near Tampa for almost four years, Graham was given his first preaching assignments and was ordained a Baptist minister. He then attended Wheaton College in Illinois to study anthropology. It was there that he met his future wife, Ruth Bell, a fellow student who was the daughter of the well-known missionary to China, Dr. Nelson Bell. His first pastorate was at the tiny United Gospel Tabernacle of Wheaton, a small independent church. From there he went to the Western Springs Baptist Church. A pastor friend told him about a Chicago radio program, *Songs in the Night*, that was about to be canceled because of a lack of funding. Graham rescued the program with the financial assistance of his church members at Western Springs. He recruited a Canadian-born singer named George Beverly Shea as his soloist on the radio ministry. Graham's meteoric rise is history.

By 1949, Graham was being recognized as a major figure in American religion. He had his first major crusade in Los Angeles in 1949, which introduced his name to the rest of the nation. By 1950, the weekly magazine *Newsweek* gushed that he was "America's greatest living evangelist." He conducted more than 400 crusades in 185 countries and territories on six continents. An outgrowth of his evangelistic campaigns was the nationally broadcast *Hour of Decision* evangelistic program. Graham's life and ministry has been the subject of numerous biographies. One of the very best is the authorized biography titled *Billy Graham* by John Pollock originally published in 1966. But *Just As I Am* is the only autobiography. It was originally published in 1997 and was revised and updated in a tenth anniversary edition in 2007 that includes his historic 9/11 sermon preached at the National Cathedral in Washington D.C. on September 14, 2001.

One could go on and on about the life and ministry of Billy Graham. His preaching career spanned seven decades. However, there are several things that set him apart from other evangelists and pastors of his time. First of all, I have been impressed by his financial integrity. In 1948 Graham and his evangelistic team established the Modesto Manifesto which outlined "a shared commitment to do all we could to uphold the Bible's standard of absolute integrity and purity for evangelists" (Graham, 128). They detailed a series of shared resolutions, an informal understanding among members of the team as to how they would conduct the Lord's business. There would be accountability for finances. Out of this he formed the Billy Graham Evangelistic Association. From the beginning, there were several stipulations in place to regulate the financial aspect of the ministry. There were no "love offerings" to be taken and Graham, himself, would be paid as a regular employee at a regular salary commensurate with that of the ministers of large city churches. His team members would be paid in the same way. Their evangelistic services were offered free of charge. All costs for each conference such as conference hall rental and publicity would be met locally by churches supportive of cooperative evangelism.

Another practice that set Graham apart was his determination to pursue sexual purity. He committed to never be alone with any woman other than his wife. What is remarkable is that over his many decades of preaching ministry, Billy Graham and his organization has never had even a whiff of a financial or sexual scandal. Considering that many prominent evangelical leaders have had dramatic downfalls because of financial or sexual abuses, that is something to celebrate.

One of Graham's boldest moves was to promote reconciliation and integration between the races years before the United States was ready for such an approach. Although Graham's early crusades were segregated, his approach changed in the 1950s, a full decade before the Civil Rights Movement was in full swing. He did this at the risk of losing considerable financial support from whites. His friendship with Martin Luther King, Jr. has been well-documented.

Finally, Billy Graham headed the committee that spearheaded the Lausanne International Congress on World Evangelization, held in Switzerland in 1974. It was attended by more than 2,200 evangelical leaders representing 150 countries and resulted in the Lausanne Covenant. That meeting was seminal in that for the first time it was acknowledged that a majority of evangelicals were not from the West, but from the Third World, and that Western domination of the church could not be sustained. There were many conflicting voices heard at the congress from poor Third World representatives demanding social action to wealthy Westerners who were satisfied with the status quo. What cannot be denied is that without the steadying hand of Graham, the Congress would not have happened, and it was realized that evangelism and social concern were not mutually exclusive concerns, thus, paving the way for evangelicals to engage in both.

In *Just As I Am*, we hear about Billy Graham from his own perspective. This is very much his own story as he wanted to tell it. There are many fine biographies about his life, but my favorite is his own story told in his way. It is a story that will certainly challenge you and stretch you.

Some of Graham's other books that you may want to explore are Peace with God (1953), Freedom from the Seven Deadly Sins (1955), Angels: God's Secret Agents (1985), The Holy Spirit (1978), Till Armageddon (1981), Approaching Hoofbeats (1983), Facing Death and the Life After (1987), and Hope for the Troubled Heart (1991).

42. BORN AGAIN

By Charles Colson

Christians love to hear stories about dramatic conversions. Saul, on the road to Damascus, a fanatical fire-breathing Pharisee, is confronted by the Risen Christ and is dramatically transformed from a persecutor of Christians into the Apostle Paul. John Newton, a captain of slave ships who underwent a sudden conversion, went on to become an abolitionist, an Anglican cleric, and the writer of such beloved hymns as *Amazing Grace* and *Glorious Things of Thee Are Spoken*. Augustine of Hippo, also known as Saint Augustine, was a sensuous youth who also was influenced by the philosophies of his day, in particular Manichaeism. He was converted dramatically to Christianity at age thirty-three in large part because of a praying mother. There are many others such as Clement of Alexandria, an early church father, and Nicky Cruz, who was the leader of a brutal Puerto Rican New York City gang before meeting David Wilkerson who led him to faith in Jesus Christ.

Born Again tells the story of one man's spiritual journey from the White House to prison, from the penthouse to the outhouse, from damnation to salvation. The origins of this book can be traced to 1974 in the aftermath of President Richard Nixon's resignation in disgrace. The United States government, as Colson describes it, was in "disarray" and the country in "numbed shock." At the time, Colson said, he was "languishing in an Alabama prison." He writes, "My own spirit was crying out in agony. How could all this have happened?" He concluded that he, along with Haldeman, Ehrlichman, Mitchell, and Nixon, had been ensnared by "their own pretensions of power, victims of their own human frailties."

Born Again is a fascinating and enlightening look at the inner workings of the Nixon White House. Colson peels away the layers and separates fact from fiction. But even more than that, it is a penetrating gaze into the inner workings of a man's conscience and the regeneration of his soul. If ever there was a dramatic conversion story, *Born Again* is it and Charles Colson a most unlikely convert. "Born again" is "an overworked Protestant cliché," but in 1974 it was not widely known or used except in certain of the more fundamentalist religious circles. With the publication of this book, it became a part of the common language.

During a conversation with his old friend, Tom Phillips, he came to the startling realization that his friend had come to a saving knowledge of Jesus Christ. As Colson wrote, "He had struck a raw nerve—the empty life" (Colson,93). In a later meeting with Phillips, Colson was urged to examine the claims of Christ and to make a commitment to him. He gave him a copy of the C. S. Lewis classic, *Mere Christianity* (See Chapter III)), to help him on his spiritual journey. Colson at that time was wrestling with such foundational questions such as "Is there a God?" He began reading the book and found, in Lewis, an intellectual kinship. Colson wrote, "I opened *Mere Christianity* and found myself . . . face-to-face with an intellect so disciplined, so lucid, so relentlessly logical that I could only be grateful I had never faced him in a court of law" (Colson, 121).

Colson's disenchantment with the Nixon White House was a gradual process, not an instantaneous one. He slowly came to realize during the nation's Vietnam War protest demonstrations that "presidents rule not by fiat, but by the sufferance of free men" (Colson, 139). It was at this point in his life that he began to reevaluate the morality of many of his actions such as authoring the memo listing Nixon's major political opponents and his instigation of the AFL-CIO leaders into carrying out the so-called Hard Hat Riot in 1971. He was greatly challenged by the impeccable logic in the writings of Lewis. The rightness or wrongness of each side was "irrelevant if moral leadership could not be regained" (Colson, 40). That was, to Colson, the key. He was most impressed by Lewis's arguments about moral

law. His thinking at that time was undergoing a radical transformation. Nixon's "hatchet man" was learning how to bury
the hatchet.

Colson was moved by the love of Christ. As he ruminated on
the nature of love, he wrote, "Yet love, which no one sees or
touches, moves men and nations in limitless ways. Love caused
one man to renounce a kingdom in my lifetime. Another kind
of love causes a soldier to hurl his body over a grenade which
has fallen into the midst of his buddies. Love has incomparably
greater force than any engine of known horsepower" (Colson,
122).

I was moved to tears time and again as Colson made peace with
old adversaries. For example, his relationship with Senator
Harold Hughes, a man Colson despised, was transformed from
enemies into brothers in Christ. Colson relates Hughes' first
reaction to the news of Colson's conversion, "There isn't anyone I dislike more than Chuck Colson. I'm against everything
he stands for." But the love of Christ was too strong to allow
mutual animosities to exist. As Colson writes, "Harold lum-
bered toward me, a smile slowly spreading over his face. As he
wrapped his arms around me in a great bear hug, I needed no
further explanation of what *fellowship* meant" (Colson, 150).
Out of the ruins of the Watergate scandal, something wonderful was happening in the center of America's power. Describing a weekly prayer meeting Colson attended, he wrote, "God's
Spirit was working in powerful ways all over strife-torn Washington. Each Monday morning when we met—someone would
report another miracle, old adversaries coming together as
brothers, new fellowships begun, prayer groups revived, unlikely men seeking a relationship with Christ" (Colson, 187).

Prison life was not an easy adjustment for Colson. Although he
lived at the prison camp at Maxwell Air Force Base where inmates are housed in dormitories instead of cells, he found dor-
mitory living "a horror" in that there is constant noise and
overcrowding. He was advised to not think, conform, and build

an island around himself. None of these prescriptions was he able to do. He wrote, "I am learning how God can break us in order to remake us" (Colson, 12). In addition to his Bible reading, Colson worked through the Navigators *Design for Discipleship* Bible course to help him grow in his newfound faith. He also felt a spiritual kinship with Dietrich Bonhoeffer whose *Letters and Papers from Prison* he read while at Maxwell. Bonhoeffer was executed by the Nazis at the concentration camp Flossenburg in 1945 just two weeks prior to its liberation by the Allied forces.

During his time in prison, Colson was shocked to learn that some inmates were unable to read and that some didn't even understand why they were in prison. They were unable to comprehend the charges that were brought against them. He was appalled at how shoddy some of the legal work had been. Despite warnings not to practice law while incarcerated, he worked tirelessly to help the plight of inmates by writing letters and working on their behalf behind the scenes. As he neared the end of his sentence, Colson's attitude had changed so much that after a prayer meeting to heal a fellow inmate believer, he prayed, "Thank you for letting me be here. Thank You, thank You. This moment is worth it all" (Colson, 329). Colson was released from prison in 1975, and the story of *Born Again* ends there. But that is hardly the end of the story.

Soon after his release from prison, Colson founded the non-profit ministry Prison Fellowship and then Prison Fellowship International. According to their website, the ministry "exists to serve all those affected by crime and incarceration and to see lives and communities restored in and out of prison—one transformed life at a time." Within prisons the ministry organizes evangelism events, Bible study, discipleship course, life-skills training, mentorship, and reentry programs. It is active in all fifty states and has more than 268,000 volunteers. It also facilitates classes with 26,000 prisoners participating cach month. But that is not the end of the story. The Chuck Colson Center for Christian Worldview is a research, study, and networking center to help Christians grow in their understanding of a Christian worldview. It produces a daily radio commentary, *BreakPoint*, which is heard on more than 1,000 stations in the United States. John Stonestreet is its current voice.

Although Colson died in 2012, he very much lives through his many books and the work he established. *Born Again* is very much a must read. It is imperative that Christians realize that being broken by God is not the end of the story. It is just the beginning as Colson proved so convincingly. You don't believe in jailhouse conversions? You need to rethink that position. Discover the reality of 2 Corinthians 5:17: "Therefore, if anyone is in Christ, he is a new creation; the old has gone, the new has come!" That verse describes *Born Again* and Charles Colson in a nutshell. The book describes the joy of conversion and how Jesus Christ can transform a life. But don't stop with *Born Again*. Other works by Colson are worth a read: *Life Sentence, Loving God, Kingdoms in Conflict, Against the Night: Living in the New Dark Ages*, and *God and Government.*

CHAPTER VI:
BIBLE AND CHURCH HISTORY AND BIBLICAL ARCHAEOLOGY

There is an old maxim generally attributed to writer and philosopher George Santayana, "Those who cannot remember the past are condemned to repeat it." This has been demonstrated to be true over and over again in the twentieth and twenty-first centuries with respect to world powers as well as with individuals. What the United States should have learned in Vietnam about intervening to fight proxy battles has come back to haunt us in the Middle East as conflict has become protracted. Similarly on an individual level, married couples who do not learn from their mistakes and conflicts do not mature and often break up.

One of the longest running gags in the *Peanuts* cartoon strip written by Charles Schultz is that of Charlie Brown running up to kick a football held by Lucy. At the last micro-second, Lucy invariably snatches the ball away and Charlie falls on his posterior. Charlie Brown, it seems, never learned from history. In one particular episode from September 21, 1958, Charlie says to Lucy, "All right. I'll trust you. I have an undying faith in human nature." After the inevitable occurs again and Charlie Brown falls with a big WUMP!, Lucy says to him, "Charlie Brown, your faith in human nature is an inspiration to all young people." It has been said presumably by Albert Einstein, and I paraphrase a bit, the definition of insanity is doing the same thing over and over again expecting different results.

A 2004 Common Core survey of 1,200 seventeen-year-olds showed that fewer than half of American teenagers knew when the Civil War was fought. About a quarter of them believed that Columbus sailed to the New World sometime after 1750. About a quarter of them did not know that Hitler was the Chancellor of Germany during World War II. The survey concluded that a significant proportion of them live in "stunning ignorance." When I taught high school students, I often asked similar questions just for fun to similar effect. Most were unable to place the Civil War and the American Revolution in the correct centuries.

As I transitioned to teaching adults on the college and graduate levels as well as teaching adult Bible studies and Sunday school classes, I discovered that Christian adults do not fare any better with respect not only to the content of the Bible, but to biblical history and church history. This is particularly true not only when we, twenty-first century believers, approach the subject of biblical history as well as the history of the Christian church. It was also true of the Israelites of the Old Testament who continually failed to learn from their past sins and failures and each generation tested God anew. Moses warned the Israelites just before they crossed the Jordan River to enter into the Promised Land. "Only be careful, and watch yourselves closely so that you do not forget the things your eyes have seen or let them slip from your heart as long as you live. Teach them to your children and to their children after them" (Deut. 4:9). The prophets warned them over and over again. "Do not be like your forefathers, to whom the earlier prophets proclaimed: This is what the Lord Almighty says: 'Turn from your evil ways and your evil practices.' But they would not listen or pay attention to me, declares the Lord" (Zech. 1:4).

Ignorance about biblical history is rampant. Popular books such as *The Da Vinci Code* and the furor surrounding them have amply demonstrated this. Some pastors and academics, rather than cursing the darkness, have decided to shed some light on the matter either from the pulpit or in books of rebuttal. But the problem remains. Christians easily fall prey to such drivel as *The Da Vinci Code* (not to mention the *Left Behind* series of books).

Why is it so important for Christians to know biblical history? Let me give you one example. If you read the Old Testament post-exilic books of Ezra, Nehemiah, and Esther, it is almost impossible to understand the events and basic themes unless we are able to locate their respective places in biblical and world history. It is not an exaggeration to say that there are some believers who cannot place the time of these books and the events described in them within a thousand years of their occurrence. How sad! In 586 B.C., the Babylonian king, Nebuchadnezzar destroyed Jerusalem, burned the temple to the ground, and carried thousands of the Jews of Judah into exile. This was all a judgment of God and a direct fulfillment of Deuteronomy 28: 15, 36, and 64. In fact, it was during those years of exile into Babylon that God's people came to be known as Jews, having taken their name from Judah, their homeland. The same can be said for church history and its importance to Christians.

Bible archaeology has been called the key to understanding the history of the Bible. Many people and places are only mentioned in the Bible and not in secular history. Were it not for the science of archaeology, there would be no corroborating evidence for these people and places. It is impossible to overestimate the importance of biblical archaeology to the study of the Bible. As the legendary New Testament scholar, F. F. Bruce once wrote in his Foreward to *The Bible and Archaeology*, "There is no finality in biblical archaeology. As more pieces of the jigsaw puzzle come to light, we see that we have sometimes put previously discovered pieces in the wrong place and produced a distorted pattern" (Thompson, viii). Thus, the job of the biblical archaeologist as well as the biblical scholar is never

completed. Their findings are constantly subject to repeated re-
vision and further study.

The following books will help the reader to understand the
fields of biblical and church history, as well as the science of
biblical archaeology. They are written on a level, in my opinion,
that they can be understood by the average reader.

43. A SURVEY OF ISRAEL'S HISTORY

By Leon J. Wood

This book was my textbook while taking a lower-level seminary class on the historical books of the Old Testament almost a half century ago. I found it to be an authoritative, thoroughly enjoyable walk through the history of Israel from the time of the Patriarchs to the close of Old Testament history. In the intervening decades, other histories of Israel have been published, several of them quite good, but this one gets my nod as a must-read for today's Christian.

There may be more up-to-date histories than this one and there may be better ones from a scholarly point of view, but this one has been a particular favorite of mine for decades. The edition that I read while a student was published in 1970. It was revised and enlarged by David O'Brien in 1986 adding a section on the Intertestamental Period. I used the updated version while teaching a seminary class a few years ago with great success. I have to say that this book fits me like an old shoe. I don't tend to throw away old shoes for the latest style if they still fit and are serviceable. Wood's history is easy-to-read, well-written, and extremely informative. It has established itself as a popular textbook in colleges and seminaries and is enormously helpful to anyone trying to get a grasp on Old Testament history.

Leon Wood (1918-1977) was a beloved and almost legendary professor of Old Testament Studies and Dean of Grand Rapids Baptist Seminary. There are many stories told by his students of his teaching prowess. Wood had many academic pursuits. In addition to his prolific legacy of books including the fine *Distressing Days of the Judges*, he served as one of the translators of the *Berkeley Version of the Old Testament* as well as a translator and editor for the acclaimed *New International Version* (NIV). Wood was also a controversial figure in that he advocated the "gap theory" of creation science, which has been widely debunked by scholars.

As the cover of the 1970 edition states, "In fifteen poignant chapters, *A Survey of Israel's History* explores the questions of Israel and her prominence in the course of human events." Wood provides a comprehensive and complete examination of the biblical source material as well as relating it to the pertinent archaeological data. Wood explains the importance of Old Testament history as well as the importance of its handmaiden, archaeology. "The Old Testament is not a history book as such. Its purpose is to portray God's interest in, and preparation for, His redemptive provision for sinful man. When man in his representative head, Adam, sinned in the Garden of Eden, need for such a provision came into existence. The Old Testament is God's record of how He prepared for and affected that provision as culminated in Jesus Christ, working particularly through the nation of Israel. The history involved is what is narrated in the Old Testament. Accordingly, that historical material which was pertinent to this preparation was included, and that which was not pertinent was normally omitted. For this reason, though the history is remarkably complete in many respects as noted, omissions occur which a book of history would include. Happily, there is another source of information which helps to fill in these omissions and supply general background. That source is archaeological research" (Wood, 18, 1970 edition).

Wood's book is a lively exploration of the people of Israel and their relationship to the ancient Near East. There are maps, charts, and diagrams to supplement the written text. Wood encourages the reader to consult the many Bible references that are provided because this history, as carefully written as it is, cannot substitute for the Scriptures themselves. In this book, historical events are no longer dry and boring and historical personages are not just names from a long-ago era. In Wood's capable hands, the characters that inhabit the Old Testament become living personalities that almost jump off the page. They are no longer just names from a bygone era.

It is important that Christians know from whence they came. That is why it is so necessary for believers to have a solid understanding of the foundation of Christianity. That foundation is Israel and God's dealing with that nation. Reading this book will introduce you to the Old Testament in a way that will be fun and in no way arduous. I think you will enjoy it.

44. BIBLE ARCHAEOLOGY

By Alfred Hoerth and John McRay

&

45. ARCHAEOLOGY & THE NEW TESTAMENT

By John McRay

I have decided to bundle these two books together because of the similarity of material and the common authorship. The stated purpose of *Bible Archaeology* is to cover "the most significant archaeological data relevant to the people and places named in the Old and New Testaments. The authors' aim is to provide historical, geographical, and literary material that will enrich the knowledge of everyone who is interested in a fuller understanding of the Bible in its cultural setting and thus provide a basis for a deeper faith and appreciation for what God has done throughout history to bring about the fulfillment of his promises" (Hoerth and McRay, 6). Although it purports to examine both Old Testament and New Testament data, its main thrust seems to be towards the former, which is why I have included the McRay text, *Archaeology & the New Testament.*

Bible Archaeology is subtitled *An Exploration of the History and Culture of Early Civilizations.* It begins with a chapter titled "Archaeology and the Bible," which not only defines just what archaeology is; it explains just why the field of study is important to biblical studies. The authors write, "Archaeology is especially valuable in supplying information about objects, places, and activities for which no historical data exist" (Hoerth and McRay, 10). They further explain, "Biblical archaeology is a scientific discipline, which, when properly employed, can contribute to the placement of the Old and New Testament narratives in their correct historical and cultural settings for more accurate interpretation of the biblical text" (Hoerth and McRay, 11).

The next eight chapters cover in order the following topics: Mesopotamia and the Bible, Egypt and the Bible, Palestine and the Bible: Old Testament, Persia and the Bible: New Testament, Anatolia and the Bible, Greece and the Bible, and Italy and the Bible. This book is an informative and engaging basic introduction to the field of biblical archaeology written in such a way that the non-specialist can benefit greatly from reading. The accompanying full-color maps, photographs, and diagrams walk the reader through important archaeological digs and helps make those places come alive for the reader and place them in their historical context. This is the one book to read if you want to walk vicariously in the sandals of such biblical figures as Abraham and Moses, and Jesus and his disciples including the Apostle Paul.

Archaeology & the New Testament builds upon the foundation *Bible Archaeology* lays and provides the reader with a fuller examination of how archaeology fits in with the New Testament. Whereas the Hoerth and McRay text attempted to cover both testaments within the compass of about 280 pages, *Archaeology & the New Testament* is much more comprehensive at roughly 375 pages. Here McRay demonstrates the influence of society, architecture, and religion on the people of the first century. He begins, much as his Old Testament book along with Hoerth did, with an introduction that surveys the role and method of archaeological excavation. After noting some of the contributions that archaeological investigations have made to the study of the New Testament, he then briefly discusses how modern technology such as magnetometers and infrared photography are useful in locating sites underground and how computers now aid in the analysis of data. He then walks the reader through the basic method of excavation and how materials are dated.

McRay then discusses the architecture of New Testament times. His extremely informative and fascinating presentation gives equal time to city layouts and civic structures as well as to religious and domestic structures. The next section demonstrates the large amount of evidence pertaining to Herod the Great. Of particular interest to the Christian reader would be the Temple Mount and the areas around the Temple, the judgment pavement of Pilate, and the water supply.

The final two sections discuss in great detail archaeology and the life of Christ and how it all applies to the early Church. Galilee and Judea are covered with respect to the movements of Jesus through those areas with added discussions about the cities of Eastern and Central Asia Minor, cities in Western Asia Minor, Macedonian cities and Athens, and Corinth and Rome and how they relate to the Apostle Paul. The reader is able to tour archaeological sites associated with the ministry of Jesus, the journeys of Paul, and the seven churches of the book of Revelation.

This book is a veritable feast of information that includes numerous helpful diagrams, maps, and charts as well as 150 photographs. A very helpful glossary can be found at the back of the book that defines technical terms so as not to bog down the reader in details. Under McRay's expert tutelage, the life and times of Jesus and the Apostle Paul come alive for the reader of the New Testament.

The authors of these two books are highly respected in their respective areas of expertise. Alfred Hoerth taught at Wheaton College for over thirty years where he was director of archaeology. John McRay also taught at Wheaton and is professor emeritus of New Testament and archaeology at the Wheaton Graduate School.

46. FOXE'S BOOK OF MARTYRS

By John Foxe

Foxe's Book of Martyrs is the popular title for *Actes and Monuments of these Latter and Perilous Days, Touching Matters of the Church*. It is a Protestant account of the history of martyrs by the English historian John Foxe. The book was first published in 1563 by the press of John Day. It purported to tell the story of Christian martyrs throughout Western history, but mainly provided a very biased account of the suffering of Protestants in England and Scotland under the Roman Catholic Church. Thus, it was highly incendiary and quite influential in its time and helped form perceptions of Catholicism in those countries. It was widely distributed and read particularly by the English Puritans and helped shape British opinion for centuries. The book's title is well-known, but it is little read today.

The Book was published during the reign of Queen Elizabeth I five years after the death of the Roman Catholic Queen Mary I and details the period of religious conflict between the Church of England and the Roman Catholic Church. Foxe's work was instrumental in turning the tide of popular opinion against the latter in favor of the former as a viable entity and not simply a modern cult religion.

John Foxe (or Fox) was born in Lincolnshire in 1517, where his parents were said to have provided a stable home despite the loss of his father at an early age. His mother soon remarried and he remained in his parent's home. He was very studious and was said to have read the Greek and Latin Church Fathers by the time he turned thirteen and was apparently very competent in the Classical Hebrew of the Old Testament. He entered Brasenose College, Oxford, when he was about sixteen years of age and then Magdalen College the next year in 1535. After graduating with a bachelor's degree in 1537 and a master's degree in 1543, he lectured in logic. He must have been a junior instructor until he received the latter degree. Foxe resigned from his college in 1545 after becoming a Protestant rather than take the obligatory holy orders. The primary reason for his resignation was his opposition to the vow of celibacy, which all priests had to make. He regarded clerical celibacy as "self-castration" and was bitterly opposed. Thus, ended his promising career as an academic. But his opposition to the Roman Catholic Church would fuel his writing and the publication of *Book of Martyrs*.

The book went through four editions during the lifetime of John Foxe. The first edition was beautifully illustrated with sixty woodcut drawings and was at that time the largest publishing venture in England's history, surpassing that of even the Bible. Of course, this was still several decades before the publication of the famous Authorized Version to which King James I had his name affixed. The 1570 edition was published in two volumes with 150 woodcuts. One woodcut is of William Tyndale, just before being strangled and burned at the stake, who cries out, "Lord, open the king of England's eyes!" That second edition was vehemently attacked by Roman Catholics who claimed that it was full of falsehoods. Interestingly, the second edition attempted to delete the inaccuracies of the first and refute the charges brought against it resulting in a book that was nearly twice the size of the original.

When Mary I became Queen of England in 1553, the situation became untenable for Foxe. Eventually, he moved to Frankfurt in Germany and then to Basel in Switzerland. He received reports from England about the ongoing religious persecution in his native country. He finally returned home after the death of Bloody Mary in 1558. Upon his return, Foxe became acquainted with John Day, the printer. He was ordained a priest by the Bishop of London, but he had Puritan leanings and refused to wear clerical vestments. No doubt the persecutions were not far from anyone's mind.

Foxe begins his book with a history of Christian martyrs to the first persecutions under Nero. In this opening chapter, he details the martyrdom of Stephen, the crucifixions of Phillip, Jude the brother of James, Peter, Simon, and Andrew. Thomas was supposedly "thrust through with a spear." Luke was reportedly hanged on an olive tree.

Foxe then chronicles the ten persecutions under Nero, Domitian Trajan, Marcus Aurelius, Severus, Maximus, Decius, Valerian, Aurelian, and finally Diocletian in A.D. 303. He informs us that the persecutions under Diocletian, for example, lasted ten years and were widespread against all Christians. Foxe writes, "It is impossible to ascertain the numbers martyred, or to enumerate the various modes of martyrdom. Racks, scourges, swords, daggers, crosses, poison, and famine were made use of in various parts to dispatch the Christians" (Foxe, 25). Those "lucky" ones who were not killed, "were respited from execution, but though they were not put to death, as much as possible was done to render their lives miserable, many of them having their ears cut off, their noses slit, their right eyes put out, their limbs rendered useless by dreadful dislocations, and their flesh seared in conspicuous places with red-hot irons" (Ibid.).

Before arriving at the Inquisition, Foxe lingers briefly discussing the persecutions of Christians in Persia and the Papal persecutions against the Waldenses in France and the Albigenses. He recounts the St. Bartholomew massacre at Paris in 1572. The edition that I own is a 1926 one edited by William Byron Forbush that includes the 1761 martyrdom of John Calas, a merchant from the city of Toulouse.

The Inquisition depicts the horrors that professed Christians can inflict upon other believers. Even for those who know little of church history, when they hear the word Inquisition, it conjures up ghastly images of saints being burned at the stake. The

Medieval Inquisition was a series of inquisitions in the twelfth and thirteenth centuries established to combat what the Roman Catholic Church considered to be heretical movements particularly in France and Italy. Unfortunately, history repeated itself and there were many inquisitions to follow. As Foxe informs us, "Upon all occasions the inquisitors carry on their processes with the utmost severity and punish those who offend them with the most unparalleled cruelty" (Foxe, 61). The descriptions that Foxe makes of the tortures and executions are sobering.

Foxe focuses mainly on the persecutions in England and Scotland, but he relates outrageous behavior in other countries such as Germany, Italy, Spain, Ireland and the Netherlands. He tells the story of Galileo's near brush with death and the recantation of his scientific theories about the earth and the sun. There is also an entire chapter devoted to the life and persecutions of John Wycliffe. The edition that I own edited by Forbush adds numerous chapters dealing with such topics as the persecutions of John Bunyan, the life of John Wesley, the persecutions and sufferings of the Quakers, and the massacres of 1641 in Ireland.

This is a book that is disturbing and not for the faint of heart. If a movie were made of the *Book of Martyrs*, it would certainly merit at least an R for violence.

Foxes Book of Martyrs is a book that will never die. It is one of the greatest Christian classics and deserves to be read and re-read each generation. It is a gripping and fascinating story that is told with great passion and pathos and recounts a sad history that reads better than fiction. If you read it alongside Bruce Shelley's *Church History in Plain Language*, you will begin to get a more rounded picture of the history of the Christian Church. It has been well said that the blood of the martyrs was the seed of the Church. Unfortunately, we still have martyrs today and that bloody seed is still being nourished in other parts of the world. It is a part of our history that we dare not ignore.

47. CHURCH HISTORY IN PLAIN LANGUAGE

By Bruce Shelley

The September 4, 1974 *Peanuts* cartoon by Charles Shultz begins with Sally sitting at a table with Charlie Brown looking on beginning to write an essay titled "Church History." In the second frame she stops to think about her subject, and then in the third frame, she writes, "When thinking about church history, we have to go back to the very beginning." In the final frame she writes, "Our Pastor was born in 1930." A bemused Charlie Brown looks on.

The late Bruce Shelley, an eminent professor of Church History and Historical Theology at Denver Theological Seminary until his death in 2010, writes, "Many Christians today suffer from historical amnesia. The time between the apostles and their own day is one giant blank" (Shelley, xi). The Bible is full of reminders to the people of God to remember the past. For example, in the Old Testament, Moses relates what Yahweh told him just prior to the Exodus. "On that day tell your son, 'I do this because of what the Lord did for me when I came out of Egypt. And it will be like a sign on your hand and a symbol on your forehead that the Lord brought us out of Egypt with his mighty hand" (Ex. 13:8, 13). "Now these things occurred as examples to keep us from setting our hearts on evil things as they did" (1 Cor. 10:6).

Shelley believes that a good working knowledge of church history is important for believers today. He writes, "As a consequence of our ignorance concerning Christian history, we find believers vulnerable to the appeal of cultists. Some distortion of Christianity is often taken for the real thing" (Shelley, xi). Knowing church history is not a panacea for naiveté, but it can help to guard against a kind of spiritual *hubris*. It can be helpful to know that other Christians faced some of the same problems in the past as we do today.

The Christian story is divided by Shelley into nine great ages of the church. They are: (1) the age of Jesus and the Apostles, (2) the age of Catholic Christianity, (3) the age of the Christian Roman Empire, (4) the Christian Middle Ages, (5) the age of the Reformation, (6) the age of reason and revival, (7) the age of progress, (8) the age of ideologies, and (9) the age of global expansion and relocation.

Church History in Plain Language, first published in 1982, is now in its fourth edition and was revised by R. L. Hatchett, a professor of Theology and Philosophy at Houston Baptist University, to bring it up to date. He includes information on Gnosticism and how that age-old heresy is still relevant today. Shelley's book is very well-written, concise, and really gets to the heart of the matter. What I really like about Shelley's treatment of church history is his easy-to-read style and sense of humor. He writes in such a way that the entire field of study comes alive for the reader. It should easily be the first choice for the lay reader. That is a "no brainer."

Church history is not an easy subject to cover. It is a vast area of study that covers over 2,000 years. Consequently, numerous multi-volume works on the subject have been published over the years, some easier to read than others. One of the finest and better-known works is the magisterial eight-volume *History of the Christian Church* by Philip Schaff. It is well-written and easy to read, but it was written in the nineteenth century. The set that I own is a wonderful reprint published in 1910 by Eerdmans and ends at the Swiss Reformation. This certainly limits its usefulness. One obstacle for the modern reader is that its eight volumes include a whopping 6,848 pages of text alone. I confess to often wading in its waters, but I have never swum its entire length. Hopefully, I will have time left in this life to read it from cover to cover. Another superb work is Kenneth Scott

Latourette's two-volume *A History of Christianity* published in 1953 (revised edition). However, with at least 2,184 pages of text, it is still a handful. Latourette, a professor for many years at the Yale Divinity School, also wrote a highly-regarded seven-volume work, *A History of the Expansion of Christianity.*

It is for good reason that this book has sold over 300,000 copies, which is phenomenal for an academic history book. As the back cover states, "The continuing popularity of this book attests to its success in achieving its purpose—to make church history clear, memorable, and accessible to every reader." Yes, read the books by Schaff and Latourete if you have the time (lots of it) and the inclination, but for a user-friendly one-volume church history, Shelley's book is a clear first choice.

CHAPTER VII:
CHRISTIAN DOCTRINE AND THEOLOGY

I am a firm believer that Christians ought to know something about their faith, why they believe as they do. The study of Christian doctrine and theology helps the believer to do just that. In my 2021 book, *The Layperson's Library: Essential Bible Study Tools for the Man and Woman in the Pew*, I made the case for studying Christian doctrine. I wrote, "Christian doctrine, or systematic theology as the scholars usually refer to it, often has a bad reputation in the church at large. In fact, decades ago, systematic theology was even called 'dogmatics' or 'dogmatic theology.' That may make you smile as you remember someone who was very dogmatic in his theology" (Yost, 250). In fact, systematic theology can be defined as simply 'an attempt to reduce religious truth to an organized system' (Demarest, 1064). As I further note in *Layperson's* Library, "the words 'theology' and 'doctrine' do not occur anywhere in the Bible. Christian doctrine, or systematic theology, is simply a way that theologians use to order God's truth in a way that makes sense. Although many in the church tend to think that the words 'doctrine' and 'theology' are synonyms for boredom, Christians need to know what they believe and why they believe it" (Yost, 250).

The following nine books will go a long way to helping you to understand the whys and wherefores of your beliefs.

48. CHRISTIANITY AND LIBERALISM

By G. Gresham Machen

Do you embrace the orthodox tenets of the Christian faith? Do you believe in the deity of Christ, his death, burial, and bodily resurrection, the Trinity, the inerrancy of Scripture, the substitutionary atonement of Christ, and his second coming? A century ago, these traditional beliefs were under vicious attack by theological liberals. A courageous seminary professor by the name of G. Gresham Machen took a stand against the liberals of his day resulting in the publication of this book.

A century ago, G. Gresham Machen was a lonely voice crying in the wilderness. In the great fundamentalism-liberalism controversy, he became the somewhat reluctant spokesman for the fundamentalist cause even though he didn't like to be referred to as one. He certainly had his differences with many in the movement and didn't adhere to all of their beliefs. What he and the fundamentalists did have in common was an allegiance to the Bible as the Word of God and the historic orthodoxy of the Christian faith. However, Machen had great credibility in the academic world as a graduate and later professor at the prestigious Princeton Theological Seminary. Whereas many in the Fundamentalist movement were considered unsophisticated and backward, Machen was a bona fide intellectual with all the credentials. In any event, *Christianity and Liberalism* caused a backlash of seismic proportions that still reverberates today.

What possible bearing could a book that was published a century ago have on the average Christian reader today well into the twenty-first century? If G. Gresham Machen was writing to combat the theological liberalism of his day, which he also termed "modernism," what application could that have on a new era of church history in which the "modernism" of that century is no longer the "modernism" of today? Machen wrote, "The great redemptive religion which has always been known as Christianity is battling against a totally diverse type of religious belief, which is only the more destructive of the Christian faith because it makes use of traditional Christian terminology" (Machen, 2). Is that not precisely what we are facing in the church today? A new more destructive "Christian" faith using the same terminology and wearing sheep's clothing. In fact, the church which I observe today hardly resembles the church of my youth, much less the one that Machen observed and commented upon.

Machen's stand on the authority of the Word of God and its historic doctrines made him a threat within the Presbyterian church. Machen was a take no prisoners, zero compromise, iconoclast who called for the dismissal of liberals within his own denomination, the United Presbyterian Church in the United States of America. He also led the revolt against modernism at Princeton Theological Seminary which led to the establishment of the Westminster Theological Seminary in Philadelphia in 1929. As the UPCUSA continued to stray from its biblical foundations and its adherence to the Westminster Confession of Faith, he led a group of conservatives out of the church and formed the Orthodox Presbyterian Church in 1936. This led to a further split with a new denomination, the Bible Presbyterian Church, breaking off from the Orthodox Presbyterian Church in 1937 due to the influence of Carl McIntire, J. Oliver Buswell, Allan McRae, and Francis Schaeffer. Machen died on January 1, 1937, at the age of fifty-five, but in his relatively short life, he wielded tremendous influence.

J. Gresham Machen is rightly regarded as the last in the line of great Princeton theologians in the mold of Archibald Alexander, Charles Hodge, and B. B. Warfield. Although not technically a theologian—he was a New Testament scholar—his theological contributions were enormous and he is considered by conservatives as one of the luminaries produced by that seminary.

The theological trends which Machen observed a century ago were, he opines, rooted in naturalism. He rightly understood these trends in naturalism as shaped by the history of the 100 or so years previous to the writing of the book. If anything, the innovations and changes of the past century up until our own time have become even more radical. Can you imagine how the people of the early twentieth century would have reacted to jet airplanes, space travel, men on the Moon, nuclear power and weapons, and the Internet? All of these developments have in some way, directly or indirectly, shaped the theology and praxis of our day. Machen believed that the theological developments of his day were a complete departure from the historic Christian faith. He writes, "Christianity is battling against a totally diverse type of religious belief, which is only the more destructive of the Christian faith because it makes use of traditional Christian terminology" (Machen, 2). Machen believed that this new doctrinal departure was not a variation of the Christian faith, but something else altogether. He explains, "Modern liberalism not only is a different religion from Christianity but belongs in a totally different class of religions" (Machen, 7).

In his chapter titled "Doctrine," Machen immediately sounded the alarm. He saw the differences between the two theological camps as more than technical theological nuances, but as having tremendous implications for the church at large. It was a "grass roots" issue. He writes, "Modern liberalism in the Church, whatever judgment may be passed upon it, is at any rate no longer merely an academic matter. It is no longer a matter of theological seminaries or universities. On the contrary its attack upon the fundamentals of the Christian faith is being carried on vigorously by Sunday-School 'lesson-helps,' by the pulpit, and by the religious press" (Machen, 19). He counters those who would argue that doctrine is unimportant and that it makes no difference in how Christians live their daily lives. He explains, "On the contrary, it makes all the difference in the world. From the beginning, Christianity was certainly a way of life; the salvation from sin appeared not merely in a blessed hope but also in an immediate moral change" (Machen, 47). Machen repudiates those who feel that doctrine is unimportant and cites Martin Luther's example. Luther famously drew the theological lines at the Diet of Worms after which he said, "Here I stand, I cannot do otherwise." Machen concludes, "Indifferentism about doctrine makes no heroes of the faith" (Machen, 51).

Machen hits the high points of the controversy in his subsequent chapters. He writes about God and Man and in doing so attacks the modernist view of the universal fatherhood of God and its corollary, the brotherhood of man. He wonders, "It is very strange how intelligent persons can speak in this way. It is very strange how those who accept only the universal fatherhood of God as the sum and substance of religion can regard themselves as Christians or can appeal to Jesus of Nazareth" (Machen, 59). When the universal fatherhood of God is taught, there is no need for other Christian doctrines such as atonement, sin, repentance, justification, et al. There is no need for a cross in such a religion. Machen was adamant, "The modern doctrine of the universal fatherhood of God is not to be found in the teaching of Jesus" (Machen, 60).

In his chapter titled "The Bible," he sets forth the biblical doctrines of inspiration and inerrancy. The modernists of Machen's day were attacking the authority of Scripture claiming that it was a merely human book and full of errors. Machen countered, "A Bible that is full of error is certainly divine in the modern pantheizing (sic) sense of 'divine,' according to which God is just another name for the course of the world with all its imperfections and all its sin. But the God whom the Christian worships is a God of truth" (Machen, 74-75). He points out that the liberals of his day didn't even believe in the authority of Jesus because they did not trust the veracity of the sayings and works of Jesus. They also denied the miraculous elements of Jesus' ministry such as the virgin birth. Machen concludes, "It is no wonder that liberalism is totally different from Christianity, for the foundation is different. Christianity is founded upon the Bible. It bases upon the Bible both its thinking and its life. Liberalism on the other hand is founded upon the shifting emotions of sinful men" (Machen, 79). The twentieth century saw a plethora of books published supporting the doctrine of biblical inerrancy and documenting what happens when the church departs from it, but Machen said it first and nobody said it better.

In *Christianity and Liberalism* Machen hits the major points of contention between the modern liberalism of his day and the orthodox Christian faith. His logic is incisive and his writing compelling. Over a century ago, much was changing both in society and the church. The Scopes "monkey" trial was world-wide news and the Bible was under attack even by those sup-posedly in the Christian camp. Machen's book was a bugle call rallying the conservative wing of the church to action. It was articulate and well-written and still packs a punch today mainly because not much has changed. The actors and the script may have changed, but the battle is still being fought. Christians owe it to themselves to know what the battle is and where it is being fought. This is a seminal book that defined the battle lines and still deserves to be read today.

49. THE KNOWLEDGE OF THE HOLY

By A. W. Tozer

A. W. Tozer spent thirty years as the pastor of the Southside Alliance Church (Christian and Missionary alliance) in Chicago, but it was not as a pastor or preacher that he made his reputation. It was his writing ministry that left an indelible impression on those who encountered him and he still speaks to generations today. His biographer, David J. Fant, Jr. wrote that "so impressed were people with this man that they applied to him such descriptive terms as oracle, seer, Christian mystic" (Fant, 6). Warren Wiersbe, a Tozer admirer, once wrote that he "functioned as the conscience of evangelicalism at large" (Wiersbe, 163). He was a remarkable man and he left a literary legacy that has been surpassed by only a few.

Tozer correctly begins with God and that we must think rightly about him or the battle is already lost. Therefore, what a person or the Church thinks about God is not inconsequential; it is paramount. He writes, "Without doubt, the mightiest thought the mind can entertain is the thought of God, and the weightiest word in any language is its word for God" (Tozer, 8). Our ideas about God must conform to the reality of what the Scriptures reveal him to be and not something "Buried under the rubbish of conventional religious notions" (Ibid.). Tozer believed that "the Church has surrendered her once lofty concept of God and has substituted for it one so low, so ignoble, as to be utterly unworthy of thinking, worshiping men" (Tozer, 5).

Tozer published this book in 1961. I shudder to think what he would say about the twenty-first century church. His analysis is spot on and prescient and he doesn't spare anyone's feelings. Lest you think that such discussions about God should be limited to theologians confined to their "ivory towers" with zero practical value, Tozer would argue that such is foundational to daily Christian living. He writes:

> "A right conception of God is basic not only to systematic theology but to practical Christian living as well. It is to worship what the foundation is to the temple; where it is inadequate or out of plumb the whole structure must sooner or later collapse. I believe there is scarcely an error in doctrine or a failure in applying Christian ethics that cannot be traced finally to imperfect and ignoble thoughts about God" (Tozer, 8).

If we construct a God in our own image, it will certainly be beneath the dignity of the Most High God. As Tozer concludes, "perverted notions about God soon rot the religion in which they appear" (Tozer, 10). This can be illustrated again and again in the histories of the Israelite nation and the Christian church.

The first attribute that Tozer discusses and the title of the second chapter is "God Incomprehensible." He writes that the feeble efforts of inspired men of God to express the inexpressible "has placed a great strain upon both thought and language" (Tozer, 13). This is seen repeatedly in Scripture when the writer, in order to convey what he sees, employs words such as "likeness," "appearance," and the like. His evaluation of the modern church is scathing in that he says that our conceptualized "God" is "only slightly superior to the gods of Greece and Rome" (Tozer, 15). The conundrum is that we yearn to know a God who cannot be known, to comprehend what is incomprehensible, and touch and taste that which is unapproachable.

Tozer then pauses to define just what an attribute is. He writes, "An attribute of God is whatever God has revealed as being true of Himself" (Tozer, 18). He then muses on the question of how many attributes God has. He concludes his pondering by simply agreeing with Charles Wesley who wrote in his great hymn, *God of a Thousand Attributes*, that "Glorious all and numberless."

The rest of the book is more suggestive than exhaustive. The reader will wish that Tozer had written more. His insights are illuminating, often profound. He briefly discusses the mystery of the Trinity. Then he expounds briefly in turn God's self-existence, his self-sufficiency, his eternality, his infinitude, his immutability, his divine omniscience, his wisdom, his omnipotence, his divine transcendence, and his omnipresence. Tozer dips his toe in the water when we wish he would simply jump in. We get just a taste, but oh, what a taste it is! He concludes with brief chapters on God's faithfulness, goodness, justice, mercy, grace, love, holiness, and sovereignty. If you would like to read a more comprehensive and exhaustive work and are up for the challenge, read Stephen Charnock's 1797 masterpiece, *The Existence and Attributes of God*. At 802 pages, it will keep you busy, but oh so blessed. It is a classic! For those wanting a more distilled version, check out A. W. Pink's *The Attributes of God*. At ninety-two pages, it is much more manageable than Charnock and you will get a different perspective than Tozer.

The Knowledge of the Holy is not, at 124 pages, a long book and each brief chapter can be read in about five-minute increments in your easy chair. I suggest that you read slowly and let Tozer's words sink in. But let me warn you! Reading Tozer is like playing with fire. He may or may not warm your heart, but he will certainly light a fire under you.

50. YOUR GOD IS TOO SMALL

By J. B. Phillips

Too many people go through life with a distorted view of God. According to J. B. Phillips, "The trouble with many people to-day is that they have not found a God big enough for modern needs" (Phillips, 7). He argues that we are crippled by a limited idea of God. This book was published in 1952, the year of my birth. However, in the roughly seven decades since its writing, I have seen God grow smaller and smaller. If Phillips thought that God was small when he wrote this book, he would likely be astonished by how he has shrunk in the intervening years.

John Bertram Phillips was an English Bible scholar, Bible trans-lator, and Anglican clergyman who is perhaps best-known for his landmark translation of the epistles of the New Testament, *Letters to Young Churches*, which was published in 1947. Later he added translations of the gospels, the Acts of the Apostles, and the Book of Revelation, which was compiled into the 1958 publication, *The New Testament in Modern English*. Up until that point, the main alternatives for Protestants who wanted to read the Bible were the *King James Version* and the *Revised Standard Version*. Phillips opened up the pages of the Bible to the average person who wanted to explore the pages of the New Testa-ment. He infused life and freshness into a text that was, for the English reader, full of stilted phraseology and archaic language. He also utilized the paragraph in his translation often ignoring the individual verses of older translations. His rendering of Ro-mans 12:2 has been oft-quoted and is unforgettable, "Don't let the world around you squeeze you into its own mold."

Phillips' purpose in writing this book was twofold. "First to ex-pose the inadequate conceptions of God which still linger unconsciously in many minds, and which prevent our catching a glimpse of the true God, and secondly to suggest ways in which we can find the real God for ourselves" (Phillips, 8-9). In the first half of the book, he discusses about a dozen "Unreal Gods," or misconceptions that people have of God. For example, he talks about God as the resident policeman (conscience), the parental hangover, the grand old man, and meek-and-mild. Of the latter he writes, "Why *mild*? Of all the epithets that could be applied to Christ this seems one of the least appropriate" (Phillips, 27). He explains the prevailing notion behind this view of God. "There will probably linger at the back of his mind an idea that Christ and the Christian religion is a soft and sentimental thing which has nothing to do with the workaday world. For there is no doubt that this particular 'inadequate god.' The mild and soft and sentimental, still exists in many adult minds" (Phillips, 28).

Phillips also describes the God of absolute perfection and how Christians have insisted that such a God requires a standard of 100% obedience. That is not too difficult to swallow as today we hear athletes routinely talking about giving 110% and even 120% in their respective sports. The only problem is that nobody is able to measure up to such lofty standards. Phillips writes, "This one-hundred-per-cent standard is a real menace to Christians of various schools of thought, and has led quite a number of sensitive conscientious people to what is popularly called a 'nervous breakdown.' And it has taken the joy and spontaneity out of the Christian lives on many more who dimly realize that what was meant to be a life of 'perfect freedom' has become an anxious slavery" (Phillips, 30). He explains further. "But the conscientious, sensitive, imaginative person who is somewhat lacking in self-confidence and inclined to introspection, will find one-hundred-per-cent perfection truly terrifying" (Phillips, 31).

Other gods that Phillips describes are the Second-hand God, the grand old man, the heavenly bosom, the pale Galilean, and my favorite, the God in a box. He describes those who adhere to this view of God. "They seem to him to have captured and tamed and trained to their own liking Something that is really far too big ever to be forced into little man-made boxes with neat labels upon them" (Phillips, 37).

The legalist, of course, will always impose the standard as a set of rules to be enforced rather than as a "shining ideal" to be followed. Jesus referred to his yoke as "easy" and his burden "light." Even the Apostle Paul, an anal-retentive saint if there ever was one, wrote that he was pressing toward the mark and had not already attained it.

Then there is the God of perennial grievance. This God has somehow failed in some way its adherents. "The people who feel that God is a Disappointment have not understood the terms on which we inhabit this planet. They are wanting a world in which good is rewarded and evil is punished—as in a well-run kindergarten. They want to see the good man prosper invariably, and the evil man suffer invariably, here and now" (Phillips, 50). As Phillips explains, "Glaring injustices and pointless tragedy will sometimes be quite beyond our control and our understanding" (Ibid.). He concludes, "You cannot worship a Disappointment" (Ibid.).

If it appears that Phillips has spent too much time on the inadequate conceptions of God (about half of the book), he assures us that it was absolutely necessary. He explains:

> "We shall never want to serve God in our real and secret hearts if He looms in our subconscious mind as an arbitrary dictator or a Spoil-sport, or as one who takes advantage of His position to make us poor mortals feel guilty and afraid. We have not only to be impressed by the 'size' and unlimited power of God, we have to be moved to genuine admiration, respect, and affection, if we are ever to worship Him" (Phillips, 63).

Phillips believes:

> "We can never have too big a conception of
> God." He writes, "It is rather to see the
> immensely broad sweep of the Creator's
> activity, the astonishing complexity of His
> mental processes which science laboriously
> uncovers, the vast sea of what we can only call
> 'God' in a small corner of which man lives and
> moves and has his being" (Phillips, 63-64).

Having deconstructed many false conceptions of God, Phillips
in the second part of the book goes on to provide us with a
grand picture of an adequate God. He explains why he takes
this approach. "We shall never want to serve God in our real
and secret hearts if He looms in our subconscious mind as an
arbitrary Dictator or a Spoil-sport, or as one who takes advantage of His position to make us poor mortals feel guilty and
afraid. We have not only to be impressed by the 'size' and un-
limited power of God, we have to be moved to genuine admiration, respect, and affection, if we are ever to worship Him"
(Phillips, 63).

This leads to a question or two. First of all, how big is God?
Second, how does such a big God, and eternal being, make himself known to us. He writes, "There must obviously be an almost unbelievable 'scaling-down' of the 'size' of God to match
the life of the planet" (Phillips, 73). This was accomplished in
the person of Jesus Christ who became a man in the Incarnation and walked upon this earth. Phillips argues, "For complete
dependability, for universal appeal, for a personally guaranteed
authenticity to which all other truth is to be related, God must
do it Himself" (Ibid.). So, Jesus Christ, the second member of
the Godhead, came to earth and lived a perfect life while suffering, being tempted, being hungry and thirsty, being fatigued,
and finally dying the agonizing death of a criminal on a Roman
cross. Jesus Christ invaded our world to show us a true picture
of who God is. As Phillips explains, "Christ's claim to be not

only God but Representative Man has had an almost incredible magnetic power" (Phillips, 109).

That is the God that Phillips describes in this book. "The Character of God is focused in Christ" (Phillips, 117). He lived upon this earth and died a sacrificial death to reconcile sinful man to God. But he also was raised from the dead and lives today. This is a historical fact that ought to have transformative power in our lives. Phillips writes, "It is impossible to exaggerate the importance of the historicity of what is commonly known as the Resurrection. If, after all His claims and promises, Christ had died and merely lived on as a fragrant memory, He could only be revered as an extremely good but profoundly mistaken man. His claims to be God, His claims to be Himself the very principle of Life, would be mere self-delusion" (Phillips, 111).

Such is the true conception of God and the difference between him and the inadequate God of so many today. Perhaps Phillips would lament how small God has become in the minds of so many some seven decades after the publication of this book. How did we get to this point? What is the difference between our modern conceptions of God and the life-transforming God of the early followers of Christ? Again, Phillips is spot on in his analysis.

> "We may here point out the great difference that has come to exist between the Christianity of the early days and that of today. To us it has become a performance, a keeping of rules, while to the men of those days it was, plainly, an invasion of their lives by a new quality of life altogether" (Phillips, 119).

Your God Is Too Small is a book whose title is often quoted even today, but is seldom read. I encourage you to read this wonderful little book and ponder its profound teachings. I recently re-read it and found it to be as fresh today as it was when it was written so many years ago. You owe it to yourself.

51. KNOWING GOD

By J. I. Packer

The most important endeavor in life is knowing God. "In fact," according to J. I. Packer, "it is the most important practical project anyone can engage in. Knowing about God is crucially important for the living of our lives" (Packer, 14). He begins his book using the example of an Amazonian tribesman being flown to London and plopped down in Trafalgar Square without explanation and without teaching him to speak English. That would be cruel. Likewise, we are being "cruel to ourselves if we try to live in this world without knowing about the God whose world it is and who runs it" (Ibid.). Packer explains why,

> "The world becomes a strange, mad, painful place, and life in it a disappointing and unpleasant business for those who do not know about God. Disregard the study of God, and you sentence yourself to stumble and blunder through life blindfolded, as it were, with no sense of direction and no understanding of what surrounds you. This way you can waste your life and lose your soul" (Packer, 14-15).

One of the most memorable television advertising campaigns in the United States was from the late 1970s and early 1980s for the brokerage firm E. F. Hutton. Invariably the commercials would depict people doing the normal everyday things such as attending a dinner party or out jogging or commuting on a train. One person would say to the other, "My broker is E. F. Hutton and E. F. Hutton says..." All of a sudden, the world would come to a crashing halt. People on the other side of the restaurant or at the far end of the train would drop everything and crane their ears to hear what was being said. It was so successful and so well-known that even leadership guru John

257

Maxwell titled his fifth leadership law, "The Law of E. F. Hutton."

Now, having said that, when J. I. Packer says something, I tend to listen very carefully, and so should you. The late J. I. Packer—he died in 2020—was one of the most influential evangelical thinkers of the past half century.

Packer's evangelical roots and the influences that shaped his burgeoning theological mind were the Puritans, in particular John Owen and Richard Baxter. He was also greatly influenced by D. Martyn Lloyd-Jones, the pastor at the historic Westminster Chapel in London. Packer's reputation was established with the 1958 publication of *Fundamentalism and the Word of God*. The Word of God would become the major theme of his writing as it most assuredly is in *Knowing God*.

Packer has long been one of my favorite evangelical writers. He is such an interesting person. He was an unlikely candidate, in my opinion, to become either a theologian or one of the leading spokesmen for the evangelical movement. While studying at Corpus Christi College at Oxford in the forties, he played clarinet in the Oxford Bandits, a jazz band. His early influences were not so much Augustine or John Calvin or Martin Luther as they were King Oliver, Louis Armstrong, Morton Becket, and Willie Gary "Bunk" Johnson. Even after his conversion, he continued to believe that the New Orleans jazz of the 1920s was North America's greatest cultural contribution to emerge in the twentieth century. Later, after his conversion, he decided to forgo his jazz career. Using 1 Corinthians 6:12 as his guide, continuing to play would have been lawful for him, but not expedient. Packer was hugely influential in my life. I went through much the same mental process in deciding to stop playing electric guitar as I began my seminary studies back in the seventies. I thought I was going to be the next Eric Clapton or Jimi Hendrix. I, too, decided it was not expedient for me. In Packer's case, he went on to become one of the foremost evangelical thinkers and writers of the twentieth century and beyond.

Packer deals with many of the attributes of God in this book. Some of the highlights are the chapters outlining his majesty, his wisdom, his love, his grace, and his judgment and wrath.

An essential element of knowing God is an understanding of his majesty. Packer believes that we have lost a sense of the majesty of God. He writes, "That is one reason why our faith is so feeble and our worship so flabby. We are modern men, and modern men, though they cherish great thoughts of man, have as a rule small thoughts of God" (Packer, 73-74). He opines that "we are poles apart from our evangelical forefathers at this point" (Packer, 74). Packer explains, "When you start reading Luther, or Edwards, or Whitefield, though your doctrine may be theirs, you soon find yourself wondering whether you have any acquaintance at all with the mighty God whom they knew so intimately" (Ibid.). Sadly, in the modern emphasis that God is personal, we have lost a vital sense of his majesty.

Packer spends two of the twenty-two chapters of the book on the wisdom of God. He understands wisdom to be "the practical side of moral goodness" (Packer, 80). He returns to the Word of God as the source of wisdom for the believer. He writes:

> "These things were written for our learning: for the same wisdom which ordered the paths God's saints trod in the Bible times orders the Christian's life today. We should not, therefore, be too taken aback when unexpected and upsetting and discouraging things happen to us now. What do they mean? Why, simply that God in His wisdom means to make something of us which we have not attained yet, and is dealing with us accordingly" (Packer, 86).

Packer believes that one of the attributes that man lost in the Fall was wisdom. He writes, "The moral qualities which belonged to the divine image were lost at the Fall; God's image in man has been universally defaced, for all mankind has in one way or another lapsed into ungodliness" (89-90). However, according to Packer, God can repair the damage done by the fall by "communicating these qualities to them afresh" (Packer, 90). The apostle Paul wrote that we are being renewed in the image of Christ (2 Cor. 3:18). One way to do this is to seek wisdom from God. Unfortunately, Packer opines, "It is to be feared that many Christians spend all their lives in too unhumbled and conceited a frame of mind ever to gain wisdom from God at all" (Packer, 91). The book of Proverbs in the Old Testament is classified as Wisdom Literature. Its basic theme is that we should seek wisdom as it contrasts that with the way of the fool. Packer writes, "Wisdom consists in choosing the best means to the best end. God's work of giving wisdom is a means to His chosen end of restoring and perfecting the relationship between Himself and men for which He made them" (Packer, 97).

The apostle John's repeated statement, "God is love," is the subject of one of Packer's chapters. He calls it one of the greatest statements in Scripture, but he also says it is also "one of the most misunderstood." Packer exposes the weak and insipid concepts of God's love many have. He writes, "So the God who is love is first and foremost light, and sentimental ideas of His love as an indulgent, benevolent softness, divorced for moral standards and concerns, must therefore be ruled out from the start. God's love is holy love" (Packer, 110). He explains, "God's love is stern, for it expresses holiness in the lover and seeks holiness for the beloved. Scripture does not allow us to suppose that because God is love we may look to Him to confer happiness on people who will not seek holiness, or to shield His loved ones from trouble when He knows that they need trouble to further their sanctification" (Ibid.). Having dealt with some of the common misconceptions about God's love, Packer then goes on to define just what it is. He says, "God's love is *an exercise of His goodness towards individual sinners whereby, hav-*

ing identified Himself with their welfare, He has given His Son to be their Saviour, and now brings them to know and enjoy Him in a covenant relation" (Packer, 111). Packer says that the love of God was so unique that the writers of the New Testament "had to introduce what was virtually a new Greek word *agape* to express the love of God as they knew it" (Packer, 112).

With respect to the grace of God, Packer contends that the average modern Christian's understanding is superficial at best. He writes, "There do not seem to be many in our churches who actually believe in grace" (Packer, 116). He cites the examples of the apostle Paul and his conflicts with the Judaizers, Augustine and the Pelagians, and Martin Luther and the Reformers. He writes, "But many church people are not like this. They may pay lip-service to the idea of grace, but there they stop. Their conception of grace is not so much debased as non-existent" (Packer, 116-17). Packer lists four crucial truths that form the foundation for the doctrine of grace. He says that because many reject them, "It is not to be wondered at, therefore, that faith in grace is a rarity today" (Packer, 117). They are: "1. The moral ill-desert of man. 2. The retributive justice of God. 3. The spiritual impotence of man. 4. The sovereign freedom of man" (Packer, 117-19). Only when one understands these four truths can the believer begin to grasp the fullness of God's grace.

Commonly misunderstood about God are two aspects of his character that must be considered together: his judgment and his wrath. The two are intimately intertwined and cannot be separated. About God's wrath, Packer writes, "The fact is that the subject of divine wrath has become taboo in modern society, and Christians by and large have accepted the taboo and conditioned themselves never to raise the matter" (Packer, 134). He explains, "The modern habit throughout the Christian church is to play this subject down. Those who still believe in the wrath of God (not all do) say little about it; perhaps they do not think much about it. To an age which has unashamedly sold itself to the gods of greed, pride, sex, and self-will, the Church mumbles on about God's kindness, but says virtually nothing about his judgment" (Ibid.). God's judgment springs logically from his wrath. However, many today tend to downplay the judgment of God. Packer asks the reader whether he believes in divine judgment? To which he replies, "Many, it seems, do not. Speak to them of God as a Father, a friend, a helper, one who loves us despite all our weaknesses and folly and sin, and their faces light up; you are on their wavelength. But speak to them of God as Judge, and they frown and shake their heads. Their minds recoil from such an idea. They find it repellent and unworthy" (Packer, 125). Such is the mindset of modern man. But, as Packer reminds us, "there are few things stressed more strongly in the Bible than the reality of God's work as Judge" (Ibid.). He explains, "The Bible leaves us in no doubt that God loves righteousness and hates iniquity, and that the ideal of a judge wholly identified with what is good and right is perfectly fulfilled in Him" (Packer, 128). The view of God as a benevolent being "without severity is the rule rather than the exception among ordinary folk today" (Packer, 144). Packer is correct in stressing that believers must not ignore God's wrath and his judgment. As he reminds us, "God's wrath in the Bible is always *judicial*" (Packer, 137).

The famous first question of "The Shorter Catechism" of *The Westminster Confession of Faith* asks "What is the chief end of man?" To which it replies, "Man's chief end is to glorify God, and to enjoy him forever." What Packer has done in *Knowing God* is given Christians a user guide to doing just that. There is so much ignorance today about God's character and nature. Packer's book is an important correction to that kind of fuzzy thinking.

52. FOUNDATIONS OF THE CHRISTIAN FAITH

By James Montgomery Boice

It takes a remarkable scholar and preacher to fill the shoes of men such as the famous Presbyterian pastors, Donald Grey Barnhouse, and his successor, Mariano DiGangi. James Montgomery Boice was such a man. Barnhouse actually influenced Boice as a young man by encouraging him to attend the important Christian prep school, Stony Brook. This major educational decision ultimately led to degrees from Harvard University and Princeton Theological Seminary, culminating in a Doctor of Theology degree from the University of Basel in Switzerland. In addition to Barnhouse, Boice was spiritually molded and shaped by such evangelical luminaries as Carl Henry and Frank Gaebelein. In 1968, the circle was complete when Boice became the senior pastor at the historic Tenth Presbyterian Church in Philadelphia, the very same church where Barnhouse served for so many years. He ministered there until his untimely death in 2000.

In addition to being the pastor for over thirty years at one of the most influential Presbyterian churches in the United States and the voice of *The Bible Study Hour* radio broadcast, Boice was also a prolific scholar and writer and an important voice in the evangelical world. He, along with such notable figures such as John Gerstner, J. I. Packer, R. C. Sproul, Norman Geisler, Greg Bahnsen, and J. Barton Payne, was instrumental in launching the International Council on Biblical Inerrancy (ICBI). The authority of Scripture was a main focus of his ministry. The ICBI wrote three creedal documents, published books, conducted "Authority of Scripture" seminars, and sponsored the lay "Congress of the Bible I," which met in Washington, D.C., in September 1987.

Foundations of the Christian Faith is a comprehensive and readable theology of the Christian faith. It is a long book at just
over 700 pages, but it is easy reading. Originally it was published in four separate volumes: *The Sovereign* God, *God the Redeemer, Awakening to* God, and *God & History*. I commend InterVarsity Press for its decision to collect all four books into
one handy volume.

The first section of the book, "The Sovereign God," begins with
"The Knowledge of God" and covers important topics such as
the Word of God, his attributes, and his creation. The second
section, "God the Redeemer," covers the fall of man and God's
provision for sin, Jesus Christ. Within the compass of just 100
pages, Boice deftly provides a beautiful summarization of the
person and work of Christ, a complete course in Christology.
The third section, "Awakening to God," walks the reader step
by step through the Holy Spirit, how God saves sinners, the life
of the Christian, and the work of God in salvation. The final
section, "God and History," is very important for our understanding. I love how Boice introduces his discussion of time
and history. He asks the question, "What's wrong with me?"
Then he smoothly transitions to "Christ, the focal point of history," and the Church of God. His discussion titled "A Tale of
Two Cities" will be immediately recognized by anyone who
has read the Dickens classic, but his topic is not the French
Revolution. His subject matter will spark the interest of anyone
who is familiar with Augustine's *The City of God* because that
is his focus here: the secular city, the secular church, God's city,
and church and state. How timely! Finally, Boice concludes his
magnum opus with a brief discussion of the end of history. I
love how he invites the reader with his title "How will it all
end?" Certainly, we all want to know the answer to that question.

Boice published over fifty books during his lifetime, including
a collection of hymns. By all means, don't limit your reading to
Foundations of the Christian Faith. Once you have a taste for the
simple and clear writing style of this exceptional man of God,

you likely will want to read further. Some of the books you might want to explore include *Parables of Jesus, Christ's Call to Discipleship, Renewing Your Mind in a Mindless World: Learning to Think and Act Biblically,* and *Ordinary Men Called by God: A Study of Abraham, Moses, and David.* He also published numerous expositional commentaries that are very accessible to a lay audience. Some of my favorites are his studies on the Minor Prophets, the Sermon on the Mount, the Gospel and Epistles of John, and Romans.

Foundations of the Christian Faith is not the kind of book that you take to the beach for some light reading. It is not heavy reading, mind you, but the subject matter is very serious. If I were to read this book again, I would begin at the first section, "The Knowledge of God," and read a chapter a day and in no time at all I would be through the book and in the process, I would have finished a complete course in systematic theology—almost painlessly. Then you will have a reference book that you can consult time and time again when you are researching a topic or even if you simply have a question about the afterlife or some other subject. In my academic and personal life, I have read many books about Christian doctrine. This is the best one-volume summarization of the subject that I have ever seen, and believe me, I have read most of the standard works on the subject. Do yourself a favor and jump in. The water is fine.

53. THE HOLINESS OF GOD

&

54. CHOSEN BY GOD

&

55. EVERYONE'S A THEOLOGIAN

By R. C. Sproul

The late R. C. Sproul has for a long time been one of my theological heroes. He had the wonderful gift of being able to distill complex theological topics and make them understandable to the average person. If there were such a thing as *An Idiot's Guide to Christian Doctrine*, R. C. Sproul would most assuredly have been the author. The fact that I am recommending that you read three of his books speaks to the fact that I highly respect his writings. I could have easily included another half dozen.

A personal note: I heard him preach in person back in the 1980s when I was a Presbyterian pastor attending my denomination's annual business meetings. He spoke on 1 Samuel 5 about the ark in Dagon's temple after it had been captured by the Philistines. I never forgot that sermon. Sproul has always reminded me of the television character Columbo. He always struck me as a bit disheveled, but always the smartest guy in the room. "Oh, one more thing!" He was hugely influential in my life as a Presbyterian pastor and later as a seminary professor and academic dean as well as to countless others.

Sproul was greatly influenced by John Gerstner while pursuing his theological studies at Pittsburgh Theological Seminary. Gerstner, professor of Church History at Pittsburgh and an expert on the life and theology of Jonathan Edwards, was the resident conservative at a very liberal institution and something of an iconoclast. Gerstner's formative influence helped shape the direction that Sproul's ministry would take. After graduation from seminary, Sproul taught himself the Dutch language and completed his doctoral studies in theology in 1969 at the Free University of Amsterdam where he studied under the esteemed theologian G. C. Berkouwer. Aside from the more than 100 books that he wrote, Sproul is perhaps best known as the founder of the Ligonier Valley Study Center in western Pennsylvania, which is now known as Ligonier Ministries and is located just outside of Orlando, FL. Throughout his ministry, Sproul has been a staunch defender of the Calvinistic approach to theology as well as biblical inerrancy and has stressed the sovereignty of God as well as his holiness.

With the publication of *The Holiness of God* in 1985, Sproul began to become a household name among evangelicals outside of Presbyterian and Reformed circles. It has been called a modern classic by some. Sproul believed that the holiness of God was being downplayed by many in the world of evangelicalism and that other "priorities" such as evangelism, or social action, or spiritual nurture were receiving top billing. Sproul wrote, "How we understand the person and character of God the Father affects every aspect of our lives" (*Holiness*, 25). He felt that Christians really had no idea just what the holiness of God meant. He wrote, "When the word *holy* is applied to God, it does not signify one single attribute. On the contrary, God is called holy in a general sense. The word is used as a synonym for his deity. That is the word *holy* calls attention to all that God is. It reminds us that his love is holy love, his justice is holy justice, his mercy is holy mercy, his knowledge is holy knowledge his spirit is holy spirit" (*Holiness*, 57). It also suggested the transcendence of God. "When we speak of the transcendence of God, we are talking about a sense in which God is above and beyond us" (*Holiness*, 55).

My favorite chapter in *The Holiness of God* is titled "The Insanity of Luther." Martin Luther was so obsessed with God's holiness and so fixated on his own personal failures that he spent literally hours every day in confession. Confession was a requirement for all monks, but not every day. Luther once spent six hours confessing his sins, which drove his Father Confessor to distraction. Although Luther certainly went overboard with his obsession with sin and confession, he probably had a better grasp on the holiness of God than most of us do. Sproul wrote, "He (God) is concerned about our deepest motivations. For a good deed to pass the standard of God's goodness it must flow out of a heart that loves God perfectly and loves our neighbor perfectly as well. Since none of us achieves that perfect love for God and our neighbor, all of our outwardly good deeds are tarnished. They carry the blemish of the imperfections of our inner motivations" (*Holiness*, 120-21).

Many of my readers are able to remember the 1967 self-help bestseller by psychiatrist Thomas Anthony Harris, *I'm OK, You're OK*. It was hawked as a practical guide to transactional analysis as a method for solving life's problems. Sproul wrote *The Holiness of God* to reiterate the message that I'm not OK, and you are not OK. We are sinners and we offend the holiness of God. He writes, "The most mysterious aspect of the mystery of sin is not that the sinner deserves to die, but rather that the sinner in the average situation continues to exist. . . . The issue is not why does God punish sin, but why does He permit the ongoing rebellion of man" (*Holiness*, 153). The answer as Sproul explains it is that God is patient, forbearing, and gracious. However, as he warns us, "We experience the grace of an infinite God, but grace is not infinite. God sets limits to His patience and forbearance. He warns us over and over again that someday the ax will fall and his judgment will be poured out" (*Holiness*, 168). That is a message that the world sorely needs to hear.

Another important book by Sproul is his 1986 follow-up to *The Holiness of God* titled *Chosen By God*. It is basically a primer on the biblical doctrine of predestination. Predestination is perhaps the most controversial doctrine in the Bible and has spurred endless arguments on the one hand. On the other hand, it is a doctrine that some people just don't want to talk about. As Sproul writes, "It is linked to despairing notions of fatalism and somehow suggests that within its pale we are reduced to meaningless puppets. The word conjures up visions of a diabolical deity who plays capricious games with our lives" (*Chosen* 9). The controversy in a nutshell is predestination versus free will. Sproul comes down convincingly on the side of predestination, which he identifies as the Reformed or Calvinistic view.

Sproul expertly walks the reader through the controversy in a clear, engaging fashion. He identifies well known scholars and Christian leaders on both sides of the issue. He explains that the doctrine is logically connected with the doctrine of the sovereignty of God. He writes, "From the mass of guilty humanity, God sovereignly decides to give mercy to some of them. What do the rest get? They get justice. The saved get mercy and the unsaved get justice" (*Chosen*, 37-38). Sproul argues, "If human freedom and divine sovereignty are real contradictions, then one of them, at least, has to go. If sovereignty excludes freedom and freedom excludes sovereignty, then either God is not sovereign or man is not free" (*Chosen*, 41). He solves the conundrum by providing an alternative that makes perfect sense. He says, "We can keep both sovereignty and freedom if we can show that they are not contradictory" (Ibid.). He then goes on to argue that the confusion comes down to the misconception most people have when they think of free will. It is not free will that is negated by sovereignty; it is autonomy. He writes, "At a human level we readily see that people can enjoy a real measure of freedom in a land ruled by a sovereign monarch. It is not freedom that is canceled out by sovereignty; it is *autonomy* that cannot coexist with sovereignty" (Ibid.).

It is clear that the controversy over predestination and free will is an apparent paradox. It is one of those mysteries, of which there are many, in Scripture. Both cannot be correct, can they? Or is the problem with our limited human perspective? Some of Sproul's chapter titles are "Foreknowledge and Predestination," "Double, Double, Toil and Trouble: Is Predestination Double?" and "Can We Know that We Are Saved?" He concludes with a helpful chapter in which he answers questions and precludes objections.

Chosen By God is an intelligent, convincing discussion about an issue that has raged for centuries and is not going away. Sproul is a master at breaking down difficult theological concepts into their component parts. Predestination is a biblical doctrine that is denied by some, misunderstood by many, and called demonic by a very few. Read this book to discover why notables such as Billy Graham, C. S. Lewis, and Francis Schaeffer had different views on the subject. It is by far the best book that I have ever read about a difficult, often confusing subject. See for yourself. For those whose interest in the topic is piqued, read the author's *Willing to Believe: The Controversy over Free Will.*

Everyone's A Theologian is Sproul's introduction to systematic theology. It is a brief and concise, but still comprehensive, summary of the subject that makes theology real and vital for the average person. Without dumbing it down, he makes it simple and approachable for just about anybody. Sproul himself admits that many people "are comfortable with the word *theology* but cringe when they hear the qualifying term *systematic*" (*Theologian*, 4-5). He gives the purpose for this helpful volume, "As I engage in systematic theology, I never cease to be amazed by the specific, intricate coherence of the scope of divine revelation. Systematic theologians understand that each point in theology addresses every other point. When God speaks, every detail He utters has an impact on every other detail. That is why our ongoing task is to see how all the pieces fit together into an organic, meaningful, and consistent whole" (*Theologian*, 7).

If you have ever reacted negatively to the word "theology," this book is for you. Guess what? If you are a Christian, like it or not, you are a theologian. Hence the title, *Everyone's A Theologian*. Theology is exciting and this book is anything but a dull, dry survey of the field. Read it and discover for yourself.

56. THE CHALLENGE OF THE CULTS AND NEW RELIGIONS

By Ron Rhodes

It is often difficult to define just what a cult is. For example, is Seventh Day Adventism a cult? Some in the evangelical world say yes and some say no. How about Jews for Jesus? The Jewish community certainly considers them a dangerous cult. As you can see, whether a movement is a cult or not depends much upon one's perspective, but it also depends upon the criteria one is using.

According to Ron Rhodes, "Prior to 1850, cultists were practically unheard of in America" (Rhodes, 14). He estimated back in 2001 when *The Challenge of the Cults and New Religions* was published that "there are well over twenty million Americans involved in the cults and the occult" (Ibid.). That incredible figure is just for America; it doesn't include Canada, Europe, and other parts of the world. What is clear is that membership in cults is growing and they are flourishing.

In the twentieth century there was a proliferation of books published on the subject of cults. Some were good and some not so good. Probably the definitive work on cults in the twentieth century was Walter R. Martin's *The Kingdom of the Cults*, which was published in 1965. Martin defined a cult as "any religious group which differs significantly, in some one or more respects as to belief or practice, from those religious groups which are regarded as the normative expressions of religion in our total culture." Martin included chapters on Unitarian Universalism, Christian Science, the Church of Jesus Christ of Latter-Day Saints (Mormons), Seventh Day Adventism, Jehovah's Witnesses, the Bahai Faith, Black Muslims, Scientology, and Armstrongism, in addition to some minor groups including various New Age groups and those based on Eastern religions. He concluded that although the Seventh Day Adventists exhibited some cultlike appearances, their core beliefs fit within the mold of historic Christianity. It is usually considered to be a classic in the field and is in its sixth updated edition as of 2019.

Although Martin's book is a quite useful tools for those who encounter the cults, since the publication of this book, the perception of cults has become increasingly negative. In Martin's listing of cults were some groups who have made valuable contributions to society such as the Unitarians. Towards the end of the twentieth century, cults have generally been viewed negatively with socially deviant beliefs and practices often revolving around a charismatic leader who lures impressionable youths into their group. Extreme examples of this would be Jim Jones of the People's Temple and David Koresh of the Branch Davidians.

Much has changed since Martin wrote in the 1960s. Ron Rhodes deplores several trends that have swept across America's religious landscape over the final decades of the twentieth century. He sees "rapidly eroding spiritual foundations, with a huge percentage of the public rejecting any concept of absolute truth" and "a majority of people holding to moral relativism" (Ibid.). In the church, he says, there are "a significant number of impotent and lifeless Christian churches that have produced indifference, lack of commitment, spiritual dryness, doctrinal immaturity, and biblical illiteracy among members, thus rendering them open to seeking out other religious groups" (Rhodes, 14-15). Along with that, there is a crisis among the youth of our country with a "shifted family structure, with many children growing up in single-parent households" (Rhodes, 15) and "a pervasive disillusionment and lack of direction among many of America's youth, rendering them vulnerable to cultic leaders" (Ibid.). They are particularly open to being led into the psychological bondage that cults offer.

I included *The Challenge of the Cults and New Religions* in my list of 100 books that are must-reading because the cults are so prevalent and they are rapidly growing. The average cultist is much more aggressively evangelistic than the average garden variety Christian. That is one reason that membership in the cults is increasing. What do you say when a pair of Jehovah's Witnesses knock on your front door? Do you know what to say to them? Do you simply refuse to answer the door as so many do? Or do you have a trap door that you pull leading down to a pit of hungry alligators? That might work very well, but it is not very Christlike. The subtitle of Rhodes' book is *The Essential Guide to Their History, Their Doctrine, and Our Response.* It is imperative that Christian know about the cults and how to respond to them. That is what Rhodes does very well. He not only tells us their history and what they believe, he tells us how to challenge their belief systems.

Rhodes begins his book with chapters titled "Defining Cults" and "Defining Cultic Growth." He then includes chapters on the Church of Jesus Christ of Latter-day Saints, Jehovah's Witnesses, the Mind Sciences, the New Age Movement, the Church of Scientology, Hindu-Based Cults, the Unification Church, The Baha'i Faith, Unitarian Universalism, Oneness Pentecostalism, Freemasonry, and Satanism.

The chances are good that you have encountered someone in a cult or know someone involved in a cult. Do you know what the differences are between their cult beliefs and orthodox Christian beliefs? This book is an excellent, essential resource for all Christians unless you live in an enclosed bubble or live in a cave isolated in the dessert. Rhodes writes in an engaging and compelling manner. It should be on every believer's bookshelf.

CHAPTER VIII:
DAILY DEVOTIONAL AND
PRAYER

DAILY DEVOTIONAL

Many Christians use a daily devotional guide alongside their everyday Bible reading. There are many excellent ones available. What they all share in common is a basic theme for the day, a Scripture reading, and a brief thought-provoking devotional message. Over the years I have explored many of the better-known guides such as L. B. Cowman's *Streams in the Desert*, Charles Spurgeon's *Morning and Evening*, Warren Wiersbe's *Giants Step: Daily Devotions from Spiritual Giants of the Past*, and Sarah's Young's *Jesus Always: Embracing Joy in His Presence*. Frankly, I recommend all of them. But my two "must reads" are the classic by Oswald Chambers, *My Utmost for His Highest*, and one that is a bit different by Eugene Peterson, *Praying with the Psalms*. Both are wonderful.

57. MY UTMOST FOR HIS HIGHEST

By Oswald Chambers

For about the last quarter century, I have read this book cover to cover every year. I can truthfully say that with the exception of the Bible, this book has had the most profound impact upon my spiritual life. Every year that I read it, I find new insights and truths that touch me in different ways. In the past, I have used many daily devotional guides such as those by Spurgeon, Cowman, Piper, and Wiersbe from time to time, but I always come back to this classic. It has become the best-selling devotional work of all time.

My Utmost for His Highest contains brief daily devotional readings for every day of the year. The readings always follow a verse or partial verse of Scripture. The book was originally published posthumously in 1933 by the author's wife from a compilation of his preaching and teaching to students and soldiers. Most of the teachings contained in this book were initially shared with students as lectures at the Bible Training College in Clapham, England, from 1911 to 1915. Additional material came from devotional talks given during World War I to soldiers guarding the Suez Canal while he was serving with the Y.M.C.A. in Zeitoun, Egypt. Chambers died suddenly after a bout of appendicitis in 1917 at the age of forty-three, but his wife, Bibby, didn't begin to compile the shorthand notes from his talks until 1924. It is said that Chambers refused to go to a hospital on the grounds that the beds would be needed by men wounded in battle. He was buried with full military honors in Cairo.

Chambers was born to Christian parents in 1874 in Aberdeen, Scotland. His father was in full-time vocational Christian service which led to the family moving from place to place. His travels with his family took him to different locales in Scotland before the family moved to London in 1889. As a teenager he was known for his mature spirituality and for his great aptitude in music and art. He studied at the National Art Training School (now the Royal College of Art) from 1893 to 1895. He continued his studies in art at the University of Edinburgh where he came under the influence of the great preacher, Alexander Whyte, the pastor of Free St. George's Church. Whyte is probably best-known for his magisterial six-volume *Bible Characters* (See Chapter IV). Chambers felt the call to ministry while in Edinburgh which led him to Dunoon College near Glasgow. It wasn't long before Chambers was teaching classes at the college and working in administration. In 1911 Chambers founded the Bible Training College in Clapham Common near London, which proved to be fertile ground for much of the material contained in *My Utmost for His Highest*. The Bible Training College was open to anyone wanting to serve the Lord Jesus Christ regardless of economic resources. It is said that nobody went away empty-handed whether in need of money, food, or clothing. Chambers is one of my spiritual heroes. He occupies a place high in the pantheon of spiritual giants.

Following are some of my favorite nuggets from the book.

> "The lasting value of our public service for God is measured by the depth of the intimacy of our private times of fellowship and oneness with Him" (January 6).

> "A warning which needs to be repeated is that 'the cares of this world and the deceitfulness of riches,' and the lust for other things, will choke out the life of God in us" (January 27).

> "The resounding evidence of the Holy Spirit in a person's life is the unmistakable family likeness

to Jesus Christ, and the freedom from everything which is not like Him" (February 8).

"Drudgery is one of the finest tests to determine the genuineness of our character" (February 19).

"If a child gives in to selfishness, he will find it the most enslaving tyranny on earth" (March 14).

"To be unspiritual means that other things have a growing fascination for you" (April 2).

"The good is always the enemy of the best" (May 25).

"Crises always reveal a person's true character" (September 10).

"It is piercing to realize that God not only knows where we live, but also knows the gutters into which we crawl" (October 4).

My suggestion is that you use the updated edition edited by James Reimann and published by Discovery House Publishers in 1992. All of my quotations are taken from this edition. Because the English language is in a state of constant flux, there was a need for an updated edition which would reflect some of the linguistic changes over the last century or so. Reimann has taken great care to convey the essential message of Oswald Chambers while making it more readable and easily understood. I began reading Chambers in the original version, but switched to Reimann's edition about fifteen years ago and find it exceedingly easy-to-understand. He has also given the same updating treatment to Spurgeon's two classics, *Morning by Morning* and *Evening by Evening*, as well as Cowman's *Streams in the Desert*. You can't go wrong using any of these books along with your daily Bible reading. But you owe it to yourself to read and reread *My Utmost for His Highest*.

58. PRAYING WITH THE PSALMS

By Eugene H. Peterson

According to Eugene Peterson, everybody prays after a fashion. He contends in the Introduction to this book, "It's our most human action. At the deep center of our lives, we are connected somehow or other with God." That deep center may often get buried under the hustle and bustle and endless debris of our daily lives, but it is always there. As Peterson explains, "We pray because it is our most human response. We're made by and for the voice of God—listening to and answering that voice is our most characteristic act. We are most ourselves when we pray" (Introduction).

For some reason or a variety of reasons, I have somehow missed the obvious connection between prayer and the Psalter. Oh yes, I knew that David often cried out to the Lord in praise, confession, and supplication, but I never made the connection that I should also be praying the Psalms. I have to admit that at times I am a bit dense and need to be hit over the head with a sledgehammer. *Praying with the Psalms* was that sledgehammer for me. Dietrich Bonhoeffer introduced me to the concept of praying the Psalms, but Eugene Peterson has become my muse. In his wonderful book, *A Long Obedience in the Same Direction* (see Chapter X), Peterson opines, "I knew that following Jesus could never develop into a 'long obedience' without a deepening life of prayer and that the Psalms had always been the primary means by which Christians learned to pray everything they lived, and live everything they prayed over the long haul" (Peterson, *Long Obedience*, 12).

Peterson was puzzled because the Christians around him didn't pray the Psalms. He asked himself, "Christians have always

prayed the Psalms; why didn't my friends and neighbors"
(Ibid.)? He concluded that the language, or phraseology, ca-
denced and beautiful and harmonious, seemed remote from
their jerky and messy and discordant everyday lives" (Ibid.). He
decided to "translate them from their Hebrew original and convey the raw, rough, and robust energy that is so characteristic
of these prayers (Ibid.). The result can be seen in *Praying with
the Psalms* as well as in his wonderful translation *The Message:
The Bible in Contemporary Language*.

In *Praying with the Psalms*, that is exactly what Peterson does.
He provides a fresh translation of a brief section of the Psalter.
He begins with a title and a scriptural reading from the Psalms.
There is an entry for each day of the year. Peterson then provides a translation of one or two of the verses from that day's
reading along with a brief two or three sentence exposition. He
then concludes with a prayer based upon that psalm.

The late Eugene Peterson is the perfect guide to our explo-
rations in praying the Psalms. Who better to walk alongside us
as we learn to use the Psalms of the Old Testament as our
model for prayer and to meditating on the words of David? Peterson was a beloved Presbyterian pastor in Bel Air, Maryland
for twenty-nine years. But he was best -known for *The Message*
as well as the more than thirty books published in his lifetime.
He was a true scholar with a pastor's heart. He earned a Master
of Arts degree in Semitic languages from Johns Hopkins University and demonstrated that scholarly bent in all of his writings. This wonderful little book is one of the fruits of those
labors.

Peterson suggests that we use his book as an "entrance into
praying the psalms." He writes, "The focused meditation and
prayer is an opening into a large interior. Step briskly through
the entrance and then take your time. Settle into the spacious
interior. Make yourself at home in the psalm. Once inside there
is so much more to listen to, so much more to say" (Introduction). By doing this, he explains, "That is why praying with

David is the chief way we have of cultivating fluency in this our most human language" (Introduction). I would suggest that you read and re-read this book. It certainly bears reading over and over again. But first, step into the vestibule and make your way into the interior.

An example of a daily reading is the one from January 24 titled "The Earth Reeled and Rocked." The reading is from Psalm 18:7-15 and includes his translation of verse 7.

> "Then the earth reeled and rocked;
>> The foundations also of the mountains trembled
>> And quaked, because he was angry."

His comments on the passage: "Earthquake, thunder lightening, volcanic eruptions—sudden, violent dislocations of nature's routine—are images of the God who is tremendously active beneath the surface of casually observed life."

His prayer for that day:

> "Lord, in my little faith, I try to reduce you to a convenient size and harness your attributes to my requirements. I need your thundering word to lay the foundation of my world bare so I can see that you are not a convenience to use, but the very rock on which I stand. Amen."

Another example is from March 26 titled "I Am Sorry for My Sin" using Psalm 38:15-22 as its starting point.

> "For I am ready to fall,
>> And my pain is ever with me.
> I confess my iniquity;
>> I am sorry for my sin."

His comments on the passage: "Sin frequently sets off an inordinate amount of excuse-making and blaming of others. But not here. In this prayer I learn to accept responsibility for my own sin (see v. 5), make an honest confession, and then look to God for deliverance."

His prayer for that day: "O Lord, the next time I look for someone else to blame for the troubles my own sins have caused, recall to me the words of this psalm. Help me bravely to acknowledge my faults, submit myself to your judgments and hope in your grace, through Jesus Christ my Lord and Savior. Amen."

From these two examples, I hope you can see how this little book can be your entryway into the world of praying the Psalms. Peterson is both simple and yet profound. Read it and see if you agree.

PRAYER

As the United States Senate Chaplain, Peter Marshall, once prayed before that august body of legislators, "If we are too busy to pray, we are far busier than we have any right to be." Prayer is universally recognized by Christians as an essential component of the spiritual life. In my 2021 book, *The Layperson's Library: Essential Bible Study Tools for the Man and Woman in the Pew*, I wrote, "If reading God's Word is like eating for the Christ follower, then prayer is like breathing. Unfortunately, prayer is more discussed than actually practiced. What is even worse is that when it is practiced, it is often practiced incorrectly and selfishly" (Yost, 218). John Calvin referred to prayer as "the soul of faith." A life that is biblically-based and evangelical will always be nurtured by prayer. It is an absolutely necessary component of the Christian life.

In his classic daily devotional, *My Utmost for His Highest*, Oswald Chambers has a great deal to say about the subject of prayer. He writes, "Prayer is not a normal part of the life of the natural man. We hear it said that a person's life will suffer if he doesn't pray, but I question that. What will suffer is the life of the Son of God in him, which is nourished not by food, but by prayer. When a person is born again from above, the life of the Son of God is born in him, and he can either starve or nourish that life. Prayer is the way that the life of God in us is nourished" (August 28). The great nineteenth century Scottish preacher, Alexander Whyte in his classic work on the subject, *Lord, Teach Us to Pray*, once wrote, "Prayer, at its best, is the noblest, the sublimest, the most magnificent, and stupendous act that any creature of God can perform on earth or in heaven" (Whyte, 51).

The four books that follow will help you get your prayer life onto a firm foundation. The Murray and Whyte books are well over 100 years old and absolute treasures. The Keller one is a contemporary treatment of the subject from a well-known and beloved Presbyterian pastor and the Marshall collection is a particular favorite of mine by the subject of the wonderful biography, *A Man Called Peter*, who was also the United States Senate Chaplain. You will be greatly blessed by reading the works of these well-respected authors.

59. WITH CHRIST IN THE SCHOOL OF PRAYER

By Andrew Murray

This book is another devotional classic by the South African pastor, teacher, and writer who was raised by Dutch Reformed missionary parents in the nineteenth century (see Chapter IX under *Absolute Surrender* for more biographical information). It is a collection of thirty-one brief lessons as taught by the Lord Jesus Christ himself. It certainly qualifies as one of the best known and beloved prayer classics of all time.

Murray begins his book with a brief Preface in which he holds up our Lord as the model for our prayers. He believes that prayer, particularly intercessory prayer, is the highest calling of the Christian. He laments that many do not understand its importance. He writes, "As long as we view prayer as simply the means of maintaining our own Christian lives, we will not fully understand what it is supposed to be" (Murray, 5). We must view it as vital to our spiritual lives and as essential as breathing.

There is so much richness in Murray's teaching about prayer. Murray begins each chapter with a verse or verses from Jesus followed by a brief exposition ending with a specific prayer by the author himself. Following are a few highlights.

One of Murray's early chapters is titled "Alone With God" in which he quotes Jesus's teaching in Matthew 6:6 about praying in secret. Murray writes, "Thus we are taught at the very beginning of our search for the secret of effective prayer to remember that it is in the inner chamber, where we are alone with the Father, that we learn to pray properly" (Murray, 27). He then concludes the chapter with this prayer. "May the place of secret prayer become the most beloved spot on earth to me" (31)! He concludes by praying that all Christians learn to regard prayer "as the highest privilege of their lives—a joy and a blessing" (Murray, 32).

Many Christians pray, but feel that God does not answer. Murray's chapter titled "The Certain Answer to Prayer" addresses that issue. He quotes Christ's words in Matthew 7:7-8 and then James in James 4:3, "Ye ask, and receive not, because ye ask amiss." Murray comments, "He (Jesus) wants to impress this one truth deeply on our minds: we may and must most confidently expect an answer to our prayers" (Murray, 43). It is Murray's contention that "the chief thing in prayer: the assurance that prayer will be heard and answered" (Ibid.). He believes that the main reason believers pray and receive no answer is because they "have not learned to pray properly" (Murray, 45).

In his chapter titled "The Infinite Fatherliness of God," Murray begins his chapter prayer thus, "Blessed Lord, though this is one of the first and simplest lessons in Your school, it is one of the hardest for our hearts to learn. We know so little of the love of the Father. Lord, teach us to live in such a way that the Father and His love may be nearer, clearer, and dearer to us than the love of any earthly father. Let Your assurance of His hearing our prayers give us much more confidence in Him than in any earthly parent, because He is infinitely greater than man" (Murray, 57).

In the chapter titled "The Boldness of God's Friends," Murray explores one of the oft-forgotten relationships that God's children have with him. He writes, "Let us confine ourselves to this chief thought: prayer is an appeal to the friendship of God" (Murray, 71). Murray is particularly focusing on our appeals when engaging in intercessory prayer and how sometimes we need to persevere when we do not receive an immediate answer. He argues, "Intercession is part of faith's training school. There our friendship with men and with God is tested. It is seen whether our friendship with the needy is so real that we would sacrifice our rest and go even at midnight to obtain what they needed" (Murray, 74).

In his chapter titled "Prayer Must Be Definite," Murray deplores the prayers that we make that are generic and not specific. He opines, "Our prayers must be a distinct expression of definite need, not a vague appeal to His mercy or an indefinite cry for blessing" (Murray, 87). He notes, "So much of our prayers are vague and pointless. Some cry for mercy, but do not take the trouble to know exactly why they want it. Others ask to be delivered from sin, but do not name any sin from which deliverance can be claimed" (Ibid.). Murray deplores such general prayers.

One of Murray's most powerful chapters is titled "The Cure of Unbelief" in which our Lord uses the grain of mustard seed as an example. Murray says that we must have faith when we pray. He writes, "Though faith is the simplest exercise of the spiritual life, it is also the highest" (Murray, 114). Murray also believes that fasting and prayer go hand in hand. "And so He teaches us two lessons of deep importance in regard to prayer. The one is that faith needs a life of prayer in which to grow and keep strong. The other is that prayer needs fasting for its full and perfect development" (Murray, 115). He explains, "Prayer is the one hand with which we grasp the invisible. Fasting is the other hand, the one with which we let go of the visible. In nothing is man more closely connected with the world of sense than in his need for, and enjoyment of, food" (Murray, 117).

In his chapter titled "Prayer and Love," Murray references Mark 11:25: "And when ye stand praying, forgive, if ye have ought against any: that your Father also which is in heaven may forgive your trespasses." Murray suggests a practical way to do just that. He writes, "If great injury or injustice occurs, try first of all to assume a godlike disposition. Avoid the sense of wounded honor, the desire to maintain your rights, and the need to punish the offender. In the little annoyances of daily life, never excuse a hasty temper, a sharp word, or a quick judgment with the thought with the thought that we mean no harm, or that it is too much to expect feeble human nature to really forgive the way God and Christ do" (Murray, 125). The reason that this is so important, according to Murray is that "Jesus speaks of love as the root of forgiveness. It is also the root of believing prayer" (Murray, 128).

A powerful chapter is titled "The Power of United Prayer." Murray explains, "As a tree has its roots hidden in the ground and its stem growing up into the sunlight, so prayer needs secrecy in which the soul meets God alone and public fellowship with those who find their common meeting place in the name of Jesus" (Murray, 131). He argues that our bonds with our fellow believers are "no less real and close than that which unites him to God" (Ibid.). Murray's prayer at the end of the chapter is compelling. "Grant especially, blessed Lord, that your church may believe that it is by the power of united prayer that she can bind and loose in heaven, cast out Satan, save souls, remove mountains, and hasten the coming of the kingdom" (Murray, 137).

Finally, Murray's chapter titled "Our Boldness in Prayer" quotes 1 John 5:14-15. "And this is the confidence we have in him, that, of we ask any thing according to his will, he heareth us: and if we know that he hears us, whatsoever we ask, we know that we have the petitions that we desired of him." He explains why so many lack boldness when they pray. "One of the greatest hindrances to believing prayer is undoubtedly this: many don't know if what they ask is according to the will of God. As long as they are in doubt on this point, they cannot have the boldness to ask in the assurance that they will certainly receive" (Murray, 260). He then explains why 1 John 5:14-15 should counter that kind of thinking. "This is the very opposite of John's purpose in writing this. He wanted to stir boldness and confidence in us, until we had he full assurance of faith in prayer" (Murray, 261). Murray is distressed by Christians who lack boldness and who feel that their prayers are not in line with the will of God. He writes, "If Christians could only see what incalculable harm they do themselves by thinking that because their prayers are possibly not according to God's will, they must be content without answers" (Murray, 266).

What I have shared with you is only the tip of the iceberg. There are thirty-one brief chapters, each one a vital lesson from Jesus on how to pray. Each chapter is a treasure and the reader will find many golden nuggets along the way. You will also strengthen your prayer life as you learn from the Master. My prayer for you as you read this book is the one that Murray prayed, "May my prayer be its echo, so that the Father hears me in You and You in me" (Murray, 241). Amen! And Amen!

60. LORD, TEACH US TO PRAY

By Alexander Whyte

The stately Alexander Whyte was the greatest Scottish preacher of the nineteenth century and is considered to be a giant among the masters of the pulpit. His life is covered more completely in Chapter IV. His magisterial *Bible Characters* (See Chapter IV) is not to be missed along with other treasures such as *The Walk, Conversation, and Character of Jesus Christ Our Lord*, *The Spiritual Life: The Teaching of Thomas Goodwin*, and *The Nature of Angels*. His classic study on prayer was actually a series of sermons preached at Free St. George's Church in Edinburgh and what a collection of sermons they were! Whyte was a master preacher, but he was first and foremost a man of prayer. This volume is an outgrowth of his life of prayer. The title of the book comes from the request the disciples made in Luke 11:1, "Lord, teach us to pray."

Whyte begins with the magnificence of prayer, Whyte declares, "Once you begin to think aright of Him Who is the Hearer of prayer; and Who waits in all His magnificence, to be gracious to you—I absolutely defy you to live any longer the life you now live" (Whyte, 6). He talks about the great privilege of prayer and how there are some who would rather die than not pray. He writes that what is important to a person is what that person will do. "You need no omniscience to tell you that man's true value. If he lets his Bible lie unopened and unread: if he lets God's Throne of Grace stand till death, idle and unwanted; if the depth and the height, the nobleness and the magnificence, the goodness and the beauty of divine things have no command over him, and no attraction to him—then, you do not wish me to put words upon the meanness of that man's mind. Look yourselves at what he has chosen: look and weep at what he has neglected, and has for ever lost" (Whyte, 10)!

Two of my favorite chapters in the book are about Elijah and Habakkuk. In one of the most powerful chapters in the book titled "Elijah—Passionate in Prayer," Whyte describes the great prophet thus, "Elijah towers up like a mountain above all the other prophets. There is a solitary grandeur about Elijah that is all his own. There is an unearthliness and a mysteriousness about Elijah that is all his own. There is a volcanic sudden-ness—a volcanic violence indeed—about almost all Elijah's movements, and about all Elijah's appearances" (Whyte, 66).

Whyte talks about Elijah's passion as perhaps his defining characteristic. The apostle James tells us in his epistle that "Eli-jah was a man just like us. He prayed earnestly that it would not rain and it did not rain on the land for three and a half years" (James 5:17). Whyte writes, "We never see Elijah but he is in a passion, as we say. In a passion of anger at Ahab. In a passion of scorn and contempt at the priests of Baal. In a pas-sion of fury and extermination against all idolatry, and against all organized uncleanness. In a passion of prayer and interces-sion" (Whyte, 67). He also describes him that he had "a whirl-wind for a heart. Elijah did nothing by halves. What he did, he did with all his heart. And what a heart it was" (Whyte, 68)!

Whyte goes on to say that Elijah was not unique in that he had passions; everybody has passions. He had a passion for prayer. Whyte then goes on to point out the difference between Elijah and most other people. He opines, "You have plenty of passion if you would make the right use of it. You are all vicious or vir-tuous men, prayerful or prayerless men; and, then, you are effectual or unavailing in your prayers—just as your passions are. You have all quite sufficient variety and amount of passion to make you mighty men with God and with men, if only your passions found their proper vent in your prayers. You have all passion enough—far too much in other things. What an ocean of all kinds of passion your heart is" (Whyte, 70-71)! The problem, according to Whyte, is that we have made our passions "the occasions of our self-destruction." The reason? "Your heart in your religion is dead as a stone" (Whyte, 72). Whyte pulls no punches in his denunciation of Christians who are passionate in other things, but not their faith. He continues, "Yes: you have passions enough to make you a saint in heaven, or a devil in hell: and they are every day making you either the one or the other. We all have plenty of passion, and to spare: only, it is all missing the mark. It is all sound and fury, a tale told, a life laid out and lived by an idiot" (Whyte, 71), to borrow a thought from Shakespeare's character Macbeth. It is little wonder that Alexander Whyte was one of the most powerful preachers of the nineteenth century English-speaking world.

Another favorite chapter is titled "Habakkuk—On His High Tower." Habakkuk himself tells us in his little Old Testament book, " I will stand upon my watch, and set me upon the tower." Whyte describes eloquently Habakkuk's tower and its meaning, " The truth and the faithfulness and the power of God— these things were the deep and broad foundations of Habakkuk's high tower, into which he continually escaped, and from the high top of which he was wont to look out upon the land, and to his God. God's grace and mercy and long-suffering were the doors and stairs, were the walls and battlements, of Habakkuk's high tower; and God's sure salvation was the golden and far-shining roof of it" (Whyte, 103).

Whyte bids us to consider the man, Habakkuk. He describes Habakkuk's method of retreat and compares him to the prayer warriors of our present day. "Look, now at that man of God who is like Habakkuk in our own days. Look at that prophet upon his tower in our own city. He has climbed up far above us, his fellows, into a calm and clear air: and he has so climbed by means of much prayer, and by means of much meditation, and by means of much secret self-denial of many kinds. He has a time and place of retreat, and of purification, and of exaltation of mind, that we know nothing of" (Whyte, 108-109). Whyte deplores both prayerlessness in Christians and improper prayer. He writes, "There are men among us who do not neglect prayer, and yet who sadly neglect to watch and wait for God's promised answer to their prayers. Prayer, when we think about it, and perform it aright—prayer is a magnificent thing—and a venturesome—for any man to do. For prayer builds, and fits out, and mans, and launches a frail vessel of faith on the deep and wide sea of God's sovereignty: and sets her sails for a harbour nothing short of heaven" (Whyte, 109).

According to Whyte, there can be many reasons why God does not seem to answer prayer. Sin is foremost among them. "There is no tyranny so terrible, there is no invasion and captivity of the soul one-thousandth part so horrible, and so hated of all God's saints, as their captivity to their own sins" (Whyte, 107). But Whyte also argues that we lose many answers to prayer because we do not wait and watch for God's answer. He writes, "I am convinced, my brethren, that we lose many answers to our prayers,—not so much because we do not pray, as because we do not go up to our tower and watch for and welcome God's answers to our prayers" (Whyte, 110). He concludes that "Habakkuk never made a holier or a more fruitful resolve than when he said, 'I will stand upon my watch, and set me upon the tower, and will watch to see what He will say unto me'" (Ibid.). What powerful preaching! Oh, that we had preachers today with such power and precision in their words!

There is so much more to this wonderful book. Warren Wiersbe calls it one of the great volumes on prayer. You will encounter chapters with titles such as "The Geometry of Prayer," "Imagination in Prayer," "Concentration in Prayer," "Our Lord in the Garden," "The Man Who Knocked at Midnight," and "The Costliness of Prayer." It is possible that your prayer life might need a bit of a jump start. This thoughtful volume by an absolute prince of the pulpit is just what the doctor ordered. I dare you to read it. It will convict your heart and stir your conscience.

61. THE PRAYERS OF PETER MARSHALL

Compiled and edited by Catherine Marshall

Let me begin by saying that I have been a fan of Peter Marshall ever since I was a wee lad after I saw the 1955 movie *A Man Called Peter* starring Richard Todd and Jean Peters. That led to my reading the book on which the movie is based, *A Man Called Peter* by his wife, Catherine Marshall. I then found a 33 rpm recording of two sermons by him, *The Trumpet of the Morn* and *Trial by Fire*, and I was hooked. I had never heard such passion and power in preaching. At that time, I was a young student in seminary and I knew then that I would model my preaching after the fine example of this remarkable man of God. I lamented that he had died at such a young age and that I would never hear him preach in person.

While still in seminary, I searched for and read every book by Peter Marshall that I could find. I haunted the used book stores and found and read *Mr. Jones, Meet the Master* and *John Doe, Disciple*. These two books were compilations of sermons by Peter Marshall edited by his wife. Then, of course, I found this book, *The Prayers of Peter Marshall*. This book transformed my prayer life, much as the preaching of Peter Marshall had transformed my preaching aspirations. But more about the book later.

Peter Marshall was a thirty-one-year old bachelor serving as the pastor of the Westminster Presbyterian Church in Atlanta when he met his future wife, Catherine, who was a twenty-year old student at Agnes Scott College. She, like many young people from Atlanta's five large educational institutions (Agnes Scott College, Georgia Tech, Emory University, Oglethorpe University, and Columbia Seminary), flocked to hear his powerful preaching characterized by his thick Scottish brogue. Marshall came to the United States in 1927 at the age of twenty-five from his native Scotland where he was raised in poverty by his mother and stepfather. His ambition, inspired by Hudson Taylor, was to become a missionary to China. His passage to America was funded by a cousin who wanted him to receive a proper ministerial education. He began his theological studies at Columbia Theological Seminary in 1929 and was ordained a Presbyterian minister after graduation. He served briefly at a small rural church in Covington, Georgia, before being called to the Westminster Presbyterian Church in Atlanta in 1933. It was there that he met Catherine and was smitten by her. They were married in 1936.

The year after Peter and Catherine were married, 1937, he accepted a call to the historic New York Avenue Presbyterian Church in Washington, D.C. It was there that Marshall gained fame and a wider audience. In 1946, he was appointed to serve as the U.S. Senate Chaplain. He served until his untimely death from a heart attack two years later.

Ironically it was Marshall's Senate prayers, not his preaching, that attracted a great deal of national attention. These were not your garden-variety multipurpose prayers. If Marshall's preaching was life-transforming, his prayers were like opening the door of a blast furnace. His prayers stepped on toes and pierced consciences. As the old saw goes, he comforted the afflicted and afflicted the comfortable. But most importantly, he led them to God. This book contains 276 prayers of Peter Marshall. Pastoral prayers that he delivered at his congregations in Covington, Atlanta, and Washington, D.C. comprise eighty-four of this collection; the remaining 192 are prayers that were delivered from 1947-49 before the U.S. Senate. In *A Man Called Peter*, Catherine relates that people began to flock to hear his prayers. He even received fan mail from all over from people who had read the *Congressional Record*. She writes, "More and more Senators began leaving their offices and committee rooms early in order to hear the opening prayer. Visitors in the gallery, pressmen, even the page boys began looking forward to those prayers" (Marshall, 233). In a city of self-important men with impressive titles, Marshall's primary aim was to point them to a higher wisdom than their own." This was a radical notion that hit a nerve in the capital city. Senators began to believe that God could actually direct just how they should vote. Sadly, Marshall did not write out his prayers and few were recorded on tape and are available today. These prayers represent only the tip of the iceberg

Peter Marshall's life was sadly all too brief, but his life's example, sermons, and prayers live on and still have a tremendous impact on people today. If you are tired of hearing the same old rote public prayers that regurgitate the same trite phrases over and over again, this book will be a breath of fresh air. Each prayer exudes warmth, wisdom, and humanity that will touch you in new ways and help to transform your own prayer life. If you enjoy this book of prayers, I suggest that you read his biography, *A Man Called Peter*, and then also read his books of collected sermons edited by his wife. You can also listen to several of his sermons online, the aforementioned *Trial by Fire* and *Trumpet of the Morn*. Also available is *Were You There?* delivered in the late 1940s. Peter Marshall was on intimate terms with God and his prayers are a model of what real prayer ought to be. To him, we are greatly indebted.

A few snippets from the book should whet your appetite.

> "So, deliver us from the blasphemy of optimism that is mere wishful thinking" (March 9, 1948).

> "We confess, our Father, that we know in our hearts how much we need Thee, yet our swelled heads and stubborn wills keep us trying to do without Thee. Forgive us for making so many mountains out of molehills and for exaggerating our own importance and the problems that confront us" (June 16, 1947).

"Lord. We are ashamed that money and position speak to us more loudly than does the simple compassion of the human heart. Help us to care, as Thou dost care, for the little people who have no lobbyists, for the minority groups who sorely need justice" (June 4, 1948).

"Save us from the sin of worrying, lest stomach ulcers be the badge of our faith" (May 8, 1947).

"Deliver us, we pray Thee, from the tyranny of trifles. May we give our best thought and attention to what is important, that we may accomplish something worthwhile" (May 12, 1947).

"Where we are wrong, make us willing to change, and where we are right, make us easy to live with" (May 14, 1947).

"Let us have less talking and more thinking, less work and more worship, less pressure and more prayer. For if we are too busy to pray, we are far busier than we have any right to be" (June 3, 1947).

"May we never fail to do the very best we can. Help us to pray in the knowledge that it all depends on Thee. Help us then to work as if it all depended on us" (March 25, 1947).

"Teach us economy in speech that neither wounds nor offends, that affords light without generating heat" (March 20, 1947).

"Deliver us, O Lord, from the foolishness of impatience" (January 22, 1947).

"With all the resources of an infinite God available to them that ask Thee, forgive us, O Lord, for our lack of faith that begs for pennies when we could write checks for millions, that strikes a match when we could have the sun" (February 26, 1947).

"Save these, Thy servants, the chosen of the people, from the tyranny of the nonessential, from the weary round of that which saps strength, frays nerves, shortens life, and adds nothing to their usefulness to Thee and to this Nation" (February 10, 1947).

"May we be more concerned that we are on Thy side, than that Thou art on ours" (February 11, 1947).

"Let us not break faith with any of yesterday's promises nor leave unrepaired any of yesterday's wrongs" (February 17, 1947).

"So long have we been riding on the balloon tires of conceit, for our own good we may have to be deflated, that on the rims of humility we may discover the spiritual laws that govern our growth in grace" (June 19, 1947).

"Our Father, we are beginning to understand at last that the things that are wrong with our world are the sum total of all the things that are wrong with us as individuals. Thou hast made us after Thine image, and our hearts can find no rest until they rest in Thee" (June 26, 1947).

62. PRAYER

By Timothy Keller

It is an unfortunate truth, but many Christians just don't know how to pray. They have heard for years that prayer is the most powerful way to experience God in the fullest, but few have even the faintest idea how to go about it and sadly they have never been taught. This book, written by an experienced Presbyterian pastor, examines just what prayer is, and more importantly, explains how to do it. Timothy Keller anchors his teaching on prayer in the Psalms of the Old Testament and shows how the ancient psalmists expressed their prayers to God. He also mines some of the riches of the writings of spiritual giants from the past such as Augustine, Martin Luther, John Calvin, and Jonathan Edwards,

The late Timothy Keller was a prominent New York City (Redeemer Presbyterian Church) pastor and author who has been an influential voice in the evangelical world for the past several decades. He is the author of *God's Wisdom for Navigating Life*, *Making Sense of God*, *The Meaning of Marriage*, *The Reason for God*, *The Prodigal God* (See Chapter IV), and *A Shepherd Looks at Psalm 23*, *Counterfeit Gods*, and *Generous Justice* to name just a few of his many books. Keller's books have helped millions of Christians worldwide. In addition, Redeemer Presbyterian Church has planted more than 300 churches throughout the world.

In his Introduction, Keller admits that he "didn't have a first book to give someone who wanted to understand and practice prayer" (Keller, 1). He admits that there are numerous great books on prayer, many of them classics, but most are older and "written in an archaic idiom" (Ibid.). In addition, he felt that most such books were "primarily theological or devotional or practical" (Ibid.), but very seldom did they combine all three elements. He wanted a book on prayer that combined the "theological, experiential, and methodological" in one volume written in contemporary English usage. That led to the writing of this book. Keller explains his rationale. "Nearly all the classic books on prayer spend a fair amount of time warning readers about practices of their day that were spiritually unhelpful or even damaging. Such cautions must be updated for readers in each generation" (Ibid.). Keller has certainly closed the gap with this delightful volume.

Keller divides his book into five logical sections, each one building upon the others before it. He begins with a section titled simply "Desiring Prayer." Keller explores both the necessity of prayer as well as its greatness. He notes the recent interest among Christians. "Within the Christian church, there has been a similar explosion of interest in prayer. There is a strong movement toward ancient meditation and contemplative practices. We now have a small empire of institutions, organizations, networks, and practitioners that teaches and coaches in methods such as centering prayer, contemplative prayer, 'listening' prayer, *lectio divina*, and many others of what are now called 'spiritual disciplines'" (Keller, 13).

Keller shares how in the crucible of his cancer treatment, he changed his approach to prayer. He made four practical changes in his private devotions the first of which was an intense study of the Psalms, which led naturally to praying through them. Then he began to use meditation as a transitional discipline between Bible reading and prayer. He also upped the frequency of prayer. Instead of only praying in the morning, he added evening prayers and prayed with greater expectation. He writes, "An encounter with God involves not only the affections of the heart but also the convictions of the mind. We are not called to choose between a Christian life based on truth and doctrine *or* a life filled with spiritual power and experience. They go together" (Keller, 16-17).

Keller admits that prayer is not an easy topic for writing. "Prayer is nonetheless an exceedingly difficult subject to write about. That is not primarily because it is so indefinable but because, before it, we feel so small and helpless" (Keller, 18). Although he confesses to his own inadequacy, he states without qualification that "Prayer is the only entryway into genuine self-knowledge. It is also the main way we experience deep change—the reordering of our loves. Prayer is how God gives us so many of the unimaginable things he has for us. Indeed, prayer makes it safe for God to give us many of the things we desire. It is the way we know God, the way we finally treat God as God. Prayer is simply the key to everything we need to do and be in life. We must learn to pray. We have to" (Ibid.).

In his discussion on the greatness of prayer, Keller references some of the giants of the faith such as John Owen, John Calvin, Jonathan Edwards, Austin Phelps, and George Herbert and how integral prayer was in their lives. He writes, "The infallible test of spiritual integrity, Jesus says, is your private prayer life" (Keller, 23). Keller sees prayer as central to the Christian life. "Giving priority to the inner life doesn't mean an individualistic life. Knowing the God of the Bible better can't be achieved all by yourself. It entails the community of the church, participation in corporate worship as well as private devotion, and instruction in the Bible as well as silent meditation. At the heart of all the various ways of knowing God is both public and private prayer" (Ibid.).

Keller likens prayer to a journey and says that there is "a longing in prayer that is never fulfilled in this life, and sometimes the deep satisfactions we are looking for in prayer feel few and far between" (Keller 30). Yet, at the same time he assures us, "Even in spiritually lean times, prayer can serve as a kind of heavenly 'Manna' and quiet 'gladness' that keeps us going, just as the manna in the wilderness kept Israel moving toward its hope" (Ibid.). However, Keller cautions, we must approach prayer in the proper frame of mind. He warns, "An arrogant spirit cannot rightly use the power of prayer's siege engines"

(Keller, 31). He summarizes this section by saying that "prayer is awe, intimacy, struggle—yet the way to reality. There is nothing more important, or harder, or richer, or more life-altering. There is absolutely nothing so great as prayer" (Keller, 32).

In his second section, "Understanding Prayer," Keller explains how with all the confusion that the great monotheistic religions of Islam, Judaism, and Christianity throw at us with regard to prayer, we can define and discern what real prayer actually is. He explains that the relationship between us and our encounter with God in prayer is rooted in the Bible. He writes, "We can define prayer as a *personal, communicative response to the knowledge of God*" (Keller, 45). He tells us how that is accomplished. "In the Bible, God's living Word, we can hear God speaking to us and we respond in prayer" (Ibid.). Keller further defines prayer. "What is prayer, then, in the fullest sense? Prayer is continuing a conversation that God has started through his Word and his grace, which eventually becomes a full encounter with him" (Keller, 48). Why, then, are some prayers insipid and ineffective? He explains, "The power of our prayers, then, lies not primarily in our effort and striving, or in any technique, but rather in our knowledge of God" (Keller, 49).

Keller urges, as does Eugene H. Peterson in his *Praying with the Psalms*, that we immerse ourselves in Scripture, particularly the Psalms. He writes, "If the goal of prayer is real, personal connection with God, then it is only by immersion in the language of the Bible that we will learn to pray" (Keller, 55). He explains, "Without immersion in God's words, our prayers may not be merely limited and shallow, but also untethered from reality. We may be responding not to the real God but to what we wish God and life to be like. Indeed, if left to themselves our hearts *will* tend to create a God who doesn't exist. People from Western cultures want a God who is loving and forgiving, but not holy and transcendent" (Keller, 62). How true!

In his third section titled "Learning Prayer," Keller turns to Augustine, Martin Luther, and John Calvin for what he describes as "three master classes" on the subject. He cites the personal letters of Augustine and Luther to individuals on how to pray as well as an excerpt from Calvin's magisterial *Institutes of the Christian Religion*, which constitutes the third master class. Calvin identified them as "the rules for prayer." His first rule is what Keller calls "the principle of reverence." Keller, in echoing Calvin, implies that many believers approach the discipline of prayer without "a due sense of the seriousness and magnitude of what prayer is" (Keller, 97). He minces no words when he states, "It is a personal audience and conversation with the Almighty God of the universe" (Ibid.). Thus, approaching prayer and God, according to Keller, without a corresponding sense of awe is the absolute worst thing that a Christian can do.

Calvin's second rule for prayer can be summarized as having a sense of spiritual humility. It includes both an awareness of our utter dependence on God as well as a "readiness to recognize and repent our own faults in particular" (Keller, 99). Calvin believed that we should approach God in prayer with the "disposition of a beggar."

Calvin's third and fourth rules for prayer are really two sides of the same coin. We must have a submissive trust in God. That was Christ's attitude during his Passion in the Garden of Gethsemane. "Not my will, but thy will be done." But at the same time, we pray with confidence and hope.

The ultimate "Master class," according to Keller, is what is commonly called the Lord's Prayer found in Matthew 6:9-13. He writes, "The Lord's Prayer may be the single set of words spoken more often than any other in the history of the world. Jesus Christ gave it to us as the key to unlock all the riches of prayer. Yet it is an untapped resource, partially because if is so very familiar" (Keller, 109). He further states, "The whole world is starving for spiritual experience, and Jesus gives us the means to it in a few words" (Ibid.). Keller then examines the prayer phrase by phrase gleaning some of the highlights of the wisdom of Augustine, Luther, and Calvin. This is a beautiful section.

In his fourth section, Deepening Prayer, Keller uses two common words to describe prayer: a conversation and an encounter. He first discusses how prayer and meditation go together and how the believer can enhance the former by "listening to God's voice through meditation on the Scripture" (Keller, 145). He calls meditation "the gateway to prayer." He writes differentiating the biblical discipline from the "mantra meditation" of the popular Transcendental Meditation. "Christian meditation, however, stimulates our analysis and reflection—and centers it on the glory and grace of God" (Keller, 150).

Prayer is also an encounter with God where we seek his face. Keller writes, "Prayer is a conversation that leads to encounter with God" (Keller, 165). That is the ultimate goal. However, he warns that "if the beauty and glory of Christ do not capture our imaginations, dominate our waking thought, and fill our hearts with longing and desire—then something else will" (Keller, 177). According to Keller, it is possible to go through life as a church goer going through the motions and never finding the heart's joy in God. How sad!

In his final section, Doing Prayer, Keller deals with the actual act of prayer itself. He says that "there are three basic kinds of prayer to God" (Keller, 189). He begins with what he terms "upward prayer," which focuses on God himself. Another way of describing this kind of prayer is the "prayer of awe." "Inward" prayer focuses on self-examination and confession. Finally, there is "outward prayer," which are supplication and intercession. I have often used the ACTS acronym for teaching how to pray: Adoration, Confession, Thanksgiving, and Supplication. Keller's method is very similar to that.

Timothy Keller's writings have profoundly affected my Christian walk in so many ways. I firmly believe that you will find him helpful, too. This is the one book I would give to a believer who wants to learn the nuts and bolts of prayer or who wants to deepen his prayer life. By reading this book, you will discover new and powerful ways to experience God through prayer.

CHAPTER IX:
CHRISTIAN LIVING

It would be nice, wouldn't it, if after coming to a saving knowledge of Jesus Christ, God would somehow whisk us to heaven in a chariot of fire with horses of fire like he did with Elijah. However, the flashy exit from this world is not the way most of us go home. We patiently await the coming of our Lord and Savior Jesus Christ and along the way we live full lives, experience trials and tribulations, and eventually we pass from this life in less than dramatic fashion.

Salvation has been described by theologians as having three components. We have been saved; we are being saved; and we shall be saved. Those who are born again Christians and still living on this planet have already experienced the first part and are now working on the second. The apostle Paul wrote to the Philippians, "Continue to work out your salvation with fear and trembling, for it is God who works in you to will and to act according to his good purpose" (Phil. 2:12-13). Another way to describe this is the Christian life, or as the theologians describe it technically, the sanctification process. That is where we are now as we await the grand finale, glorification. Along the way we experience the trials and vicissitudes of life as we live the Christian life here on earth. Sometimes it is not easy. We have setbacks; we have temptations; we have illness; and sometimes it seems as if we are not growing in the Christian faith as much as we would like.

I am grateful for the many helpers I have had who have assisted me along the way as I, along with Bunyan's character

305

Pilgrim, make this Christian pilgrimage called the Christian life. Some of them I have never met except through their writings, but they have been invaluable friends just the same. Of the ten friends whose books have helped me immeasurably along the way and are included in this chapter, I have met only two, Warren Wiersbe and Fitzsimmons Allison. But all are wonderful guides to making sense of and living the Christian life.

63. ABSOLUTE SURRENDER

By Andrew Murray

Andrew Murray, who lived from 1828 to 1917, was a South African pastor, teacher, and writer. He was the child of Dutch Reformed Church missionaries sent from Scotland to South Africa. It is estimated that he wrote approximately fifty books and dozens of gospel tracts over the course of his lifetime. He studied at the University of Aberdeen in Scotland for his initial education and the University of Utrecht where he studied theology. He was influenced greatly by the ministries of Robert Murray McCheyne and Horatius Bonar and the Scottish revival meetings. Of his many books, several are considered to be modern devotional classics including *Absolute Surrender* and *With Christ in the School of Prayer* (see Chapter VIII). They continue to be printed and read and re-read today over a hundred years after Murray's death.

Absolute Surrender is a compilation of nine sermons that appeal to Christians to give themselves entirely to the Lordship of Jesus Christ. Murray served several churches, all in South Africa, and was a leader in the Keswick Movement. His writings on the "inner life" were very influential in that movement. His theology, which included faith healing and the continuation of the apostolic gifts, made him one of the forerunners to the Pentecostal movement of the twentieth century.

In the first chapter or address aptly titled the same as the book, Murray argues that "the condition of God's blessing is absolute surrender into His hands" (Murray, 7). He says that the believer should say to God, "I am thine, and all that I have, as the words of absolute surrender with which every child of God ought to yield himself to his Father" (Ibid.). Murray's contention is that the idea of absolute surrender is grounded in the very nature of God, who is the "Fountain of life" and the "Source of existence."

He reasons that if all creation is surrendered to God, shouldn't we as well? He writes, "God has created the sun, the trees, and the grass; and are they not all absolutely surrendered to God" (Murray, 9)?

Murray's second chapter is "The Fruit of the Spirit is Love." In this address he expounds upon the meaning of the apostle Paul's statement in Galatians 5:21. Murray contends that when Christ promised the Holy Spirit to his disciples, he did it with the end in view "that they might have power to be witnesses" (Murray, 21). But they were also to love one another as a mark of the indwelling Christ. Murray laments the absence of true love among believers. "Oh, if this were true in the Church of Christ how different her state would be! May God help us to get hold of this simple, heavenly truth that the fruit of the Spirit is a love which appears in the life, and that just as the Holy Spirit gets real possession of the life, the heart will be filled with real, divine, universal love" (Murray, 22). He admits how difficult this can be particularly with those hard to love Christians. "Oh, friend, you have not learned the lesson that Christ wanted to teach above everything. Let a man be what he will, you are to love him. Love is to be the fruit of the Spirit all the day and every day. Yes, listen! If a man loves not his brother whom he hath seen—if you don't love that unlovable man whom you have seen, how can you love God whom you have not seen" (Murray, 31)? What a challenge for us!

The other seven chapters are "Separated Unto the Holy Ghost," "Peter's Repentance," "Impossible with Man, Possible with God," "O Wretched Man that I Am," "Having Begun in the Spirit," "Kept By the Power of God," and "Ye Are the Branches." According to Murray, it is possible for every believer to live in an intimate relationship with the Lord Jesus Christ and to ex-perience spiritual victory. The secret is found in the chapters of this book. Each chapter title is from a verse of Scripture and uncovers guidance into the path of spiritual victory. For exam-ple, the Apostle Paul's famous words in his epistle to the Ro-mans, "O wretched man that I am," indicate that we must begin with a sober assessment of ourselves before we can expect to experience spiritual progress. As Murray writes, "There you have the words of a man who has come to the end of himself" (Murray, 71). Murray reminds us that these are the words of a regenerate man, who is also an impotent man as well as wretched. His only hope is, as the title of the next chapter indicates, in the power of the Holy Spirit ("Having Begun in the Spirit"). Although his views were not shared by everyone of his day, he believed that it was possible for the believer to receive the fullness of the Holy Spirit. In that sense, he was a forerunner of the Charismatic movement of the twentieth century.

Murray believed that God had already done everything for the Christian to experience the power of God in their lives. He argued that the reasons that so many believers failed to do this could be traced to a half-hearted surrender to God, unbelief in the power of the Holy Spirit, and a failure to harness the power of prayer. He explores the latter problem in his classic *With Christ in the School of Prayer*. He taught that the greatest curse to the effective spiritual life was attention to "self."

Murray's writings have been read and loved by many over several generations. The fact that so many of his books are still in print and still being read after over a century attests to that fact. Untold numbers of Christians have been blessed by his simple writing which unfolds the secrets of absolute surrender and the successful spiritual life. Murray's plea in this book is simple as he tells his readers, "Oh! I advise you Christians, *bring everything into relationship with Jesus*" (Murray, 126). Please allow this book to lead you into a more successful, intimate relationship with your Lord and Savior. Learn from one of the pioneers of the "Inner Life" movement.

64. THE PURSUIT OF GOD

By A. W. Tozer

The pen of A. W. Tozer produced more than three dozen books, two of which are considered to be classics today, *The Knowledge of the Holy* and *The Pursuit of God*. I was first introduced to Tozer over forty years ago by Warren Wiersbe in his wonderful book, *Walking with the Giants*. Since that day, Tozer's writings have seared themselves upon my heart and changed the way that I regard the world, the modern church, and its people. For more about Tozer, see my review of *The Knowledge of the Holy* in Chapter VII: Christian Doctrine & Theology.

Tozer begins his book with the observation that within the evangelical movement of his day, there was "to be found increasing numbers of people whose religious lives are marked by a growing hunger after God Himself" (Tozer, IX). He notes that "they are thirsty for God, and they will not be satisfied until they have drunk deep at the fountain of living water" (Ibid.). He believed that this hunger was largely ignored by the religious leaders and Bible teachers of his day. He writes, "Current evangelicalism has (to change the figure) laid the altar and divided the sacrifice into parts, but now seems satisfied to count the stones and rearrange the pieces with never a care that there is not a sign of fire upon the top of lofty Mount Carmel" (Tozer, IX-X). Ouch! And he was writing in the late 1940s. How much more true this is today. He laid the blame squarely at the feet of the leaders and Bible teachers of his day who, though orthodox in their doctrines, beliefs, and teaching were "strangely unaware that there is in their ministry no manifest presence, not anything unusual in their personal lives" (Tozer, X).

In chapter 1, "Following Hard after God," Tozer addresses the doctrine of prevenient grace, which he describes as "before a man can seek God, God must first have sought man" (Tozer, 1).

He attacks the conversion accounts of his day as basically sterile and not rooted in Scripture. He opines, "The whole transaction of religious conversion has been made mechanical and spiritless. Faith may now be exercised without a jar to the moral life and without embarrassment to the Adamic ego" (Tozer, 2). In fact, Tozer questions the whole procedure of "accepting" Christ as being without scriptural foundation. When I was a wee lad, I used to wonder why people were told to accept Christ. Nowhere in the Bible is anyone ever told to "accept" Christ.

Tozer also wonders, and rightly so, how it is possible to be "saved' without a corresponding hunger for God. He writes, "The man is 'saved,' but he is not hungry or thirsty after God. In fact, he is specifically taught to be satisfied and encouraged to be content with little" (Ibid.). He accuses Christians of spiritual complacency when he writes, "The modern scientist has lost God amid the wonders of His world; we Christians are in real danger of losing God amid the wonders of His Word" (Tozer, 2-3).

Tozer suggests that the saints of the past give us exemplars of those who eagerly sought after God. He writes of David that his life "was a torrent of spiritual desire, and his psalms ring with the cry of the seeker and the glad shout of the finder" (Tozer, 5). He believed that the Christians of his age and time erred in that emphasis was made on conversion, but not so much sanctification. He writes, "We have been snared in the coils of a false logic which insists that if we have found Him, we need no more seek Him" (Tozer, 6). He believes that such smug satisfaction with conversion and "no more" would have been anathema to the great saints of the past such as Augustine, Samuel Rutherford, and David Brainerd. Tozer sadly concludes, "I want deliberately to encourage this mighty longing after God. The lack of it has brought us to our present low estate. The stiff and wooden quality about our religious lives is a result of our lack of holy desire. Complacency is a deadly foe of all spiritual growth. Acute desire must be present or there will be no manifestation of Christ to His people" (Tozer, 7).

Tozer's second chapter is titled "The Blessedness of Possessing Nothing," which deals with the way that our possessions often come between us and God. He calls this "the tyranny of things." He writes, "Our woes began when God was forced out of His central shrine and 'things' were allowed to enter. Within the human heart, 'things' have taken over. Men have now, by nature, no peace within their hearts, for God is crowned there no longer, but there in the moral dusk, stubborn and aggressive usurpers fight among themselves for first place on the throne" (Tozer, 11-12). He uses the patriarch Abraham as a role model in this regard. He writes of Abraham, "He had everything, but *he possessed nothing*. There is the spiritual secret. There is the sweet theology of the heart, which can be learned only in the school of renunciation" (Tozer, 17). He concludes that the way to a deeper relationship with God is through spiritual and physical poverty. He writes, "The way to deeper knowledge of God is through the lonely valleys of soul poverty and giving up of all things. The blessed ones who possess the kingdom are they who have repudiated every external thing and have rooted from their hearts all sense of possessing. These are the 'poor in spirit'" (Tozer, 13).

Using Hebrews 10:19 ("Therefore, brethren, since we have confidence to enter the holy place by the blood of Jesus.") as his jumping off point, Tozer talks about "removing the veil." He discusses the reluctance of saints in the Old Testament to enter into the presence of God and contrasts that with the New Testament teaching. "Ransomed men need no longer pause in fear to enter the Holy of Holies. *God wills that we should push on into His presence and live our whole life there*" (Tozer, 24). He puts his finger squarely on what the problem was in the church of his day. "The world is perishing for want of His presence. The instant cure of most of our religious ills would be to enter His presence in spiritual experience, to become suddenly aware that we are in God and that God is in us" (Tozer, 26).

Tozer speaks of the prophets of old and asks where they are. He wonders where those whose hearts have broken have gone. He laments that we have an abundance of orthodox teachers, but few prophets. He writes, "Men of the breaking hearts had a quality about them not known to or understood by common men. They habitually spoke with spiritual authority. They had been in the presence of God and they reported what they saw there. They were prophets, not scribes" (Tozer, 30). Tozer was such a one crying out in the spiritual wilderness of his day. Tozer calls for the veil to be removed, not the Old Testament veil in the temple, but "the veil of our fleshly fallen nature that lives on, unjudged within us, uncrucified, and unrepudiated" (Tozer, 31). He calls these sins "self-sins." He explains, "To be specific, the self-sins are these: self-righteousness, self-pity, self-confidence, self-sufficiency, self-admiration, and a host of others like them. They dwell too deep within us and are too much a part of our natures to come to our attention until the light of God is focused upon them. The grosser manifestations of these sins—egotism, exhibitionism, self-promotion—are strangely tolerated in Christian leaders, even in circles of impeccable orthodoxy" (Tozer, 32). He even goes so far as to say that "they appear these days to be a requisite for popularity in some sections of the church visible" (Ibid.). Is there any wonder that Tozer was considered to be a twentieth century prophet? Jeremiah or Isaiah could not have said it better. Tozer said, "Self is the opaque veil that hides the face of God from us" (Tozer, 33).

So, what is the solution to this? Tozer gives us the answer in the title to this book, *The Pursuit of God*. He suggests first apprehending God. He wonders why so few believers have a close walk with God. He asks, "Why do they know so little of that habitual conscious communion with God which the Scriptures seem to offer. The answer is our chronic unbelief" (Tozer, 37). The difference is as wide as the gulf between intellectual knowledge and exercising that knowledge in saving faith. He says of such Christians, "Their ideas are brain-deep, not life deep. Wherever life touches them, they repudiate their theories and live like other men" (Tozer, 39). Tozer considered himself an "evangelical mystic," which I think is reflected in his musings on the spiritual world. He writes, "The world of sense intrudes upon our attention day and night for the whole of our lifetime. It is clamorous, insistent, and self-demonstrating. It does not appeal to our faith; it is here, assaulting our five senses, demanding to be accepted as real and final. But sin has so clouded the lenses of our hearts that we cannot see that other reality, the city of God, shining around us. The world of sense triumphs. The visible becomes the enemy of the invisible, and the temporal, of the eternal. That is the curse inherited by every member of Adam's tragic race. At the root of the Christian life lies belief in the invisible. The object of the Christian's faith is unseen reality" (Tozer, 41-42). Thus, we need to apprehend God. Tozer explains, "As we begin to focus upon God, the things of the spirit will take shape before our inner eyes" (Tozer, 43).

Tozer also suggests that we discern the "universal presence of God." He quotes Psalm 139:7, "Where can I go from your Spirit? Or where can I flee from your presence?" Please keep in mind that Tozer was not only an evangelical, he was a mystic. When you read this, don't think that he was an odd duck who saw visions and heard voices. According to Warren Wiersbe in his chapter on Tozer, "A mystic is simply a person who: (1) sees a real spiritual world beyond the world of sense; (2) seeks to please God rather than the crowd; (3) cultivates a close fellowship with God, sensing His presence everywhere; and (4) relates his experience to the practical things of life" (Wiersbe, 165). Tozer writes, "God dwells in His creation and is everywhere individually present in all His works. This is boldly taught by prophet and apostle and is accepted by Christian theology generally; that is, it appears in the books, but for some reason it has not sunk into the average Christian's heart so as to become a part of his believing self. Christian teachers shy away from its full implications, and, if they mention it at all, mute it down until it has little meaning" (Tozer, 45).

Tozer then asks why it is that "some people 'find' God in a way that others do not" (Tozer, 50)? "Why does God manifest His presence to some and let multitudes of others struggle along in the half-light of imperfect Christian experience" (Ibid.)? He examines the lives of great saints from the past from Bible characters such as Moses, David, Elijah, and Isaiah to later ones such as Saint Francis, Luther, and Charles Finney. He sees one great commonality in all of these great saints: "spiritual receptivity." Tozer explains, "Something in them was open to heaven, something which urged them Godward" (Tozer, 50-51). What was there in them that was different from you and me? He says, "They differed from the average person in that when they felt that inward longing, they *did something about it.* They acquired the lifelong habit of spiritual response. They were not disobedient to the heavenly vision" (Tozer, 51). Tozer sees the failure to do this as "the cause of a very serious breakdown in modern evangelicalism" (Tozer, 52). Christians become complacent with their spiritual lives and they do not seek the best that God has in store for them. Tozer writes, "The tragic results of this spirit are all about us. Shallow lives, hollow religious philosophies, the preponderance of the element of fun in gospel meetings, the glorification of men, trust in religious externalities, quasi-religious fellowships, salesmanship methods, the mistaking of dynamic personality for the power of the Spirit: These and such as these are the symptoms of an evil disease, a deep and serious malady of the soul" (Tozer, 53). Ouch! Had Tozer been an Old Testament prophet, no doubt he would have been stoned or lowered into a muddy cistern. His message would not have been tolerated by the status quo.

Tozer provides several remedies for this sorry state of the church. First, he says we must listen to the voice of God. It is sad that so many in our day fail to read the Word of God. That is the primary way in which God speaks to us. Tozer writes, "The voice of God is a friendly voice. No one need fear to listen to it unless he has already made up his mind to resist it" (Tozer, 63). He claims, "The Bible will never be a living book to us until we are convinced that God is articulate in His universe" (Tozer,

64). Second, we must cultivate the habit of what he calls the "gaze of the soul." It is, he explains, "a continuous gaze of the heart at the triune God" (Tozer, 72). It is "a habit of soul . . . which will become after a while a sort of spiritual reflex requiring no more conscious effort on our part" (Ibid.). Tozer reflects, "When we lift our inward eyes to gaze upon God, we are sure to meet friendly eyes gazing back at us, for it is written that the eyes of the Lord run to and fro throughout all the earth" (Tozer, 73).

Tozer also calls for us to restore the creator-creature relation. To say that this has been out of balance in recent decades is a gross understatement. Keep in mind, of course, that Tozer was writing over seventy years ago. He also, turning to the Beatitudes, calls for meekness and rest. He says that the human race can be seen by taking the Beatitudes and turning them wrong side out. Tozer believes that nothing that Jesus spoke about in the Sermon on the Mount can be seen in "the world of men."

Finally, Tozer calls for Christians to treat life as a sacrament. He deplores the tendency of most believers to separate the sacred and the secular. He writes, "This is the old sacred-secular antithesis. Most Christians are caught in its trap. They cannot get a satisfactory adjustment between the claims of the two worlds. They try to walk the tightrope between two kingdoms and they find no peace in either. Their strength is reduced, their outlook confused, and their joy taken from them" (Tozer, 100-01). The solution is to turn our entire lives into a sacrament.

When I first began to preach, someone told me that my task was twofold: to comfort the afflicted and afflict the comfortable. When you read Tozer, you will certainly be challenged. You will never be the same.

65. TRUE SPIRITUALITY

By Francis A. Schaeffer

What is true spirituality? What does it mean to be truly spiritual? When I was growing up, true spirituality was often couched in negative terms. I was taught to see spirituality as a list of what Christians did not do, not so much what they were or what they did. Spiritual Christians did not engage in certain behaviors. For example, they did not drink alcoholic beverages. They did not smoke cigarettes. They did not go to movie theaters. They did not use playing cards. So much emphasis was placed on the negatives that there was little said about the positives. Unfortunately, this focus on the negative gave me a false understanding of what true spirituality really is. It was not until many years later that I was "cured" of this "fake news" about spirituality and sanctification and came to a more biblical understanding.

Francis Schaeffer is a trustworthy guide to what true spirituality actually is. He was the twentieth century's patron saint to the multitudes of restless and questioning youth of many cultures who made their way to his legendary L'Abri in the Swiss Alps and were transformed through his logical mind and faithful application of biblical principles. For more about this remarkable man and his influential international ministry, please see Chapter XI. Francis Schaeffer had a huge impact on me as a searching university student a half century ago. *True Spirituality* is a wonderful summation on how to live the Christian life.

This book is organized into two major sections each roughly the same length. Section I, "Freedom Now from the Bonds of Sin," looks at true spirituality from three perspectives. First, Schaeffer lays out some basic considerations such as the centrality of death and the power of the Holy Spirit. Second, he examines true spirituality as it relates to biblical unity. Finally, he discusses the moment-by-moment practice of true spirituality and how it relates to sanctification. In Section II, "Freedom Now from the Results of the Bonds of Sin," Schaeffer handles the problems of man's separation from himself and also from his fellowman.

Schaeffer begins his book with a chapter that sets out in positive fashion an introduction to all that follows as he capsulizes just what the Christian life is. He writes, "1. The true Christian life, true spirituality, does not mean *just* that we have been born again. It must begin there, but it means much more than that. 2. It is not just a desire to get rid of taboos in order to live an easier and a looser life. Our desire must be for a deeper life. 3. True spirituality, the true Christian life, is not just outward, but it is inward. 4. It is positive; positive inward reality" (Schaeffer, 16-17).

Schaeffer believed that much of the modern Christian's problem with regard to spirituality has to do with his mentality. He writes, "We are infiltrated by the world with its attitudes, rather than the attitudes of the perspective of the Kingdom of God" (Schaeffer, 27). What should the mentality of the believer be? He answers, "What is being presented to us here is the question of the Christian's mentality in all of life, and the order stands: rejected, slain, raised" (Schaeffer, 26). One of the themes of Schaeffer's writing is renunciation of self, death to self, as the starting point in growing in Christ. He is quite clear that justification, being "saved," is just the beginning, not the end. He explains, "But if we want to know anything of reality in the Christian life, anything of true spirituality, we must 'take up our cross daily.' The principle of saying 'no' to self lies at the heart of my attitude toward the world as it maintains its alien stand in rebellion against the Creator" (Schaeffer, 29-30).

Schaeffer also talks about a resurrection after the rejection of self. He writes, "in our thoughts and lives now we are to live *as though we had already died, been to heaven, and come back again as risen*" (Schaeffer, 41). The only way we can accomplish this, according to Schaeffer, is "in the Spirit's power." He writes, "The Holy Spirit is specifically introduced to us here as the agent of the power and the person of the glorified Christ" (Schaeffer, 57).

Schaeffer covers another of the themes in his writing and teaching career, that of the naturalism of this age creeping into the values of modern Christians. He writes, "I am impressed with the number of times I am asked by Christians about the loss of reality in their Christian lives. Surely this is one of the greatest, and perhaps *the* greatest reason for a loss of reality: that while we say we believe one thing, we allow the spirit of the naturalism of the age to creep into our thinking, unrecognized" (Schaeffer, 60). Therefore, according to Schaeffer, we must strenuously resist the idea of a purely naturalistic universe. He adamantly proclaims that "we live in a personal universe in which there is a personal God who objectively exists" (Ibid.). It is a supernatural universe in which we live. Thus, Schaeffer sums up how we are to live in this supernatural universe. "This is the Christian life, and this is true spirituality. *In the light of the unity of the Bible's teaching in regard to the supernatural nature of the universe,* the 'how' is the power of the crucified and risen Christ, through the agency of the indwelling Holy Spirit, by faith" (Schaeffer, 70). That, in essence, is the secret of the successful Christian life.

One of the things I like about Schaeffer's book is that he recognizes the fact that salvation is not only a past event, but has a present and a future aspect. I remember hearing over and over in my youth that salvation was something that happened in the past. There was a tremendous emphasis on getting people "saved." Once they were saved, it was as if they had arrived. However, we are presently being saved; that is sanctification. Plus, we shall be saved; that is glorification. Schaeffer also writes that once we trust in Christ as our Savior, "we are immediately in a new relationship with God the Father. God the Fa-

ther is immediately *our* Father. He is 'Abba'—Daddy—to us"
(Schaeffer, 80).

In Section II of this book, Schaeffer explains what it means to
be free from the results of the bonds of sin. He first considers
man's separation from himself and how we can now have freedom from conscience and in the thought-life. Jesus taught that
what we think, we are. Many believers are defeated in their
Christian lives because of they cannot control evil thoughts.
Schaeffer also writes about the healing of psychological problems as well as the whole person.

Finally, Schaeffer concludes this brief book with a discussion of
how man is separated from his fellowman and he explains how
we can have healing in personal relationships and in the
Church. This is needed today because of the increasing polarization in the United States in politics and religion.

Many people today consider themselves to be "spiritual," but,
in reality, have no idea just what that means. Francis Schaeffer
had been a Presbyterian pastor for over a decade when he wondered whether being a Christian really made a difference in
how people behaved. This book was the result. Schaeffer lays
out for us exactly what true spirituality is and how we can
model it in our lives. It is another "must read" by this extraordinary man of God and Christian thinker.

66. ORDERING YOUR PRIVATE WORLD

By Gordon MacDonald

When *Future Shock* was published over a half century ago in 1970, American futurist Alvin Toffler envisioned a world fast-approaching in which change would occur so rapidly that it would be impossible for people and societies to keep pace. In fact, he defined the term "future shock" as a psychological state of individuals and societies in which they perceived to be on the receiving end of "too much change in too short a period of time." Mind you, this was before the age of the personal computer, the Internet, smart phones, and the like. His book resonated with many because they felt that as the title suggested, they were experiencing "future shock." They felt that their lives were spinning out of control. Certainly, in the fifty or so years since the book's publication, the situation has gone from bad to worse and Christians are not immune to the changes. I must confess that I felt a lot of future shock after I finally made the transition from the VHS format to DVD for movies only to be told by my children that nobody uses DVDs anymore. In any event, there are many Christians who feel as if their private world is spinning out of control. This book is for them and for anyone else who has difficulty managing time.

The name, Gordon MacDonald, is a familiar one in the evangelical world. He served for many years as the senior pastor at the megachurch, Grace Chapel, in Lexington, MA, before moving on to many other prestigious positions such as head of Intervarsity Christian Fellowship, Chairman of World Relief, Editor at Large for *Leadership Journal,* and Chancellor as well as interim president at Denver Seminary. He is Pastor Emeritus of Grace Chapel. He is also a prolific author having written or co-written over a dozen books. I was most impressed with Mac-

Donald's preaching when I heard him speak at a Moody Pastor's Conference in Chicago back in the 1980s.

In my judgment, *Ordering Your Private World* is the most important book that MacDonald has written and one of the most important published in the twentieth century about how to live the Christian life. The problem is that many, if not most people, live in a state of constant inner disorder. Their lives appear to be lived in constant disarray. They have difficulty finding the time for Bible reading and prayer. This seems to be particularly true for some Christians. They live lives of constant anxiety and little spiritual growth. Their lives are lived in perpetual disorder. MacDonald argues that, using the experiences and writings of the great saints as well as the writings of more contemporary sages, the inner life can be ordered and regulated. When that occurs, there can be tremendous personal growth, character development, and Christian witness.

I will never forget the time of my life when this book first appeared in print. It was 1984 and I was winding down my first full-time pastoral position in a church in Michigan and preparing to move to a little Presbyterian church in North Carolina. My life was disorder upon disorder. Prior to moving to Michigan, I was a full-time seminary student working three jobs and struggling to pay the bills. *Ordering Your Private World* was just what the doctor ordered and could have been written exclusively for me and my situation. I devoured the book and tried to incorporate what MacDonald was saying into my own frantic and disordered life.

MacDonald describes the perilous situation many Christians who have disordered lives find themselves in by comparing it to a sinkhole. His chapter titled "The Sinkhole Syndrome" likens their lives to one of Florida's sinkholes, which appear seemingly out of nowhere where solid ground once was. I live in central Florida and will never forget my first year here when the parking lot at a local grocery story and K-Mart suddenly collapsed into a large sinkhole. One day it was a regular parking lot; the next day it was a sinkhole. He describes the existence of some Christians who "too often live on the verge of a sinkhole-like collapse" (MacDonald, 15). Such a believer is "a person whose inner world is in shambles, whose life is caving in" (Ibid.).

A differentiation is made between those who are called and those who are driven. MacDonald points out that Jesus called people who were drawn to him and avoided the driven types of individuals. Jesus didn't ask for volunteers, only those whom he called. He writes, "How can you spot a driven person? Today it is relatively easy. Driven people show the marks of stress. Look for symptoms of stress, and you have probably found some driven men and women" (MacDonald, 29). Driven people are candidates for broken private worlds. MacDonald describes them as being gratified only by accomplishment, preoccupied with the symbols of accomplishment, caught in the uncontrolled pursuit of expansion, have a limited regard for integrity, possess limited or undeveloped people skills, tend to be highly competitive, often possess volcanic tempers, and are abnormally busy" (MacDonald, 31-36). He concludes that King Saul, a man whose life was a personal shipwreck if there ever was one, exhibited all of the characteristics of being driven. He writes, "From the very beginning Saul had been a driven man, and he had never cultivated the order of his private world" (MacDonald, 40).

Two chapters that I found particularly helpful are titled "Has Anyone Seen My Time? I've misplaced it!" and "Recapturing My Time." These two chapters are worth reading and re-reading. MacDonald discusses the symptoms of disorganization and what such a life looks like. When he talks about the cluttered appearance of a desk and the condition of a car, I feel as if he is writing about me. He writes, "The central principle of all personal organization of time is simple: *time must be budgeted!*" (MacDonald, 68). MacDonald draws an analogy between money and time. He explains, "When money is limited, one budgets. And where time is in limited supply, the same principle holds. The disorganized person must have a budgeting perspective. And that means determining the difference between the fixed—what one *must* do—and the discretionary—what one would *like* to do" (Ibid.). He uses Jesus as an example of someone who had tremendous demands on his time, but was never hurried or disorganized. Two insights that he shares about Jesus' personal organization of time are invaluable. First, *"He clearly understood His mission,"* and second, *"He understood His own limits"* (MacDonald, 70). MacDonald wisely suggests that we examine the life of Jesus for clarity on how to use our time wisely.

MacDonald shares his own personal struggles in the area of time management. "I wanted to make sound decisions about the budgeting of my time, and I wanted to be free of that frantic pitch of daily life in which one is always playing catch-up. Was it possible? Not the way I was going" (MacDonald, 72)! He compiled the lessons that he had learned and systematized them into what he calls "MacDonald's Laws of Unseized Time" (MacDonald, 74). They should be heeded by anyone who has difficulty in this area. They are "Law #1: Unseized Time Flows Toward My Weakness. Law #2: Unseized Time Comes Under the Influence of Dominant People in My World. Law #3: Unseized Time Surrenders to the Demands of All Emergencies. Law #4: Unseized Time Gets Invested in Things that Gain Public Acclamation" (MacDonald, 74-78). Having analyzed time wasters, he then suggests ways to recapture "my" time. Very penetrating analysis!

In Chapter 8, MacDonald talks about the need for Christians to discipline their minds. Here he covers some of the ground that Mark Noll does in his *The Scandal of the Evangelical Mind.* For example, he writes, "Although evangelical Christians have made an outspoken commitment to Christian education, there has not always been a high enough value placed upon the development of the mind" (MacDonald, 93). In so doing, Christians do cut corners and as a result, MacDonald concludes "there is an essential laziness and internal disorganization in many Christian lives" (MacDonald, 94). He believes that some Christians "appear to be afraid to think" and that they "mistake the gathering of facts, doctrinal systems, and lists of rules for thinking. They are uneasy when dealing with open-ended questions. And they do not see the significance of wrestling with great ideas if they cannot always come up with easily packaged answers. The consequences are a drift toward mediocrity in personal living and mental activity and a loss of much that God meant for His children to enjoy" (MacDonald, 97).

In Chapter 9, MacDonald builds upon the foundation he laid in the previous one. He titles it "The Sadness of a Book Never Read." Here he lays out three objectives for people to place themselves into a "growth mode." He calls these objectives for "developing the intellectual dimension of our private worlds." "Objective One: The mind must be disciplined to think Christianly" (MacDonald, 101). "Objective Two: The mind must be taught to observe and appreciate the messages God has written in creation" (MacDonald, 102). "Objective Three: The mind must be trained to pursue information, ideas, and insights for the purpose of serving the people of my public world" (MacDonald, 103). He then suggests several disciplines in which we can engage which will help us grow intellectually. Very stimulating! He compares books to people. A book may show outer marks of wear and tear, but may have never been read. Likewise, people have large areas of their private worlds that "remain unopened." MacDonald opines, "They are disorganized within because they have never stretched and conditioned their minds to handle the information and challenges of the age" (MacDonald, 112).

MacDonald suggests that Christians cultivate the inner life. He calls it "Order in the Garden." He fears that for many believers the inner life is neglected. He warns about the consequences of such neglect. "A disorganized spirit often means lack of inner serenity. For some, what should be tranquility is in fact only numbness or emptiness" (MacDonald, 116). What this means is that we often have nothing in the tank for a reserve in time of crisis. He writes, "A neglected, disordered spiritual center usu-ally means that, we have little *reserve or resolve for crisis mo-ments* such as failure, humiliation, suffering, the death of a loved one, or loneliness" (MacDonald, 120).

MacDonald also suggests that Christians rediscover the spiri-tual disciplines of the Christian faith. These spiritual disci-plines go back hundreds, and even thousands, of years, but have been neglected by many believers of the past two cen-turies. He writes, "We strengthen the innermost strands . . . by making sure that God's words are entering the garden of our private worlds. Our first step in spiritual discipline is finding solitude and silence; the second step is learning to listen to God. The third step . . . is done through *reflection and medita-tion*" (MacDonald, 139-40). He also recommends reading Chris-tian classics. "Reading the great classics of Christian literature is a must for spiritual growth" (MacDonald, 141). I have been banging that drum for a number of years as has Warren Wiersbe. Amen to that!

At the end of each of the book's fourteen brief chapters is a one-sentence declaration titled "Memo to the Disorganized." Each memo begins with the words, "If my private world is in order," and offers a helpful piece of advice to the harried. For example, at the end of Chapter 5, the memo reads "If my pri-vate world is in order, it will be because I have made a daily determination to see time as God's gift and worthy of careful investment." Another helpful memo reads, "If my private world is in order, it will be because I see myself as Christ's steward and not master of my purpose, my role, and my identity" (Mac-Donald, 50). There is also a study guide appended to the back of the book by Leslie H. Stobbe that includes helpful questions for reflection on each chapter.

This is a book that is fun and easy-to-read. The chapters are brief enough that each one can be easily read in five or ten min-utes in an easy chair. That is how I did it. In our hurried and harried world, there are many Christians who live disordered lives and whose private worlds are in a state of disarray. Mac-Donald has written a book that will help believers avoid the "sinkhole syndrome" and live spiritual lives of calm and order.

67. THE GOLDEN COW: MATERIALISM IN THE TWENTIETH CENTURY CHURCH

By John White

Allow me to begin by saying how much John White's books helped me during my seminary years and when I was a young pastor. He published his first books, *The Cost of Commitment* and *The Fight: A Practical Handbook for Christian Living*, during my first year of seminary. I read them along with all the other books that were required for my seminary classes and couldn't wait for more. During my years of seminary, White published about one book per year which I eagerly snapped up and read: *Eros Defiled: The Christian and Sexual Sin* (1977), *Daring to Draw Near: People in Prayer* (1977), *The Golden Cow: Materialism in the Twentieth-Century Church* (1979), *Parents in Pain: Overcoming the hurts and Frustration of Problem Children* (1979), *Flirting With the World: A Challenge to Loyalty* (1982), and *The Masks of Melancholy: A Christian Physician Looks at Depression & Suicide* (1982). Even though I had plenty of required reading as well as Hebrew and Greek studies, I began to look forward to the next John White book as much as my wife and I now look forward to the next John Grisham novel.

John White (1924-2002) was well-qualified to write on the vast array of topics he tackled. Although he was best-known as a Christian author and international speaker having worked with the International Fellowship of Evangelical Students of Latin America, he was also a medical doctor with a specialty in psychiatry. He was born in Liverpool, England, but moved to Canada in 1965, where he completed his residency in psychiatry and was associate professor of psychiatry at the University of Manitoba. He also served as pastor of Church of the Way. White had a very interesting and adventurous life. He served during World War II in the British Fleet Air Arm as a reconnaissance photographer and served in several short-term mission endeavors including behind the Iron Curtain as a Bible smuggler and in Bolivia with New Tribes Mission.

Later in life, he became associated with the national Association of Vineyard churches and helped to start the Surrey Vineyard of Vancouver, British Columbia.

But back to *The Golden Cow*. When I read the book soon after its publication in 1979, it was like being hit over the head with a sledgehammer. I saw so many parallels between the modern church in the West and the money changers Christ drove out of the temple. I saw parallels between our church and the Israelites in the Old Testament whom the prophets accused of idolatry and prostitution. I began to realize that we in the Western church had begun worshiping a golden cow of our own of materialism and success.

The Golden Cow begins with Jesus—where else could it begin—in the temple court. He is enraged because of the buying and selling and money changing taking place there. He cried out, "Is it not written, 'My house shall be called a house of prayer for all nations? But you have made it a den of robbers.'" White continues with the Old Testament prophet Isaiah who thundered against the Jerusalemites of his day who were guilty of commercial dishonesty such as "exploitation of the consumer, legal corruption, and violent oppression" (White, 17). They are described using different images: "rebellious sons, stubborn asses, forgetful oxen, and an unrighteous harlot" (White, 18). He writes, "The images used have one point in common: God's people, in sinning as they do, have forgotten *who they are to whom they belong*" (Ibid.). The prophets Jeremiah and Ezekiel also vilify Israel for her harlotry. He points out that Jesus used a whip of cords and the prophets a whip of words.

White believed that materialism was not just practiced by the ancient Israelites up to the time of Christ and in the Western world today. It is ubiquitous. He writes, "We live in a materialistic world divided by iron and bamboo curtains into two materialistic camps, those of capitalist materialism and of communist materialism" (White, 37). However, he saw a big difference between Christians in the West and those in other parts of the world. He says that Christians who live in places "much less affected by the temptation of our kind of materialism" seem to evidence a spirit of joy and that our Western Christianity seems hollow by comparison.

White is scathing in his portrayal of the modern church, at least the church of the 1970s when the book was written. He believed that we have sold ourselves out to mammon. He claims that even our decision-making processes such as in the matter of the construction of a church building is "governed more by the mass psychology of church members than by prayerful planning" (White, 81). He guesses that "we do not in fact build beautiful buildings for a spirit of worship but for prestige and pride" (White, 86). He concludes, "At the heart of the matter lies our dependence upon material things. We take them for granted. We accumulate them. We go into debt to acquire them, work longer hours to earn them. They enslave us. They enslave not only our bodies but our hearts which no longer have room for the crying of the needy, the starving and the dying" (White, 94). He applies our spirit of harlotry even to the pittances we give to our pastors and missionaries by way of "support." He writes that the church must "look carefully at the monster we have created" (White, 95). "We are part of a Christian world into which the worship of the golden cow has infiltrated more widely than most of us could ever dream. The church has become a harlot because her religion has become an industry. It is itself big business" (Ibid.).

But, White says, religion is not a business. However, were we to visit the average Christian bookstore, we would have to wonder as we wander aisle after aisle filled with "Jesus Saves" pencils and "John 3:16" coffee mugs, "I love Jesus" tee shirts and bumper stickers. White suggests that an antidote to this kind of materialism is teaching a biblical view of stewardship, which is not the same as fund raising. Pastors, elders, and teachers have a major responsibility to do this. "Christian leaders have a duty to teach God's people both the responsibility and the joys of giving. Such teaching has a spiritual goal. Its aim is not to raise money but to set Christians free from their bondage to money, to teach them the liberty of liberality and thus to increase their joy in the Lord" (White, 116).

White concludes his book by comparing many of our evangelism efforts to the consumer culture. We are so acclimated to the world around us that we never see its values creeping into the church. White writes, "We humans get desensitized quickly to things which horrify us" (White, 130). In that regard, perhaps we are like the proverbial frog in the pot of boiling water. He writes, "Christ is not a product to be marketed, nor are those to whom you witness customers" (White, 150).

White calls for a radical transformation in our way of thinking and values. He calls for us to examine our own hearts and "ask ourselves whether we have been lured into the seats of the moneychangers" (White, 134). And ask yourself this: If you think the Western church was materialistic in 1979 when this book was published, have our values improved or gotten worse? I think we all know the answer, hence the need to read this book.

68. RESPECTABLE SINS

By Jerry Bridges

Jerry Bridges (1929-2016) was a prolific conference speaker and author who wrote more than a dozen books and is perhaps best-known for his million selling *The Pursuit of Holiness*. But for my money, this book is the one that I recommend the highest. I think the subtitle of this book says it all, *Confronting the Sins We Tolerate*. As the author puts it so well in his Preface, "Conservative evangelicals . . . have become so preoccupied with some of the major sins of society around us that we have lost sight of the need to deal with our own more 'refined' or subtle sins."

Bridges was a staff member of the Navigators headquartered in Colorado Springs, CO. The Navigators is a para-church organization whose emphasis is discipleship training with a special interest in training others to share their faith in Jesus Christ with others. They are quite active on college and university campuses and are known for providing exceptional resources such as Bible study booklets and study aid materials. Bridges was particularly well-known internationally for his books on personal holiness.

In *Respectable Sins*, Bridges, in returning to his favorite theme of holiness, tackles the tough sins, the sins that many Christians do not consider to be sins, or at least not the really all that serious sins. I once heard Warren Wiersbe call them the "sins in good standing in the church." They are the sins that we tolerate because we all do them. In fact, many do not even consider them to be sins at all. Bridges begins his book with sin, or the lack of sin. His chapter is titled "The Disappearance of Sin." He laments, "The whole idea of sin has virtually disappeared from our culture. Unfortunately, the idea of sin is all but disappearing from many churches as well" (Bridges, 18). The reason for this, Bridges argues is "that the entire concept of sin has . . . been softened, even within many of our churches to accommodate modern sensibilities" (Bridges, 18-19). It is true, he says, that Christians deplore the sins of those in the world, "but on the whole, we appear to be more concerned about the sins of society than we are the sins of the saints. In fact, we often indulge in what I call the 'respectable' or even 'acceptable sins' without any sense of sin'" (Bridges, 19). He then gives several common examples such as the gossip about a brother or sister in Christ or the hurts we harbor over "wrongs long past." He concludes the chapter with a chilling indictment. "There is also a vast multitude who are quite judgmental toward the grosser sins of society but who seem pridefully unaware of their own person sins" (Bridges, 22).

Bridges then moves on to a discussion of the malignancy of sin. He compares sin to cancer, which "often invokes a sense of despair and sometimes even hopelessness" (Bridges, 23). As some cancer patients are in denial about their disease, some Christians are the same about their sins. "We who are believers tend to evaluate our character and conduct relative to the moral culture in which we live" (Bridges, 24). He then compares our own attitudes toward sin with those of the Puritans, who were not afraid to call a sin what it was. He challenges us. "Shall we presume on God's grace by tolerating in ourselves the very sin that nailed Christ to the cross" (Bridges, 29)? Bridges argues that we must deal with our sins, even the respectable ones! "Make no mistake. Dealing with sin is not an option. We are commanded to put sin to death" (Bridges, 36). He informs the reader that it is possible with the power of the Holy Spirit and then Bridges tells us step by step how that can be done.

The bulk of Bridges' book deals with a dozen clusters of specific sins that Christians have characterized as "respectable." He laments the fact, citing numerous studies, that "there is little difference between the values and behavior patterns of Christians and non-Christians" (Bridges, 58). He explains why this has happened. He writes, "Living one's daily life without regard to God probably doesn't seem like sin to many people" (Bridges, 60). One thing that I really like about this book is that over and over again, Bridges addresses one of my pet peeves, the driving habits of Christians. Some believers blissfully drive ten to twenty miles above the speed limit just like unbelievers. The only difference between the Christian and the non-Christian is that the Christian may have an *icthus* (fish) decal on his bumper or a sticker that says "God is my co-pilot." Some Christians apparently do not believe that speeding in our automobiles or blowing through stop signs are ethical issues even though the Apostle Paul is very clear in Romans 13 that we are to be subject to the governing authorities. Bridges makes very plain his meaning. "We are not only to eat to the glory of God, we are to drive to the glory of God, we are to shop to the glory of God, and we are to engage in our social relationships to the glory of God. Everything we do is to be done to the glory of God. That is the mark of a godly person" (Bridges, 57).

Bridges then explores a litany of sins. He begins with anxiety and frustration. He then explains why they are indeed sins. He defines frustration as being upset or angry "at whatever or whoever is blocking our plans" (Bridges, 69). Then he discusses discontentment and what he calls "unthankfulness." Again, these are sins that ingrained in us and in our church culture. Rather than beating us over the head with this, Bridges writes, "The primary purpose of this book is to help us face the presence of many of these subtle sins in our lives and to recognize the fact that, to a large degree, they have become acceptable to us. We tolerate them in our lives with hardly a second thought" (Bridges, 73).

Bridges continues with an expose of other common sins such as pride, selfishness, lack of self-control, impatience and irritability, and anger. His admonition with respect to self-control is important and should be heeded by every Christian. "What is self-control? It is a governance or prudent control of one's desire, cravings, impulses, emotions, and passions. It is saying no when we should say no. It is moderation in legitimate desires and activities, and absolute restraint in areas that are clearly sinful" (Bridges, 110). Bridges believes that the virtue of self-control is often overlooked by Christians and "receives little *conscious* attention." He explains, "We have boundaries from our Christian culture that tend to restrain us from obvious sins, but within those boundaries we pretty much live as we please" (Ibid.).

Towards the end of the book, Bridges includes a brief chapter on judgmentalism. He discusses what we wear to church services, alcohol use among Christians, doctrinal correctness, and interestingly enough contemporary music. The latter has been a hot button issue in many churches. The church that I grew up in did not have drums and guitars in the worship service. In fact, today's average church service appears radically different from the church of a half century ago. Many older worshipers, grew up with the old hymns and dislike the newer "praise songs." I am probably one of those "old fogies." Bridges writes, "It's true that a lot of contemporary music is shallow and human-centered. But there is much that is as God-honoring and worshipful as our traditional hymns. So let's avoid being judgmental" (Bridges, 142).

Envy, Jealousy, and related sins are dealt with next. Bridges talks quite frankly about his own struggles with envy. Then he talks about my favorite, sins of the tongue. He writes, "In this category, we must also include lying, slander, critical speech (even when true), harsh words, insults, sarcasm, and ridicule. In fact, we would have to say that any speech that tends to tear down another person—either someone we are talking about or someone we are talking to—is sinful speech" (Bridges, 159).

Finally, Bridges concludes his litany of respectable sins with worldliness. He defines it as follows: "Worldliness means accepting the values, mores, and practices of the nice, but unbelieving, society around us without discerning whether or not those values, mores, and practices are biblical. Worldliness is just going along with the culture around us as long as that culture is not obviously sinful" (Bridges, 166). Bridges then discusses three ways that worldliness manifests itself in the life of the believer: through money, through immorality, and through idolatry. Bridges is very clear on this. "What a warning this should be to all of us. We can be very learned in our theology or very upright in our morality and yet fail to display the gracious qualities of Christian character that Paul called the fruit of the Spirit" (Bridges, 101).

Bridges' *Respectable Sins* is a book that should be read by all Christians. We all practice these sins which we don't include under the category of sin. Yet, they are very clearly sin and we often fall prey to them. Bridges, according to the back cover, "writes not from a height of spiritual accomplishment but from the trenches of his own battles with sin." I dare you to read this book and not see your own face in the mirror that Bridges holds up to us. Could it be that we have gotten too comfortable with our own "respectable sins?"

69. CHRISTLESS CHRISTIANITY

By Michael Horton

When I first read this book several years ago, I was totally blown away. It was like being hit over the head with a sledge-hammer. I was captivated by his first paragraph in which he shared the scenario that Presbyterian minister Donald Grey Barnhouse proposed on his nationwide broadcast on CBS over sixty years ago. Horton writes, "Barnhouse speculated that if Satan took over Philadelphia, all of the bars would be closed, pornography banished, and pristine streets would be filled with tidy pedestrians who smiled at each other. There would be no swearing. The children would say, 'Yes, sir' and 'No, ma'am,' and the churches would be full every Sunday . . . *where Christ is not preached* " (Horton, 15). At that point I was hooked.

Horton, the J. Gresham Machen Professor of Systematic Theology and Apologetics at Westminster Theological Seminary in California who received his doctoral degree from the University of Cambridge, believes that the church in America today is well on its way to becoming a church where Jesus Christ is merely an afterthought. He writes, "I think that the church in America today is so obsessed with being practical, relevant, helpful, successful, and perhaps even well-liked that it nearly mirrors the world itself. Aside from the packaging, there is nothing that cannot be found in most churches today that could not be satisfied by any number of secular programs and self-help groups" (Horton, 16-17). He believes that the church has drifted away from being Christ-centered to being human-centered. The regular diet in these churches in America today is "do more, try harder." The church is shallow and self-absorbed. He says, "The focus still seems to be on us and our activity rather than on God and his work in Jesus Christ. . . . there is a tendency to make God a supporting character in our own life movie rather than to be rewritten as new characters in God's drama of redemption" (Horton, 18). "It is not heresy as much as silliness that is killing us softly. God is not denied but trivialized" (Horton, 24). This is very strong stuff indeed!

In an email exchange with the author, Horton confided to me that out of all the books he has written, this 2008 one was his least favorite to write. I asked him what led to the writing of the book. He answered, "There were lots of trends I think that were distracting from the core message—speculative and sensational end times scenarios, the signs and wonders movement, prosperity movement, culture wars, etc. The Bible is an unfolding drama with Christ as the central character—and not just any Jesus we prefer (American Jesus, Jesus the Therapist/Life Coach, Business Guru, etc.), but 'the Lamb of God.' If theological liberals crave the acceptance of academic fashion, evangelicals tend to court the approval of pop culture. That divide between two different types of worldliness has only widened and worsened in the last decade, as the church mirrors either progressivism or populism. MSNBC churches and FOX churches have a home in about one-half of the US population, but churches that take the gospel for granted today will exchange it for another 'gospel' tomorrow. If I'm more interested in my church's position on masks than its view of the Trinity, justification by Christ's imputed righteousness, gospel-driven holiness, the means of grace and Christ's glorious bodily return, I need to rethink my priorities (April 12, 2022).

According to Horton, the church today mirror's contemporary society. He writes, "Grab all the glory now. No cross, no wrath, no judgment. Just be all that you can be. We are constantly bombarded by appeals to our native narcissism" (Horton, 91). "Flitting like a bumblebee from flower to flower of religious, spiritual, moral, psychic, and even familial and sexual identities, our generation actually finds it plausible that there can be genuine communities on the Internet" (Horton, 186). He is particularly scathing in his evaluation of the Prosperity Gospel theology of Joel Osteen and his ilk. He writes, "Salvation is not a matter of divine rescue from the judgment that is coming, but rather a matter of self-improvement in order to have your best life now" (Horton, 74). Of course, his denunciation also applies to other adherents of the so-called Prosperity Gospel. Horton sees the gospel that Osteen preaches as Christless and cross- less. He writes, "Because he does not face the bad news, Osteen does not really have any good news" (Horton, 99). He con- cludes, "If the central message of Christianity were how to have your best life now or become a better you, then rather than heralds we would need life coaches, spiritual directors, and motivational speakers. Good advice requires a person with a plan; Good News requires a person with a message" (Horton, 195). "In its therapeutic milieu, sin is failing to live up to our potential, not falling short of God's glory. It is 'sin' not to be- lieve in ourselves, and the wages of sin is missing out on our best life now" (Horton, 71). Horton weighs in on God's reason for his existence in the gospel according to Osteen. "Basically, God is there for you and your happiness. He has some rules and principles for getting what you want out of life, and if you follow them, you can have what you want. Just *declare it* and prosperity will come to you. God as *personal shopper*" (Horton, 68).

Horton pulls no punches in his indictment against the insipid Christianity that many in the United States practice. Here is a sample of his well-intentioned barbs. "The Bible is the constitu- tion for God's covenant people, not a textbook of general prin- ciples" (Horton, 207). "The central message of Christianity is not a worldview, a way of life, or a program for personal and societal change; it is a gospel" (Horton, 105). "If we are slaves, it is not to an external oppressor but to our own trivial desires" (Horton, 239). "We are the walking dead, forgetful that our de- signer-label fashions of religion and morality are really a death shroud. To paraphrase Jesus, we go through life like corpses with lipstick, not even aware that all of our makeovers and self- improvement are just cosmetic" (Horton, 241). "How could we ever have imagined that the best way to win the world to

Christ is to surrender the only legitimate tools that God has given for the breakthrough of Christ's kingdom in the very heart of this world's history of vanity?" (Horton, 248) ". . . proponents of the prosperity gospel (T.D. Jakes, Benny Hinn, Joel Osteen, and Joyce Meyer) are purveyors of a pagan worldview with a peculiar American flavor" (Horton, 68). "Evangelicals are as likely . . . today to talk about pop psychology, politics, or moralism instead of the gospel" (Horton, 30).

Thankfully, Horton doesn't simply identify the sickness in the evangelical church in America today. He actually has a cure. He summons the Church to find its true calling. We should be "scattered as salt and light throughout the week" and he reminds us that when we gather together, we have one calling: "to deliver (and receive) Christ through preaching and sacrament" (Horton, 209). He also reminds that we need to learn to feed ourselves. Many believers who have been Christians for decades are still spiritual babies in Christ and need to be bottle-fed and have their diapers changed. Horton says, "Our people need to learn to feed themselves through personal spiritual practices that allow them to deepen their relationship with Christ" (Horton, 193). The idea is to transition the church's role from that of a spiritual babysitting service to a spiritual coach. That is what disciple-making is all about. Finally, he says that we need to be less narcissistic and more Christ-centered and missional. He writes, "The answer to narcissism is not more talk about us, but bringing God's Word to the world" (Horton, 254).

Michael Horton is a first-rate theologian who is also quite a prolific writer. If Christless Christianity has whetted your appetite, you might be eager to read some of his heavier theological works. Be ready for some challenging reading. But the results will be worth the effort. Some books that are worth your time and attention are Recovering Our Sanity: How the Fear of God Conquers the Fears that Divide Us, The Christian Faith: A Systematic Theology for Pilgrims on the Way, Pilgrim Theology: Core Doctrines for Christian Disciples, Rediscovering the

Holy Spirit, For Calvinism, The Gospel-Driven Life: Being
Good News People in a Bad News World, and Core Christianity: Finding Yourself in God's Story. But by all means, read
Christless Christianity. You will be challenged, but you will not
be disappointed.

70. TRUST IN AN AGE OF ARROGANCE

By C. FitzSimons Allison

Christopher FitzSimmons Allison is a retired American Anglican clergyman who was formerly the Bishop of the Episcopal Diocese of South Carolina. He is perhaps best known for his role in the Anglican realignment and his opposition to the blessing of same-sex unions by the Episcopal Church. Born and raised in South Carolina, he was educated at Virginia Theological Seminary and then later at Oxford University where he received the Doctor of Philosophy degree in 1956. He became known as one of the remaining evangelical conservatives and something of an iconoclast in the increasingly liberal American Episcopal Church. He courageously stood for the authority of the Word of God when so many in his denomination were abandoning that position. I had the distinct honor and privilege of interviewing Bishop Allison prior to writing this description of his book. I can say this without hesitation that at ninety-five years of age, he is still as sharp as a tack.

On a personal note, I had the pleasure of meeting Bishop Allison some years ago when he preached at my home church, Westminster Presbyterian Church in Charlotte, N.C. His son, John, and daughter-in-law, Courtney, both attorneys, were attendees in my adult Sunday school class.

Bishop Allison's book is about trust and how it has been lost both in society and in the Church. Trust is such an essential commodity that when it has been lost or misplaced, it leads to disastrous consequences. As Allison writes on the back cover, it "causes cheating, lying, litigation, divorce, wars, genocide, and human misery. Western civilization is giving up trust in the promise of God's mercy, justice, and forgiveness and replacing it with trust in the goodness of man." Many have lost trust in the political systems of their countries; spouses have lost trust with their mates; and Christians have lost trust with their leaders in the wake of too many sexual and financial scandals to count.

At the center of all this is how Allison begins his book with the introductory chapter titled "The Center: I am Not and God Is." He rejects the writings of Ayn Rand and echoes those of William Temple when he writes, "We are not only born self-centered and are in rivalry and conflict with others who are also self-centered, but we are naturally at enmity with the true center, God" (Allison, xv). In *Trust in an Age of Arrogance*, Bishop Allison takes aim at two ancient approaches to religion that have infected the Church today: that of the Pharisees and of the Sadducees. He is scathing in his denunciation of both of them. He sees both of them as cancers in today's Church. He writes, "The biblical Sadducee is a near equivalent of today's secular humanist who believes that this world is all there is" (xvi). He defines his modern counterpart as "characterized by a low view of God, an unconcern with heaven or hell, and a commitment to self-esteem at the expense of transformation, salvation, and true unity with God" (Allison, xxviii). The Pharisee represents the other side of the coin. He disagrees with the Sadducee in many substantial ways, but this disagreement leads to self-righteousness and legalism. Allison sounds a clarion call of warning about the yeast of both the Sadducees and the Pharisees in the modern Church. He believes that they have contributed to the bondage of sinful arrogance that has no parallel in history. He writes, "Even pagans believed that hubris in the face of the gods would bring judgment and destruction. Awe, fear, trembling, dread, reverence, and even respect are almost absent today from the human posture before God" (Allison, 2).

Allison argues that those of us who live in modern (and postmodern) times have a different view of God than those of earlier centuries. He writes, "We have arrogated to ourselves the attributes of deity and given to God the responsibility to justify himself, repent, change, or disappear as irrelevant" (Allison, 1). He says that such a turn of events is unprecedented. "At no time in the history of either Christian or pagan religions has a people shown such hubris toward God or to the gods. Even pagans believed that hubris in the face of the gods would bring judgment and destruction. Awe, fear, trembling, dread, reverence, and even respect are almost absent today from the human posture before God" (Allison, 1-2). How do we learn to trust God again in such an age of arrogance? You see, the yeast of the Sadducees and the Pharisees has permeated our society and even the Church.

Allison argues that the yeast of the Sadducees leads to idolatry. He writes, "With the denial of resurrection and the loss of transcendent judgment, hopes this side of the grave become final hopes and therefore idolatrous" (Allison, 37). This is further demonstrated in *The Golden Cow* by John White. Their yeast has also led to a denigration of doctrine. Looking at the Church in the United States, I see that Allison is correct. We have become churches filled with people who are doctrinally generic. It is deemed petty to insist on certain doctrinal standards and creeds. What this leads to is distressing. Allison writes, "As virtues are reduced to values, values reduced to mere preferences, all objective standards are lost. Loyalty and morality are no longer seen as solid benchmarks for behavior but only as options for what seems to work for an individual" (Allison, 50). He also takes aim at the so-called "prosperity gospel." "Some distortions of Christianity, with their tit-for-tat heavenly rewards as motives for earthly virtue, promises of prosperity, 'naming and claiming' material rewards, express a religion of less virtue than that of the Stoic. The latter is willing to do the right thing with no expectation of reward because of this belief in objective, if unseen, reality of virtues that are not mere preferences. But the promise of prosperity is a distressing distortion of the Christian hope" (Ibid.).

Allison wonders why the yeast of the Sadducees is so seductive to us. He outlines four factors. The first is accommodation to the age in which we live. For his main illustration, he goes back in history many hundreds of years, even before the Sadducees were formed, to that of the ancient Israelites. "From the beginning, Israel's unfaithfulness in accommodating to the surrounding culture was condemned by God through the prophets" (Allison, 61). Another factor is a sense of the loss of the justice of God. He defines this as "the haunting absence in the secular mind of the justice of God. We live in a climate that has, to a considerable extent, lost its hope for justice" (Allison, 64). Allison cries out to the Church. "The urgent task at hand is to make sure authentic Christianity is again proclaimed. The justice, mercy, and love promised by Christian faith is largely unknown to many, even in churches, because it has been badly distorted and fatally misrepresented by both the Sadducean and Pharisaic yeast warned against by Jesus" (Allison, 66).

With respect to the yeast of the Pharisees, Allison explains that their religious tradition is "more complex than conventionally appreciated" (Allison, 67). The Pharisees in Jesus' time were strict legalists and hypocrites on top of that. Jesus was usually much harder on them than the Sadducees. Allison writes that in a modern context "Pharisees would have set clear boundaries and limits for the media, TV, movies, and publications. They may have been attracted by pornography, but they would have legislated against it, or fought for family values while having an affair" (Allison, 69). Why do the Pharisees attract us so? Allison explains that "Pharisaism, a pervasive counterfeit of the Christian faith, panders to our universal thirst for self-righteousness" (Allison, 81). Does this sound at all familiar? The antidote? Allison says the Sermon on the Mount "is the necessary, rigorous, and devastating purging of the Pharisee yeast. It's chemotherapy for the Pharisee cancer" (Allison, 73).

Allison takes no prisoners in this book and he spares no one, not even members of his Anglican faith tradition. In his chapter titled "Anglican Pharisees," he has his Anglican/Episcopal colleagues in his sights. He begins by writing, "Pharisaism, a pervasive counterfeit of the Christian faith, panders to our universal thirst for self-righteousness" (Allison, 81). He points out that classical Anglicanism had a "profound grasp of grace" as evidenced in the writings of such luminaries as Lancelot Andrews (c. 1555-1626), John Donne (c. 1571-1631), Richard Hooker (c. 1554-1600), George Herbert (c. 1593-1633), and John Davenant (c. 1593-1633). However, William Law, the author of *On Christian Perfection* (1726) and the influential classic *A Serious Call to a Devout and Holy Life* 1728), was deficient in that his "teaching lacked the full dimension of grace" (Allison, 83). He also took aim at the esteemed Bishop Jeremy Taylor (1613-1667), whose *Holy Living* and *Holy Dying* have been revered by generations of believers, not just in the Anglican tradition. He writes that Taylor's widespread acceptance is "conclusive evidence that the Christian gospel has been misrepresented and obscured" (Allison, 87).

Allison carefully documents the Pharisee yeast throughout the Church from John and Charles Wesley to Roman Catholicism and the Council of Trent. With respect to Roman Catholicism, he writes, "Works of supererogation and indulgences ... are the logical and historical result of the claim that we are worthy before God by virtue of the righteousness within us, a righteousness we can add to for merit" (Allison, 98). Allison is equal opportunity as he exposes the yeast in the Methodists and the Presbyterians. I admit to feeling a bit uncomfortable to reading about my own tradition, Presbyterian, being skewered. Allison writes, "The Pharisaic corruption within the Presbyterian tradition is especially ironic as few traditions have been as careful about how precisely to fashion the doctrine of grace and justification. The devil is indeed an equal opportunity deceiver" (Allison, 116).

Trust in an Age of Arrogance is the kind of book that may leave you feeling a bit uncomfortable. Os Guinness states in his cover endorsement of the book, "I started this book in an arm chair and finished it on my knees." When you read it, it may be like looking into a mirror and you will see yourself. It will likely drive you to self-examination and repentance. I can guarantee that you will not be the same after reading it. You may, indeed, finish it on your knees.

71. WHY US? WHEN BAD THINGS HAPPEN TO GOD'S PEOPLE

By Warren W. Wiersbe

In 1981, an interesting book appeared on the *New York Times* best-seller list. It was a curious thing because, first of all, it was a religious book. Religious books just did not make it onto secular best-seller lists. The second thing that was strange about this book was that it dealt with a profound theological problem. In fact, it attempted to grapple with one of the oldest and most vexing theological problems known to man. The title was *When Bad Things Happen to Good People* and its author was a Jewish rabbi, Harold S. Kushner.

As a young theology student and later as a rabbi, Harold Kushner was perplexed by the message of the book of Job in the Old Testament even as he studied and taught the book a number of times. As a young rabbi, he used the book to counsel people in his congregation about grief and pain. However, it was not until his three-year-old son, Aaron, was diagnosed with progeria, a disease that causes rapid aging, that what were formerly abstract theological beliefs became personal for him. Aaron died of his disease two days after his fourteenth birthday. According to Kushner, his son was a bright and happy child who began to gain weight and lose his hair as a toddler. Medical specialists informed Kushner and his wife that Aaron "would never grow much beyond three feet in height, would have no hair on his head or body, would look like a little old man while he was still a child, and would die in his early teens" (Kushner, 2).

Before Aaron's death, Kushner believed in a just world superintended by an all-powerful God. Good people were protected and rewarded and evil people were punished. Kushner had believed in "an image of God as an all-wise, all-powerful parent who would treat us as our earthly parents did, or even better" (Kushner, 3). After Aaron's diagnosis and subsequent death, he began to reexamine his views. What had happened to Aaron, in Kushner's mind, contradicted everything he had been taught about God, and so, after much study and thought on the matter, he came to the conclusion that God is well-meaning, but not omnipotent and cannot intervene in the daily affairs of the world. That led to the writing of his bestseller. He talks of a beneficent God who is limited in his powers. In fact, one of the chapters in the book is titled "God Can't Do Everything, But He Can Do Some Important Things."

The publication of Kushner's book produced a firestorm of negative reviews particularly from the evangelical Christian world. Kushner's God resembled more a kindly old man God-figure; picture George Burns from the 1977 movie *Oh, God!*, than the God of the Old Testament who is described as a "consuming fire." One evangelical leader, Charles Colson (see Chapter V, *Born Again*) was particularly scathing in his denunciation of the book. Evangelicals believed that Kusher's view of human suffering was not biblical and it was not orthodox. While many may have found Kushner's book comforting, many others found it heretical. I read the book soon after it was published and was aghast at Kushner's conclusions.

Enter Warren W. Wiersbe, a name that is very familiar in the evangelical world. He was an American pastor (Moody Memorial Church), Bible conference speaker, prolific author, and the successor to Theodore Epp as director and speaker of the *Back to the Bible* ministry. He is well-known to Christian readers as the author of widely-read *Be* series (*Be Mature, Be Joyful, Be Obedient*, etc.). Wiersbe has been hugely influential in my own life. I would guess that I have read his *Walking with the Giants* over a dozen times and each reading blesses me anew. His death in 2019 was a blow to evangelicals around the world.

In this book Wiersbe tackles the difficult question of why God allows suffering in the lives of his people. The title of this book published in 1984, *Why Us? When Bad Things Happen to God's People*, is a direct and, in my mind, not too thinly disguised refutation of Rabbi Harold Kushner's book, *When Bad Things Happen to Good People*. Wiersbe writes with a pastor's heart and offers spiritual insight for Christians dealing with pain, suffering, and death in their lives.

Wiersbe addresses his first chapter, "To You Who Hurt," to hurting people, those who are in emotional pain and/or physical pain. He references Kushner's book and concludes that both he and the rabbi had the same purpose in writing: "to help people who hurt and who are perplexed by the problems of life" (Wiersbe, 12). Wiersbe admits that he has wrestled with the same questions and that he has come to some biblically based conclusions: "1. Our answers to the problem of suffering must have intellectual integrity. 2. People live by promises, not by explanations. 3. We must live. 4. We must live for others. 5. The resources for creative suffering are available" (Wiersbe, 13-14). He warns the reader, "Suffering is not a topic for speculation; it is an opportunity for compassion and involvement. The mind grows by taking, but the heart grows by giving out" (Wiersbe, 15).

In Chapter 2, Wiersbe asks the really big question: "Why do bad things happen to good people?" He clarifies the issue by stating that there are several assumptions behind the question. He infers that the sincere inquirer actually believes certain things. For example, "There are values in this universe; the universe is logical and orderly; people are important; life is really worth living; and we can find answers that will help us" (19). That means that "the really big question is not 'Why do bad things happen to good people?' but 'What is the purpose of life'" (Wiersbe, 19)?

Wiersbe seemingly goes against the grain of much modern thinking in declaring "that happiness is not the major goal in life, but instead is a wonderful by-product" (Wiersbe, 20). After all, Kushner's book was widely-praised by theologians, psychiatrists, and counselors across the board. Wiersbe departs from Kushner's line of thought when he explains that "Bad things not only happen to *good* people, but they also happen to a select group of 'good people'—God's people. The fact that we know God as our Father and Jesus Christ as our Savior doesn't exempt us from the normal burdens of life, or from those special trials that surprise us at times. In fact, our faith could even make us a special target for enemy attack" (Wiersbe, 21). Kushner's view of a limited God who is not in control seems heretical to me. The title of his seventh chapter, to me, says it all: "God Can't Do Everything." Kushner asks, "Are you capable of forgiving God even when you have found out that He is not perfect" (Kushner, 148)? Huh??? Forgiving God?? Kushner's view of God is entirely deficient and decidedly un-Christian, not to mention un-Jewish.

Perhaps the most helpful and informative chapter in Wiersbe's book is titled "Pictures of Pain." Wiersbe goes through the Bible and describes some of the metaphors that describe pain and suffering in Scripture. He explains why they are so effective. "Why do we use...metaphors as we discuss the important things of life? For one thing, these pictures help us get our hands on some complex experiences. It's much easier to talk about 'the storms of life' than to go into the painful details" (Wiersbe, 54). Wiersbe, first of all, lists some of the obvious metaphors such as the furnace, the storm, and warfare. Then he discusses a less obvious one, the harvest. However, the ideas of threshing and the winnowing fork are certainly familiar to us. Wiersbe writes, "Of course, one of the obvious lessons from this agricultural metaphor is that we reap what we sow. We not only reap *what* we sow, but we also reap *in proportion* as we sow" (Wiersbe, 62).

Wiersbe also discusses the subject of pruning, which is most illuminating. It is absolutely necessary to understand this if we want to understand suffering in the life of the believer. The picture is of God as a gardener with a big set of pruning shears. Wiersbe writes, "Suffering is not always punishment for sin, in spite of what Job's friends may say. Sometimes our suffering is a pruning experience during which God carefully removes *good* things so that we may become more useful to Him and to others" (Wiersbe, 64). He also criticizes those who fail to comprehend these basic agricultural images. "How strange it is that people should accept the laws of nature, such as sowing, reaping, or pruning, and learn to cooperate with them and yet reject these same principles when they are applied to the spiritual life. If I enjoy my breakfast juice, cereal, and toast, it's because some seeds died and produced a harvest. Should I be so selfish that I refuse to permit God to 'plant' me, grind me in the mill, or crush me in the press, so that my life may feed others" (Wiersbe, 64-65)?

Wiersbe also explains the metaphors of travail and birth, running the race, and trial. He concludes this chapter with six lessons that these metaphors teach us that can help us in times of suffering: "(1) God has not promised to make us comfortable, but He has determined to make us conformable. (2) The battles of life are not easy, but God has given us the equipment we need to succeed. (3) We need patience. (4) Times of travail can be times of birth. (5) The storms are frightening, but God can speak to us out of the whirlwind. (6) Yield to the pruning knife; it will make you more fruitful" (Wiersbe, 72).

The basic problem with Kushner's book is that he argues for a limited God, who lacks the ability to do all things. In response to this deficient view of God, Wiersbe cites Psalm 103:19, "The Lord has established his throne in heaven." He writes, "That doesn't describe a 'limited God' in the process of becoming infinite" (Wiersbe, 82). Wiersbe also suggests that prayer is an exercise in futility if God is not in control. He argues, "If God is not in control, there is no sense talking to Him about your needs" (Ibid.). Wiersbe argues forcefully for an omnipotent God who is most certainly in control of everything in the universe.

Wiersbe includes several brief chapters dealing with such diverse topics as how to pray when life falls apart, character, hope, and dealing with disaster. He includes two helpful appendixes at the end of the book. The first is titled, "Questions You May Be Asking." In Appendix 1 he shares common questions that people have shared with him as well as his answers. Some of the questions asked are: "Why must innocent infants and children suffer? (Wiersbe, 150) "A friend of mine claims that there is 'healing in the atonement,' and that every Christian has the right to claim healing and perfect health because of the Cross. Do you agree with this?" (152) "What about the Holocaust" (Wiersbe, 153)? Appendix 2 is titled "A Little Anthology" and includes thirty-three pithy quotations that Wiesrsbe has used in preaching and counseling. These quotations come from such varied writers as Samuel Rutherford, Matthew Henry, Dwight L. Moody, St. Augustine, Ralph Waldo Emerson, Martin Luther, and Phillips Brooks.

Suffering is part and parcel of the human condition and is a result of the Fall. Christians are not magically immune from the trials and tribulations that afflict all people simply because they are believers. Children die tragically; drunken drivers plow into cars killing pregnant women and their child; seemingly good people suffer terribly from the ravages of cancer. Rabbi Kushner's book brought comfort to thousands of people wondering why these things happen. But it is a false comfort because it is based on a false premise. Warren Wiersbe has done a service to Christians everywhere in that he has provided a biblical response to Kushner's false teaching. You may have suffered sometime in your life or know someone who is or has. You owe it to yourself to read this book.

CHAPTER X:
DISCIPLESHIP AND CHRISTIAN DISCIPLINES

DISCIPLESHIP

Christian discipleship is a term that is rarely discussed outside of Christian circles. The second word, discipleship, comes from the root word, disciple (*mathetes*) from the verb *manthano*, which means "to learn." Hence, a disciple is a learner who follows the precepts of a teacher. However, it means much more than simply the transfer of information. A disciple was more than just a pupil; he was an adherent. The disciple/teacher relationship implies much more than that; it connotes a relationship. Jesus called his disciples so that they might be with him. Christ's disciples not only learned from him; they followed him, absorbed his values, and reproduced his teachings. In fact, that is what the Great Commission of Matthew 28 calls believers to do—to make disciples.

In the New Testament, Christian discipleship was a costly affair. It required disciples to count the cost and change their way of living. It required them to deny themselves, take up their crosses, and follow Jesus. Discipleship, then, is not to be taken casually or in a cavalier fashion. It is deadly serious. Of the three books included in the first part of this chapter, the first two are by the German pastor and theologian, Dietrich Bonhoeffer, who knew how to count the cost and was executed in a German concentration camp during World War II for his stand for the Gospel. They are absolute gems and classics! The third is by an American Presbyterian pastor who writes deeply and profoundly on the subject. All three books will enthrall you and challenge you.

72. LIFE TOGETHER

&

73. THE COST OF DISCIPLESHIP

By Dietrich Bonhoeffer

On April 9, 1945, by special order of Heinrich Himmler, Dietrich Bonhoeffer was executed at the concentration camp at Flossenburg mere days before it was liberated by allied forces. A tablet in the church in Flossenburg displays the following inscription which was unveiled on Easter Monday, 1953: "Dietrich Bonhoeffer was a witness of Jesus Christ among his brethren. Born February 4, 1906, in Breslau. Died April 9, 1945, in Flossenburg." Bonhoeffer's untimely death was yet another reminder of the truth so eloquently expressed by the early church father, Tertullian, "The blood of the martyrs is the seed of the Church." From his brief time of thirty-nine years on this earth, Bonhoeffer left an example and a literary legacy that is matched by few and still lives on and cries out loudly for us to listen.

Bonhoeffer spent his formative years in Berlin, where his father distinguished himself as a physician and became the first to occupy a chair of psychiatry in Germany. He grew up in a close, tightly-knit family where he learned that one's Christian walk could never be simply an intellectual exercise or at the opposite end of the spectrum, mystical emotion. He discovered that a walk with Jesus Christ must be lived out in concrete, tangible ways both in public and in private. He was an athletic youth who also played the piano skillfully and had among his childhood friends children of the scholar Adolf von Harack and the historian Hans Delbrück.

At age sixteen, Bonhoeffer committed himself to study theology which he did at Tübingen and Berlin, where he studied under such great scholars as Holl, Seeberg, Lietzmann, and Lütgert. He completed his doctoral dissertation, *Sanctorum Communio*, which was a theological study of the sociology of the church. He concluded that the church was "Christ existing as community," out of which *Life Together* was born.

In Berlin, Bonhoeffer lectured in systematic theology, served as a pastor to students at a technical school, and published his first book, *Creation and the Fall*. In 1933, he delivered over Berlin radio a scathing rebuke to the German public for their naïve acceptance of Adolph Hitler. The broadcast was cut off before he was allowed to finish. When Hitler's accension appeared to be inevitable, Bonhoeffer, refusing to collaborate in any way with the Nazi government, moved to London having accepted a pastoral call to two German congregations.

Bonhoeffer returned to Germany having interrupted his plans to visit Gandhi in India in his pursuit of pacifism. He had received a call from the Confessing Church to lead an illegal clandestine seminary in Pomerania. In 1935, he moved to Zingst and then to Finkenwalde. His experiences at Finkenwalde where he lived communally with twenty-five vicars were described and documented in his 1938 book, *Gemeinsames Leben*, which translated means "life together." He was forbidden by the Nazis to write or publish and his "underground" seminary was closed by the Gestapo.

Bonhoeffer moved briefly to the United States in 1939, but he refused the safety and comfort and returned to his native country to serve Jesus Christ by working with the Confessing Church and the Resistance movement. He spent his time moving about the country illegally preaching, teaching, and writing all of which he had been expressly forbidden to do. It was during this time that he wrote his classic work *Ethics*. In April 1943, he was arrested and sent to Tegal, a military prison, where friendly guards secretly allowed him to minister to prisoners. These guards also preserved his papers, essays, and the like and found a way to transport them outside the prison where they would be preserved. He was then transferred from Gestapo prison to prison and spent time in Buchenwald and Schonberg before finally landing in Flossenburg where he would be executed in 1945.

Life Together was written while Bonhoeffer taught at an underground seminary. He observed, "Among earnest Christians in the Church today there is a growing desire to meet together with other Christians in the rest periods of their work for common life under the Word. Communal life is again being recognized by Christians today as the grace that it is, as the extraordinary, the 'roses and lilies' of the Christian life" (21). Thus, this book grew directly out of his personal experiences of Christian community in the underground seminary. Throughout the book he stresses the centrality of Christ and points out that the Church is the meeting place of Christ and what it ought to be doing when it gathers together. He wrote, "Christian community means community through and in Jesus Christ. On this presupposition rests everything that the Scriptures provide in the way of directions and precepts for the communal life of Christians" (*Life*, 24). Keep in mind that this book arose out of the crucible of personal experience in Nazi Germany when the discovery of their fellowship would have meant prison and even death. He is not talking about the once per week fellowship meal at the church building where everyone goes back home to a comfortable existence. They found real community with one another. Bonhoeffer wrote, "The physical presence of other Christians is a source of incomparable joy and strength to the believer" (*Life*, 19). This book is for Christians who are hungry for real fellowship, not the plastic version we so often play at in the United States of the twenty-first century.

The fellowship and community that Bonhoeffer describes is deadly serious with deadly consequences. Yet, he is able to find some humor in the foibles of human personality. In writing about unison singing, he writes, "There is no place in the service of worship where vanity and bad taste can so intrude as in the singing" (*Life*, 60). He describes a couple of his comrades who sound coincidently like some of the good folks in my own church choir. He writes, 'There is the bass or alto who must call everybody's attention to his astonishing range and therefore sings every hymn an octave lower. There is the solo voice that goes swaggering, swelling, blaring, and tremulant from a full chest and drowns out everything else to the glory of its own fine organ" (Ibid.). Who knew that Bonhoeffer had such a sense of humor?

Bonhoeffer had a profound understanding of true spiritual love. He wrote of the differentiation between human and spiritual love. "Human love is directed to the other person for his own sake, spiritual love loves him for Christ's sake" (*Life*, 34). He also comprehended the necessity to be inclusive in the church. He wrote, "The exclusion of the weak and insignificant, the seemingly useless people, from a Christian community may actually mean the exclusion of Christ; in the poor brother Christ is knocking at the door" (*Life*, 38). This is a lesson that the twenty-first century evangelical desperately needs to learn.

In his chapter titled "The Day with Others," Bonhoeffer places great emphasis on communal practices. He points out that the New Testament commanded "speaking to yourselves in psalms" (Eph. 5:19). From there he points out that "we can and we should pray the psalms of innocence as Christ's prayer for us and to us" (*Life*, 48). I personally have been rediscovering this ancient practice to great spiritual enrichment. He writes, "The more deeply we grow into the psalms and the more often we pray them as our own, the more simple and rich will our prayer become" (*Life*, 50). Second, he opines that the prayer of the psalms ought to be followed by the reading of Scripture. The reading should be "brief, selected verses which are to form the guiding thought for the day" (Ibid.). He also advocates the consecutive reading of biblical books. He writes, "We must learn to know the Scriptures again, as the Reformers and our fathers knew them. We must not grudge the time and the work that it takes. We must know the Scriptures first and foremost for the sake of our salvation" (*Life*, 54).

I found Bonhoeffer's third chapter, "The Day Alone," to be of great help to me. He includes helpful discussions on solitude, but what really blessed me as well as stung me were his remarks on prayer. He writes, "The most promising method of prayer is to allow oneself to be guided by the word of the Scriptures, to pray on the basis of a word of Scripture. In this way we shall not become the victims of our own emptiness" (*Life*, 84). But it is his discussion of intercessory prayer that really hit me over the head. "I can no longer condemn or hate a brother for whom I pray, no matter how much trouble he causes me. His face, that hitherto may have been strange and intolerable to me, is transformed in intercession into the countenance of a brother for whom Christ died, the face of a forgiven sinner. This is a happy discovery for the Christian who begins to pray for others. There is not dislike, no personal tension, no estrangement that cannot be overcome by intercession as far as our side of it is concerned. Intercessory prayer is the purifying bath into which the individual and the fellowship must enter every day" (*Life*, 86). To me that is nothing short of profound. He ends with, "Who can really be faithful in great things if he has not learned to be faithful in the things of daily life" (*Life*, 87)?

Bonhoeffer's fourth chapter is titled "Ministry" and it offers some profound insights. He argues that "service should govern the Christian community." He says, "Once a man has experienced the mercy of God in his life he will henceforth aspire only to serve. The proud throne of the judge no longer lures him; he wants to be down below with the lowly and the needy, because that is where God found him" (*Life*, 94). About the ministry of helpfulness, he writes, "We must be ready to allow ourselves to be interrupted by God. God will be constantly crossing our paths and canceling our plans by sending us people with claims and petitions. We may pass them by, preoccupied with our more important tasks, as the priest passed by the man who had fallen among thieves, perhaps—reading the Bible" (*Life*, 99). Ouch!!

Some other gems from *Life Together*:

> "We pray for the big things and forget to give thanks for the ordinary, small (and yet really not small) gifts."

> "Let him who cannot be alone beware of community.... Let him who is not in community beware of being alone.... Each by itself has profound perils and pitfalls. One who wants fellowship without solitude plunges into the void of words and feelings, and one who seeks solitude without fellowship perishes in the abyss of vanity, self-infatuation and despair."

> "The person who loves their dream of community will destroy community, but the person who loves those around them will create community."

The Cost of Discipleship is, in the opinion of many, Bonhoeffer's most important work. In the book, he condemns cheap grace and calls for a radical discipleship. It was groundbreaking in its day, but still packs a punch. It is largely a commentary on the Sermon on the Mount (Matt. 5-7) with an addendum covering the charge of Jesus to his disciples (Matt. 10). His opening salvo sets the tone for the rest of the book. He begins the book, "Cheap grace is the deadly enemy of our Church. We are fighting today for costly grace" (*Cost*, 45). His words on the next page seem to describe the Church of the twenty-first century to a tee. But he was writing in the 1930s in Nazi Germany. "In such a Church the world finds a cheap covering for its sins; no contrition is required, still less any real desire to be delivered from sin" (*Cost*, 46).

Bonhoeffer's book, *The Communion of the Saints* was based on his 1930 doctoral dissertation, *Sanctorum Communio: A Theological Study of the Sociology of the Church*. In that important book, Bonhoeffer began to set out his vision of the church and its responsibility to judge society and its trends. He was not hesitant to critique the church and particularly his own Lutheran brand of Protestantism. He writes, "We Lutherans have gathered like eagles round the carcase (sic) of cheap grace, and there we have drunk of the poison which has killed the life of following Christ" (*Cost*, 57).

Of course, *The Cost of Discipleship* is about discipleship and what it should mean to the Christian? In his introduction, he asks, "What did Jesus mean to say to us? What is his will for us today? How can he help us to be good Christians in the modern world" (*Cost*, 37)? He then talks about the theological word "grace" and what it meant to Christ and what it should mean to the believer. He writes, "The grace which gave itself to him was a costly grace, and it shattered his whole existence" (*Cost*, 51). Bonhoeffer goes right to the source of what Jesus said and did, the Gospels, particularly the Sermon on the Mount. That is the major substance of this book (Matthew 5-7) along with Christ's charge to his disciples (Matthew 10). He believed that the Christians of his day had substituted a different gospel for the one revealed by Christ in his most famous sermon.

Bonhoeffer pulls no punches with his first sentence. "Cheap grace is the deadly enemy of our Church. We are fighting today for costly grace" (*Cost*, 45). A few lines further down, he says, "Grace without price; grace without cost" (Ibid.). Bonhoeffer further describes cheap grace. He writes, "The grace which amounts to the justification of sin without the justification of the repentant sinner who departs from sin and from whom sin departs. Cheap grace is not the kind of forgiveness of sin which frees us from the toils of sin. Cheap grace is the grace we bestow on ourselves" (*Cost*, 47). He ridicules the folly of such cheap grace. "Well, then, let the Christian live like the rest of the world, let him model himself on the world's standards in every sphere of life, and not presumptuously aspire to live a different life under grace from his old life under sin" (*Cost*, 46). He then explains why cheap grace is an oxymoron and why it is so costly. "Grace is costly because it compels a man to submit to the yoke of Christ and follow him" (*Cost*, 48). Bonhoeffer then asks, "Is there a more diabolical abuse of grace than to sin and rely on the grace which God has given" (56). The effect of all this is that "the word of cheap grace has been the ruin of more Christians than any commandment of works" (*Cost*, 59).

Bonhoeffer then discusses the ramifications of the call of Christ to discipleship. He cites the example of Levi (Matthew) the tax collector as a model of the call. He explains, "This encounter is a testimony to the absolute, direct, and unaccountable authority of Jesus. There is no need of any preliminaries, and no other consequence but obedience to the call" (*Cost*, 62). Discipleship, then, is no abstract, doctrinal concept, but the living essence of Christianity. He says, "Christianity without the living Christ is inevitably Christianity without discipleship, and Christianity without discipleship is always Christianity without Christ" (*Cost*, 63-64). He again cites the example of Levi at the receipt of custom and that of Peter at the nets. They both walked away. According to Bonhoeffer, the first step of discipleship is always walking away. He argues that it "cuts the disciple off from his previous existence. The call to follow at once produces a new situation. To stay in the old situation makes discipleship impossible" (*Cost*, 67). Thus, that initial step is of absolute importance. Everything depends upon it. Peter must leave his nets. Levi must leave his table. The rich young man must forsake his wealth. Bonhoeffer pulls no punches when he writes, "Only the obedient believe. If we are to believe, we must obey a concrete command. Without this preliminary step of obedience, our faith will only be pious humbug, and lead us to the grace which is not costly" (*Cost*, 70). The call of Christ leads to the inevitable and as Bonhoeffer put it so well, "He bids him come and die."

Christian discipleship is not for sissies and it is not for the halfhearted. *The Cost of Discipleship* is an argument for costly grace, costly because a man had to die to obtain it and we have to give up our lives to confirm it. Dietrich Bonhoeffer was only thirty-nine years of age when he paid the ultimate price for his faith, but the profound impact made through his life and death and brilliant writings continue to inspire us many decades after his death.

I have a confession to make. While still a student in seminary, I was a bit leery of the writings of Dietrich Bonhoeffer. What a fool I was. We learned to read the German theologians very critically and warily because of their tradition of liberal theology. Billy Sunday, the fiery evangelist of the early twentieth century, once stated that "if you turn hell upside down, you will find 'Made in Germany' stamped on the bottom." But that was before I had actually read the writings of Bonhoeffer. And once I did that, I fell in love with his heart for God. I believe you will too.

74. A LONG OBEDIENCE IN THE SAME DIRECTION

By Eugene H. Peterson

The thoughtful reader might inquire as to why I have included a book in my list of 100 that at one time apparently nobody wanted to read and almost nobody wanted to publish. In the late 1970s before its eventual publication in 1980, seventeen publishers had given Eugene Peterson the "thumbs down" to this book telling him variously that either there was no "niche" in the market or it was "irrelevant to the concerns of contemporary North Americans" (Peterson, 202). Had InterVarsity not decided to take a risk with a middle-aged Presbyterian pastor with zero books to his credit, one of my favorite writers might have grown discouraged and quit. Thankfully, the publication of this book gave Peterson a "foothold" in the publishing world and the confidence to continue. Had he not continued, we likely would not have been blessed with some of the most delightful books of the past few decades, such as *Praying with the Psalms* (see Chapter VIII), *The Message: The Bible in Contemporary Language, Run with the Horses: The Quest for Life at Its Best*, and *Eat This Book: A Conversation in the Art of Spiritual Reading* among many others.

Although the title of this book may appear to be a bit ambiguous to some and wordy to others, the subtitle explains it all: *Discipleship in An Instant Society*. Simply put, this is a book about discipleship and how to do it. The title, while perhaps unfamiliar to some, actually comes from a quotation by Friedrich Nietzsche from his 1907 book *Beyond Good and Evil*. Peterson, then, understands the Christian walk as a long one that proceeds in one direction, hence the title.

This book is a unique approach to Christian discipleship in that he likens the modern Christian's spiritual pilgrimage to that of the ancient Israelites and their thrice annual journeys "up" to Jerusalem to attend the great worship festivals. They often had to travel long distances. Since Jerusalem topographically was the highest city in Palestine, on their pilgrimages pious Hebrews would sing songs from the Psalter. These were the psalms numbered 120 through 134 and they came to be known as the Songs of Ascents, or in Hebrew *shiray hammaloth*. As Peterson explains, "The ascent was not only literal, it was also a metaphor: the trip to Jerusalem acted out a life lived upward toward God, an existence that advanced from one level to another in developing maturity" (Peterson, 18). Hence, this is a book about discipleship, but quite unlike any that I have ever read. Peterson examines each psalm in order and assigns it a title or theme. For example, Psalm 120 is titled "Repentance," which he calls "the first word in Christian immigration, [and] sets us on our way to traveling in the light. It is a rejection that is also an acceptance, a leaving that develops into an arriving, a no to the world that is a yes to God" (Peterson, 33).

According to Peterson, two terms encapsulate the Christian journey. The first comes from the New Testament, disciple (*mathetes*), which according to him in the plural form "are people who spend our lives apprenticed to our master, Jesus Christ. We are in a growing-learning relationship, always. A disciple is a learner, but not in the academic setting of a schoolroom, rather at the work site of a craftsman" (Peterson, 17). The second term, pilgrim, describes a person who is going someplace. Peterson describes Christians as people who realize that the world is not our home. We are simply passing through on a spiritual pilgrimage with the patriarch Abraham as "our archetype." I'm reminded of the gospel song I sang as a child, "This world is not my home, I'm just a passing through, My treasures are laid up somewhere beyond the blue."

As pilgrims and disciples in this world, Peterson argues that we face numerous difficulties in this world that fall under three categories: the world, the flesh, and the devil. He writes, "Their temptations have a definite shape and maintain a historical continuity. That doesn't make them any easier to recognize" (Peterson, 15). He also says that Christians have been negatively influenced by the instant society in which we live and our shortened attention spans. Peterson opines, "We assume that if something can be done at all, it can be done quickly and efficiently" (Peterson, 16). That is not how discipleship works. He discusses the "terrible attrition rate" of people who have made "decisions" for Christ. He explains, "Many claim to have been born again, but the evidence for mature discipleship is slim. In our kind of culture everything, even news about God, can be sold if it is packaged freshly; but when it loses its novelty, it goes on the garbage heap. There is a great market for religious experience in our world; there is little enthusiasm for the patient acquisition of virtue, little inclination to sign up for a long apprenticeship in what earlier generations of Christians called holiness" (Ibid.).

This book is a treasure trove of spiritual insights that is a delight to read. Peterson writes so beautifully that I am tempted to be envious. I cannot share everything with you, but following are a few of the highlights.

From Psalm 121, Peterson derives lessons on the biblical doctrine of providence. He translates the first verse, "I look up to the mountains; does my strength come from mountains?" I had never really given this verse much thought and I confess to you that I have been teaching the Psalms and Hebrew poetry in a graduate level setting for almost forty years. Like so many readers of Scripture, we simply gloss over the details and ignore the obvious. Why would the ancient Hebrews look to the mountains, or to "the hills" as the NIV translates it? As they traveled up towards Jerusalem, what would they see around them? Obviously, they would see hills, but it was what was on those hills that provided the temptation to doubt God. Peterson explains, "During the time this psalm was written and sung, Palestine was overrun with popular pagan worship. Much of this religion was practiced on hilltops. Shrines were set up, groves of trees were planted, sacred prostitutes both male and female were provided; persons were lured to the shrines to engage in acts of worship that would enhance the fertility of the land, would make you feel good, and protect you from evil" (Peterson, 40). That is why there are so many prohibitions in the Old Testament against the "high places." What would the Hebrews see all around them? Shrines dedicated to Baal and Asherah and dozens of others! The psalmist asks, "Does my strength come from the mountains?" In other words, does it come from Baal? Asherah? The sun priest? The moon priestess? What does the modern believer see today on his spiritual journey? There are numerous trials and temptations and help comes only from the Lord. Peterson writes, "No literature is more realistic and honest in facing the harsh facts of life than the Bible. At no time is there the faintest suggestion that the life of faith exempts us from difficulties. What it promises is preservation from all the evil in them" (Peterson, 42).

Another favorite chapter is the one titled "Perseverance" based on Psalm 129. Peterson translates verse 2, "They've kicked me around ever since I was young, but they could never keep me down." On a long journey, people become fatigued and want to quit. People take wrong turns or have flat tires. I remember one year traveling from North Carolina to Florida as we began our vacation. We made a wrong turn and lost about an hour of time. How frustrating it was! Peterson writes, "The psalms are not sung by perfect pilgrims. The pilgrims of old made their mistakes, just as we make ours. *Perseverance* does not mean 'perfection.' It means that we keep going. We do not quit when we find that we are not yet mature and there is a long journey still before us" (Peterson, 131). Thankfully, my family and I got back on the right road and made it to our destination, albeit an hour or so later than anticipated, and had a wonderful week of vacation. It would have been foolish to get angry and return to North Carolina because of one silly mistake. Peterson writes, "The central reality for Christians is the personal, unalterable, persevering commitment God makes to us. Perseverance is not the result of *our* determination; it is the result of God's faithfulness" (Peterson, 132-33).

The penultimate psalm that Peterson examines is Psalm 133 which he titles "Community." This is a well-known brief chapter of Scripture that talks about the anointing oil that flows down Aaron's head and beard to the collar of his priestly robes. He translates the first verse, "How wonderful, how beautiful, when brothers and sisters get along!" Peterson lays it on the line. "Our membership in the church is a corollary of our faith in Christ. We can no more be a Christian and have nothing to do with the church than we can be a person and not be in a family" (Peterson, 175). In my acquaintance, there are some who claim to be Christian, but do not attend church and do not feel that it is necessary to be part of a faith community. They want to be what I call "Lone Ranger Christians," which is an oxymoron if there ever was one. The Bible does not recognize such a person. As Peterson writes, "Scripture knows nothing of the solitary Christian. People of faith are always members of a community" (Peterson, 176-77).

In his final chapter, Peterson writes that he sometimes amuses himself by imagining Friedrich Nietzsche, the German philosopher and avowed atheist who proclaimed the death of God in the eighteenth century and also provided the title for this work, appearing in his study while he is writing his books. He writes that Nietzsche "was convinced that Christians, by promoting the weak and ineffectual Jesus to keep the weakest, spiritually diseased, morally unfit and inferior parts of the population alive and reproducing, were a malign influence on civilization and would be the ruin of us all" (Peterson, 206). He thought he had dealt a death blow to Christianity and Peterson imagines "him standing there angry and appalled, beard smoking, astonished that these weak, inadequate, ineffectual and unfit Christians are still alive, and still reproducing" (Ibid.).

Were Nietzsche here today, he would likely be flummoxed at this book, particularly its title. He might even refuse to read it.

But you, dear Christian, should read it. Eugene Peterson's beautiful book will be good for your soul.

CHRISTIAN DISCIPLINES

Mention the Christian disciplines or its similar term spiritual disciplines to the average twenty-first century Protestant believer and you will usually get a blank look. Images are immediately conjured in the mind of a monk living secluded in a desert cave or a mountain monastery. One often thinks of some mystical Roman Catholic practices that have no connection to the real world. These thoughts are unfortunately based on misconceptions and bear little resemblance to the truth.

In reality, many of the spiritual disciplines have been practiced by thoughtful believers for centuries. Practices such as prayer, study, submission, service, confession, worship, and celebration have been part and parcel of the average Christ-follower's daily regimen for spiritual growth. They just haven't identified them as spiritual disciplines.

Thomas Hume, the eighteenth-century Scottish philosopher and thinker, wrote in his *Enquiry into Morals*, "Celibacy, fasting, penance, mortification, self-denial, humility, silence, solitude, and the whole train of monkish virtues: for what reason are they everywhere rejected by men of sense, but because they serve to no manner of purpose; neither advance a man's fortune in the world, nor render him a more valuable member of society; neither qualify him for the entertainment of company, not increase his power of enjoyment" (Cited in Willard, 132). We might update Hume's words for the past few decades by adding a few references to hot tubs, fast cars, drinking craft beer, and gorgeous women and we would not be too far off the mark.

Why have modern Christians adopted such negative attitudes toward the classical spiritual disciplines? Why are those disciplines that were so central to the lives of Jesus Christ and the

Apostle Paul in the first century and John Wesley, John Knox, Martin Luther, and George Fox in later centuries so little regarded today by the majority of those who call themselves Christ-followers? Why do so many today regard those who practice the spiritual disciplines as fanatical and trite? Why is it that we think we can reap a spiritual harvest without sowing spiritual seed? Our modern Western society has produced instant Christians who are a mile wide and an inch deep.

The classical spiritual disciplines are God's way of producing deep Christians. They are God's way of sanctifying believers and enhancing spiritual growth. They are one means that God uses of sowing unto righteousness. The writings of Henry J. M. Nouwen, Richard J. Foster, and Dallas Willard in the twentieth century sparked a renewed emphasis on the Christian disciplines and have inspired generations of believers to reexamine their own spiritual practices and seek a closer walk with Jesus.

75. THE WAY OF THE HEART

By Henri J. M. Nouwen

Why does a book by a Roman Catholic priest, that was inspired by the ancient teachings of St. Anthony and the Desert Fathers, belong on this list of 100 "must reads"? If I had to include one book by Henri Nouwen, why not his much better known 1972 classic *The Wounded Healer*? The short answer is that this little book affected me in a way that few have. We in the twenty-first century have a tendency to live in the moment and anything that is twenty years old, or even ten years, or five years, is out of date—laptop computers, cell phones, iPads, and the like. What can this book, which was published in 1982, which was based on *The Sayings of the Desert Fathers*, who lived in the Egyptian desert during the fourth and fifth centuries, possibly say to the modern Christian and why do I stake my reputation by urging you to read it?

First of all, I would answer this by saying that the classic spiritual disciplines have enjoyed something of a renaissance among Protestant Christians since the publication of Richard Foster's 1978 book *Celebration of Discipline*. Dallas Willard followed Foster's book with *The Spirit of the Disciplines* as have others. It is completely apropos for Protestants to talk about and practice the spiritual disciplines. Second, the spiritual disciplines were never just a Roman Catholic trend practiced by a few monks who sequestered themselves in monasteries. No, Protestants had already been practicing at least some of them such as prayer, meditation, and Bible study and there has been a growing movement in recent decades against our materialistic culture and towards simplicity. So, the spiritual disciplines are not to be shunned as being only for Roman Catholics. Since they are modeled after the life and practices of Jesus himself, they are for everybody and there is no stigma of Roman Catholicism attached to them. At this writing, I am teaching an adult Sunday school class on the spiritual disciplines at my own local church, a Presbyterian church mind you, and I can assure you that my students are not going off *en masse* to shave their heads and go off to live in caves or monasteries.

Henri Nouwen was not just any run-of-the mill Roman Catholic parish priest when he published his best-known work, *The Wounded Healer*, in 1972. He was born in 1932 in the Netherlands, studied at the Catholic University of Nijmegen and earned a doctorandus degree. He spent two years as a fellow in the Religion and Psychiatry program at the Menninger Clinic in Topeka, KS, and then taught for twenty years at several prestigious institutions including the University of Notre Dame, Yale Divinity School, and Harvard. He also served as scholar-in-residence at the Pontifical North American College in Rome. He believed it was possible to integrate spiritual ministry with modern psychology. In fact, this book is an outgrowth of his teaching at Yale Divinity School. It came out of a seminar on the spirituality of the desert fathers of the fourth century.

So, what do the desert fathers have to say to us who live in the frantic twenty-first century? Is there anything they can teach us? Actually, there is. Quite a lot. Nouwen laments, "Many of us have adapted ourselves too well to the general mood of lethargy" (Nouwen, 2). We even have a term for a certain type of that species, "couch potato." Nouwen addresses three means through which the desert fathers (and mothers, too) connected with God, through solitude, silence, and prayer.

Nouwen regarded Anthony, "the father of monks," to be the best guide into understanding the role of solitude in the life of the Christian. The story of Anthony demonstrates that "we must be made aware of the call to let our false, compulsive self be transformed into the new self of Jesus Christ. It also shows that solitude is the furnace in which the transformation takes place" (Nouwen, 10). Thomas Merton, who wrote the cele-brated autobiography *The Seven Storey Mountain* (See Chapter V), wrote that the desert fathers regarded society as "a ship-wreck" and everybody had to swim for his life. Nouwen be-lieved that the core of the problem with society is that it "is not a community radiant with the love of Christ, but a dangerous network of domination and manipulation in which we are eas-ily entangled and lose our soul" (Nouwen, 11). Jesus said that we are to be in the world, but not of the world, but the sad truth is that too many of us are very much of the world. Sometimes we need to separate ourselves from the world for a time of soli-tude. It is well known that Jesus often went alone into the desert (or wilderness). It has been said that we must be a part, or we will fall apart.

Nouwen saw solitude as "the furnace of transformation" and that without it "we remain victims of our society and continue to be entangled in the illusions of the false self" (Nouwen, 15). He regarded solitude not as a "private therapeutic place" where a person can rest and take it easy. He wrote, "Solitude is the place of the great struggle and the great encounter—the strug-gle against the compulsions of the false self, and the encounter with the loving God who offers himself as the substance of the new self" (Nouwen, 16). He saw it as "the place of conversion . . . where the old self dies and the new self is born" (Nouwen, 17). Finally, he saw that the fruit of solitude is compassion which he calls "the basis of all ministry" (Nouwen, 24). We are able to "enter into solidarity with those who suffer" (Nouwen, 25). He wrote, "Solitude leads us to the awareness of the dead person in our own house and keeps us from making judgments about other people's sins" (Nouwen, 27).

The second way that the desert fathers connected with God was through silence. Nouwen believed that "silence completes and intensifies solitude" (Nouwen, 35). He quotes Arsenius who said, "I have often repented of having spoken, but never of having remained silent" (Nouwen, 36). We have all heard jokes about monks in monasteries and their rules of silence, but the truth is that silence is something that we might all benefit from utilizing more. Silence is in reality simply a fasting (another spiritual discipline) from words. Nouwen is not saying that we need to retreat to a monastery or to the desert and never speak again, but he is suggesting that we sometimes talk so much that our words have lost their "creative power." He writes, "A word with power is a word that comes out of silence" (Nouwen, 48). Many people are afraid of being silent. They feel uncomfortable with it and feel that they must say something, anything. Nouwen writes, "One of our main problems is that in this chatty society, silence has become a fearful thing. For most people, silence creates itchiness and nervousness. Many experience silence not as full and rich, but as empty and hollow. For them silence is like a gaping abyss which can swallow them up" (Nouwen, 52). Why should we practice silence more? Because Nouwen says, "The Word of God is born out of the eternal silence of God, and it is to this Word out of silence that we want to be witnesses" (Nouwen, 40). May God deliver us from words that are inauthentic and shallow. Amen.

The third way that the desert fathers connected with God was through prayer. Nouwen distinguishes between prayer of the mind and prayer of the heart and suggests that the latter is superior. He writes, "One of these demonic ruses is to make us think of prayer primarily as an activity of the mind that involves above all else our intellectual capacities" (Nouwen, 68). He laments the fact that for most prayer is simply talking to God and that is usually a one-sided conversation. He writes, "The crisis of our prayer life is that our mind may be filled with ideas of God while our heart remains far from him. Real prayer comes from the heart" (Nouwen, 71). He continues, "The prayer of the heart is a prayer that does not allow us to limit our relationship with God to interesting words or pious emotions" (Nouwen, 76). Nouwen says that prayer of the heart is characterized by several things. They are short and simple, unceasing, and all-inclusive.

What can we learn from the desert fathers so many centuries removed from their much different cultural milieu and why should you read Henri Nouwen's brief guidebook? "Solitude, silence, and unceasing prayer form the core concepts of the spirituality of the desert" (Nouwen, 91). With Nouwen showing us the way, we too can learn to practice these very current and much needed spiritual disciplines.

76. CELEBRATION OF DISCIPLINE

By Richard J. Foster

"Superficiality is the curse of our age. The doctrine of instant satisfaction is a primary spiritual problem." That is the opening salvo of Richard Foster's 1978 *Celebration of Discipline*. We who are Christians would immediately nod our heads and add a hearty "Amen, brother!" to that. However, we don't like to think that we are superficial, that we, too, are as shallow as our unsaved neighbors. We like to perceive ourselves as somehow being deeper and more complex than those "who are of the world."

In my experience, I have observed that many Christians are not appreciably different from their non-Christian friends and neighbors. They watch the same mindless drivel on their television screens. Christians fall into the same trap of consumerism as they do. They read the same trashy novels. Many adopt the very same worldview that unbelievers do. In fact, if you examine the life of the average Christian in the U.S., you would often have to wonder what is it that distinguishes him from the non-Christian.

When *Celebration of Discipline* was published in 1978, it created a firestorm towards the end of the "Me Decade," which would soon give way to the increased consumerism of the 1980s. It was a wonderful time "to be all that you could be." In fact, beginning in the 1980s, this slogan would be a vital component of the U.S. Army's recruiting. Commercials on television touted this over and over again. It was seemingly OK to find full self-expression and to make as much money as you could.

When Foster wrote this book, he was like a voice crying in the wilderness. He said that Christians needed to get back to the basics, to the spiritual disciplines of the faith. Up until then, most Protestants were just a little bit suspicious of spiritual disciplines. Of course, they believed and practiced reading the Bible and prayer (at least some of them did, when it was convenient), but spiritual disciplines sounded too Roman Catholic for their tastes. They were for the Desert Fathers who lived centuries ago or for some monks who lived on a mountainside in a remote monastery. But for the average evangelical Christian, spiritual disciplines were a foreign concept. It scared them; it was too edgy.

The interesting thing about the author of this book, Richard J. Foster, is that he was not a Roman Catholic monk writing for Roman Catholics who wanted to cloister themselves. He was writing for the average Christ followers who wanted to grow deeper in their spiritual lives. Plus, Foster was one of us Protestant evangelicals. Well, sort of. He was a Quaker having spent his formative years in Southern California in small Friends gatherings. He graduated from George Fox College (a Friends institution) and Fuller Theological Seminary. He then became the pastor of Woodland Avenue Friends Church in Canoga Park, CA where became acquainted with the late Dallas Willard, a church member who was also an influential Christian philosopher and professor at the University of Southern California. His influential book, *The Spirit of the Disciplines* (See Chapter X), was published ten years after Foster's. Two of his other masterpieces, *Renovation of the Heart* and *The Divine Conspiracy*, are included the Appendix.

Foster utilizes the analogy that the Apostle Paul used in Gal. 6:8, "But he who sows to the Spirit will from the Spirit reap eternal life," and combines it with the illustration of a farmer sowing seeds. "The Disciplines are God's way of getting us into the ground; they put us where He can work within us and transform us. By themselves the Spiritual Disciplines can do nothing; they only get us to the place where something can be done" (Foster, 6). The book is divided into three parts. Part I includes the Inward Disciplines such as meditation, prayer, fasting, and study. Part II deals with the Outward Disciplines: simplicity, solitude, submission, and service. He concludes the book with Part III, the Corporate Disciplines, which the church practices corporately: confession, worship, guidance, and celebration.

Celebration of Discipline is not some dry, dusty tome describing what the spiritual disciplines are and their place in history. Rather, it is an eminently practical book telling us how to put these disciplines into practice and make them a part of our everyday lives. Furthermore, Foster gives examples from his own life and those of others to demonstrate just how they can work. I have read this book from cover-to-cover three times and parts of it many times over. It has changed my approach to the Christian life as it has for multitudes of Christians worldwide. It has proven to be a game-changer for them. *Celebration of Discipline* is a book that begs to be read . . . and practiced. You will never be the same.

77. THE SPIRIT OF THE DISCIPLINES

By Dallas Willard

This is a book for Christians who are serious about their faith and who want to live like Jesus did. It is a clarion call to discipleship using the classical spiritual disciplines of the Christian faith. Richard Foster first sounded the call in 1978 with *Celebration of Discipline* to the broader evangelical world and got people talking about the spiritual disciplines. This book came ten years later and provided the essential biblical and theological justification for why we should do them. So, in a sense, *The Spirit of the Disciplines* is a companion volume to Foster's book. It is a detailed and profound look at how God changes lives. Salvation, Willard asserts, is much more than forgiveness for sin; it is a complete and utter transformation.

Willard saw modern Christians as basically anemic in their spiritual lives. He wrote, "Modern thinking has come to view the Christian faith as powerless, even somehow archaic, at the very least irrelevant" (Willard, viii). The remedy is living the way Jesus did. According to Willard, "If we have faith in Christ, we must believe that he knew how to live. We can, through faith and grace, become like Christ by practicing the types of activities he himself engaged in, by arranging our whole lives around the activities he himself practiced in order to remain constantly at home in the fellowship of his Father" (Willard, ix). He sees the alternative all too clearly. "To depart from righteousness is to choose a life of crushing burdens, failures, and disappointments, a life caught in the toils of endless problems that are never resolved. Here is the source of that unending soap opera, that sometimes horror show known as normal human life. The 'cost of discipleship,' though it may take all we have, is small when compared to the lot of those who don't accept Christ's invitation to be a part of his company in The Way of life" (Willard, 2). "In other words, we must develop a psychologically sound theology of the spiritual life and of its disciplines to guide us" (Willard, xi).

Dallas Willard is a name that might be unfamiliar to many, but he was one of Christianity's most brilliant and influential thinkers of the past fifty years and he left behind a legacy of books on spiritual formation that should prove helpful to believers for centuries. He and Richard Foster were close friends. Willard mentored him when Foster was a young man just beginning in ministry and helped shape his fledgling ideas. That led to a lifetime friendship and collaboration. They both saw a need for a renewal of the spiritual disciplines.

When Willard looked around him at contemporary society and the church, he observed, "Our communities and churches are thickly populated with people who are neurotic or paralyzed by their devotion and willing bondage to how they feel. Drug dependence and addiction is epidemic because of the cultural imperative to feel good" (Willard, 99-100). He saw a qualitative difference between the modern church and the early Christians. He writes, "So, wherever early Christians looked they saw examples of the practice of solitude, fasting, prayer, private study, communal study, worship, and sacrificial service and giving—to mention only some of the more obvious disciplines for spiritual life" (Willard, 100). He concludes, "These early Christians really did arrange their lives *very* differently from their non-Christian neighbors, as well as from the vast majority of those of us called Christians today" (Ibid.).

In the ancient Roman world of Paul's day, it was simply assumed that physical exercise and intense training were necessary to succeed as an athlete. Completing the physical training analogy, Willard argues that "just as with the physical, there is a specific round of activities we must do to establish, maintain, and enhance our spiritual powers. One must *train* as well as *try*. An athlete may have all the enthusiasm in the world, he may 'talk a good game.' But talk will not win the race" (Willard, 98).

The big question for Christians is how we achieve spirituality. What is the methodology? Willard discusses how many believers are satisfied with "regular church attendance and faithfulness to commonly recognized religious duties" as means of radically transforming their spiritual lives. But as Willard observes, "Good effects often come from these. They are to be used and not despised. But their track record for actual transformation of individuals into Christlikeness is not impressive" (Willard, 69). He then suggests a way of achieving spirituality that is from Scripture. "But the Bible also informs us that there are certain *practices*—solitude, prayer, fasting, celebration, and so forth—we can undertake, in cooperation with grace, to raise the level of our lives toward godliness" (Ibid.). Willard believes that the modern mind-set works against the use of the spiritual disciplines. Do we actually have to follow the first-century practices of Jesus and Paul? He argues, "But today we are insulated from such thinking. Our modern religious context assures us that such drastic action as we see in Jesus and Paul is not necessary for *our* Christianity—may not even be useful, may even be harmful" (Willard, 107). Willard's conclusion is compelling. "His (Paul's) crucifixion of the flesh, and ours, is accomplished through these activities such as solitude, fasting, frugality, service, and so forth, which constitute the curriculum in the school of self-denial and place us on the front line of spiritual combat" (Willard, 109).

Central to our understanding of the spiritual disciplines is a definition of "spiritual life" as well as its disciplines. According to Willard, "A 'spiritual life' consists in that range of activities in which people cooperatively interact with God and with the spiritual order deriving from God's personality and action. And what is the result? A new overall quality of human existence with corresponding new powers" (Willard, 67). So, what are the disciplines for the spiritual life? "The disciplines are activities of mind and body purposefully undertaken, to bring our personality and total being into effective cooperation with the divine order. They enable us more and more to live in a power that is, strictly speaking, beyond us, deriving from the spiritual realm itself" (Willard, 68).

Willard has a somewhat different arrangement of the spiritual disciplines than Foster does. Whereas Foster separates the disciplines into three divisions (inward, outward, and corporate) and spends the greater bulk of his book on a detailed examination of each discipline (meditation, prayer, fasting, study, simplicity, solitude, submission, service, confession, worship, guidance, and celebration), Willard devotes only one chapter to the disciplines themselves. He divides the disciplines into two broad areas: disciplines of abstinence and disciplines of engagement and he lists fifteen main disciplines (solitude, silence, fasting, frugality, chastity, secrecy, sacrifice, study, worship, celebration, service, prayer, fellowship, confession, and submission), whereas Foster lists only twelve.

Willard discusses the Apostle Paul's psychology of redemption "as a progressive sequence of real human and divine actions and events that resulted in the transformation of the body and the mind. For him these were actions—events—real experiences we humans have, real parts of our lives, so real we cannot ignore them" (Willard, 111). These experiences, of course, go hand and hand with the spiritual disciplines. However, he argues that Protestants have generally overreacted against "ascetic or disciplinary practices." Even practitioners in the psychoanalytic tradition of Sigmund Freud tend to dismiss Christian experience. As Willard notes, they "still regard treatment as having failed if the client retains belief in God" (Willard, 110).

Willard includes a lengthy chapter towards the end of the book in which he addresses the exclusion of poverty from the list of spiritual disciplines. He writes, "Possessions and money cause uneasiness today in the minds of many sincere Christians" (Willard, 193). He then discusses the feelings of guilt that so many affluent Christians experience. He explains, "They are haunted by the more radical thought that their service to God would be better if they were poor—or at least if they owned nothing beyond what is required to meet their day-to-day needs. They are troubled by the idea that the very possession of surplus goods or money is evil" (Ibid.). Willard cites two of the biblical texts most commonly used when the issue of wealth is raised: James 1:9-10 and 1 Timothy 6:17-19. He concludes, "The idealization of poverty is *one of the most dangerous illusions of Christians in the contemporary world*. Stewardship— which requires possessions and includes giving—is the true spiritual discipline in relation to wealth" (Willard, 194).

Richard Foster's *Celebration of Discipline* and this book by Willard are bookends and deserve to be read together. They complement one another and the authors are two peas in a pod. Dallas Willard is an important writer who deserves to be read again and again. I also suggest his *Renovation of the Heart* and *The Divine Conspiracy*. His writings will stretch your mind and challenge your spirit. You owe it to yourself to discover what this man of God has to say to you. He may change your life.

Some gems from Dallas Willard:

> "Our world is hungry for genuinely changed people. . . . Let us be among those who believe that the inner transformation of our lives is a goal worthy of our best effort" (Willard, 9).

> "In contemporary society our Adversary majors in three things: noise, hurry, and crowds" (Willard, 13).

> "There is a progression in the spiritual life. It is not wise to tackle the Mt. Everest of the soul before having had some experience with lesser peaks" (Willard, 24).

"In a culture where the landscape is dotted with shrines to the Golden Arches, and an assortment of Pizza Temples, fasting seems out of place, out of step with the times" (Willard, 41).

"Constantly the Bible deals decisively with the inner spirit of slavery that an idolatrous attachment to wealth brings" (Willard, 72).

"If we had only a tinge of the sense of revulsion that God feels toward sin, we would be moved to holier living" (Willard, 130).

CHAPTER XI:
CHRISTIANS, CULTURE, AND SCIENCE

CHRISTIAN INTERACTION WITH CULTURE

How should Christians interact with the culture in which they live? That is the question that a lot of believers are asking today. It is helpful to remember that we live in a fallen world. As the society and culture around us become seemingly more and more godless, what are we who are Christ-followers to do? Jesus was very helpful on this issue. He told us that "we are to be in the world but not of the world." Therefore, although we may not agree with many of the values espoused by the culture around us, we are still very much a part of it. Unless one is willing to completely separate from the culture as the ancient Desert Fathers did, we are part of it, like it or not for better or for worse. Thus, we need to engage our culture as part of our responsibility implicit in the Great Commission.

There is no shortage of books that deal with the topic of Christians and culture. Two of the most commanding voices of the twentieth century writing on the subject were Francis A. Schaeffer and John R. W. Stott. Both wrote passionately and extensively on how Christians should engage the culture around them. Some other leading lights, no less insistent, were Carl F. H. Henry, Mark A. Noll, and Os Guinness. The latter two continue to carry on this mission into the twenty-first century. All have written books that the thoughtful Christian should read and ponder. It is with much delight that I commend them to you.

78. THE UNEASY CONSCIENCE OF MODERN FUNDAMENTALISM

By Carl F. H. Henry

First of all, let me confess that I am a recovering fundamentalist and have been since about 1970. My formative years were spent in a fundamentalist church that was the epitome of the "fighting fundie." I have long much preferred the gentler term, "evangelical." Second, although the book is talking about a fundamentalism that many might think is long past, a museum piece, there is much in the book that is fresh and challenging even to our day. As Richard Mouw states in his Foreword, "It is clearly a book written for the late 1940s." Published in 1947, the book caused quite a stir then and it still packs a punch today.

In the early decades of the twentieth century, fundamentalists were in a "war" with theological liberals, who attacked both the credibility and authority of Scripture, but also posited a "social gospel." Fundamentalists saw themselves as contending for the faith and there was little interest in social issues. I well remember those days growing up in the 1950s and 1960s being in a local church that preached more about separation than any kind of involvement in redeeming society and culture. There was a bunker mentality amongst us and we were suspicious of anyone who strayed from our mindset. But Henry wrote, "Fundamentalism in revolting against the Social Gospel seemed also to revolt against the Christian social imperative" (Henry, 22).

Carl Henry was the right man to challenge this kind of fuzzy thinking. He was a Baptist minister who earned bachelor's and master's degrees from Wheaton College, the citadel of evangelical education, as well as two doctoral degrees, a Doctor of Theology from Northern Baptist Theological Seminary and a PhD from Boston University. He certainly had the credentials. He taught at Northern Baptist Theological seminary from 1942 to 1947 and was part of the establishment of the National Association of Evangelicals and served on its board for several years. In his spare time, he helped to establish the Fuller Theological Seminary in 1947 and was its first acting dean. In 1949, Henry met with evangelical scholars who proposed the need for an organization "to promote serious academic discussion" and even suggested the name by which it would be known, the Evangelical Theological Society. I have been a member since the mid-1970s. In 1956, Henry became the first editor-in-chief of the magazine launched by Billy Graham, *Christianity Today*. Henry was a leading evangelical scholar and certainly the right man to challenge the status quo.

The Uneasy Conscience of Modern Fundamentalism was a clarion call to fundamentalists to rise above their bunker mentality, get their heads out of the sand, and "separate" themselves from separatist fundamentalism and reclaim their proper role in influencing society and culture. It was a challenge to preserve a doctrinal focus on the Bible while at the same time rejecting theological liberalism. It critiqued both fundamentalism's disengagement from society and its separatist rigidity. It was a call to change. As Henry put it, "Whereas once the redemptive gospel was a world-changing message, now it was narrowed to a world-resisting message. Out of twentieth century Fundamentalism of this sort there could come no contemporary version of Augustine's *The City of God*" (Henry, 19). He was one of them, an insider, writing, "Fundamentalism is the modern priest and Levite, bypassing suffering humanity" (Henry, 2). Ouch!

Henry ably discussed the curious reluctance of many fundamentalists of his day to steer clear of the kingdom message because "a *kingdom now* message is too easily confused with the liberal social gospel, and because a *kingdom then* message will identify Christianity further to the modern mind in terms of an escape mechanism" (Henry, 46). He wonders how the modern believer can proclaim the kingdom at all, and why this should even be an issue since the kingdom of God was Christ's most frequent subject of preaching. Henry wrote, "no study of the kingdom teaching of Jesus is adequate unless it recognizes His implication both that the kingdom is here, and that it is not here. This does not imply an ultimate paradox, but rather stresses that the kingdom exists in incomplete realization" (Henry, 48). Even today the kingdom of God is the subject of much fuzzy thinking and practice. As Henry explained, "The main difference between the kingdom of God *now* and the kingdom of God *then* is that the future kingdom will center all of its activities in the redemptive King because all government and dominion will be subjected to Him" (Henry, 49). He concluded that the nature of a future earthly reign, over which Christians have argued vehemently, should be overshadowed by what we should be doing now in that "the kingdom is a present spiritual reality in the lives of believers, being coextensive with the outworked redemptive and regenerative plan of God."

Henry believed that in the contemporary church of his time, the salt had lost its savor. Whereas in the eighteenth century the church had been the forerunner for social and moral reform, in the present day it had lost its way. He challenged contemporary evangelicalism to "reawaken to the relevance of its redemptive message to the global predicament" (Henry, 54). It had lost its way and was "a stranger, in its predominant spirit, to the vigorous social interest of its ideological forebears" (Henry, 39). Sadly, he wrote about the evangelical church, "It has ceased to challenge Caesar and Rome, as though in futile resignation and submission to the triumphant Renaissance mood" (Ibid.). He concluded, and it is sadly still applicable to the twenty-first century evangelical church in many respects that "the challenge of modern Fundamentalism to the present world mind is almost nonexistent on the great social issues" (Henry, 30).

Henry challenged the evangelical church of his day, but many of his concerns still ring true today. His arguments and agenda still deserve our careful attention. Henry's book was read and his message was heeded. Not long after *Uneasy Conscience* was published World Vision began its ministry as well as the World Relief Commission. The National Association of Evangelicals, which Henry helped to form, came into being and began to grapple with some of these concerns. Henry's words written so many decades ago still speak to us today. "If historic Christianity is again to compete as a vital world ideology, evangelicalism must project a solution for the most pressing world problems" (Henry, 65). To those words, I conclude with a hearty "Amen."

79. A CHRISTIAN MANIFESTO

&

80. THE GREAT EVANGELICAL DISASTER

By Francis A. Schaeffer

How does a man overcome a working-class upbringing in "a home with no books and little culture" to become one of the most beloved evangelicals of the twentieth century and a seminal Christian thinker? By almost any standard of measurement, Francis Schaeffer stands as one of the most intriguing, influential, and interesting figures in the evangelical world in the twentieth century. He has been called the "pastor to modern youth and Christian interpreter of the twentieth century" (Catherwood, 113). He was one of a few outliers in the 1960s who were fighting for the intellectual integrity of Christianity. During the fifties and sixties many were railing against smoking and drinking and for biblical separation. But then in 1968, he published the seminal work, *The God Who Is There*, a book that attacked modern liberal theology, neo-orthodoxy, and much of the philosophy of that time. It was the first book that Schaeffer had written without using transcripts from his previous lectures. But the book gave Schaeffer a wide following and intellectual respectability.

It was a rocky road for Schaeffer and his wife, Edith. They were Presbyterian missionaries in Switzerland after several small Bible Presbyterian pastorates in the United States. They became interested in international youth ministries, specifically in Europe, which in 1947 was suffering the aftermath of World

War II. They arrived in Geneva, Switzerland, in 1948, and settled in nearby La Rosiaz, which Schaeffer used as a base of operations for his preaching throughout Europe on the dangers of liberalism, including the neo-orthodox teachings of Karl Barth. It was not long before their three children became ill, one son contracting polio, the dread disease of that time. Then their mission board withdrew support and they were ordered to leave Switzerland by the government. To say that it was a difficult time would be an understatement. But the Schaeffers believed that God was calling them to a new ministry, an *abri*, which was a French word for "the shelter."

After the Swiss government cancelled the edict to leave the country in a miraculous turn of events that can only be described as providential, they established in 1955 L'Abri, which was to serve as both a spiritual community as well as a philosophy seminar. Clearly philosophy played a central role in the mind of Francis Schaeffer. As one writer puts it, his "analysis of the disciplines of art, music, and theology is patterned after his interpretation of theology" Ruegsegger, 107). His references to philosophers such as Plato, Aristotle, Thomas Aquinas, Kant, Hegel, and Kierkegaard are numerous in his books. He analyzed trends in modern thought going as far back as the Middle Ages in particular noting Aquinas, Kierkegaard and Hegel.

In the day-to-day running of their endeavor, the Schaeffers were greatly influenced by Hudson Taylor's faith principles. According to Catherwood, "They would live by prayer, and operate on four principles: They would not ask for contributions but would rather make their needs known to God alone. They would not recruit staff but would rely on God to send them the right people. Plans would be made day by day and not far ahead, in order to allow for God's sovereign guidance to them. They would not publicize themselves but would trust the Lord to send them people truly seeking and in need" (Catherwood, 123). And come they did—by the thousands, from as far away as Central America and Asia. One of those attracted to L'Abri was my friend and colleague, the late R. K. McGregor Wright, professor and theologian. Over lunch one day, he regaled me and my wife with stories of his time backpacking through Europe as a disaffected youth and turning up at L'Abri, where he was greatly influenced by the Schaeffers.

In 1982, Crossway Books provided a tremendous service to the Church by compiling the twenty-two books that Schaeffer wrote into a five-volume set. The wide range of issues upon which he wrote can be roughly split into five areas coinciding with each of the five volumes; (1) A Christian View of Philosophy and Culture, (2) A Christian View of the Bible as Truth, (3) A Christian View of Spirituality, (4) A Christian View of the Church, and (5) A Christian View of the West. *A Christian Manifesto* and *The Great Evangelical Disaster* fall into the last two categories respectively and were published in 1981 and 1984.

A Christian Manifesto was intended as a Christian response to *The Communist Manifesto* published in 1848 and *The Humanist Manifesto* documents published in 1933 and 1973. Schaeffer believed that the decline of Western civilization was due to the rise of pluralism in society. He writes, "Pluralism has come to mean that everything is acceptable. The new concept of pluralism suddenly is everywhere. There is no right or wrong; it is just a matter of your personal preference" (*Manifesto*, 46). He stated that humanism and Christianity were diametrically opposed to one and antithetical to each other. He writes, "We should be utterly ashamed that this is the fact" (*Manifesto*, 20). He deplores the gradual drift of society and views the larger picture. "They (Christians) have very gradually become disturbed over permissiveness, pornography, the public schools, the breakdown of the family, and finally abortion. But they have not seen this as a totality—each thing being a part, symptom, of a much larger problem. They have failed to see that all of this has come about due to a shift in world view—that is, through a fundamental change in the overall way people think and view the world and life as a whole" (*Manifesto*, 17).

In this book, Schaeffer explains why this cosmic shift has occurred. He shows how we have been blind to how the entire
foundation of society has shifted radically from our traditional
Judeo-Christian heritage to a humanistic view of the world. He
calls for Christians to change the course of history by a return
to biblical truth and values. Schaeffer concludes that when the
state defies the absolute law of God, it then becomes illegiti-
mate and its authority no longer in force. He calls for Christians to resist the state when that happens by any means necessary. He calls for legal and political action as well as civil disobedience as a last resort.

Civil disobedience has meant different things to Christians in
different times and different circumstance. To Christians living
during the time of the Roman Empire, it meant a horrible death
in the arena being eaten by lions. To believers living in the
twentieth century behind the Iron Curtain or in other totalitarian countries, the prospect of Civil disobedience was faced every day of their lives and could lead to prison or worse. Dietrich Bonhoeffer was hanged by the Nazis in 1945 for his civil
disobedience. Civil disobedience in the United States means far
softer enforcement. We do not fear the physical oppression that
Christians in other countries face on a daily basis. Soviet labor
camps in Siberia have replaced the lions the early Roman believers faced. Ostracism by friends and neighbors are some of
the consequences faced by those of us in the United States. In
recent years, lawsuits have even been brought about against
believers for upholding their beliefs, such as the famous case in
Colorado in 2016 involving Jack Phillips of Masterpiece
Cakeshop who was ordered by the Civil Rights Commission to
bake a cake for a same-sex wedding.

In *A Christian Manifesto*, Schaeffer sounds the cry, a clarion call
for change with Christians leading the charge. He says, "It is
not too strong to say that we are at war, and there are no neutral parties in the struggle. One either confesses that God is the
final authority, or one confesses that Caesar is Lord" (*Manifesto*, 116). This is a powerful book.

When Schaeffer wrote *The Great Evangelical Disaster* in 1984, he called the issues about which he was writing "the greatest problem we who are Christians face in our generation" (*Disaster*, 13). He wrote that believers have compromised their stand on truth and morality to the point that there is almost nothing that they will oppose. He believed that the evangelical branch of Christianity had sold itself out to the world. The title of the book speaks loudly for itself. Schaeffer clarifies his meaning, "Here is the great evangelical disaster—the failure of the evangelical world to stand for truth as truth. There is only one word for this—namely *accommodation*: the evangelical church has accommodated to the world spirit of the age" (*Disaster*, 37).

Schaeffer exposes the spirit of compromise and accommodation in the Church today. He writes, "Accommodation, accommodation. How the mindset of accommodation grows and expands. The last sixty years have given birth to a moral disaster, and what have we done? Sadly, we must say that the evangelical world has been part of the disaster. More than this, the evangelical response itself has been a disaster. Where is the clear voice speaking to the crucial issues of the day with distinctively biblical, Christian answers? With tears we must say that largely it is not there and that a large segment of the evangelical world has become seduced by the world spirit of this present age" (*Disaster*, 141). Schaeffer believed that it was easy for Christians to accommodate to the current trends of the age, but that accommodation led to more accommodation which led to more of the same.

Schaeffer believed that the twentieth century saw a great shift from a basic biblical consensus of moral values to those without foundation. He writes of the moral drift, "The freedom that once was founded on a biblical consensus and a Christian ethos has now become autonomous freedom, cut loose from all restraints. Here we have the world spirit of our age—autonomous Man setting himself up as God, in defiance of the knowledge and the moral and spiritual truth which God has given. Here is the reason why we have a moral breakdown in every area of life. The titanic freedoms which we once enjoyed have been cut loose from their Christian restraints and are becoming a force of destruction leading to chaos" (*Disaster*, 22). He believed that Christians "are locked in a battle of cosmic proportions. It is a life and death struggle over the minds and souls of men for all eternity, but it is equally a life and death struggle over life on this earth" (*Disaster*, 23).

The Great Evangelical Disaster is a book that needs to be read. It cries out to be read. If anything, the trends of which he wrote have become exacerbated and evangelicals have become even more accommodating in the twenty-first century. Read it and see if you agree.

81. INVOLVEMENT: BEING A RESPONSIBLE CHRISTIAN IN A NON-CHRISTIAN SOCIETY

&

82. INVOLVEMENT: SOCIAL AND SEXUAL RELATIONSHIPS IN THE MODERN WORLD

By John Stott

The late John Stott has done the Church a tremendous service by writing these two volumes. They are a gift to us that ought to be read and heeded. He remarks that one of the "most notable features of the worldwide evangelical movement" in recent years (He published them in 1984 and 1985.) "has been the recovery of our temporarily mislaid social conscience" *(Responsible,* 13). He points out that in the early decades of the twentieth century up until about 1970, evangelicals had been preoccupied with the attacks of liberalism against the authority of Scripture and the historic Christian faith as well as its "social gospel." He believes that evangelicals are now playing catch-up in the area of social responsibilities. He offers these two volumes as his "contribution to the catching-up process." They are must reading for any believer who wants to be "a responsible Christian in a Non-Christian society."

These two books grew out of a series of sermons preached at All Souls in London under the title "Issues Facing Britain Today." They subsequently morphed into a series of lectures given at the London Institute for Contemporary Christianity. The two volumes which I commend to you were the result of those sermons and lectures. Stott's *raison d etre* is given in his Introduction to the first volume. He writes, "Some Christians, anxious above all to be faithful to the revelation of God without compromise, ignore the challenges of the modern world and live in the past. Others, anxious to respond to the modern world around them, trim and twist God's revelation in their search for relevance. I have struggled to avoid both traps. For the Christian is at liberty to surrender neither to antiquity nor to modernity. Instead, I have sought with integrity to submit to the revelation of yesterday within the realities of today" (*Responsible*, 14).

Stott begins in the first chapter of the first volume to lay the groundwork for the social involvement of Christians. He asks, "Involvement: Is it our concern?" For those who might be leery of social involvement, he writes, "Evangelism and social concern have been intimately related to one another throughout the history of the church" (*Responsible*, 19). He then gives examples from our own history of how this came about. One shining illustration of this was the influence of John Wesley, the founder of Methodism. Stott writes, "And if that social conscience, admittedly, was the offspring of more than one progenitor, it nonetheless was mothered and nurtured by the Evangelical Revival of vital, practical Christianity—a revival which illuminated the central postulates of the New Testament ethic, which made real the Fatherhood of God, and the Brotherhood of men, which pointed to the priority of personality over property, and which directed heart, soul, and mind, towards the establishment of the Kingdom of Righteousness on earth" (*Responsible*, 20-21).

Stott then gives the biblical basis for social concern. He asks a pertinent question, "Why should Christians get involved" (*Re-

sponsible, 34)? He answers, "In the end there are only two possible attitudes which Christians can adopt towards the world. One is escape and the other engagement" (Ibid.). He then deplores the fact that evangelicals in the twentieth century have largely chosen escapism. He explains, "Too many of us evangelicals either have been, or maybe still are, irresponsible escapists. Fellowship with each other in the church is more congenial than service in an apathetic and even hostile environment outside. Of course, we make occasional evangelistic raids into enemy territory (that is our evangelical specialty); but then we withdraw again, across the moat, into our Christian castle (the security of our own evangelical fellowship), pull up the drawbridge, and even close our ears to the pleas of those who batter on the gate" (*Responsible*, 35). Such a scathing indictment of so many of us!!

Stott continues to lay the groundwork for social involvement in Volume I in chapters two through four. He discusses pluralism and asks whether we Christians should impose our views. He concludes, "In social action . . . we should neither try to impose Christian standards by force on an unwilling public, nor remain silent and inactive before the contemporary landslide, nor rely exclusively on the dogmatic assertion of biblical values, but rather reason with people about the benefits of Christian morality, commending God's law to them by rational arguments. We believe that God's laws are both good in themselves and universal in their application because, far from being arbitrary, they fit the human beings God has made" (*Responsible*, 52). Stott then discusses the kind of influence Christians should have in society. He uses Christ's teachings from the Sermon on the Mount and calls believers to be salt and light in society. He concludes that "truth is powerful when it is argued; it is even more powerful when it is exhibited" (*Responsible*, 110).

In the second part of Volume I, Stott discusses global issues that are still germane today. He first lays out the nuclear threat and includes such topics as the arms race and arms expenditure, nuclear proliferation, the consequences of nuclear war, and finally offers some theological and moral reflections including some different positions held by Christians on the subject of war. Stott then includes a chapter on the environmental crisis facing our planet. He opines on the reasons for concern as well as the biblical perspective. Essentially, he says that it boils down to a matter of stewardship. Unfortunately, we, as Christians have been among the worst examples of this and have been very poor stewards of the planet. He concludes, "Trusteeship includes conservation. The greatest threat to mankind may prove in the end to be not nuclear war but a peace-time peril, namely the spoilation of earth's natural resources by human folly or greed" (*Responsible*, 159).

The final two chapters of Volume I deal with north-south inequality and human rights. He first examines the inequities between north and south economically particularly in terms of use of natural resources. He reiterates the biblical prophecy that "nation will rise against nation." He reminds us that "the multiplicity of mutually hostile nations with mutually incomprehensible languages is a consequence of God' judgment on man's disobedience and pride" (*Responsible*, 176). He then elucidates the biblical principle of equality and how it should be not only a spiritual reality in the lives of Christians, but an economic one as well.

Finally, Stott discusses human rights and gives pertinent examples of human rights violations. He then discusses how believers should be concerned for both human rights and human dignity as well as equality and the Christian's responsibility. He writes using the Israelites as an example, "Far from exploiting them, God's people were to be the voice of the voiceless and the champion of the powerless, including their enemies" (*Responsible*, 199).

Volume II deals with social and sexual relationships in the modern world. It is divided into two parts: social issues and sexual issues. Under social issues Stott deals with topics as diverse as work and unemployment, industrial relations, the multiracial dream, and poverty, wealth, and simplicity. Under the umbrella of the multiracial dream, Stott discusses the issue of slavery in America's past and its racial problems today. He also uses as examples German anti-Semitism and South African Apartheid. Although slavery, Nazism, and Apartheid have been long abolished, the residual effects remain and the root hatred which led to them unresolved.

Stott's chapter on poverty, wealth, and simplicity are particularly interesting to me as I have written on those subjects extensively. He discusses how Christians ought to respond to poverty in the modern world and offers three approaches. He then suggests three options for rich Christians using the examples and teaching of Jesus and that of the early Church. He concludes this chapter, "May God help us to simplify our life-style, grow in generosity, and live in contentment" (*Relationships*, 123).

Part II, Sexual Issues, includes in-depth discussions on issues as diverse as the role of men and women in society and Christian ministry, marriage and divorce, abortion, and homosexual partnerships. In the chapter about men and women, Stott discusses the rise of feminism, and then different views on the relationship between the sexes: equality, complementarity, and responsibility. Finally, he examines the role of women in ministry. He agrees "that women are called by God to ministry hardly needs any demonstration" (*Relationships*, 148). He qualifies that by saying, "The only question is what form women's ministry should take, whether any limits should be placed and in particular whether women should be ordained" (*Relationships*, 149). Many denominations have already decided on this issue. Stott concludes, "If God endows women with spiritual gifts (which he does), and thereby calls them to exercise their gifts for the common good (which he does), then the church must recognize God's gifts and calling" (*Relationships*, 156).

In Chapter Six, Stott tackles the changing attitudes of society and Christians toward divorce. He then sets forth the Old Testament teaching on the subject, as well as that of Jesus and the Apostle Paul. He takes a rather traditional view on this difficult issue in writing, "We may on occasion feel at liberty to advise the legitimacy of a separation without a divorce, or even a divorce without a remarriage, taking 1 Corinthians as our warrant. But we have no liberty to go beyond the permissions of our Lord" (*Relationships*, 185).

In Chapter 7, Stott writes about the abortion dilemma. His opinion on the subject needs no explanation. "Any society which can tolerate these things, let alone legislate for them, has ceased to be civilized" (*Relationships*, 191). He sees the key issue as being both moral and theological. Stott firmly believes that the fetus is not merely "a lump of jelly or blob of tissue," but a human being made in the image of God.

Finally, Stott concludes Volume II with a chapter titled "Homosexual Partnerships." He sets the context for his discussion by stating three facts. "First, *we are all human beings* (*Relationships*, 215). He states, "That is to say, there is no such phenomenon as a 'homosexual.' There are only people, human persons, made in the image and likeness of God, yet fallen, with all the glory and the tragedy which the paradox implies, including sexual potential and sexual problems" (Ibid.). Then he writes, "Secondly, *we are all sexual beings*" (Ibid.). "Thirdly, *we are all sinners*" (Ibid.). Stott then goes on to examine the biblical prohibitions against homosexual behavior. He discusses the stories of Sodom and Gibeah as well as the Leviticus texts. He moves from there to the New Testament statements of the Apostle Paul in Romans 1:26-27, 1 Corinthians 6:9-10, and 1 Timothy 1:9-10. Finally, he covers the purpose of sex and marriage as the Bible teaches. He deplores the homophobia and lack of love the Church has often exhibited towards homosexuals and then throws a jab at Western culture that "inhibits the development of rich same-sex friendships by engendering the fear of being ridiculed or rejected as a 'queer'" (*Relationships*, 244). One topic that Stott does not address, and understandably so in that the book was written in the 1980s, is that of transgender identities.

More than ever before, Christians need to be salt and light in society. The discussions in these two volumes, though written decades previously, are just as important as when they first appeared in print. Jesus called us to be "in the world, but not of the world." Stott shows the reader how that can be done. I strongly commend these books to you. You will not be disappointed.

83. THE SCANDAL OF THE EVANGELICAL MIND

By Mark A. Noll

When this book was first published almost thirty years ago, it was a scathing indictment of the anti-intellectual trends within the evangelical camp. The question is what has changed as we are now almost twenty-five years into the twenty-first century? If anything, the trends have only intensified and the issues exacerbated. As Noll writes in the Preface to this new 2022 edition, he almost seems to be shaking his head in bewilderment as he laments, "These evangelicals have been least likely to seek vaccination against the coronavirus, least likely to believe that evolutionary science actually describes the development of species, and least likely to believe that the planet is really warming up because of human activity" (Noll, x). Yet, these are the same evangelicals who steadfastly adhere to the authority of Scripture. He writes, "White evangelicals appear as the group most easily captive to conspiratorial nonsense, in greatest panic about their political opponents, or as most aggressively anti-intellectual" (Ibid.). Sadly, he is talking about some people in the church that I know.

Although there is a deep well of respected evangelical scholarship, there is a seeming disconnect between them and evangelicals at large. It is indeed unfortunate that the broader evangelical population has been prone to have "a special fascination for slipshod reasoning disseminated on Twitter" (Noll, xi) rather than solid evangelical scholarship. He asks, "Are the Christian colleges and universities failing? Or are they just spitting into a whirlwind" (Ibid.)?

Evangelicals historically have been rather dismal on social issues. Many evangelicals, even today, dismiss any progressive political or cultural ideas as attacks on anything that is God-fearing or smacking of apple pie and red-blooded American-ism. Evangelicalism has been particularly blind with respect to the civil rights struggle in America and has been more likely to accept Jim Crow segregation than campaign against it. Evangelicals also as a whole have also viewed with great skepticism what are considered by most to be the well-documented conclusions of modern science. To say that evangelicals are obscurantists is for the most part quite generous.

Noll concluded that in the current American climate, it is possible to regard "evangelical intellectual life" a lost cause. Yet, he was not quite ready to withdraw from the evangelical camp. Therefore, this book is not so much intended to educate as to incite to action. That is the primary reason I included this book in my list of 100 "must reads."

Mark Noll was the perfect person to sound the alarm. With advanced degrees from both Trinity Evangelical Divinity School (M.A.) and Vanderbilt University (Ph.D.), he certainly had the academic credentials. In addition, he spent twenty-seven years teaching at Wheaton College and then was named the Francis A. McAnaney Professor Emeritus of History at the University of Notre Dame before landing his current position as Research Professor of History at Regent College. He was considered to be one of us as a highly respected professor with an impressive list of books to his credit including *A History of Christianity in the United States and Canada* and *The Civil War as a Theological Crisis.*

Noll begins his book with the distressing news, "The scandal of the evangelical mind is that there is not much of an evangelical mind" (Noll, 3). He notes that there is much good in the evangelical world, but an intellectual bent is not one of them. He writes, "Despite dynamic success at a popular level, modern American evangelicals have failed notably in sustaining serious intellectual life. They have nourished millions of believers in the simple verities of the gospel but have largely abandoned the universities, the arts, and other realms of 'high' culture" (Ibid.). Francis Schaeffer had been banging a similar drum for decades as had several others. Noll admits that North American evangelicals have enjoyed a rich theological harvest and have made great inroads in the area of biblical scholarship, but that scholars have failed in their "effort to articulate a theology that is faithful both to the evangelical tradition and to modern standards of academic discourse" (Noll, 6). He defines the problem, "By an evangelical 'life of the mind' I mean more the effort to think like a Christian—to think within a specifically Christian framework—across the whole spectrum of modern learning, including economics and political science, literary criticism and imaginative writing, historical inquiry and philosophical studies, linguistics and the history of science, social theory and the arts" (Noll, 7).

Noll sees the problem as an intellectual one that grew "out of the historical development of America's distinctly evangelical culture" (Noll, 15). He details a culture where "intense, detailed, and precise efforts have been made to understand the Bible. But it is not a culture where the same effort has been expended to understand the world or, even more important, the processes by which wisdom from Scripture should be brought into relation with knowledge about the world" (Ibid.). Noll is particularly unsparing and forthright in his criticism of fundamentalism, dispensational premillennialism, the Higher Life movement, and Pentecostalism as contributors to this failure. Although he paints a very bleak picture of the evangelical scene, he challenges the evangelical community to right its ship and turn the situation around. He writes, "Fidelity to Jesus Christ demands from evangelicals a more responsible intellectual existence than we have practiced throughout much of our history" (Noll, 27).

Noll reaches back to the roots of the Protestant Reformation to John Calvin and later the Puritans as well as Jonathan Edwards and the Great Awakening to trace a much different intellectual scene. He writes, "In science, public life, the arts, and still other spheres, these early Protestants were attempting, in other words, to develop a Christian mind" (Noll, 39). Although often-

times the Puritans get a bad rap nowadays, Noll sees their contribution as largely positive. He writes, "The distinguishing
characteristic of Puritanism was its effort to unite the theology
of the Reformation with a comprehensive view of the world. . .
. The key contribution of the Puritans to the intellectual life of
later evangelicals is their gift of a mind as well as a theological
position, a set of principles concerning society as well as a
stance toward the church, a worldview as well as spirituality"
(Noll, 41). He argues, and I heartily agree, that we evangelicals
are descendants of the Puritans. Noll is greatly enamored of
Jonathan Edwards whom he considered the "greatest evangelical mind in America" (Noll, 60), but alas, he feels, the Great
Awakening did not produce worthy successors.

Noll spends considerable time on a chapter titled "The Intellectual Disaster of Fundamentalism." He criticized its tendency to
interpret the Bible haphazardly including "a weakness for treating the verses of the Bible as pieces in a jigsaw puzzle that
needed only to be sorted and then fit together to possess a finished picture of divine truth" (Noll, 126). This was particularly
true of dispensationalism. However, the book is about more
than how evangelicals approach the Bible, and here he seems to
echo Francis Schaeffer in so many ways, "but about evangelical
intellectual life, especially evangelical efforts to think in a
Christian manner about society, the arts, the human person,
and nature. For that kind of thinking the habits of mind fundamentalism encouraged can only be called a disaster" (Noll, 132).
Back in the 1970s while I was a student in seminary, I preached
at a fundamentalist church in Maryland that had a huge "end-
times" chart on one of the walls that traced history from the creation to the millennial kingdom. Noll criticizes this kind of
muddled thinking. "I believe that the major point of biblical
prophecy is to reveal affective and cosmological dimensions of
redemption in Christ and to provide believers with a complete
and detailed preview of the end of the world" (Noll, 142). And
yet, prophecy conferences continue to draw large crowds and
the Left Behind series of novels continue to be best sellers.

Noll does not believe that all is lost. While writing in the early 1990s, he felt that the evangelical ship could be righted. He writes, "The problem of fundamentalism was that the worst features of the nineteenth-century intellectual situation became the methodological keystones for mental activity in the twentieth century. If this analysis is correct, it means that fruitful evangelical thinking must come to grips not only with the excesses of the fundamentalist past but with the compounded damage done when those excesses were grafted on to even longer-lived intellectual weaknesses" (Noll, 130).

Noll also spends considerable time in reflecting on philosophy, politics, and science. With respect to politics, Noll seems almost prescient in his evaluation of the American scene particularly in light of the aftermath of the 2020 presidential election. One study conducted by the American Enterprise Institute discovered that more than twenty-five percent of white evangelicals believe that Donald Trump has been in a battle with a group of child sex traffickers that include prominent Democrats and certain Hollywood moguls. Statistics about voter fraud and who was responsible for the violence in the Capitol riot suggest widespread belief in conspiracy theories among evangelicals, not to mention skepticism about the COVD-19 vaccine. One might well ask: How did the Protestant church wind up here? To many the answer may seem obvious. The cultivation of the life of the mind, so important during much of the history of the Church, has been abandoned in the past 200 years.

Noll's reflections about science are particularly disturbing. While admitting that there are some fine evangelical scientists, he admits, "With some notable exceptions, the way for most evangelical scientists to get along was to go along in silence about the contested, highly controversial theoretical issues that dominated scientific discussion in the evangelical movement. The result has been a catastrophe for scientific thinking among evangelicals" (Noll, 178). Noll is critical of modern creation science, but he admits that "Creation scientists have performed an excellent service by denying the vast cosmological claims about the self-sustaining, closed character of the universe can ever arise from scientific research itself. They are just as insightful when claiming that such grand conclusions are as much an act of faith as any other large-scale religious claim" (Noll, 186). On-the-other hand, he lambasts creation scientists for some fuzzy thinking. He opines, "The mentality of fundamentalism lives on in modern creation science, even if some of the early fundamentalists were by no means as radical in their scientific conclusions as evangelicals have become in the last forty years" (Noll, 189). He writes further, "Creation science has damaged evangelicalism by making it much more difficult to think clearly about human origins, the age of the earth, and mechanisms of geological or biological change. But it has done more profound damage by undermining the ability to look at the world God has made and to understand what we see when we do look" (Noll, 196). Noll laments in his Afterword written in 2022, "Otherwise, except for the hard sciences, it is now an intellectual Wild West" (Noll, 263).

The Scandal of the Evangelical Mind has been called "an epistle from a wounded lover." Noll felt betrayed by what he saw going on around him in the evangelical world. This is an important book that provides both sober analysis of the issues and sounds the battle cry for evangelicals. It was named "Book of the Year" by the influential *Christianity Today* magazine. In my opinion, it is one of the most important Christian books published within the last three decades. It will not be the easiest reading for the average layperson, but it is extremely valuable and well worth persevering. The problems he described so well in 1994 eventually have trickled down from the colleges and seminaries to the church itself and finally to the pew. You owe it to yourself to be informed and Noll is just the person to do it. If you were ever tempted to paint Joel Osteen and T. D. Jakes and Charles Swindoll with the same brush and identify them indiscriminately by the term "evangelical," you absolutely need to read this book.

84. THE AMERICAN HOUR

By Os Guinness

Os Guinness has written a provocative book that brilliantly provides a careful and searching analysis of the strength of the American republic towards the end of what has been called the "American Century." Published in 1993, *The American Hour* (like the author's previous works *The Dust of Death* and *The Gravedigger File*) demonstrates how America's current crisis of cultural authority impacts our country at its very heart. The subtitle of the book gives us insight into the direction Guinness takes, *A Time of Reckoning and the Once and Future Role of Faith.*

This book is about America's crisis of cultural authority, what led up to it, and "what is likely to affect the outcome." Guinness believed at the time of writing that we are at a pivotal point in our nation's history. He writes, "The present moment is therefore the American Century's American Hour. It is an authentic *Kairos* moment, one of those great times of reckoning in which Americans judge themselves and for which America will always be judged" (Guiness, 6). He explains, "Under the impact of modernity, the beliefs, ideals, and traditions that have been central to Americans and to American democracy—whether religious, such as Jewish and Christian beliefs, or civic, such as Americanism—are losing their compelling cultural power. The crisis is not a crisis of legitimacy, like that of the Soviet Union, but a crisis of vitality that goes to the heart of America's character and strength" (Guinness, 4).

Os Guinness, though born in China to medical missionary parents and then raised and educated in England at the University of London (Bachelor of Divinity) and Oriel College, Oxford (Ph. D.), has lived in the United States since 1984. He was mentored by Francis Schaeffer at L'Abri in the 1960s where he served as a leader in that community, and then after moving to the United States as a Guest Scholar at the Woodrow Wilson Center and Visiting Fellow at the Brookings Institute. He was the lead drafter of The Williamsburg Charter in 1986, a document on the role of religion in the public life of the United States. He served as the Executive Director of the Williamsburg Charter Foundation from 1986-89. He has also served as a Senior Fellow with the Trinity Forum, the EastWest Institute in New York, and the Oxford Centre for Christian Apologetics. His books offer penetrating analyses into the cultural, political, social, and religious contexts in which we live. He is the author of more than two dozen books and the editor of eight additional ones. I can think of nobody more qualified to write this book. He continues in the tradition of his teacher, Francis Schaeffer, as well as Carl Henry, R. C. Sproul, and numerous others whose books are reviewed in this volume. An interesting sidenote is that Guinness is the great-great-great grandson of Arthur Guinness, the Dublin brewer of Guinness Stout fame.

The United States enjoyed unprecedented international prestige after World War II. The contribution of the United States to the Allied war effort was substantial, but the glow did not last forever. Guinness explains that in the years preceding the publication of this book, leading up to and including the Reagan years, "the newly emerging multipolar world is no longer America's oyster" (Guinness, 12). His assessment: "After a great sea-change in American life over the past few decades, the republic is approaching the climax of a generation-long crisis of cultural authority" (Guinness, 18).

Guinness argues that an understanding of "the present significance of faith in America" is of paramount importance and that we must "assess their social, national, and international consequences" (Guinness, 20). The author identifies his readership and what he hopes to accomplish. "This book is written principally for thoughtful Americans who love their country deeply, who appreciate America's unsung strengths and virtues as well as her recent successes but who realize that all is not well with America as recent celebration may suggest. What the book offers are three things: an analysis from an international perspective of what is currently America's deepest problem (the crisis of cultural authority), a proposal setting out a constructive solution to a key part of that problem (the reforging of a public philosophy for a civil public square), and a discussion of the prospects for an American renaissance" (Ibid.). Guinness insists most emphatically that he is NOT engaging in "an exercise in pessimism, blaming, or doom-crying" and that his analysis is non-partisan in that he does not intend to "bash" either the liberals or the fundamentalists. There is enough blame to go around.

Part One of the book is titled "The Cultural Revolution." It is clear, according to Guinness that "the United States is experiencing a transformation or restructuring" (Guinness, 25). This observation is not unique to the author, but has been expressed in articles, books, and commentaries over the years that the United States "is at a historic turning point, decisive for itself and perhaps also for the world" (Ibid.). This has been obvious to anyone over the past several generations who has not had his head in the sand. Guinness explains precisely what this crisis of cultural authority is. "Under the impact of modernity, the beliefs, ideals, and traditions that have been central to Americans and to the character of American democracy—whether religious, such as Jewish and Christian beliefs, or civic, such as Americanism—are losing their cultural compelling power" (Guinness, 27). Amazingly, this observation comes from someone who was born in China and lived in the United Kingdom for his formative years. He writes, "American beliefs, ideals, and traditions are fast becoming a lost continent to many Americans" (Guinness, 29). I recently read for the second time Tom Brokaw's fascinating book, *The Greatest Generation*, and it is so interesting that he laments some of the same social trends as Guinness. As Guinness points out echoing Brokaw, "Thus almost across the board, beliefs, ideals, and traditions, which once both inspired and restrained Americans, are losing their binding address. No longer self-evident in theory or culturally compelling in practice, they lack their former integrity and effectiveness in decisively linking belief to behavior, private life to public life" (Guinness, 30).

Guinness argues that this crisis of cultural authority that we are experiencing in the United States has already moved beyond the first stage, "perplexity, irritation, and rebellion against authority." He also believes that we have almost completed the second stage—and please keep in mind that the book was published in 1993, almost thirty years ago—"that of nostalgia for authority and attempted restoration." He warns that we will one day, and I personally believe we are already there, we will reach "the moment of reckoning when effective cultural authority either revives or sinks into oblivion, with dire consequences for the nation" (Guinness, 32). I believe we are at that point where civic and religious ideals have lost their power to influence the lives of Americans.

Guinness provides a fascinating overview of several influential decades in American life. He walks us through the fifties, sixties, seventies, and eighties to trace the development of the growing crisis. Because I lived through those decades, these chapters were of particular interest to me. According to Guinness, the first phase of cultural conflict began in the fifties and climaxed in the decade of the sixties with something of a counter-revolution in the eighties during the Reagan presidency.

Although the fifties in the United States might seem an unlikely place to begin examining the crisis of cultural authority, Guinness believes that the foundation for what we face now was laid in that decade. Although many today look back upon that decade with nostalgia, he claims that there were already pitfalls that led to the tumultuous sixties. In contradistinction to what he termed "The Golden Fifties," what followed was "The Seismic Sixties." Guinness observes, "The sixties earthquake was certainly the result of a long, slow buildup of violently colliding forces. But the reason the crunch was so shattering was not simply that new realities collided with conservative traditions—these were already weakened—but that, as we saw, the new realities collided with liberal illusions at the height of their strength and influence" (Guinness, 93).

Guinness titles his next chapter "The Second-thought Seventies," a decade that is often overlooked in the examination of cultural conflict. Those years are often seen as a period of malaise, a time that was often characterized as the "Me decade." Guinness, however, sees the seventies as having significant links to the sixties and "therefore a hinge decade with a critical significance" (Guinness, 102). It led to what he termed "The Empty Eighties." A decade in which "its conservative counter-revolution balances the cultural revolution of the sixties" (114). He sees the Reagan years as a period when there was a "surge of optimism." He writes, "Conservatism was confident and in control" (Guiness, 116). Among other trends in society, Guinness sees the financial scandals of the eighties as the outgrowth of the prosperous eighties. He writes, "For all the effort to revive moral order, the eighties finished as spiritually devastated as the seventies, though without the dreaded term 'malaise'" (Guinness, 119).

Guinness is led to speculate on how the nineties would play out. He is not optimistic and his concerns have proved to be prophetic. He writes, "Nothing epitomizes popular postmodernism better than MTV and the hand-held remote controls through which American adolescents nibble and dabble their way toward lostness, grazing at will in the flickering pastures of one greener channel after another" (Guinness, 129). What would he think of today's adolescents, and even adults, who appear to have cell phones surgically implanted and appear to move through life, even while driving a vehicle, totally fascinated with what is on the screen rather than the world outside?

In Part Two, which is titled "The Civil Public Square," Guinness begins with the American Civil War Battle of Antietam where 23,000 men fell on September 17, 1862, as a metaphor for the cultural wars we are facing today. In this war, there is a "take no prisoners" approach. He writes, "A new irrepressible tension between equally opposing and enduring forces is building up. The house of the American republic is dividing again" (Guinness, 136). Guinness concedes the fact that Americans are "extraordinarily religious" that understanding its role in society is crucial. He writes, "Understanding American religion is a necessity for understanding American history and culture, whether to Americans or non-Americans. Describing American society without religion is like describing Switzerland without the Alps" (Guinness, 141). If our country is sharply divided as Guinness argues so strenuously, everyone shares in the blame and should be part of the solution. He writes, "To an important degree, all Americans share in the responsibility for rebuilding the civil public square. It is certain that if it is not done all Americans will share the cost" (Guinness, 146). He believes our country is at a crossroads and that delay would spell disaster.

Guinness writes at length about how the culture war in America has become so uncivil and that both religious conservatives and liberals share the blame for this increasing polarization. He observes, "The culture-wars rhetoric is one of all-engulfing crisis and conflict, yet a large part of the controversy is not serious in quite the way the rhetoric makes it out to be. In the first place, the direst warnings of an extreme sacred square and an extremely naked sacred square have not proved true—as evidenced by the fact that each side reads opposite conclusions from the same set of facts" (Guinness, 163). He deplores the false civility exhibited by both sides of the fight and alludes to G. K. Chesterton's comment that tolerance is the virtue of people who don't believe anything.

In his next two chapters, Guinness poses some pointed questions to religious conservatives and then to religious liberals whom he calls the first and fourth faiths. He steps on the toes of religious conservatives such as myself when he argues, "Unquestionably it is Protestant evangelicals and fundamentalists

who have caused a great part of the confusion and must bear a
large measure of the responsibility" (Guinness, 179). He explains, "At best, Evangelicals and fundamentalists should recognize that 'Christian America' is a loaded term, charged with
emotions, historical baggage, and the specter of a revived dis-
crimination if it is applied today" (Guinness, 182). He points to
the long line of enemies/scapegoats that we have had. "Secular
humanists, New Agers, and Trilateral Commissioners are only
the latest in a long roll call of scapegoats, such as masons,
Catholics, Mormons, Jews, and international bankers. What
might have been legitimate concern over principled differences
has given way to an unprincipled politics of resentment"
(Guinness, 186). Ouch! Guinness believes that much of the
problem lies in "that much conservatism Christian activism is
a combination of righteous cause and unrighteous strategies"
(Guinness, 189). He explains, "A large part of the opposition
aroused by fundamentalism has to do with its style of public
engagement as much as its positions" (Ibid.). He describes a
fundamentalist as being a person "who talks of standing on the
rock of ages, but acts as if he were clinging to the last piece of
driftwood" (Guinness, 195). Guinness concludes, "Without a
clear commitment to the common vision for the common good,
evangelical and fundamentalist engagement in the public
square serves neither America's interests nor their own"
(Guinness, 197).

His questions are just as scathing for the religious liberals. He
describes them thus, "Preoccupied with the splinter in the eye
of the fundamentalist, they overlook the plank in their own"
(Guinness, 216). He observes that they often simplify arguments by resorting to stereotypes and the like. He writes, "The
problem with stereotypes is not that they offend sensitivities.
It is that indulgence in stereotypes and cliches is a telltale sign
of the lazy thinking that causes historical and cultural blindness" (Guinness, 217).

Guinness asks, "What is "the greatest danger facing the United
States?" The traditional response to this question has been ex-

ternal forces. Guinness points to the study by Arnold Toynbee "that all great civilizations were destroyed from within" (Guinness, 285). Guinness writes, "Similarly, I contend that, while America's outward problems, such as poverty, drugs, air contamination, and health care costs are massive and growing, they are no more important than America's inward problems, such as broken families, mediocrity in education, alienation in meaning, and nihilism in popular culture" (Ibid.). He discusses in detail three aspects of this problem: the crisis of national identity, the crisis of public philosophy, and the crisis of republican character. Guinness observes, "Compared with its prominent place in the past, talk of republican character makes only a feeble sound in the public discussion today" (Guinness, 288). He argues, "Yet for all the sophisticated disdain, there is a definite resurgence of interest in virtue among philosophers and educators" (Ibid.).

Guinness examines the hollowness, or weightlessness, of our culture and concludes that it "results from the erosion of the sense of personhood and truth in American society" (Guinness, 290). He identifies it as "the degenerative disease brought on by the crisis of cultural authority" (Guinness, 290-91). Guinness then traces the disease through literature going back to Walt Whitman's comment about America's "hollowness of heart" and T. S. Eliot's poem "The Hollow Men" through the emptiness of the eighties as seen in Tom Wolfe's *The Bonfire of the Vanities*. He argues that weightlessness "shows up clearly in its effects on personhood and truth" (Guinness, 292). This leads quite naturally to certain eventualities. He writes echoing Nietzsche, "If God is dead, we must face the fact that nature is morally indifferent, rationality is only a tool of power, and human rights are a fiction" (294). Guinness writes further, "If there are no absolute truths or absolute standards, if grand political differences are only a matter of 'cultural differences,' and if tolerance itself is relative, then Western democracy becomes as hollow an ideology as Communism" (Guinness, 294-95).

According to Guinness, one of the problems is that there is something of a selective blindness in American life and that we rely more upon spin than reality. He writes, "A thicket of unreality stands between Americans and the facts of life. The making of illusions has become the business of America" (Guinness, 297). And most disturbingly, Americans do not seem to care and have grown addicted to hollowness, the fiction of their lives, and "instant information." He sadly observes, "In a media-saturated society, authenticity is being spin doctor to your own artificiality. It almost seems that when modern communications and consumerism have both had their way, what is left of public speech in America will be America Lite, with all the body and flavor of a Miller Lite and all the depth and rationality of a Bud Lite commercial" (Guinness, 301).

Having considered at length the historical role of religion in American society and how it has lost its power as a vital force in shaping the moral and cultural landscape of this country and its consequences, Guinness postulates four possible scenarios for the future of America ranging from the continued decline of religion in America to a resurgence of faith. He demonstrates convincingly how each outcome could affect our society. The first two outcomes see a diminishing role of religion in public life. Only the fourth outcome, "a massive revitalization of American life," holds out hope for the restoration of spiritual vitality in the United States. Guinness then sets forth a vision for the future of America, one in which we are able to move beyond these struggles and once again provide the diverse faiths of our country with a revitalized and constructive role in the public arena. That is a goal that all Christians should desire.

The American Hour is an important book to read for all Christians who want to understand what is happening in the United States. Many are bewildered by the cultural and spiritual changes that they see and wonder how our nation has drifted so far from its first principles. As Guinness observes, "A republic that cannot return to its first principles is a republic that is in its last days" (Guinness, 276). Glaspey's evaluation of the book hits the nail on the head. "This book is marked by level-headedness, bold insight, the avoidance of extreme and simplistic formulas, and a willingness to critique all sides of the current struggle" (Glaspey, 108). It will expand your horizons and force you to confront the culture in which you live, and move, and have your being. Read it and I think you will agree.

SCIENCE AND THE BIBLE

It is not an over exaggeration to say that many of the places where science and Scripture intersect have become bitter battlegrounds. Simply put, there are numerous apparent disagreements between the Bible and the findings of modern science. Where there is conflict, it is often just assumed that science is correct. However, the truth is that science often is wrong because its findings are time-sensitive and must be updated continually based on new findings. Second, many tensions arise because of the philosophical presuppositions of unbelieving scientists rather than the scientific information itself. As John C. Lennox provocatively asks in his thoughtful book, *God's Undertaker, has science buried God?*

There are three primary areas of conflict that define the battle lines between science and Scripture: evolution, the days of creation, and miracles. The focus of the first two has been the bitter disagreement over how to interpret the first chapter of the book of Genesis. Much ink has been spilled in writing about the subject. Since the publication of Charles Darwin's *The Origin of Species* in 1859, the theory of evolution has been thought by many to be in conflict with the biblical account of the creation of mankind. Likewise, how to interpret the "days" of Genesis 1 has been the subject of much debate. The third area of conflict, miracles, has inspired bitter argumentation. Many people simply assume that science has proven the impossibility of them. Any phenomenon that contradicts the laws of physics, for example, cannot be true, they say. Examples abound in Scripture: the parting of the Red Sea in Exodus, the extended day in Joshua, the feeding of the 5,000 in all of the gospel writers, the raising of Lazarus from the dead. The list goes on and on.

The following two books deal in thought-provoking ways the relationship between science and the Bible. You likely will not agree with all that is written, but your mind will certainly be stretched by reading them.

85. GOD'S UNDERTAKER: HAS SCIENCE BURIED GOD?

By John C. Lennox

The phrase "God is dead" first appeared in 1882 in the writings of Friedrich Nietzsche, the German philosopher. He used it to express his opinion that the Enlightenment had essentially negated the existence of God. Although he was speaking some-what metaphorically, there are some more modern writers who have used the phrase in a literal sense. This movement hit its peak in the 1960s.

Is God for all practical purposes "dead?" Has modern science killed him, buried him, and left him, if not forgotten, then at least irrelevant? Is atheism the only intellectually respectable position to hold? The late John C. Lennox, Emeritus Professor of Mathematics at the University of Oxford and Emeritus Fellow in Mathematics and Philosophy of Science at Green Templeton College, Oxford University, answers these questions with an emphatic "No!" Lennox was well-qualified to rebut the assertions and offer a Christian alternative. He is the author of numerous books on the relationship between science, religion, and ethics. Of the many debates in which he participated, he is perhaps best known for his 2007 clash with Richard Dawkins, the author of *The God Delusion*, at the University of Birmingham in the United Kingdom.

In this inviting and thought-provoking book, Lennox challenges the reader to consider such questions very carefully. He writes, "It is a widespread popular impression that each new scientific advance is another nail in God's coffin" (Lennox, 14). He continues, "Perhaps it would be more accurate to say that they are convinced, not so much that science is at war with God, but that the war is over and science has gained the final victory. The world simply needs to be informed that . . . God is dead and science has buried him" (Lennox, 17).

Lennox, in an engaging and entertaining fashion, walks the reader through the major issues. He discusses the uneasy relationship religion has had with science over the centuries citing such notable scientists as Isaac Newton, Galileo, Copernicus, and Albert Einstein. He writes, "Tensions can arise when empirical evidence conflicts with the accepted scientific framework" (Lennox, 37). He gives the classic case of such obscurantism in that some in the church refused to even look through Galileo's telescope. As Lennox writes, "The implications of the physical evidence were too much to face" (Lennox, 37). Lennox draws the battle lines right off the bat. He writes, "The question that is central to this book turns out to be in essence a worldview question: which worldview sits most comfortably with science—theism or atheism? Has science buried God or not" (Lennox, 13)?

Why is it that modern religionists can now embrace the theories of Copernicus and Galileo when once they were considered heretics? Lennox asks, "What has happened to make the difference? Simply that they now take a more sophisticated, nuanced view of the Bible" (Lennox, 24). He continues, "The important lesson is that we should be humble enough to distinguish between what the Bible says and our interpretations of it. The biblical text just might be more sophisticated than we first imagined and we might therefore be in danger of using it to support ideas that it never intended to teach" (Lennox, 25). It is science, not God's Word, that that is constantly changing.

In this book, Lennox addresses topics as diverse as the scope and limits of science, designer universe, designer biosphere, the nature and scope of evolution, the origin of life, and the genetic code and its origin. He invites the reader to consider the claims of both science and Scripture. As the back cover asks, "Is it really true, he asks, that everything in science points toward atheism? Could it be possible that theism sits more comfortably with science than atheism?"

God's Undertaker is not the easiest book to read. It is not the book to take to the beach for an afternoon of light reading. But it is an important book. Many Christians appear to be baffled at the seeming impasse between their faith and the claims of modern science. Lennox will help you think through the issues and give you some intellectual ammunition to use against your atheist friends and neighbors. Don't take my word for it. Read it for yourself. You will be challenged.

86. THE LANGUAGE OF GOD

By Francis S. Collins

The name Francis Collins may not be a household name to the average person, but to those in the scientific community it is well-known and revered. As the head of the Human Genome Project, which is responsible for mapping DNA, the code of life, he is one of the world's leading and most respected scientists. But even more important than his lofty academic credentials, he is a committed Christ-follower with a strong belief in God and the authority of Scripture. Dr. Collins, unlike some in the scientific world, believes that faith in God and faith in science are not contradictory. *The Language of God* is a compelling case for God and for science.

This remarkable book traces the spiritual journey of Collins from agnosticism to a vibrant faith in Jesus Christ. Raised on a dirt farm in the Shenandoah Valley in Virginia without running water and with few amenities, Francis Collins was an unlikely candidate for receiving a Ph.D. in physical chemistry from Yale University and achieving worldwide renown. As a young man he found himself confused by his study of biology. "The overwhelming complexity of life led me to the conclusion that biology was rather like existential philosophy: it just didn't make sense" (Collins, 15). While still in medical school and confronted by a woman with severe untreatable angina, he was faced as a scientist with the important issues of life and death. He found himself, at the age of twenty-six, finally weighing the evidence for and against belief. He writes, "And yet there I found myself, with a combination of willful blindness and something that could only be properly described as arrogance, having avoided any serious consideration that God might be a real possibility. Suddenly all my arguments seemed very thin, and I had the sensation that the ice under my feet was cracking" (Collins, 20).

A turning point for Collins was, much like the experience of Charles Colson, the reading of *Mere Christianity* by C. S. Lewis. He explains the effects of the book on him. "As I turned its pages, struggling to absorb the breadth and depth of the intellectual arguments laid down by the legendary Oxford scholar, I realized that all of my own constructs against the plausibility of faith were those of a schoolboy" (Collins, 21). He said that the arguments of Lewis "rock my idea about science and spirit down to their foundation" (Collins, 22). He was also influenced by another book by Lewis, *The Four Loves*. He writes, "Agape, or selfless altruism, presents a major challenge for the evolutionist" (Collins, 27).

In his chapter titled "The War of the Worldviews," Collins muses about whether "the search for the existence of a supernatural being, so pervasive in all cultures ever studied, represent a universal but groundless human longing for something outside ourselves to give meaning to a meaningless life and to take away the sting of death" (Collins, 35). He asks, "Why do we have a 'God-shaped vacuum' in our hearts and minds unless it is meant to be filled" (38)? In response to the idea that the conception of some kind of God is just wish fulfillment, Collins responds, "In fact, one can turn this wishful thinking argument on its head. Why would such a universal and uniquely human hunger exist, if it were not connected to some opportunity for fulfillment" (Ibid.)?

Part Two of the book deals with the great questions of human existence. The chapters in this section are titled "The Origins of the Universe," "Life on Earth: Of Microbes and Man," and "Deciphering God's Instruction Book: The Lessons of the Human Genome." With respect to the origins of the universe, Collins is a firm believer in the Big Bang theory. He writes, "The Big Bang cries out for a divine explanation. It forces the conclusion that nature had a defined beginning. I cannot see how nature could have created itself. Only a supernatural force that is outside of space and time could have done that" (Collins, 67). He explains how important this is to our faith in God. "The consequences of Big Bang theory for theology are profound. For faith traditions that describe the universe as having been created by God from nothingness (ex nihilo), this is an electrifying outcome" (Collins, 66). As a scientist, Collins sees no reason that science and belief cannot coexist in harmony. He writes, "There is nothing inherently in conflict between the idea of a creator God and what science has revealed" (Collins, 81).

In his chapter about life on earth, Collins agrees, in contradistinction to those who believe in a young earth, with current scientific theory that the earth is likely 4.55 billion years old. While some in the evangelical community have almost made it an article of faith that the earth is no more than 10,000 years old, he concludes, "While the question of the origin of life is a fascinating one, and the inability of modern science to develop a statistical probable mechanism is intriguing, this is not the place for a thoughtful person to wager his faith" (Collins, 93).

Collins devotes several pages, including two helpful chart illustrations, to a sort of crash course about the discovery of and race to determine the structure of DNA. For people like me for whom science is not their strong suit, it was very helpful, an idiot's guide on the subject. His explanation is both fascinating and enlightening. For those who might fear that "naturalistic explanations are taking all the divine mystery out of the world," Collins reassures them. He explains, "Do not fear, there is plenty of divine mystery left. Many people who have considered all the scientific and spiritual evidence still see God's creative and guiding hand at work. For me, there is not a shred of disappointment or disillusionment in these discoveries about the nature of life—quite the contrary" (Collins, 106-07)! He adds, "For those who believe in God, there are reasons now to be more in awe, not less" (Collins, 107).

When Collins was asked to head the Human Genome Project, he was surprised and reluctant being already happily engaged leading the genome center at the University of Michigan. He indicated initially no interest in the position, but then reconsidered. He writes, "But the decision haunted me. There was only one Human Genome Project. This was only going to be done once in human history. If it succeeded, the consequences for medicine would be unprecedented. As a believer in God, was this one of those moments where I was somehow being called to take on a larger role in a project that would have profound consequences for our understanding of ourselves? Here was a chance to read the language of God, to determine the intimate details of how humans had come to be. Could I walk away" (Collins, 118-19)? Thankfully, he did not. Collins also felt a particular obligation as a Christian to participate in the Human Genome Project. He explains, "For me, as a believer, the uncovering of the human genome sequence held additional significance. This book was written in the DNA language by which God spoke life into being. I felt an overwhelming sense of awe in surveying this most significant of all biological texts. Yes, it is written in a language we understand very poorly, and it will take decades, if not centuries, to understand its instructions, but we had crossed a one-way bridge into profoundly new territory" (Collins, 123-24). Collins' discussion of DNA, its discovery, and its mapping is a fascinating one. He breaks it down so even those who might be weak in the sciences can understand.

In chapter four, Collins discusses the origins of life on earth. He writes, "The advances of science in the modern age have come at the cost of certain traditional reasons for belief in God" (Collins, 85). He admits that there is much we do not know such as how different types of microbial life came about on this planet. He asks, "But how did self-replicating organisms arise in the first place" (Collins, 90)? He acknowledges "the profound difficulty in defining a convincing pathway for life's origin" (Collins, 91). Some have posited that RNA and DNA were possible opportunities for divine creative action. But then again, nobody knows for certain and Collins takes a cautious approach and encourages the same. "In Summary, while the question of the origin of life is a fascinating one, and the inability of modern science to develop a statistically probable mechanism is intriguing, this is not the place for a thoughtful person to wager his faith" (Collins, 93).

Collins continues his discussion of the origins of life on earth with a survey of the evidence from the fossil record. While acknowledging the problems inherent from it and the many puzzles that have not yet been solved, Collins says "virtually all of the findings are consistent with the concept of a tree of life of related organisms" (Collins, 96). He concludes this chapter with a brief discussion of the theory of Charles Darwin and concludes, "No serious biologist today doubts the theory of evolution to explain the marvelous complexity and diversity of life. In fact, the relatedness of all species through the mechanism of evolution is such a profound foundation for the understanding of all biology that it is difficult to imagine how one would study life without it" (Collins, 99).

In chapters seven through ten, Collins proposes four possible responses to the "contentious interaction between the theory of evolution and faith in God" (Collins, 158). The first option is atheism and agnosticism. With respect to the former, he concludes, "Atheism itself must therefore be considered a form of blind faith, in that it adopts a belief system that cannot be defended on the basis of pure reason" (Collins, 165). He also sees the boundary lines between strong agnosticism and weak atheism as "blurry" and undefined.

The second option, creationism, is thoroughly investigated. Collins describes the most extreme version of this view, Young Earth Creationism. He argues that the term "creationist" has been hijacked to apply to a specific subset of believers, "specifically those who insist on a literal reading of Genesis 1 and 2 to describe the formation of life on earth" (Collins, 172). He believes that it is a dangerous position. He writes, "But the claims of Young Earth Creationism simply cannot be accom-

modated by tinkering around the edges of scientific knowledge. If these claims were actually true, it would lead to a complete and irreversible collapse of the sciences of physics, chemistry, cosmology, geology, and biology" (Collins, 173-74).
Collins sides with many other interpreters of Scripture
throughout history, such as Augustine, in concluding that the
Genesis account appears to be more like "a morality play than
an eyewitness report on the evening news" (Collins, 175). He
asks, "The intention of the Bible was (and is) to reveal the nature of God to humankind. Would it have served God's purposes thirty-four hundred years ago to lecture to His people
about radioactive decay, geological strata, and DNA" (Ibid.)?

Collins understands that Christians who feel drawn to Young
Earth Creationism have a high view of Scripture and believe
that modern scientific advances are threatening to God. He argues that those who feel that they must defend God are, in reality, dishonoring him. He asks, "Can faith in a loving God be
built on a foundation of lies about nature" (Collins, 176). He
concludes with a scathing indictment of the movement. "Thus,
by any reasonable standard, Young Earth Creationism has
reached a point of intellectual bankruptcy, both in its science
and in its theology. Its persistence is thus one of the great puzzles and great tragedies of our time. By attacking the fundamentals of virtually every branch of science, it widens the
chasm between the scientific and spiritual worldviews, just at
a time where a pathway toward harmony is desperately
needed" (Collins, 177).

Collins is also highly critical of the third option, Intelligent Design (ID). He sees it as a misguided attempt by evangelicals to
harmonize science and Scripture. He writes, "While ID is presented as a scientific theory, it is fair to say it was not born
from the scientific tradition" (Collins, 184). He explains, "On
the surface, the objections to Darwinism put forward by the ID
movement appear compelling, and it is not surprising that non-
scientists, especially looking for a role for God in the evolutionary process, have embraced these arguments warmly. But

if the logic truly had merit on scientific grounds, one would expect that the rank and file of working biologists would also show interest in pursuing these ideas, especially since a significant number of biologists are also believers. This has not happened, however, and Intelligent Design remains a fringe activity with little credibility within the mainstream scientific community" (Collins, 186-87). Why is this true? "A viable scientific theory predicts other findings and suggests approaches for further experimental verification. ID falls profoundly short in this regard" (187). Collins concludes, "The warm embrace of ID by believers, particularly evangelical Christians, is completely understandable, given the way in which Darwin's theory has been portrayed by some outspoken evolutionists as demanding atheism. But this ship is not headed for the promised land; it is headed instead to the bottom of the ocean" (Collins, 195).

Collins coins his own terminology for the fourth option, which he calls BioLogos. This is really just a fancy name for theistic evolution. Collins sees this as a more viable theory for the origin of life here on earth. He acknowledges the discomfort the topic of evolution has caused, which he sees as showing no signs of abating. However, he cautions that "believers would be well advised to look carefully at the overwhelming weight of scientific data supporting this view of the relatedness of all living things, including ourselves" (Collins, 141). Collins answers some of the critiques against theistic evolution and then answers the question, "What about Adam and Eve?" Collins cites C. S. Lewis as finding in the story of Adam and Eve more of a moral story than literal history. He posits that the Genesis account seems to allow for other people living on the earth at the same time that Adam and Eve were expelled from the Garden of Eden. He concludes that his position is "by far the most scientifically consistent and spiritually satisfying of the alternatives" (Collins, 210). Collins believes that there is a great danger in turning our backs on science as many evangelicals have done.

A word of caution to the reader: Francis Collins has been a vo-cal critic of the Intelligent Design (ID) movement and was founder of The BioLogos Foundation, a Christian Advocacy Group that believes in theistic evolution, a belief that God used the mechanism of evolution in creation. This is a view that I personally do not hold and neither do many Christians. I sug-gest that the reader read Phillip E. Johnson's 1991 *Darwin on Trial* (see my Appendix) as a counterbalance.

The words that Sam Cooke sang in 1960 might resonate with many of you as they did with me. "Don't know much about his-tory. Don't know much biology. Don't know much about sci-ence book" (*Wonderful World*). The world of science is confus-ing to a lot of folks. The *Language of God* is an important book that is elegantly written and deserves to be read by every thoughtful Christian. Some evangelicals may disagree vehe-mently with some of Collins's conclusions, but they need to at least think through his arguments to arrive at their own rea-soned views. Collins is one of us, an evangelical Christian, and there is not much on the subject about which this brilliant man has not thought deeply. This is a challenging and compelling work that will make you think and evaluate your own precon-ceived notions. Read it and see if you don't agree.

CHAPTER XII:
FICTION AND POETRY

There was once a time when the reading of fiction and poetry was considered to be frivolous for the Christian and pretty much a waste of time if not downright sinful. For example, in A. T. Pierson's classic biography of George Müller (see Chapter V), that nineteenth giant of prayer and faith, he writes of Müller's wayward youth that "the lad's studies were mixed with novel-reading and various vicious indulgences" (Pierson, 10). Even today, many believers dismiss the value of literary fiction and poetry as simply entertainment and of dubious value.

Although many genres of writing can be considered to be literature, when we use the term in its narrow sense, it is usually fiction and poetry that come immediately to mind. Fiction can be found in many forms not all written such as films on the big screen, television on the smaller screen, dramatic arts on the stage including opera, and writing in the form of novels and short stories.

Although the reading of fiction has been roundly criticized by some as an unworthy investment of time for the Christian, there is hardly a consensus of opinion on the matter. It is well-known that the Puritans considered drama and other secular entertainments to be taboo mainly because they distracted people from the worship of God. I believe that fiction in general and Christian fiction in particular are gifts that can enhance our understanding of the human condition and our faith in Jesus Christ. According to Veith, Jr., "The capacity to invent stories is a function of the creative imagination. This power of the human mind is doubtless a remnant of the divine image given us by the Creator" (Veith, 59). One look only as far as our Savior who often told stories to explain the Kingdom of God. Christ's repeated use of parables to teach spiritual truth was perhaps the hallmark of his pedagogic method. The word parable itself is simply a transliteration of a Greek compound word, *parabola*, which comes from *ballo* (to throw or to cast) and *para* (alongside). Thus, a parable is something that is thrown alongside as a means of illustration.

C. S. Lewis and J. R. R. Tolkien were twentieth century writers who used fiction, particularly science fiction, to great effect and to reinforce biblical teachings and Christian values. Yet, Lewis was often criticized. For example, his great novel *The Lion, the Witch, and the Wardrobe*, one of the seven novels that comprise the author's wonderful *The Chronicles of Narnia*, has been lambasted by those who object to the title, specifically the use of the word "witch." There are others who believe that Lewis is way off base for even suggesting that people in hell could somehow take a bus trip to Heaven, as we read in his *The Great Divorce*. Such people lack understanding, imagination, and a sense of humor and are probably scandalized by the language in the Psalms which suggests that mountains and hills break out into singing and trees clap their hands. Some dear readers of this book might be perplexed at my inclusion of Flannery O'Connor's *Wise Blood* in this collection. Her novel is strange, to say the least, and shocking, but it will haunt the reader long after reading and will serve as an indictment of sinfulness and self-deceit. Fiction has the unique capacity to do that and to point a mirror into our very souls. That is one reason that it should be read by Christians.

Poetry is a different genre of literature than prose fiction. At the risk of oversimplification, prose speaks to the mind or intellect, whereas poetry speaks more to the heart and emotions. When we read a poem about Mary and her little lamb or a Grecian urn or a man's love for his highlands of Scotland, the poem's form and language compels us to respond with our feelings and our minds in ways that prose does not. According to Veith, "Poetry, though, requires active reading. The reader must become involved more personally and actively than in other kinds of reading. The imagination must be fully engaged, the language must be taken in completely, and the feelings, associations, and ideas conjured up by the language must be allowed their full play" (Veith, 83).

There is no better recommendation for reading poetry than the fact that much of the Bible, particularly the Old Testament, is comprised of poetry. Most of the book of Job, and just about all of the Psalms, Proverbs, Ecclesiastes, and Song of Songs, not to mention huge sections of the writings of the prophets as well as in the narrative sections of the Torah and historical books, are poetry. Veith concludes that "because poetry tends to address the whole person—the mind, the imagination, and the emotions—there may be no better way to cultivate a Christian sensibility and worldview (apart from reading Scripture itself) than to saturate oneself in Christian poetry"(Veith, 80).

More than any other literary genre, poetry facilitates the Christian's attempt to meditate on God and his promises. According to Veith, "The meditation encouraged by poetry promotes concentrated thinking, heightened sensitivity, and an integrated Christian sensibility" (Veith, 85). Poetry liberally utilizes figures of speech such as simile and metaphor as well as numerous poetical devices such as alliteration, allusion, apostrophe, assonance, consonance, and meter all to create rhythm and to enhance a poem's meaning or intensify its mood.

It is unfortunate that many today eschew poetry out of hand. There are two main reasons for this. Most of us are exposed to poetry at an age when we are not mature enough to appreciate it. Middle school or high school students often ridicule poetry because of this. A second reason is that reading poetry can be somewhat difficult. The poetry of T. S. Elliot is a case in point. Reading his poems require work, but the rewards far outweigh the effort. A third reason that is not as prevalent as the first two is that some are put off by the form of the poem. I remember how I responded to the strange poetry of E. E. Cummings when I first encountered it. By the way, Cummings' first published work of poetry was rejected by publisher after publisher. It was easy for me to reject his form at first glance. I was apparently not alone. In the dedication of his first compilation of poetry published in 1923, he wrote "no thanks to" the fourteen publishing companies that rejected it. He was a pioneer in the modernist free-form poetry movement and is widely considered one of the most important poets of the twentieth century. Obviously, when I was first exposed to the writings of Cummings as an undergraduate university student, I lacked two things: maturity and an open mind.

Poetry, both classic and modern, deserves the attention of the thoughtful Christian. Where would we be without Milton's *Paradise Lost* or Dante's *The Divine Comedy*? Certainly, we would be the poorer without them as well as William Blake, T. S. Elliot. John Donne, George Herbert and many others. What if God in his infinite wisdom had not included the Psalms in the canon of the Old Testament? Our worship, prayers, and meditation would not be as rich as they are with them. Paul admonishes the Ephesian church "to speak to one another with psalms, hymns and spiritual songs. Sing and make music in your heart to the Lord" (Ephesians 5:19). When you read that, think of poetry as well. Paul's words to the Ephesians apply to us as well.

87. THE HOBBIT

&

88. THE LORD OF THE RINGS

By J. R. R. Tolkien

If I could somehow go back in time, one of my first stops would be at a little pub in Oxford, England called the Eagle and the Child around the middle of the twentieth century at an informal gathering of the Inklings. I would perhaps sidle up to C. S. Lewis and listen to him sharing ideas about his writing of *The Chronicles of Narnia* or *The Screwtape Letters.* Or perhaps I might hobnob with Owen Barfield or Charles Williams. But I would be certain to sit very close to J. R. R. Tolkien as he shared his ideas and progress on either *The Hobbit* or *The Lord of the Rings* trilogy.

The Lord of the Rings has become almost a cottage industry in the past couple of decades. First conceived as a sequel to *The Hobbit,* which was published in 1937, it evolved into something far beyond the author's initial conception. It was written in stages between 1937 and 1949 and has become one of the best-selling books of all time with over 150 million books sold. Not only have Tolkein's writings grown in popularity over the years, there have been three blockbuster movies released to a waiting public that just can't seem to get enough. *The Lord of the Rings* series is now big business indeed. It has also been adapted for radio and the stage and has been named Britain's best novel of all time by the BBC. So, of course, I need to consider both works together in this chapter.

John Ronald Reuel Tolkien, usually known as J. R. R. Tolkien, was an English writer of fantasy novels and a philologist who served as the Rawlinson and Bosworth Professor of Anglo-Saxon and a Fellow of Pembroke College, both at the University of Oxford from 1925 to 1945. He was a contemporary and close friend of C. S. Lewis and a member of the Inklings. He was hugely instrumental in the conversion of Lewis to the Christian faith from atheism.

My readers would be absolutely correct if they were to ask me why I even included *The Hobbit* in this book of "must-reads." After all, there is no mention of God; nobody prays; there are no churches, clergy, or mention of religious services. Many of the things that we might normally associate with the Christian faith are absent. Originally conceived as a bedtime story for his children, this classic has delighted young and old for generations. Tolkien's approach is much more subtle than that of his friend, C. S. Lewis. Tolkien doesn't wear his faith on his sleeve, so to speak, and yet the Christian message shines through in powerful, though subtle, ways. Certainly, his approach to weaving together fantasy and Christianity is more subtle than that of Lewis. There are at least three elements that we find in *The Hobbit* that I believe we can discern from a careful reading. First, there is a clear sense of the providence of God in the book even though his name is never mentioned nor is Jesus Christ or the Holy Spirit. That should not deter us. The canonical book of Esther never mentions God either, but the sense of his providence is overwhelming. Second, there is a clear sense of the eternal struggle between good and evil. It is blatantly obvious who the good and the bad guys are. There are no gray areas in Tolkien's fantasy world. There is a clear sense of Christian morality permeating the book. Third, there is a clear sense of Christian purpose. In one sense, Bilbo was predestined to fulfill a Christian purpose, one that he did not choose for himself. Bilbo was quite content to live in his predictable and most comfortable circumstances, but he was chosen for something greater. The dwarves needed to be returned to their homes and the Desolation of Smaug needed to be restored. Tolkien believed that reading a good fairy tale was like holding up a mirror to oneself. The thoughtful reader will likely see himself reflected in Bilbo Baggins and perhaps some of the other characters of the book.

The story of Bilbo begins with his inadvertent discovery of the One Ring and his subsequent reluctant joining of the little band of dwarves in their quest to recover stolen treasure from the great dragon Smaug. He uses the ring's powers of invisibility to assist the dwarves

When we step into the world of Tolkien's *The Hobbit*, we enter into a strange place inhabited not only by hobbits, but also elves and dwarves, dragons and goblins, and trolls and wizards among many other fantastic creatures. It is a world unlike any other. It has no apparent connection with our world except for a brief and humorous allusion to the game of golf. Bilbo, a home-loving hobbit who just wants to be left alone in the comfort of his spacious underground hobbit-hole, is soon drawn, quite against his personal inclinations, into a quest along with Gandalf the wizard and a band of homeless dwarves facing multitudinous unknown dangers including evil orcs, giant spiders, savage wolves, dragons, and the like. Finally, it is Bilbo alone—a solitary warrior and unaided—who is left to battle the evil dragon Smaug in a dramatic confrontation. In the process, it is Bilbo who has gained the most. He returns home with a treasure that is spiritual in nature and enduring.

Bilbo is quite content in the safety and comfort of his quaint little hobbit-hole when he is asked/ drafted by Gandalf's unwelcome overtures. Like Bilbo, we too often become very comfortable in our own lives and are reluctant when the call of Christ to his service comes to us. We value convenience over obedience and coziness over discipleship. There is a famous quotation by Pope Benedict XVI that well describes Bilbo's transformation from "couch potato" to man (Hobbit) of action. He said, "The world offers you comfort. But you were not made for comfort. You were made for greatness." However, Bilbo's adventures merely lay the foundation for the story told in *The Lord of the Rings* about his nephew, Frodo.

The Lord of the Rings was originally written in three stages between 1937 and 1949. It is a true epic that was originally intended to be a sequel for *The Hobbit*. But somehow, as novels often do especially if they are written by say C. S. Lewis or J. R. R. Tolkien, it took on a life of its own and evolved into a much larger book published in three volumes in 1954 and 1955. The three volumes were titled *The Fellowship of the Ring*, *The Two Towers*, and *The Return of the King*. Although the work is often referred to as a trilogy, Tolkien intended it to be part of a two-volume set along with *The Silmarillion*. Later editions, per Tolkien's original intent, were printed together in a single volume.

The setting in *The Lord of the Rings* is a pre-Christian world in which a cosmic war of epic proportions between good and evil are taking place. This work, along with *The Hobbit*, vividly demonstrates Tolkien's love for philology, myth, legend, and quest. His characters mirror medieval characters in that they, like Bilbo and Frodo, often undertake perilous adventures and in so doing prove their moral strength. Although Tolkien is best known today for his fantasy novels, his scholarly reputation was cemented with his critical studies of the Old and Middle English works, *Sir Gawain and the Green Knight* and *Beowulf*. Thus, his writings of fiction were deeply rooted in his understanding of Old and Middle English literature. We see this in the character Frodo in *The Lord of the Rings* and in Bilbo in *The Hobbit*.

It is unfortunate in the opinion of some that *Rings* does not include a true Christ-type hero character. We look in vain for one. Frodo cannot be it because he fails in his quest and is himself tainted by evil. Gandalf, the wizard, also fails in this regard because he functions more as an inspired guide, along the lines of Yoda in the *Star Wars* movie, than a savior. Although some see his "fall" in the mountains of Moria and subsequent return as a thinly-veiled allusion to Christ's resurrection, Gandalf falls short of being a savior. Samwise might come the closest to being a Christ-type hero, but simply appears to represent what a mature Christian ought to be, definitely not a savior. It is possible to see Tolkien's Roman Catholic leanings coming to bear here in favoring a works-based religion rather than one of faith alone embraced by the Reformers such as Martin Luther and John Calvin.

One decidedly Christian element in *The Lord of the Rings* is the twin principles of justice and judgment. Each character receives what he so richly deserves. As the apostle Paul put it so well in his letter to the Galatians, "Whatsoever a man sows, that shall he also reap." For example, Sauron after his cosmic program of desolation is fated to gnaw himself for eternity. In Scripture, gnawing is a symbol of eternal punishment. "Weeping, and wailing, and gnashing of teeth." This ties in with the Christian principle of individuality and responsibility. In the lands under Sauron's control, individuality is minimized as everyone is assigned a number, not a name. This tends to dehumanize. On the other hand, even someone as seemingly unimportant as a hobbit has untold potential and can topple the powerful. As Paul wrote to the Corinthians, God has chosen the weak things in this world to confound the wise. This is a profoundly Christian element even if Tolkien does not identify it as such.

There are many other Christian elements in Tolkien's great novel such as patience and perseverance. There are also humility, fidelity, and virtue. Biblical symbols are also employed such as light and bride. Although *The Lord of the Rings* is not blatantly, in your face, overtly Christian, the elements are there if one cares to look for them. Certainly, at the very least, Tolkien was a Christian who wrote a novel with Christian overtones.

I heartily recommend both *The Hobbit* and *The Lord of the Rings* to readers of all ages. The former can be read by even young readers. The latter might be a bit intense and frightening for the youngest. Readers wanting to dig deeper might also want to explore *A Hobbit Devotional* by Ed Strauss, which features sixty humorous, challenging, and encouraging devotionals, or *The Christian World of the Hobbit* by Devin Brown. But by all means, read both of Tolkien's classics. You will be magically transported into a different world and time and you will become a child again.

89. THE LION, THE WITCH, AND THE WARDROBE

&

90. THE SCREWTAPE LETTERS

By C. S. Lewis

Clive Stapleton Lewis, better known as C. S. Lewis (introduced in Chapter III), was a rather remarkable figure. In addition to being arguably the foremost Christian apologist of the twentieth century and its most influential Christian writer, he had a lifelong fascination with the ancient legends, myths, and fairy tales he learned in his childhood. Although a respected professor of medieval literature at Oxford University (and later Cambridge), he and his good friend, J. R. R. Tolkien, were members of the Inklings, an informal writer's club that met at a local pub to discuss their unfinished compositions. Other well-known regular members included Owen Barfield and Charles Williams, names familiar to many readers. The group valued narrative fiction and encouraged the writing of fantasy. The *Lord of the Rings* trilogy and this book were certainly literary outgrowths of the Inklings.

The Lion, the Witch, and the Wardrobe had its roots in the childhood of this incredibly prolific writer. The book is actually the first book in *The Chronicles of Narnia*, a collection of seven short fantasy novels that were originally published between 1950 and 1956 and illustrated by Pauline Baynes. They have been adapted for radio, television, the stage, film, and video games. It is not beyond the pale to say that the *Chronicles* has become a cottage industry. *The Lion, the Witch, and the*

Wardrobe has become one of the most beloved books of all time. The other six books in the series are in order *Prince Caspian: The Return to Narnia* (1951), *The Voyage of the Dawn Treader* (1952), *The Silver Chair* (1953), *The Horse and His Boy* (1954), *The Magician's Nephew* (1955), and *The Last Battle* (1956). The series is considered a classic of children's literature and has sold over 100 million books in forty-seven languages.

In the world of Narnia, you will encounter witches, magicians, magic rings, mythical beasts, animals that talk, and a horse that can fly. In fact, there are more talking animals than people. Battles are fought by Centaurs, Giants, and Fauns. Narnia is a fantasy world which is the setting of the unfolding drama of history in its world. In Narnia, various children play the central roles. They are all, with the exception of *The Horse and His Boy*, children from the real world who are transported magically to the land of Narnia. The seven books tell the story of the history of Narnia from its creation in *The Magician's Nephew* to its destruction in *The Final Battle*. If you see a scriptural parallel here to the unfolding story of redemption beginning in Genesis and ending in Revelation, you are not alone.

The Lion, the Witch, and the Wardrobe tells the story of four children, Peter, Susan, Edmund, and Lucy Pevensie, who have been evacuated to the English countryside from London because of the air-raids after the outbreak of World War II. They discover a wardrobe in the house of Professor Digory Kirke that has a compartment that leads to the fantasy world of Narnia. We first meet Digory Kirke as a child in *The Magician's Nephew*. When they arrive, the land is ruled by the White Witch who for over a century has held Narnia in an icy grip of perpetual winter with no Christmas. Here they meet numerous characters of this strange world—Mr. Tummus, the Faun, Mr. and Mrs. Beaver, and finally, Aslan, the lion. He is described as being very powerful and not at all tame, but very good. The children help Aslan rescue Narnia from the evil grip of the White Witch, thus inaugurating a Golden Age. The history of Narnia will continue in later books.

It doesn't take a biblical scholar to discern the religious imagery in *The Lion, the Witch, and the Wardrobe*. The Christian themes are not thinly disguised. Aslan is a Christ-figure who rescues us from evil and dies in our stead. To nobody's surprise, he rises from the dead. Does any of this sound familiar? Basically, Lewis retold the Christ story in allegory form. Along the way, the reader learns about many of the major themes and motifs of the Christian walk. We learn about the struggle between good and evil, sacrifice, loyalty, and temptation among many others. It is true that the religious and biblical allusions are obvious, but this is much more than another moralistic story that is dull and dry. The story told by Lewis is exciting and gripping, and has been much loved by children as well as adult for generations.

Was Lewis writing for children? Absolutely! Should it still be read to children and should they be encouraged to read it for themselves? Of course! But what about adults? Why have I included this book in my listing of recommended books? I am a firm believer that, although written for children, *The Lion, the Witch, and the Wardrobe*, as well as the other books of the Narnia series absolutely should be read by adults. These books reveal core truths about mankind and God and their relationship to one another. And they convey these truths in simple ways that a child, and perhaps even an adult, can understand. You owe it to yourself to read this book and the other six books in the series so that you can be conversant with one of the great epic stories of the twentieth century, whose effects continue to ripple our part of the pond. The books are very short and easily read. I think you will have fun doing so and you may rediscover some of the wonder of your childhood. One suggestion: Do not read them in publication order, but begin with *The Magician's Nephew* and go from there. In the first book, you will discover unmistakable parallels to the temptation story of Genesis three and the forbidden fruit. Have fun!

Lewis's class apologetic, *The Screwtape Letters*, is a satirical work of fiction utilizing an epistolary style that he uses master-

fully to discuss timeless Christian themes such as temptation
and how to resist it. The book is dedicated to his friend, J. R. R.
Tolkien, no stranger to fantasy himself. It began in 1940 as a
series of fictional letters that Lewis began writing from a demon named Screwtape to his pupil, Wormwood. Wormwood is
a demon apprentice who must lead a young British man,
known only as "the Patient" who has just become a Christian,
into damnation. The contents of the book were first published
in serial form by *The Guardian*, an Anglican periodical during
1941, before making their way into book form.

In the book, Wormwood consults with his uncle Screwtape, a
wise and experienced demon for advice. This book is a record
of the correspondence between the two. Their thirty-one letters
offer profound insights on subjects such as temptation and
pride. Screwtape holds an impressive administrative post in the
"Lowerarchy" of Hell. Wormwood is portrayed as an incompe-
tent bungler. After the second letter, the Patient becomes a convert to Christianity earning Wormwood a stinging rebuke from
Screwtape for allowing this. The rest of the book chronicles the
relationship between Wormwood and his uncle and the philosophical divide that marks their respective approaches to the
art of temptation. Wormwood's approach is reckless as he anx-
iously and desperately tries to tempt the Patient into sins that
are increasingly gross and wicked, but with little success.
Screwtape advises a more subtle approach, what he calls "careful handling" (Letter XII). He tells him that the Patient can outwardly appear to be a Christian as long as he remains unchanged internally. He cautions Wormwood to proceed gradually. "Indeed, the safest road to Hell is the gradual one—the
gentle slope, soft underfoot, without sudden turnings, without
signposts" (Letter XII).

The book ends in failure, as least from the perspective of
Wormwood and Screwtape. We learn in the final letter that the
Patient has been killed in the London bombings and has gone
to Heaven. Thus, the final failure for Wormwood. Screwtape is
scathing in his denunciation of Wormwood. In the first thirty

letters, Screwtape addressed his nephew as "My dear Worm-wood." In the final letter, the wording is sarcastically changed to " My dear, my very dear Wormwood, my poppet, my pigsnie" (Letter XXXI).

The Screwtape Letters is brilliant in its conception and ably demonstrates the fertile imagination of C. S. Lewis. In Lewis's world, the Oxford dons were the teachers. In the underworld of Screwtape and Wormwood, demons themselves become the professors. Although Wormwood's endeavors end in failure, Lewis's view is that the strategies of Satan are very sound and are successful much of the time. As Petersen and Petersen write, "Strangely, *The Screwtape Letters* has a ring of authentic-ity—obviously not from actual demonic correspondence, but from the experience of a man who has been tempted and has learned from it" (Petersen and Petersen, 75). Upon its publica-tion, *The Screwtape Letters* actually received a more positive re-ception from the secular market than it did from the Christian one.

My recommendation is that you read this book more than once. As you read it, you will be impressed by Lewis's cleverness and marvel at his imagination. But beyond his vehicle for getting the message across, I suggest that you see what you can recog-nize from your own life. I believe that in your reading you may even see your own reflection.

91. THE BROTHERS KARAMAZOV

By Fydor Dostoevsky

In the interests of full disclosure, this novel was not my first choice for inclusion in this book. *Crime and Punishment* was. I first read *Crime and Punishment* about a half century ago for a class I was taking at the University of Maryland and immediately it jumped to the top of my list of favorite novels. So, even though it may have been my first choice, my "experts" outvoted me. I kept seeing *The Brothers of Karamazov* turning up on numerous lists compiled by pastors and seminary professors, so my decision was to include it instead of *Crime and Punishment*. In addition, in a 2018 edition of the online newsletter *The Christian Review*, it was called the greatest novel ever written. It reaches heights of grandeur that evoke comparisons with the greatest works of Western literature.

It is my opinion that Fydor Dostoevsky towers above most novelists throughout history and has few peers. He may well be the greatest novelist of all time. But that is a subjective evaluation. For somebody who reads a steady diet of James Patterson novels or such similar literary fast food, Dostoevsky may not be to that person's liking. Suffice it to say, Dostoevsky occupies a literary stratosphere all his own. His pathos and understanding of the human condition are unmatched in world literature. His writings explored the troubled social, political, and spiritual atmospheres of Russia in the nineteenth century. Yet, as Veith so poignantly writes, "Dostoyevsky's faith, tempered by suffering and struggle, shines through the darkness he portrays" (Veith, 226).

Dostoevsky was born in Moscow in 1821, the son of a poor army surgeon. He was introduced to literature at an early age and after a brief career as an engineer, decided on a literary career. He was arrested in 1849 by czarist police while attending a meeting of his revolutionary literary colleagues whose purpose was to discuss banned books. He was condemned to death, but moments before he was to be executed, his sentence was reprieved, and he was banished to a Siberian prison camp for four years. He was classified a dangerous convict and spent his imprisonment with his hands and feet shackled. The only reading material he was allowed was his New Testament Bible, which sustained him during those difficult years. After his exile, he was to serve in the army for the rest of his life.

Pardoned by the new czar Alexander II, Dostoevsky returned to civilian status and resumed his literary career. What followed were a succession of brilliant novels written out of the crucible of his tragic life. In spite of his literary successes, he never achieved financial stability and was subject to frequent bouts of epilepsy. These factors along with the effect of his years in prison crushed his spirit and left him a melancholy and embittered man, while at the same time he was being celebrated as a national hero to the Russian masses who saw him as the chronicler of their sufferings and hopes.

It was out of a lifetime of suffering and hardship that Dostoevsky wrote *The Brothers Karamazov*, the final and crowning work of his life. The book was written in installments under intense pressure and appeared as a serial in the Moscow magazine, *Russky Vistnik*. Each installment was published to great national excitement and anticipation, which created a national furor. It is set in nineteenth century Russian and explores in great depth such questions as God, free will, and morality. Revolving around the subject of patricide, Dostoevsky explores the conflict between faith and doubt and the behaviors that are generated and their aftermath. Great themes are also explored such as forgiveness, kindness, judgment, morality, and goodness. In the conflict between faith and doubt, Dostoevsky comes down clearly and unequivocally on the side of faith, which helps to make this a great novel that should be read by

Christians. Glaspey comments, "Dostoevski's (sic) writing demonstrates a haunting awareness of the depths to which human beings can sink and the heights of self-sacrifice of which we are capable. And he tells it all with a passion that puts most other novelists to shame. Here is the Christian worldview demonstrated at its most profound with passages of awe-inspiring beauty" (Glaspey, 75).

The basic plot, which has been called the stuff of melodrama, revolves around four main characters, Fyodor Karamazov, the father, and his three sons Dmitri, Ivan, and Alexai from two marriages. Fyodor is something of a womanizer and an indifferent father. The three estranged sons return to their father's town to mediate a disputed inheritance. Set in nineteenth century Russia, the story is a mystery wrapped in an enigma as it wrestles with the question of who murdered the father, all the while dealing with questions of faith and doubt, forgiveness, justice, revenge, and repentance. Along the way, there are numerous subplots and twists and turns that reveal the life stories on minor characters. One may be thunderstruck by the sheer wonder and complexity of the novel.

One question that is set forth brilliantly in *The Brothers Karamazov* is that of the immorality of murder if there is no God. The novel states unequivocally that if there is no God, then every human behavior is allowed. Dostoevsky seems to foreshadow the tumultuous events of the twentieth century with Lenin and Stalin coming to power in the USSR with its death camps and mass killings. Stalin apparently felt that he had *carte blanche* approval to execute anyone as long as it was for the greater good of society. With God banished from the post-revolution USSR, who is there to say that what Stalin did was wrong? Dostoevsky anticipates this enigma. His answer is that we are answerable to God! It is a testament to his brilliance as a writer that he somehow manages to address almost every eternal question throughout the course of this novel. It is a masterpiece.

Many of the characters from the book are unforgettable and will stay with you long after you put the book down. One character who will live in your memory is the buffoonish Father Ferapont, a rigid ascetic who is a stereotype of the self-righteous jerk who separates himself from the world and then calls down curses upon it. He appears to be immune to the suffering of humanity. You may have encountered a Father Ferapont during your spiritual pilgrimage. Hopefully, he wasn't your pastor. The patriarch of the family is Fyodor Pavovich, a man who lives for pleasure. He is a hedonist whose main interests are drinking to excess, partying, and womanizing. He is a terrible father in that he has no interest in raising his three sons from two different marriages. He resembles too many modern men that I have known over the years. It is said that the apple doesn't fall far from the tree. Fyodor's first son, Dmitri, is proof of that old adage. His character is modeled after a prisoner Dostoevsky met during his exile in Siberia. This man was accused of killing his father for the family inheritance. What kind of offspring does such a man as Fyodor produce? Dmitri is the sad legacy such a man leaves to the world. Alexei, the second son of Fyodor from his second marriage, is a contrast to Dmitri and his father. Alexei, a committed believer and a member of the Russian Orthodox Church and monk's disciple, is the protagonist of the book and a shining light in the novel. His character provides a refreshing contrast to the two scoundrels who are his father and brother.

I will freely admit that reading *The Brothers Karamazov* is not for the faint of heart or the uncommitted. My Modern Library edition has 822 pages. By way of comparison, my Literary Guild edition of *War and Peace*, usually considered to be the standard for long novels, is 696 pages. Dostoevsky negotiated a deal with his publisher to be paid by the word. But if you are pressed for time, say you have stage four liver cancer, and you want to read a Dostoevsky novel, you surely can't go wrong by substituting *Crime and Punishment*. Both are fabulous novels. Both are monumental works of literature that scale the literary heights and also deal with Christian themes. Read either one and you will be blessed immeasurably by a rich reading experience. Or better yet, read them both.

To get a feel for the rich theology of *The Brothers Karamazov*, read the quotations below. I did not include page numbers because of the many different editions available.

> "Love is such a priceless treasure that you can redeem the whole world by it and expiate not only your own sins but the sins of others."

> "What a book the Bible is, what a miracle, what strength is given with it to man! It is like a mold cast of the world and man and human nature, everything is there, and a law for everything for all the ages. And what mysteries are solved and revealed."

> "Fear nothing and never be afraid; and don't fret. If only your penitence fail not, God will forgive all. There is no sin, and there can be no sin on all the earth, which the Lord will not forgive to the truly repentant! Man cannot commit a sin so great as to exhaust the infinite love of God."

> "Look around you at the gifts of God, the clear sky, the pure air, the tender grass, the birds. Nature is beautiful and sinless, and we, only we, are sinful and foolish, and we don't understand that life is Heaven, for we have only to understand that and it will at once be fulfilled in all its beauty, we shall embrace each other and weep."

92. THE POWER AND THE GLORY

By Graham Greene

Graham Greene has a well-deserved reputation as one of the greatest novelists of the twentieth century and *The Power and the Glory* is his universally acknowledged masterpiece. Published in 1940, the book's ethos still holds a powerful grip today, over eighty years later, and its universal conflicts could have been wrested from today's newspaper headlines or those from recent decades. Totalitarian regimes that are anti-Christ and anti-church never seem to go out of style. The martyrdom of Christians in countries that are hostile to them still goes on well into the twenty-first century. The ongoing conflict in the Ukraine with Russia in 2022 and 2023 demonstrates that the forces of evil are alive and well in our present day.

Greene's novels, of which *The Power and the Glory* sits front and center, tend to revolve around spiritual themes which he unfolds with the precision of a skilled surgeon and the subtlety of a sledgehammer. This is a book about the martyrdom of a priest in Mexico, but it could have taken place today in Russia, China, Africa, South America or a hundred other places around the globe. And it could have been about a priest, a nun, a missionary, or simply a Christian living out his faith on a daily basis. The book's title comes from the doxology recited at the end of the Lord's Prayer: "For thine is the kingdom, the power, and the glory, forever and ever. Amen."

Greene based this novel on his experiences in Mexico in 1937-38 during a time when he experienced firsthand idolatry, oppression, starvation, and casual violence. He saw life in Mexico as under the shadow of religion of either God or the Devil. He absolutely loathed his time spent there and his experiences planted the seeds from which *The Power and the Glory* sprouted. Greene travelled to totalitarian Mexico to conduct research on the socialist government's persecution of the Roman Catholic Church. The horrific effects and widespread suffering provided the core conflict for the novel. Ironically, this controversial book was condemned by the Roman Catholic Church when it was first published. According to one admirer of the book, "The novel is an unforgettable portrayal of the clash of worldviews and the unstoppable grace of God" (Veith, 127-28).

Greene's early life was difficult and unhappy which led him to attempt suicide at one point and seek treatment from a psychoanalyst. Born in 1904, he converted to Catholicism in 1926 largely because he was convinced that the existence of evil was a reality in the world. The nightmare that was his early life and the dream journals that he kept were natural bridges to the horrifying dreams that some of the characters in his novels suffered. Greene had a modest beginning as a novelist coming early under the tutelage of Joseph Conrad and John Buchan. He hit his stride with the publication of *The Power and the Glory* and *Brighton Rock* (1938), *The Heart of the Matter* (1948), and *The End of the Affair* (1951), all of which are powerful and masterful and can rightfully be considered great.

The setting of *The Power and the Glory* is a poor totalitarian Mexican state controlled by the Red Shirts. God has been outlawed and priests are public enemies. Most have been killed, but one still lives. As this priest moves from place to place trying to stay one step ahead of his would-be executioners, this man is slowly revealed to the reader.

In *The Power and the Glory*, the protagonist is an unnamed priest who is one of the only characters without a name. He drinks heavily in part to deal with his sense of failure and unworthiness. Greene believed that suffering is an inescapable part of the human condition, and we see this exemplified throughout the novel, both physical and spiritual suffering. Greene's hero, the unnamed "whiskey priest," has lost everything . . . his pride, his dignity, his self-respect, and his material possessions. He is tormented by his spiritual demons of guilt, sin, and fear, and he suffers the physical deprivations of thirst, hunger, illness, and exhaustion. He will soon lose the one thing he still possesses . . . his life. The other characters in the novel also suffer from various maladies and extreme poverty. The Church is blamed for not relieving the people's suffering, but the priest says that suffering will always be in the world. Other themes that are central to the novel are love, pride, and piety. The priest reiterates the love of God and how only God would be willing to die for such pitiable and wretched human beings as he sees. Many in the novel feel pride even when there is nothing left to be proud of. The priest's pride led him to feel superior to and callous of others; he became a drunkard, and finally conceived a child. The pride of the priest has long ago left him and he believes he is the better for it. Finally, he is able to sympathize with others and serve them. His martyrdom will be a victory of sorts.

According to Greene's profligate priest, "'I have been drunk—I don't know how many times; there isn't a duty I haven't neglected; I have been guilty of pride, lack of charity. . .' The words were becoming formal again, meaning nothing."

> "He thought: If I hadn't been so useless, useless.
> . . . The eight hard hopeless years seemed to him
> to be only a caricature of service: a few
> communions, a few confessions, and an endless
> bad example. He thought: If only I had one soul
> to offer, so that I could say: Look what I've done.
> . . . People had died for him: they had deserved
> a saint, and a tinge of bitterness spread across
> his mind for their sake that God hadn't thought
> fit to send them one" (Greene, 275).

The Power and the Glory made Time magazine's ALL TIME 100 books list ranking at number seventy-four. The list included English language novels published anywhere in the world

since 1923. There is a special Fiftieth Anniversary Edition published by Viking in 1990 with an Introduction by John Updike.
You don't need to be a Roman Catholic to appreciate the stark
beauty of Greene's prose and the priest's struggles with his
Christian faith. We have all been there and Greene tells his tale
with all the virtuosity of a master. The martyrdom of the priest
is a compelling testament to the power of the gospel. It is a
book that deserves to be read even as it fast approaches the
century mark.

93. MOBY DICK

By Herman Melville

The question of what is the Great American Novel has been debated over the years and has been the subject of much spilled ink. Is it Twain's *The Adventures of Huckleberry Finn*? Is it *The Great Gatsby* by Fitzgerald? Both are great novels, but for my money, Herman Melville's *Moby Dick* wins the prize. It has an elemental, symbolic force and is infused with biblical and theological archetypes. It is a novel that every Christian should read and be familiar with.

Actually, almost everyone appears to be familiar with *Moby Dick* on some level. They likely have never read the novel, but know that it is a story about an obsessed whaling ship captain chasing after a white sperm whale. My first exposure to *Moby Dick* was through the 1956 movie adaptation directed by the legendary John Huston and starring Gregory Peck as the deranged sea captain. Peck lent a certain dignity to the role. Of course, anytime I see a Gregory Peck movie, it is difficult for me not to see Atticus Finch (*To Kill A Mockingbird*) or a dozen other roles. But I had never read the novel until my adulthood. My, my! I never knew what I was missing!

It apparently was not Melville's intention to write a literary masterpiece. It is likely he intended it to be a cash cow in the romance-adventure genre. Unfortunately for the author (and the publisher), it was not an immediate commercial success and received a mostly lukewarm critical reception. Although lauded by the likes of Nathaniel Hawthorne and Henry Wadsworth Longfellow, sales were slow and the book was reprinted only once in America and once in England during Melville's lifetime. It was only after his death that *Moby Dick* began to attract the attention that it so well deserved.

On the surface, the book is a rollicking adventure story, slow and ponderous in parts, but with a wealth of information about life aboard a whaling ship in particular and on the eighteenth and nineteenth century whaling industry in general. On a deeper level, the book is a complex, multilayered masterpiece blended with biblical allusions and symbolism.

From the very first line of the first chapter of *Moby Dick*, the reader is immersed in a world of biblical allusions and symbolism. Melville might as well have posted a neon sign stating: "Reader Beware! Biblical literacy required." We see this clearly from the first line, "Call me Ishmael," to the final sentence, "It was the devious cruising Rachel, that in her retracing search after her missing children, only found another orphan." Other characters taken from the Bible are Ahab and Elijah as well as the names of two of the ships, *Jeroboam* and *Rachel*.

The figure of the peg-legged Ahab chasing his white whale has taken on an almost mythical quality over the years. Of course, the biblical Ahab was an evil, almost deranged, king of Israel who had a shrew for a wife, Jezebel. However, most of the attention in the book is usually directed to the symbolism of the white whale. In the Bible, the color white is a symbol of purity. Scholars and other interpreters have been divided over the precise meaning of the white whale Moby Dick since the nineteenth century. Some see the whale as evil incarnate mainly because of the earlier encounter between it and Ahab in which the sea captain lost a leg. Others have seen the whale as a symbol of good and purity. It has even been suggested that the white whale is intended to be a symbol for God himself and that Ahab's futile pursuit is not righteous at all, "but natural man's futile attempt in his hatred of God to destroy the omnipotent deity" (R. C. Sproul, 1). In the chapter titled *The Whiteness of the Whale*, the symbolism of whiteness is explored in intricate detail. In that chapter, the narrator explains, "It was the whiteness of the whale that above all things appalled me." Melville employs different terms to describe how whiteness is used in religion, history, and nature giving us one side of the coin: "elusive," "ghastly," or "transcendent horror." But he also shows us the other side of the coin: "sweet," "honorable," and "pure." Melville eloquently describes the mystifying dualism of the symbol,

> "But not yet have we solved the incantation of this whiteness, and learned why it appeals with such power to the soul; and more strange and far more portentous—why, as we have seen, it is at once the most meaningful symbol of spiritual things, nay, the very veil of the Christian's Deity; and yet should be as it is, the intensifying agent in things the most appalling to mankind. It is that by its indefiniteness it shadows forth the heartless voids and immensities of the universe, and thus stabs us from behind with the thought of annihilation, when beholding the white depths of the milky way? Or is it, that as in essence whiteness not so much a colour as the visible absence of colour; and at the same time the concrete of all colours; is it for these reasons that there is such a dumb blankness, full of meaning, in a wide landscape of snows—a colourless, all-colour of atheism from we shrink?"

In the end, *Moby Dick* is unquestionably among the greatest American novels ever written. Rich in allegory and symbolism, it is capable of being understood on different levels: as a rollicking whaling story on the high seas or as a religious allegory. Was Melville indeed correct when he wrote to Nathaniel Hawthorne that he had written an "evil story?" However you view the book, we must admit that it develops conflicts and themes that are timeless and universal. I see in the white whale a powerful symbol of an all-powerful, sovereign, pure, and transcendent God alongside the anger and frustration of a dark, sinful man who cannot comprehend deity. Good and evil, a conflict as old as the Garden of Eden and the fall of Satan. Read it for yourself and see.

94. GILEAD

By Marilynne Robinson

This book, published in 2004, is an astonishing follow-up to Robinson's 1981 debut novel, *Housekeeping*. The subject matter is different, but the beautiful prose is still the same. For fans of Robinson, it was worth the wait. It won the Pulitzer Prize for Fiction in 2005 and has regularly appeared on best book and most influential books since its publication. Former President of the United States Barack Obama regards the book as one of his all-time favorites. On September 14, 2015, President Obama interviewed Marilynne Robinson for *The New York Review of Books*, certainly a first for a sitting president. It is an important book that ought to be read by every Christian.

Gilead is not a novel with a lot of splash and dash. What Robinson gives us is a tender, beautifully written, thoughtful novel with Christian themes that resonate with the reader long after putting the book down. It begins with the title. *Gilead* may seem a strange title for a novel. Most readers will not recognize its significance. Christian readers will likely remember that it was just another place with a strange name like so many others in the Bible. Although Gilead was the name of three people in the Hebrew Bible, Robinson apparently chose the title because of its geographical significance. In the Bible, the name Gilead is often used to refer to all of the region east of the Jordan River, which was occupied by the Israelite tribes Reuben, Gad, and the half-tribe Manasseh. The town's name is referenced by the prophet Jeremiah who laments that there is no balm in Gilead, a land described as a place of war and bloodshed, that would heal the wounds of battle. In Robinson's novel, it is also a small Iowa town in 1956. It is based on the real town of Tabor, Iowa, a town located in the southwest corner of the state noted for its importance in the abolitionist movement. Toward the end of his life, John Ames, a third-generation minister who is in his mid-seventies, begins a letter to his young son, six years of age, giving him an account of his life and that of his forebears. He begins his rambling missive. "If you're a grown man when you read this—it is my intention for this letter that you will read it then—I'll have been gone for a long time. I'll know most of what there is to know about being dead, but I'll probably keep it to myself. That seems to be the way of things" (Robinson, 3).

Gilead is a tiny town that has seen better days, but it is home for Ames and he still loves it. He has preached in the same Congregationalist church for over fifty years and still does. He always preached from notes and has over fifty years of written sermons stored in boxes. Ames tells his son, "Pretty much my whole life's work is in those boxes, which is an amazing thing to reflect on" (Robinson, 18). Ames reveals his heart to his son through his stories about himself and his father and grandfather. It doesn't really read like a novel at all. That was how the book struck me when I read it a few years ago. It struck me as something that might have been written a century ago, from a time long forgotten. That is, I am certain, what Robinson intended and she accomplishes it brilliantly.

Ames and both his father and grandfather entered the clergy. Ames' grandfather was living in Maine when he had a vision of Christ bound in chains which led him to travel west to Kansas in the 1830s to join the abolitionist movement. He rode with John Brown on his abolitionist raids. He encouraged many young men to enlist in the Union cause and even lost an eye while serving as a chaplain for the Union forces during the war. Many of the anecdotes Ames tells are about his grandfather who was apparently a cross between a firebrand and an eccentric. He was a generous man who was always giving money and things away to needy people. Ames talks about growing up in "holy poverty." He speaks of his grandfather as if in awe. He relates that he was able to see better out of his one good eye than other people were able to see out of ten. He describes his grandfather, "He was just afire with old certainties, and he couldn't bear all the patience that was required of him

by the peace and by the aging of his body and by the forgetful-
ness that had settled over everything. He thought we should all
be living at a dead run. I don't say he was wrong. That would
be like contradicting John the Baptist" (Robinson, 32). Robinson based the character of the narrator's grandfather on a real-
life personage named John Todd, who was a Congregationalist
minister and also a conductor on the Underground Railroad.
He also assisted John Brown in his invasion of Missouri in 1857
to free a group of slaves.

Ames' father, unlike his radical grandfather, was influenced by
Quakers and became a Christian pacifist. He grew disillusioned
in his faith and deserted the town. Ames attempts to come to
come to grips with his feelings toward his father. Ames is a
largely sympathetic character who is very much aware of his
own limitations and failures. But he has also learned to embrace himself for who is he...warts and all.

Much of the novel seems to revolve around the Christian concept of forgiveness. Ames' best friend is the Reverend
Boughton, who is the local Presbyterian minister and a lifelong
friend. His son is John Ames Boughton (Jack) who reappears in
Gilead having left in disgrace some twenty years earlier following his shameful seduction and abandonment of a poor family
leaving a daughter who died at the age of three. Apparently, he
returns to the town seeking a balm in Gilead, healing and reconciliation. Although Jack was like a surrogate son to Ames, he
is much disliked by his father's friend. Much of the novel revolves around Ames' struggles to forgive young Jack. He
writes, "This came to my mind because of remembering and
forgiving can be contrary things. No doubt they usually are. It
is not for me to forgive Jack Boughton. Any harm he did to me
personally was indirect, and really very minor. Or say at least
that harm to me was never a primary object in any of the
things he got up to. That one man should lose his child and the
next man should just squander his fatherhood as if it were
nothing—well, that does not mean that the second man has

transgressed against the first. I don't forgive him. I wouldn't know where to begin" (Robinson, 164).

In wrestling with his feelings toward Jack, Ames also ruminates on the teachings of John Calvin. He writes to his young son, "I fell to thinking about the passage in the *Institutes* where it says the image of the Lord in anyone is much more than reason enough to love him, and that the Lord stands waiting to take our enemies' sins upon Himself. So, it is a rejection of the reality of grace to hold our enemy at fault. Those things can only be true. It seems to me people tend to forget that we are to love our enemies, not to satisfy some standard of righteousness, but because God their Father loves them. I have probably preached on that a hundred times" (Robinson, 189).

Gilead has stirred considerable controversy since its publication primarily in two areas. The first is in the area of theology, particularly the theology of John Calvin as it is portrayed in his greatest work, *The Institutes of the Christian Religion*. Robinson has been profoundly influenced by Calvin and she seeks to correct in this book some modern misconceptions regarding the doctrinal system that usually goes by the name Calvinism. Robinson interacts in many places with Calvin's theology, primarily his understanding of predestination. For example, Ames relates the occasion when he is asked his views on that doctrine. Most pastors have been asked to articulate their views in that area. He responds, "Now, that is probably my least favorite topic of conversation in the world. I have spent a great part of my life hearing that doctrine talked up and down, and no one's understanding ever advanced one iota. I've seen grown men, God-fearing men, come to blows over that doctrine. The first thought that came to my mind was, Of course he would bring up predestination" (Robinson, 149-50)! He further explains how he responds to people who ask him about it. "I tell them there are certain attributes our faith assigns to God: omniscience, omnipotence, justice, and grace. We human beings have such a slight acquaintance with power and knowledge, so little conception of justice, and so slight a capacity for grace, that the workings of these great attributes together is a mystery we cannot hope to penetrate" (Robinson, 150). Good answer! The second area of controversy is Christian multiculturalism in literature on which subject the novel has been the focus of debates.

As you read *Gilead*, you will find it saturated with Scripture and theology and some leading Christian writers and hymn writers are mentioned such as John Calvin, Isaac Watts, Jonathan Edwards, and Karl Barth. The Greek Testament is mentioned over and over in a variety of contexts as well as reading the Old Testament in Hebrew. You will meet old friends such as The Parable of the Prodigal Son as Ames works through his own breach between father and son.

This is a beautiful book that never hits the reader over the head with its revelations. Rather it allows the reader to draw conclusions slowly and thoughtfully. Robinson's prose is exquisite and subtle. The book has challenged me to write a similar letter to my own three sons. I challenge you to read the book and allow it to draw you into its magic.

95. THIS PRESENT DARKNESS

By Frank E. Peretti

"For our struggle is not against flesh and blood, but against the rulers, against the authorities, against the powers of this dark world and against the spiritual forces of evil in the heavenly realms" (Ephesians 6:12). The influence of Satan and his demons in this world cannot be denied by anyone who believes in the authority of Scripture. Christians are involved in a spiritual war, a cosmic battle of good versus evil. It is a battle of epic proportions, a life and death struggle over the souls of people that is taking place both in the heavenlies and here on earth. The Bible teaches that "the whole world is under the control of the evil one" (1 John 5:19). Unfortunately, many in the so-called Christian camp do not believe that we are in a battle at all and the reality of Satan and his minions is denied.

This Present Darkness is a book about spiritual warfare. It is not subtle in any way. Reading it is like a slap in the face. The back cover aptly summarizes the plot. "Ashton is just a typical small town. But when a skeptical reporter and a prayerful pastor begin to compare notes, they suddenly find themselves fighting a hideous New Age plot to subjugate the townspeople, and eventually the entire human race." Ashton is a small town in the Pacific Northwest just like a thousand other towns across the U.S. and its protagonists much like a million other people who inhabit these small towns. That *This Present Darkness* gives us is a compelling page turner that doesn't let up until the final page.

This Present Darkness does not rank up there with the great literary works of history such as *Moby Dick* or *The Brothers Karamazov* just as I would not rank Peretti as a novelist as being in the same class as say a Graham Greene or Fyodor Dostoevsky or in the literary stratosphere with Dante and Chaucer. But in a very real sense, Peretti is in a class all his own. He is a *New York Times* best-selling novelist whose books deal with supernatural religious themes and have sold more than fifteen million books worldwide, but that doesn't make him unique. What does make him "one of a kind" is that he basically single-handedly created his own literary genre, the Christian thriller genre. He opened the doors for other Christian writers and, for better or for worse, the *Left Behind* series. However, for Christian readers not looking for a great literary experience and who are willing to separate the wheat from the chaff, *This Present Darkness* can be a fun read.

Frank Peretti was born in Alberta, Canada, but raised in Seattle. He holds ministerial credentials in the Pentecostal Assemblies of God denomination, which is reflected in his fictional portrayals of spiritual warfare and the demonic. He has been called a "sanctified Stephen King." His books have been standard bearers for the Christian Right. You may recall that when *This Present Darkness* was published, the U.S. was experiencing the final years of the Reagan presidency along with his renewed promise for evangelicals. The editor-in-chief of Crossway Books onced quipped that Peretti's books are custom made for the Moral Majority. Although I do not believe that *This Present Darkness* is the greatest book ever written (with the exception of the Bible) as some have gushed, it is still a rollicking good tale that deserves to be read. The Christian singer Amy Grant certainly believes that it is and is a big fan. Even if you don't fit into the Christian Right target audience, it's worth reading this book to find out what all the hoopla was about almost a half century ago.

Some of Peretti's prose really soars. One passage, in particular evoked images in my mind of the time Elisha and his servant were surrounded by the Aramean army. When his servant asked, "Oh, my Lord, what shall we do?" Elisha answered, "Don't be afraid. Those who are with us are more than those with them." (1 Kings 6:15-16). After Elisha prayed for the boy's eyes to be opened, we're told, "Then the Lord opened the servant's eyes and he looked and saw the hills full of horses and chariots of fire all around Elisha" (1 Kings 6:17). Peretti writes, "Waves of spirits still poured down upon the one lone man who stood there in reasonless terror, but suddenly this man was surrounded by four heavenly warriors robed in glorious light, their crystalline wings unfurled like a canopy over their charge, their swords blurring into waving swirling sheets of brilliance" (Peretti, 222). Other passages are more workmanlike, but Peretti lets you know in no uncertain terms where he stands.

This book addresses the modern skepticism towards the existence of angels and demons. More people today, it seems, accept the reality of angels particularly with the popularity of television shows such as *Touched by An* Angel, older movies such as *It's a Wonderful* Life, and the like. But demons are another thing. There is something warm and fuzzy about belief in angels, but people do not want to talk about the other side of the coin. The book deals with this issue head on. For example, one of the characters in the book, Susan, states in a conversation with a dubious Beatrice, "Some things you're just going to have to accept for now. We've talked about God, we've toyed with the idea of angels; now let's try evil spirits, evil spirit entities. To the atheistic scientists, they might appear as extraterrestrials . . . to evolutionists they might claim to be highly evolved beings; to the lonely, they might appear as long-lost relatives speaking from the other side of the grave. Jungian psychologists consider them 'archetypal images' dredged from the collective consciousness of the human race" (Peretti, 314). Susan continued, "It's all a con game: Eastern meditation, witchcraft, divination, Science of Mind, psychic healing, holistic education—oh, the list goes on and on—it's all the same thing, nothing but a ruse to take over people's minds and spirits, even their bodies" (Ibid.)).

Peretti's theology has been criticized as being outside the mainstream of Christianity theology and reflecting a more primitive Pentecostalism. It has also been described as more dualism than theism. There have also been reservations expressed about his stereotypical portrayals of the New Age movement as being more of a straw man than actual reality. Be that as it may, it must be admitted that this novel opened the floodgates for the genre of the Christian thriller. If you read contemporary Christian fiction, *This Present Darkness* is a must read for you.

96. UNCLE TOM'S CABIN

By Harriet Beecher Stowe

If you mention the term "Uncle Tom" to somebody in the United States today, it has an extremely negative connotation particularly among Blacks. What was once a noble character in Harriet Beecher Stowe's famous novel has since degenerated into a pejorative term for a subservient black person, one who is obsequious to white people in the extreme. But that was not always so. When *Uncle Tom's Cabin* was published in 1852, it became an international best seller that sold more than 300,000 copies when it first appeared and Stowe became America's most-celebrated writer. The name, Uncle Tom, was revered then as a heroic figure, a man who never lost his human dignity even under the shadow of the dehumanizing slavery of the antebellum southern United States.

Uncle Tom's Cabin may not have started the American Civil War as legend asserts, but its publication certainly had a galvanizing effect in the North. Previously disinterested Americans could no longer ignore the dirty little issue that made legal a system of chattel slavery that had been sustained for many decades in the South. There are stories of Union soldiers marching off to war with copies of the book in their knapsacks. There is also a story, perhaps apocryphal, that when Abraham Lincoln received Stowe at the White House at the beginning of the Civil War, he declared, "So this is the little lady who started this war." Whatever the truth of this story, there is no doubt that the publication of the novel was influential in turning northern sentiments towards a war to end the institution of slavery. *Uncle Tom's Cabin* became America's first international best-seller and turned the eyes of the world on the country's slavery "problem." Despite the intrusion of a civil war upon the history of the United States and despite the outcome which led to the freeing of slaves, this same country, which was founded on such great ideals, would enact Jim Crow laws barely a dozen years later that made racial segregation legal in the southern United States and in parts of the North. In 1896 the U.S. Supreme Court made "separate but equal" the law of the land. These laws would be enforced until the social upheaval of the Civil Rights movement of the 1960s brought them finally to an end.

That Stowe wrote *Uncle Tom's Cabin* at all is something of an irony. She was a woman who would likely not escape the scrutiny of the modern "Woke" movement that has led to the dismantling of so many monuments to people once thought to be heroes in this country. While not an out and out racist along the lines of say the KKK, she definitely believed in the inferiority of blacks along the lines of Abraham Lincoln. The last time I checked, nobody is clamoring to dismantle the Lincoln Memorial. Stowe, like so many "enlightened" people of her day, believed strongly that slavery was evil, but at the same time did not believe in the true equality of blacks with whites.

Stowe, born in 1832, was the daughter of the prominent Presbyterian minister Lyman Beecher. He was the father of thirteen children of whom Harriet and Henry Ward became the most well-known. Henry Ward Beecher was a noted orator who delivered the first set of lectures at Yale in 1872, called the Lyman Beecher Lectures on Preaching. Harriet's father was a controversial figure in his day who was well-known not only as a pastor, but also as a leading figure in the temperance movement and as the president of Lane Seminary in Cincinnati. His tenure at Lane came at a time when the slavery issue threatened to divide the Presbyterian Church, Ohio, and the nation. In 1834, the seminary hosted debates about slavery that may have led to anti-abolitionist riots in 1836 and 1841. In any event, Harriet's upbringing and education were hardly typical of a girl from that time period. She attended the Hartford Female Seminary and received an excellent education there. It was during her formative years that she began to become interested in the issue of slavery. She was profoundly influenced by the actions of the abolitionists of her day as well as the reports of heinous acts committed against blacks. After she married the Reverend Calvin Stowe and they relocated to Maine, the Fugitive Slave Law was passed in 1850, which she and her husband ignored. Their home became a station on the Underground Railroad.

Uncle Tom's Cabin is a decidedly Christian novel with religious and biblical themes predominating throughout. The book is saturated with Scripture. While the main theme is the evils of slavery, it is equal parts Christian love and responsibility as well as the nature of Christian faith. It is a well-attested fact that many slaveholders were also faithful church members and claimed a vibrant Christian faith. This is one of the many hypocrisies inherent in slavery. As Stowe observes, "But you know humanity comes out in a variety of strange forms now-a-days, and there is no end to the odd things that humane people will say and do" (Stowe, 10). She clearly and compellingly argues that slavery is incompatible with the Christian faith. Stowe's mature understanding of Christian ethics and her evaluation of the inequity inherent in slavery can be seen in the following exchange between Eliza and her husband, George Harris. Eliza, who was a committed Christian and a slave, believed that her husband George should be in subjection to his master. He replied to her, "My master! And who made him my master? That's what I think of—what right has he to me? I'm a man as much as he is. I'm a better man than he is. I know more about business than he does, I am a better manager than he is; I can read better than he can; I can write a better hand—I've learned it in spite of him" (Stowe, 23). Eliza's summation of the situation is, "'Well,' said Eliza, mournfully, 'I've always thought that I must obey my master and mistress, or I couldn't be a Christian'" (Stowe, 25).

We get a feel for the unfairness and inequity of the slave issue through the eyes of George. He is a kind of anti-stereotype possessing qualities that few would believe could be embodied by a black man. After he had brilliantly invented a machine for cleaning hemp, Stowe informs us that "this young man was in the eyes of the law not a man, but a thing, all these superior qualifications were subject to the control of a vulgar, narrow-minded, tyrannical master" (Stowe, 18). Stowe also tells how a slaveowner might react to a slave who might be more intelligent or more articulate than he. "His master began to feel an uneasy consciousness of inferiority. What business had his slave to be marching around the country, inventing machines, and holding up his head among gentlemen? He'd soon put a stop to it. He'd take him back, and put him to hoeing and digging, and see if he's step about so smart" (Ibid.). Thus, George felt that his life held no future under slavery's grip. After he was cheated by his master and then insulted, he admirably restrains his impulse to retaliate.

Some believed, particularly in the South, that Stowe exaggerated the evils of slavery to gain sympathy for blacks. Most, however, believed it was spot on and were shocked. For example, it is well known from historical accounts of slavery that slaves were considered to be less human than the slaveowners. It is unclear just how human slaveowners considered them to be, but they certainly felt that slaves were on a lower level than they themselves were. For example, it was illegal in slave states to teach blacks to read and write. Prejudice was rampant. The attitude of many whites, even from the North, is illustrated by Stowe in these words by Miss Ophelia, St. Clare's cousin from Vermont, who opposes slavery, but personally finds them distasteful. "I've always had a prejudice against Negroes and it's a fact, I could never bear to have that child touch me" (Stowe, 402). Later, in an exchange with St. Clare, she says, "That's you Christians, all over!—you'll get up a society, and get some poor missionary to spend all his days among just such heathen. But let me see one of you that would take one into your house with you, and take the labor of their conversion on yourselves! No; when it comes to that, they are dirty and disagreeable, and it's too much care" (Stowe, 340).

Even slaveowners who considered themselves "Christian," often didn't believe that scriptural teaching pertained to them when dealing with blacks. For example, this is seen clearly in an exchange between Mr. and Mrs. Shelby. Mr. Shelby was the slaveowner who sold Tom to the cruel Mr. Haley to pay his debts. He states, "It's a pity, wife, that you have burdened them with a morality above their condition and prospects." Mrs. Shelby, a devout believer, replies, "It's only the morality of the Bible, Mr. Shelby." To which he replies, "Well, well, Emily, I don't pretend to interfere with your religious notions; only they seem extremely unfitted for people in that condition" (Stowe, 361). Mrs. Shelby then refers to blacks as "helpless creatures" as if they were a bit less than human.

The main character in the story is Tom, a slave who is portrayed as saintly and dignified. He has a vibrant and steadfast Christian faith that affects everyone around him. He saves the life of a little white girl, Eva, while being transported by boat to auction in New Orleans. He and Eva become close friends. She suffered from poor health and on her deathbed, she asked her father to free all of his slaves. He plans to do just that, but is killed intervening in a fight between two men. His widow refuses to honor her husband and Eva's wishes and sells Tom to the evil and brutal Simon Legree.

Legree is the main villain in the story, but he represents the greed and brutality of the institution of slavery itself. Tom is brutally beaten after refusing to whip another slave woman and refusing to divulge the whereabouts of escaped slaves. He was also beaten because he always seemed joyful and sang the "cursed Methodist hymns" that Legree despised. As Tom was again undergoing a cruel whipping, Stowe tells us, "But the blows fell only on the outer man, and not, as before, on the heart. Tom stood perfectly submissive; and yet Legree could not hide from himself that his power over his bond thrall was somehow gone. And, as Tom disappeared in his cabin, and he wheeled his horse suddenly round, there passed through his mind one of those vivid flashes that often send the lightning of conscience across the dark and wicked soul. He understood full well that it was God standing between him and his victim, and he blasphemed him" (Stowe, 259-60). Tom told Legree during a particularly brutal beating after he is told by Legree, "Ain't yer mine, now, body and soul" (509)? Tom replies, "No!, no! no! my soul an't yours, Mas'r! You haven't bought it—ye can't buy it! It's been bought and paid for, by one that is able to keep it—no matter, no matter, you can't harm me" (509).

Legree has two enslaved men, Quimbo and Sambo, who act as his enforcers enticed by the threat of punishment and reward. They habitually beat the other slaves at the behest of Legree. At the end, it is these two men who whip Tom to death. As Tom lies there dying, they express remorse and shame. Tom is certainly depicted here by Stowe as a type of Christ as he forgives the two men before he dies.

It is a well-documented fact that many slave women were sexually abused by their masters. Slave owners often purchased black women for the sole purpose of using them as sexual slaves. An attractive woman was also considered more desirable for buyers. This is illustrated by Stowe by her character, Emmeline, who is a beautiful young slave woman who is also a devout Christian. She is told to curl her hair to make her more attractive. When Simon Legree purchases Emmeline, he tells her that they will have "fine times" together. The sexual innuendo is obvious.

Under slavery a slave faced a future of perpetual degradation and misery. His only hopes were escape or death. This is perfectly described by Stowe's depiction of George. "And so fell George's last hope—nothing before him but a life of toil and drudgery, rendered more bitter by every little smarting vexation and indignity which tyrannical ingenuity could devise" (Stowe, 21). At the heart of the institution of slavery was the fact that blacks were the property of slave-holding whites, and there were no limits to the evils that could be inflicted on the enslaved.

Uncle Tom's Cabin vividly depicts the horrors of slavery and how it affected not only slaveholder and slave, but society in general. Stowe succeeded admirably in her aims, energized the abolitionist movement, and ignited a civil war. This book was of earth-shattering importance. It changed the United States radically for the better. Frederick Douglass was one of its admirers. Stowe also demonstrated graphically how slavery was incompatible with the Christian faith. It is a novel that has been much talked about in the past century or so, but little read these days. Everyone, it seems, knows the title and basically what it is about, but few have taken the time to actually read it. It is a compelling picture of everyday life during a dark period of American history. It deserves to be read by every believer. By the way, just for the record, Uncle Tom is one of my heroes of the faith.

97. WISE BLOOD

By Flannery O'Connor

Flannery O'Connor is widely considered one of America's most gifted writers of the twentieth century. She was often classified as a Southern writer in the mold of William Faulkner, Katherine Anne Porter, and Robert Penn Warren, but her writing refused to be pigeonholed. She was something of a prodigy as a writer and also an unabashed Christian who kept a handwritten prayer journal that was published. She never allowed her success as a writer to affect her relationship with God. Having said that, O'Connor utilized a Southern Gothic style in her writing and her characters were often warped individuals. The Southern regional setting contributes much to *Wise Blood's* atmosphere. It is a profoundly disturbing novel. Glaspey, a perceptive commentator, explains O'Connor's *modus operandi*, "Many will find O'Connor's stories perplexing until they understand what she was trying to do; to shock the reader into a realization of his or her own sinfulness and self-deceit...Will haunt the reader's imagination long after he or she is finished with the book" (Glaspey, 102).

O'Connor was twenty-one years old when she began writing *Wise Blood* shortly after being accepted into the prestigious Iowa Writer's Workshop at the University of Iowa. During the five years it took to complete her first novel, she had her first attack of Lupus, the disease that would eventually kill her at the age of thirty-nine. In 1946 O'Connor began keeping a handwritten prayer journal the same year she began writing *Wise Blood*. She began her journal because she felt she had to. Her father had died in 1941 after being diagnosed with systemic lupus erythematosus and her writing was not going as well as she had hoped. She struggled with feelings of mediocrity in her writing. In her struggles to become a great writer, O'Connor, a devout Roman Catholic, decided to deal with her feelings in prayer much as the ancient psalmists did. As Timothy Keller writes about her feelings in his wonderful book titled *Prayer* (see Chapter VIII), "Therefore, because O'Connor *was* a writer of extraordinary gifts who could have become haughty and self-absorbed, her only hope was in the constant soul reorientation of prayer" (Keller, 11).

O'Connor's stories are filled with unforgettable characters of which *Wise Blood* is no exception. It is, as O'Connor's stories invariably are, set in the rural South and populated by a cast of ignorant and revolting characters with little in the way of redeeming features. It is filled with hypocrites and eccentrics and opportunistic grifters looking for easy prey. You may meet a Bible salesman who steals a customer's wooden leg or a supposedly blind preacher preying on the gullible. *Wise Blood*, if not a classic tale of good and evil, at least has all of the elements. Christianity and redemption are prominent themes in O'Connor's twisted tale of moral decay in our society. Her characters all reflect that creeping decay and the influence of Satan in the world.

The novel's protagonist, Hazel Motes, is a thoroughly deplorable individual, an atheist who founds his own church called a "Church Without Christ." He has been warped by his dreadful experiences in World War II. His name is particularly significant and contributes a religious context to the novel. A mote is a small particle of dust or chaff, or a splinter of wood that might work its way into a person's eye. Jesus used the word (Matt. 7:3-5; Luke 6:41-42) in contrast with "log" or "plank" to rebuke the self-righteous Pharisees who corrected the small faults in others, while ignoring their greater ones. His name certainly fits him as he is quite judgmental about the faults of others while overlooking his own. He is able to see the "mote" in another's eye, while being blind to the glaring faults he has. He reminds me of some Christians I have known.

Wise Blood is a chronicle of the last few months of the sad and tragic life of Hazel Motes. He has just left the army and he is seriously scarred, emotionally and spiritually, from his experiences in the war. We meet Motes on the first page of the novel as a passenger on a train arriving at a town named Taulkinham. He looks like a country bumpkin and is described as having "a stiff broad-brimmed hat on his lap, a hat that an elderly country preacher would wear. His suit was a glaring blue and the price tag was still stapled on the sleeve of it" (O'Connor, 4). He takes a taxi to the address of a woman of low repute, Mrs. Leora Watts. When the driver questions him as to his intent, Motes tells him that he is not a preacher and that, in fact, he doesn't believe in anything. During his first few days in Taulkinham, he meets some peculiar characters. Two of them are the charlatan "blind" street preacher Asa Hawkes and his fifteen-year old daughter Sabbath. These two characters, along with Mrs. Watts, are all desperate people living on the fringes of society.

Motes mirrors some of the characters in Scripture in that he is desperately attempting to run away from God. His companions are thoroughly depraved individuals who inhabit the lowest rungs of human society. When Motes goes to a used car lot looking for a vehicle, he meets a boy, Enoch Emory, a teenage simpleton, who works there and whose language appalls him. "'Jesus on the cross,' the boy said, 'Christ nailed'" (O'Connor, 66). The boy continues his profanity in the background saying "Sweet Jesus, sweet Jesus, sweet Jesus" (O'Connor, 69). Finally, Motes explodes in anger and asks the car dealer in exasperation, "Why don't he shut up? What's he keep talking like that for" (Ibid.)? Veith explains O'Connor's use of profanity. "In the fictional world of the novel, the boy is being profane. And yet, O'Connor's novel is not being profane. She means the terms in their most sacred sense. The boy's profanity ironically reminds Hazel of the reality of Jesus Christ" (Veith, 41). The words of the psalmist no doubt echo in his mind, "Where can I flee from your presence" (Psalm 139:7). As Veith concludes, "The apparent profanity in O'Connor's novel is a brilliant and profound example of irony—the literary technique in which the surface meaning is contradicted by the actual meaning" (Veith, 41). Examples abound of this in classical literature.

Once Motes purchases a vehicle, he begins preaching a gospel of unbelief and attempts to attract people to his Church Without Christ, where miracles do not occur and the dead do not rise. He tries to attract crowds by preaching to the people who are attending the cinema. It is a church without Jesus, but Motes acknowledges "it needs one" (O'Connor, 140). He states his message in his crusade. "Listen you people. I'm going to preach there was no Fall because there was nothing to fall from and no Redemption because there was no Fall and no Judgment because there wasn't the first two. Nothing matters but that Jesus was a liar" (O'Connor, 101). His twisted teachings attract one disciple, Enoch, whose simple mind latches onto these teachings with glee. In some ways, Enoch's life parallels that of Motes.

There are dozens of references to the Christian faith throughout the novel. Themes such as judgment, repentance, hypocrisy, and salvation surface repeatedly. In one instance, after visiting a whorehouse with the boy from the used car lot, O'Connor writes of his conversation with the lad, "He said that what they had just done was a mortal sin, and that should they die unrepentant of it they would suffer eternal punishment and never see God" (O'Connor, 147). Here O'Connor's Catholic faith is evident. She continues demonstrating how conflicted Motes is, "Haze had not enjoyed the whorehouse anywhere near as much as the boy had and he had wasted half his evening. He shouted that there was no such thing as sin or judgment" (Ibid.). It is obvious, at least to me, that he doth protest too much and that his constant judgments of religion and the Christian faith are a thin veneer of his fear of God.

Vision is one of the central motifs in *Wise Blood*. Vision is certainly a religious concept in the broader sense. "Where there is no vision, the people perish" (Proverbs 29:18). However, in this novel the faculty of sight is particularly significant. Consider the name of the protagonist. I have already noted the significance of Motes, but consider the name, Hazel. It is a strange name for a man. However, throughout the novel he is referred to as Haze, which fits him perfectly. Haze lives the final months of his life in a perpetual spiritual haze. He is incapable of seeing the entire truth. His vision is impaired. He has eyes, but he cannot see. Finally, at the very end of the book, in a final act of desperation and futility, he blinds himself. His shortened name, Haze, is a symbol of his warped understanding of truth.

A final example of Motes' bizarre behavior is after he has blinded himself, he wraps barbed wire around his chest and walks around with his shoes lined with glass shards and rocks. This is a futile attempt to do penance to pay for his sin. When asked why he engages in such behavior, he says that he isn't clean and must pay for his sins. The influence of O'Connor's Roman Catholicism can be seen here.

Flannery O'Connor is one of America's treasures and is widely hailed as one of its greatest novelists. *The Guardian*, a British daily newspaper, in 2003 had it at number sixty-two on its list of greatest novels of all time. One warning: Reading *Wise Blood* will not leave you with a warm feeling in your heart. O'Connor's style is boldly idiosyncratic and original and may leave you feeling deeply disturbed at the depths of human behavior. O'Connor's depiction of a world without Jesus Christ is bleak and empty. But our Savior redeems such a world and promises that there is something beyond that evil and emptiness. I like the way that Veith explains O'Connor's method. "O'Connor is painting the picture of human sin in all of its inanity and ugliness. And yet, she always dramatizes in explicit terms the grace of God breaking into the hearts of sinful people and offering redemption" (Veith, 76). This is a novel that will haunt you and unsettle you, rather than soothe you. Read it and see if you agree.

More Theological Gems from Hazel Motes:

> Motes tells her, "I believe in a new kind of Jesus, one that can't waste his blood redeeming people with it; because he's all man and ain't got any

God in him. My church is the Church without Christ" (O'Connor, 119)!

"Your conscience is a trick. It don't exist though you may think it does, and if you think it does, you had best get it out in the open and hunt it down and kill it, because it's no more than your face in the mirror is or your shadow behind you" (O'Connor, 166).

98. SONGS OF INNOCENCE AND OF EXPERIENCE

By William Blake

Is there room in the Christian's library for a book of poetry? Specifically, a timeless book of poems with scriptural underpinnings by an unbelievably talented poet? There certainly is room in my library and here is why. I was introduced to William Blake in my high school English class many years ago back when the earth's crust was cooling. I was totally mesmerized when I first read those unforgettable words of Blake's *The Tyger.*

> "Tyger Tyger, burning bright, In the forest of the night;
> What immortal hand or eye, Could frame thy fearful symmetry?
> In what distant deeps or skies, Burnt the fire of thine eyes?
> On what wings dare he aspire?
> What the hand, dare seize the fire?"

It so set my heart afire that I memorized the entire poem and can still recite it over a half century later. It is said to be the most widely anthologized poem in the English language. It is heartening to know that others hold the poem in such high esteem.

Published in 1794, *Songs of Innocence and of Experience* are Blake at the height of his poetic powers. Although it sold fewer than thirty copies in his lifetime, it is the most visionary and famous of all his works. It was published with his newly invented method of etching, which he called "relief etching," which in turn produced his colored "illuminations." His visual representations of his written work have influenced artists such as the Pre-Raphaelite Brotherhood to the abstract expressionist Jackson Pollock. My personal copy is a beautiful facsimile reproduction that has an edited text on the left-hand page.

It is interesting what other poets thought of him. He was regarded as insane by William Wordsworth and a genius by Samuel Taylor Coleridge. Although Blake may have been mentally unstable, most likely from a form of mental illness, he was far from a madman. His literary influence ranges from a myriad of not only poets, but novelists and songwriters, such as Bob Dylan, John Lennon, James Joyce, T. S. Eliot, Salman Rushdie, Allen Ginsberg, Walt Whitman, and Thomas Harris (*Red Dragon*). He is widely considered the greatest poet in the English language after Shakespeare. Keep in mind that Vincent Van Gogh was not exactly a paragon of metal stability and yet we revere his paintings.

When Blake wrote, his audience was largely Christian and shared Blake's familiarity with Scripture. The imagery that he utilized was quite recognizable to them and resonated with them, but much of it would be quite foreign to many in the twenty-first century. For example, one of his most commonly used images is that of a lamb. For many, a lamb is a cute little creature with white wool. But for Christians, the lamb is symbolic of Jesus Christ. "Look the Lamb of God, who takes away the sin of the world" (John 1:29). The lamb imagery also figures prominently in the book of Revelation, also known as the Apocalypse, written by the apostle John. "Then I saw a Lamb, looking as if it had been slain, standing in the center of the throne, encircled by the four living creatures and the elders" (Revelation 5:6). This is also seen in the very same chapter where the Lamb is capitalized and of whom it is said, "Worthy is the Lamb, who was slain" (Revelation 5:12). The apostle Paul identifies him as the sacrificed Passover lamb (1 Corinthians 5:7). Of course, the lamb was an animal commonly used in the Old Testament in the Jewish sacrificial rites as laid out in the Torah. Blake's words from *The Lamb* may seem childlike, but they are powerful.

"He is called by thy name,
For he calls himself a Lamb:
He is meek & he is mild,
He became a little child."

Another common image that Blake used was that of a child which he saw as a symbol of innocence, gentleness, and purity. Isaiah's prophecy was that "a little child will lead them" (Isaiah 11:6). The child motif suggests simplicity and lack of sophistication. Jesus reinforced this imagery when he said, "I tell you the truth, unless you change and become like little children, you will not enter the kingdom of heaven" (Matthew 18:3). Blake's imagery resonated with those who had been influenced by the moralistic teaching of his day that pictured the baby and child Jesus as a figure with whom children could identify. Children were also seen as vulnerable and in danger of exploitation. Remember, that lambs were reared to be shorn and eventually eaten. Blake's words from *A Cradle Song* take on a new meaning when we begin to understand the child imagery.

"Sweet sleep with soft down.
Weave thy brows an infant crown.
Sweet sleep Angel mild,
Hover o'er my happy child.
Smiles on thee on me on all,
Who became an infant small,
Infant smiles are his own smiles,
Heaven & earth to peace beguiles."

With Blake's poetry, there is more than meets the eye. "Here then is a book that, at first sight, may appear like an eccentric, childlike naively illustrated collection of nursery home-spun verses, but which grows compellingly into one of the great works of the English Romantic imagination" (From *The Introduction* by Richard Holmes, XIV). With Blake, too, there is more to his theology and religious beliefs than is often supposed. He was a Dissenter who refused to accept the established church and it led him down some interesting paths. For example, unlike many of the Puritan tradition, he rejected the Old Testament stereotype of God as an angry and punitive deity. He also did not believe that God was transcendent and his understanding of the fall of Adam and Eve was hardly orthodox as was his view of fallen sexuality.

Why do I recommend the reading of *Songs of Innocence and of Experience*? Out of what are generally regarded as Blake's ten best poems, eight are found here: *The Tyger, The Lamb, The Chimney Sweeper, The Little Boy Lost, A Poison Tree, On Another's Sorrow, The Sick Rose,* and *London*. Blake was one of the most influential poets of his day as well as an artist of some renown. However, most of Blake's greatest champions came long after his death—such as Algernon Swinburne, William Butler Yeats, Kathleen Raine, and Allen Ginsberg. His poems are anything but childlike; they are intellectually powerful, mysterious, and complex. Reading Blake will take you back to your childhood, though, and fill you with wonder and reimagining the presence of angels and why they are here. It is one of the great works of English Romanticism and should not be forgotten. What a difference it makes having eyes of faith in viewing our world!

99. THE WASTE LAND AND OTHER POEMS

By T. S. Eliot

"This is the way the world ends, not with a bang, but a whimper." Thus, concludes T. S. Eliot's famous poem, *The Hollow Men*. Seminal lines such as that and his "April is the cruelest month" from *The Waste Land* have been a permanent part of our collective consciousness ever since he wrote those memorable lines almost 100 years ago. Eliot, widely regarded the finest modern poet, published *The Waste Land*, considered one of the best English poems ever written and the most influential of the twentieth century, in 1922, in his journal *The Criterion*. He was also a committed Christ-follower, who wrote eloquently about faith and its power to transform lives and give meaning to our mortal lives here on earth. His was a formidable intellect who wrote about spiritual themes, but also wrote about the dark side. More than anyone writing in the twentieth century, Eliot's writing pictured the hopelessness of life without God and faith in him. He believed that faith had a mysterious power to transform lives and give meaning to life here on earth. He was a committed Christian who was awarded the Nobel Prize for English in 1948 "for his outstanding, pioneer contribution to present-day poetry."

T. S. Eliot was an American-born poet, playwright, essayist, publisher, editor, and literary critic who moved to England at the age of twenty-five and lived there until his death in 1965. He became a British citizen in 1927 having renounced his United States citizenship. His best-known works were the poems *The Waste Land* and *Four Quartets* as well as his seven plays particularly *Murder in the Cathedral* and *The Cocktail Party*.

Eliot's poetry is complex, multi-layered, and often difficult. The reader seeking facile verse will be disappointed. But for those ready and willing to embrace a challenge, persevering with Eliot will be well worth the effort. Why do I include a work that admittedly is not the most accessible to the average reader? As one commentator writes, "Modern Christians are put off by the apparent strangeness of T. S. Eliot's verse, and thus neglect someone who could be one of their best allies in confronting the modern spiritual 'wasteland' with the truth of Christian orthodoxy" (Veith, 80). Of all of the great English language poets of the twentieth century including Sylvia Plath, Ezra Pound, W. H. Auden, Dylan Thomas, W. B. Yeats, Langston Hughes, Robert Frost, and Maya Angelou, Eliot is the one poet who is a "must read" by Christians. You will be in for one of the most powerful reading experiences possible.

The Waste Land arose out of the ruins and spiritual emptiness of World War I. There was a bitter mood in Europe because the war had destroyed whatever optimism Western civilization was experiencing previously. Eliot perfectly captured this mood and the spiritual emptiness of wretched people without a religious anchor who were living lives of meaninglessness. The existentialist Jean-Paul Sartre, and others like him, did much the same thing after World War II. Of course, Sartre's best-known works *Nothing and Nothingness*, *Nausea*, and *No Exit* captured the same meaninglessness of existence but without the hope that faith in Jesus Christ offers. Eliot is a singularly major poet who was also a Christian who offers that hope.

The Waste Land appears, on the surface, to be disconnected and fragmented. The poem combines two Arthurian legends, the *Holy Grail* and the *Fisher King* with satirical and lyrical depictions of British high and low society. It is divided into five sections. The first, "The Burial of the Dead," begins with the famous words:

"April is the cruellest month, breeding
Lilacs out of the dead land, mixing

Memory and desire, stirring
Dull roots with spring rain."

Thus, Eliot sets the stage for his twin themes of disillusionment
and despair. The second section, "A Game of Chess," introduces
several characters who illustrate those themes in their daily
lives. The third section, "The Fire Sermon," shows the influence
of Augustine of Hippo as well as Eastern religions. Its title
comes from a famous sermon given by Buddha popularly
known as the fire sermon. It is a meditation that deals with mature sexual themes and concludes that lust and rape are the reasons why modern society—all classes, upper, middle, and lower—have degenerated and is suffering from decay. This section
concludes with Augustine's famous prayer that God deliver
him from the fire of lust. It begins with a reference to Carthage
as the cauldron of unholy love and asks that God would save
him from the fire of lust that characterized that city.

"To Carthage then I came
Burning burning burning burning
O Lord Thou pluckest me out
O Lord Thou pluckest
burning" (lines 307-311).

Eliot is himself praying to God for the modern world's deliverance from lust, sin, spiritual decay, and death. This is particularly needed in today's world of sexual and gender confusion.
The fourth section, "Death by Water," is by far the briefest part
of the poem. Apparently, it was intended to be much longer,
but Eliot and his friend, fellow poet Ezra Pound, edited it down
to almost nothing. What is left is the account of a Phoenician
sailor, Phlebas, who has been dead for two weeks from drowning. The spiritual significance of his drowning has been much
debated. Two themes reoccur in *The Waste Land* those of water
and rebirth. Water is considered by Eliot to be spiritually important and is connected with rebirth, a New Testament Chris
tian concept. The fifth section, "What the Thunder Said," gives
the reader an image of judgment. A recurring lament is the lack

of water. In the waste land, little grows because it is a place of drought. Water is need to restore life. The thunder is a sign of coming judgment. Eliot writes,

> "Of thunder of spring over distant mountains
> He who was living is now dead
> We who were living are now dying" (lines 327-329)

There is also a reference to the journey of the two disciples to Emmaus tied in to the decay eastern Europe particularly was experiencing.

> "Who is the third who walks always beside you?
> When I count, there are only you and I together" (lines 360-61).

Finally, another clap of thunder and a flash of lightening come promising rain and ultimately rebirth. This was much needed in the aftermath of World War I. Eliot concludes the poem with three repeated words, "Shantih, shantih, shantih" (line 434). What does this mean? According to the author's notes, it means "the peace which passeth understanding" (Eliot, 54), a clear biblical allusion. For the Christian, these words need no explanation, but this line's inclusion at the end of the poem has provoked endless speculation as to the meaning. But we know, don't we?

The Waste Land deals with many Christian themes; death and rebirth certainly stand at the forefront. There are also cryptic references to Jesus Christ who died to redeem humanity. There are allusions to Augustine of Hippo and Dante's *The Divine Comedy* among many others.

100. FOUR QUARTETS

By T. S. Eliot

The Four Quartets, considered by Eliot himself to be his finest work, is a four-poem collection that expands the author's spiritual vision introduced in *The Waste Land*. The four poems, *Burnt Norton, Easter Coker, The Dry Salvages,* and *Little Gidding,* each title taken from a geographic location Eliot had visited, utilize myriad symbolic allusions and references, both literary and religious, from Western as well as Eastern thought. In this, his most spiritual work, Eliot intricately weaves together spiritual, philosophical, and personal themes to explore time and eternity and "the point of intersection of the timeless with time" and calls it "an occupation for the saint." Reading these poems is profound, almost mystical experience unlike few others. However, some critics, including the writer George Orwell the author of *1984,* were disturbed by Eliot's overt religiosity. However, time and salvation are universal themes.

Burnt Norton, a poem he wrote while working on his most famous play, *Murder in the Cathedral,* focuses on the need for people to live in the present realizing that there is a universal order. Burnt Norton was an abandoned, burnt-out country house in Gloucestershire. It had a formal garden which Eliot had visited in 1934. One of the themes of this and the other three poems in the quartet is related to the apostle Paul's biblical admonition to redeem the time because the days are evil (Ephesians 5:16). He begins this first poem with a clear reference to time.

> "Time present and time past
> Are both perhaps in time future,
> And time future contained in time past.
> If all time is eternally present
> All time is unredeemable." (lines 1-5).

These lines are also a clear echo of Augustine's question from his *Confessions* "What is time?" as well as his discussion of eternity.

There is a long passage in *Burnt Norton* that describes what happens in the garden after being lured there by a bird. Eliot focuses on the present moment while walking through a garden as well as the images and sounds such as the roses, the clouds, an empty pool, and the bird. I believe this is a description of the first human beings in the Garden. This is what I think Eliot means when he mentions "our first world." According to the narrator of *Burnt Norton*, mankind is affected profoundly by original sin and can follow one of two paths in life: either that of good or that of evil. Eliot apparently references Jesus (the *logos* or Word) and his temptation in the wilderness toward the end of the poem.

> "Will not stay still. Shrieking voices
> Scolding, mocking, or merely chattering
> Always assail them. The Word in the desert
> Is most attacked by voices of temptation." (lines 153-156).

East Coker takes its name from the hamlet in Somersetshire, Eliot's ancestral home before they immigrated to America in the seventeenth century. Eliot visited in 1937 and drew his inspiration for the poem, which originally appeared in 1940 in the *New English Weekly*. The tone is bleak and melancholy. You can feel the sadness in Eliot by the opening lines.

> "In my beginning is my end. In succession
> Houses rise and fall, crumble, are extended,
> Are removed, destroyed, restored, or in their place
> Is an open field, or a factory, or a by-pass." (lines 1-4).

When I read those words, it is hard to hold back tears as I recall my boyhood house and town and the changes that have taken place over the decades. My own children have described simi-

lar visits to the house in which they were raised even though it
was sold to new owners many years ago.

Lines 9-13 echo the words of the Preacher in Ecclesiastes 3.

"Houses live and die: there is time for building
And a time for living and for generation
And a time for the wind to break the loosened pane
And to shake the wainscot where the field-mouse trots
And to shake the tattered arras woven with a silent
motto."

There are many more literary allusions such as one to Dante
when he begins to ascend from *Purgatorio* (Eliot, line 48-49),
Milton's *Samson Agonistes* as well as the Apocalypse of John
chapter 6 (Eliot, lines 101-111), and *Ascent of Mount Carmel* by
Saint John of the Cross (Eliot, lines 135-146). In lines 147-171,
the imagery is powerful in that Jesus Christ is the wounded
surgeon (Eliot, line 147), the church the dying nurse (line 153),
and Adam the ruined millionaire (Eliot, line 158). Finally, lines
167-168 are an obvious reference to the sacrament of Holy
Communion.

"The dripping blood our only drink
The bloody flesh our only food."

This is a deeply moving poem that will enrich you spiritually.

The Dry Salvages is a poem that was written and published in
the crucible of adversity. In 1941 the Germans were bombing
England and people were taking refuge in air raid shelters. It
was under those conditions that Eliot penned this metaphoric
poem. The Dry Salvages is a small rock formation, with a bea-
con, off the coast of Cape Ann, Massachusetts, where Eliot visited as a boy. Life is described as a dreamy trip in a boat down
a river, but the travelers never arrive at their destination be
cause of their materialistic concerns about the future. The river
described at the beginning of the poem is the great Mississippi,

which runs alongside of St. Louis where Eliot was raised except for the summers when his family journeyed to the Massachusetts coast. Eliot discusses the nature of time and what our place is in time. The poet asks,

> "Where is the end of them, the fishermen sailing
> Into the wind's tail, where the fog cowers?
> We cannot think of a time that is oceanless
> Or of an ocean not littered with wastage
> Or of a future that is not liable
> Like the past, to have no destination." (lines 67-72).

As you read the poem, you may discover echoes of Psalm 130, the Doxology, Yeat's poem *Three Things*, Mary's prayer of Annunciation, Shelley's *Ode to the West Wind*, Saint Augustine, and even Krishna harkening back to Eliot's studies in Sanskrit and Hinduism at Harvard University. *The Dry Salvages* is a powerful statement against materialism and seeking financial gain.

Little Gidding is the fourth final poem in Eliot's quartet. The title comes from the name of a little English village where an Anglican religious community was founded by Nicholas Farrar in 1625. It lasted until 1647 when it was dispersed by Parliamentarians. It was comprised of a few families who had a dream of living a life devoted to prayer, work, and charity. It is said that King Charles I came there one night after his defeat by Oliver Cromwell in 1645 and prayed in the chapel. In the Anglican and Episcopal religious traditions, the community is still considered to be a model for what the Christian life should be.

The four elements—earth, air, water, and fire—are prominent in *The Four Quartets*. Fire is first seen in this poem and it becomes a major theme throughout to demonstrate the need for purification and purging from sins. Eliot references the fire of tongues that came down at Pentecost as well as the fire of hell and the fire that precedes the end of the world. There is so

much rich imagery in this poem that I cannot mention everything. However, I love the mention of the Holy Spirit (dove) in
connection with the judgement that comes from fire and water.

> "The dove descending breaks the air
> With flame of incandescent terror
> Of which the tongues declare
> The one discharge from sin and error.
> The only hope, or else despair
> Lies in the choice of pyre or pyre—
> To be redeemed from fire by fire." (lines 200-206).

Please do not be put off by the challenge of reading T. S. Eliot.
As Veith writes, "Eliot's verse is sometimes difficult, but few
poets see more deeply into the failures of modern culture, and
few have expressed the orthodox faith in poems of such sophistication" (Veith, 227). You will be richly rewarded. One suggestion: The reader might be helped by *The New Cambridge Companion to T. S. Eliot* edited by Jason Harding (New York: Cambridge University Press, 2017). There are several other excellent
books available. Also, don't miss *Murder in the Cathedral*,
which is a masterpiece of modern theater about the murder of
Thomas a Becket, a twentieth century reinterpretation of
Greek classical style.

Appendix: Other Works Considered

1. *Poems* by W. H. Auden
2. *The City of God* by Augustine
3. *A Diary of Private Prayer* by John Baillie
4. *The Love of God* by Bernard of Clairvaux
5. *Experiencing God* by Henry T. Blackaby and Claude V. King
6. *Letter and Papers from Prison* by Dietrich Bonhoeffer
7. *Diary* by David Brainerd
8. *New Testament History* by F. F. Bruce
9. *Brother to a Dragonfly* by Will Campbell
10. *If* by Amy Carmichael
11. *The Existence and Attributes of God* by Stephen Charnock
12. *Orthodoxy* by G. K. Chesterton
13. *Heretics* by G. K. Chesterton
14. *The Man Who Was Thursday* by G. K. Chesterton
15. *Kingdoms in Conflict* by Charles Colson
16. *Streams in the Desert* by Lettie Cowman
17. *Spurgeon* by Arnold Dallimore
18. *A Pilgrim at Tinker Creek* by Annie Dillard
19. *The Robe* by Lloyd C. Douglas
20. *Joni* by Joni Eareckson with Joe Musser
21. *Treatise on Religious Affections* by Jonathan Edwards
22. *The Life of David Brainerd* by Jonathan Edwards
23. *The Savage My Kinsman* by Elisabeth Elliot
24. *Studies in the Life of Christ* by R. C. Foster
25. *The Knowledge of the Holy* by John M. Frame
26. *Decision Making and the Will of God* by Garry Friesen
27. *The Return of Prayers* by Thomas Goodwin
28. *The Dust of Death* by Os Guiness
29. *The Gravedigger File* by Os Guiness
30. *The Bible and the Future* by Anthony Hoekema
31. *Hind's Feet on High Places* by Hannah Hurnard
32. *The Narnian: The Life and Imagination of C. S. Lewis* by Alan Jacobs
33. *Modern Times* by Paul Johnson

Select Bibliography

Alighieri, Dante. *The Divine Comedy.* Illustrated by Umberto Romano. Graden City, NY: Doubleday, 1947.

Allison, C. FitzSimons. *Trust in an Age of Arrogance.* Eugene, OR: Wipf & Stock, 2010.

Augustine. *The Works of Saint Augustine: A Translation for the 21st Century.* Translation, notes, and introduction by Maria Boulding. Hyde Park, NY: New City Press, 2012.

Bainton, Roland. *Here I Stand: A Life of Martin Luther.* Nashville: Abingdon Press, 1950.

Blake, William. *Songs of Innocence & of Experience.* Facsimile reproduction. London: The Folio Society Ltd., 2006.

Blomberg, Craig L. *Can We Still Believe the Bible?* Grand Rapids: Brazos Press, 2014.

Boice, James Montgomery. *Foundations of the Christian Faith.* Revised in one volume. Downers Grove, IL: InterVarsity Press, 1986.

Bonhoeffer, Dietrich. *The Cost of Discipleship.* Revised edition. New York: Macmillan, 1963.

––––––––. *Life Together.* Translated by John W. Doberstein. New York: Harper & Row, 1954.

Bridges, Jerry. *Respectable Sins: Confronting the Sins We Tolerate.* Colorado Springs: NavPress, 2007.

Bunyan, John. *The Pilgrim's Progress.* Moody Classics. Rosalie DeRosset, General Ed., 2007.

Calvin, John. *Golden Booklet of the True Christian Life.* Translated by Henry J. Van Andel. Grand Rapids: Baker, 1952.

Catherwood, Christopher. *Five Evangelical Leaders.* Wheaton, IL: Harold Shaw Publishers, 1985.

Chambers, Oswald. *My Utmost for His Highest.* Updated edition edited by James Reimann. Grand Rapids: Discovery House, 1992.

Chaucer, Geoffrey. *The Canterbury Tales.* Edited by Walter W. Skeat. New York: The Modern Library, 1929.

Chesterton, G. K. *The Three Apologies of G. K. Chesterton.* Grovetown, GA: Mockingbird Press, 2018.

Coleman, Robert E. *The Master Plan of Evangelism.* Old Tappan, NJ: Fleming H. Revell, 1963.

Collins, Francis C. *The Language of God.* New York: Free Press, 2006.

Colson, Charles W. *Born Again.* Old Tappan, NJ: Fleming H. Revell, 1976.

Dallimore, Arnold A. *George Whitefield.* 2 vols. Westchester, IL: Cornerstone Books, 1970.

Defoe, Daniel. *Robinson Crusoe.* Edited by Michael Shinagel. Norton Critical Edition. 2nd ed. New York: Norton, 1994.

Demarest, Bruce A. "Systematic Theology" in *Evangelical Dictionary of Theology.* Edited by Walter A. Elwell. Grand Rapids: Baker Book House, 1984.

Dostoyevsky, Fydor. *The Brothers Karamazov.* Translated by Constance Garnett. New York: The Modern Library, n.d.

Eliot, T. S. *Four Quartets.* New York: Mariner Books, 1943.

_____. *The Waste Land and Other Poems.* New York: Harvest Books, 1930.

Elliot, Elisabeth. *Through Gates of Splendor.* Carol Stream, IL: Tyndale House, 1956.

Fant, Jr., David J. *A. W. Tozer: A Twentieth Century Prophet.* Harrisburg: Christian Publications, 1964.

Fee, Gordon D., and Douglas Stuart. *How to Read the Bible for All Its Worth.* Fourth edition. Grand Rapids: Zondervan, 2014.

Foster, Richard J. *Celebration of Discipline.* New York: Harper & Row, 1978.

Fox, John. *Fox's Book of Martyrs.* Edited by William Byron Forbush. Grand Rapids: Zondervan, 1926.

Glaspey, Terry W. *Great Books of the Christian Tradition.* Eugene, OR: Harvest House Publishers, 1996.

Graham, Billy. *Just As I Am.* New York: HarperOne, 1997.

Guinness, Os. *The American Hour.* New York: The Free Press, 1993.

Henry, Carl F. H. *The Uneasy Conscience of Modern Fundamentalism.* Grand Rapids: Eerdmans, 1947.

Hillenbrand, Laura. *Unbroken: A World War II Story of Survival, Resilience, and Redemption.* New York: Random House, 2010.

Hoerth, Alfred, and John McRay. *Bible Archaeology.* Grand Rapids: Baker, 2005.

Hogwarts Professor. *Sobering Statistics About Readers Today.* www.hogwartsprofessor.com. Oct. 29, 2019.

Horton, Michael. *Christless Christianity.* Grand Rapids: Baker Books, 2008.

Keller, Timothy. *Prayer: Experiencing Awe and Intimacy with God.* New York: Penguin Books, 2014.

_____. *The Prodigal God.* New York: Dutton, 2008.

Kempis, Thomas à. *Of the Imitation of Christ.* Reprint ed., Grand Rapids: Baker, 1973.

Kennedy, D. James. *Evangelism Explosion.* Wheaton, IL: Tyndale House, 1970.

Kushner, Harold S. *When Bad Things Happen to Good People.* New York: Schoken, 1981.

Lawrence, Brother. *The Practice of the Presence of God.* Edited by Neil Thompson, Orlando: Christian Classic, 2021.

Lennox, John C. *God's Undertaker: Has Science Buried God?* Oxford: Lion, 2007.

Lewis, C. S. *The Complete Chronicles of Narnia.* Reprint ed., New York: HarperCollins, n.d.

_____. *Mere Christianity.* New York: MacMillan, 1943.

_____. *The Screwtape Letters & Screwtape Proposes a Toast.* New York: MacMillan, 1959.

Little, Paul E. *How to Give Away Your Faith.* Downers Grove, IL: Inter-Varsity Press, 1966.

_____. *Know Why You Believe.* Wheaton, IL: Victor Books, 1967.

Lindsell, Harold. *The Battle for the Bible.* Grand Rapids: Zondervan, 1976.

Lloyd-Jones, D. Martyn. *Studies in the Sermon on the Mount.* One-volume edition. Grand Rapids: Eerdmans, 1971.

Luther, Martin. *The Bondage of the Will.* Translated by J. I. Packer and O. R. Johnston. Grand Rapids: Baker Academic, 2012.

MacDonald, Gordon. *Ordering Your Private World.* Expanded edition. Nashville: Oliver Nelson, 1985.

Machen, J. Gresham. *Christianity and Liberalism.* Grand Rapids: Eerdmans, 1923.

Marshall, Michael. *The Restless Heart: The Life and Influence of St. Augustine.* Grand Rapids Eerdmans, 1987.

Marshall, Catherine. *A Man Called Peter.* Lincoln, VA: Chosen Books, 1951.

Marshall, Peter. *The Prayers of Peter Marshall.* Edited by Catherine Marshall. New York: McGraw-Hill, 1949.

McCray, John. *Archaeology & the New Testament.* Grand Rapids: Baker Academic, 1991.

McDowell, Josh. *Evidence that Demands a Verdict.* Colorado Springs: Campus Crusade for Christ, 1972.

Mears, Henrietta. *What the Bible Is All About.* Ventura, CA: Regal Books, 1999.

Melville, Herman. *Moby Dick.* Reprint ed., New York: The Modern Library, 1950.

Meredith, Roderick C. *Biblical Ignorance: A Real Problem!* In "Tomorrow's World." Sept.-Oct. 2006.

Merton, Thomas. *The Seven Storey Mountain.* Orlando: Harcourt, 1948.

Milton, John. *Paradise Lost.* Reprint ed., Oxford: Oxford University Press, 2005.

Morison, Frank. *Who Moved the Stone?* Reprint ed., Grand Rapids: Zondervan, n.d.

Morgan, G. Campbell. *The Crises of the Christ.* Old Tappan, NJ: Fleming H. Revell, 1936.

Morris, Robert H. ed. *Serious Joy: John Wesley's Journal.* Gainesville, GA: Old Paths Publications, 2021.

Murray, Andrew. *Absolute Surrender.* Reprint ed., Chicago: Moody Books, n.d.

_____. *With Christ in the School of Prayer.* Reprinted., New Kensington, PA: Whitaker House, 1981.

Newton, John. *Out of the Depths.* Reprint ed., New Canaan, CT: Keats Publishing, 1981.

Noll, Mark A. *The Scandal of the American Mind.* Grand Rapids: Eerdmans, 2022.

Nouwen, Heri J. M. *The Way of the Heart*. New York: Ballentine Books, 1981.

O'Connor, Flannery. *Wise Blood*. New York: Farrar, Straus, and Giroux, 1949.

Packer, J. I. *Knowing God*. Downers Grove, IL: InterVarsity Press, 1973.

Petersen, William J., and Randy Petersen. *100 Christian Books That Changed the Century*. Grand Rapids, MI: Fleming H. Revell, 2000.

Peterson, Eugene H. *A Long Obedience in the Same Direction*. Revised and expanded edition. Downers Grove, IL: IVP Books, 2000.

_____. *Praying with the Psalms*. New York: HarperOne, 1993.

Phillips, J. B. *Your God Is Too Small*. New York: MacMillan, 1961.

Pierson, A. T. *George Müller of Bristol: His Life of Prayer and Faith*. Old Tappan, NJ: Fleming H. Revell, 1899.

Rhodes, Ron. *The Challenge of the Cults and New Religions*. Grand Rapids: Zondervan, 2001.

Robinson, Marilynne. *Gilead*. New York: Farrar, Straus and Giroux, 2004.

Schaeffer, Francis A. *A Christian Manifesto*. Westchester, IL: Crossway Books, 1981.

_____. *The Great Evangelical Disaster*. Westchester, IL: Crossway Books, 1984.

_____. *True Spirituality*. Wheaton, IL: Tyndale House, Publishers, 1971.

Shelly, Bruce L. *Church History in Plain Language*. Fourth edition. Grand Rapids: Zondervan Academic, 2008.

Solzhenitsyn, Aleksandr. *The Gulag Archipelago, Volume 1*. Translated by Thomas P. Whitney. New York: Harper Perennial Modern Classics, 1976.

Sproul. R. C. *Chosen By God.* Wheaton, IL: Tyndale House Publishers, 1986.

_____. *Everyone's a Theologian: An Introduction to Systematic Theology.* Sanford, FL: Ligonier Ministries, 2014.

_____. *The Holiness of God.* Wheaton, IL: Tyndale House Publishers, 1985.

_____. *The Unholy Pursuit of God in Moby Dick.* Ligonier Ministries. https://www.ligonier.org. Aug. 1, 2011.

Stott, John R. W. *Basic Christianity.* Second edition. Downers Grove: IL: Inter-Varsity Press, 1971.

_____. *Involvement: Being a Responsible Christian in a Non-Christian Society.* Old Tappan, NJ: Fleming H. Revell, 1984.

_____. *Involvement: Social and Sexual Relationships in the Modern World.* Old Tappan, NJ: Fleming H. Revell, 1984.

Stowe, Harriett Beecher. *Uncle Tom's Cabin.* Reprint ed., New York: Doff, Mead, & Company, 1952.

Strobel, Lee. *The Case for Christ.* Grand Rapids: Zondervan, 1998.

Taylor, Dr. and Mrs. *Hudson Taylor's Spiritual Secret.* Chicago: Moody Classics, 2009.

Ten Boom, Corrie, with John and Elizabeth Sherrill. *The Hiding Place.* Old Tappan, NJ: Fleming H. Revell, 1971.

Thompson, J. A. *The Bible and Archaeology.* Grand Rapids: Eerdmans, 1972.

Tolkien, J. R. R. *The Hobbit.* Revised edition. New York: Random House, 1982.

_____. *The Lord of the Rings.* Reprint boxed ed., New York: Clarion Books, 2020.

_____. *The Lord of the Rings.* 50th Year Anniversary edition. Boston: Mariner Books, 2005.

Tozer, A. W. *The Knowledge of the Holy.* Lincoln, NB: Back to the Bible Broadcast, 1961.

Veith Jr., Gene Edward. *Reading Between the Lines.* Wheaton, IL: Crossway, 1980.

Warren, Rick. *The Purpose Driven Life.* Grand Rapids: Zondervan, 2002.

Webezahl, Robert. "Dante." *Book Page.* Jan. 2022.

White, John. *The Golden Cow: Materialism in the Twentieth Century Church*. Downers Grove, IL: Inter-Varsity Press, 1979.

Whyte, Alexander. *Bible Characters*. One-volume reprint ed., Grand Rapids: Zondervan, 1967.

_____. *Lord, Teach Us to Pray*. Reprint ed., Grand Rapids: Baker, 1976.

Wiersbe, Warren W. *Walking with the Giants*. Grand Rapids: Baker Book House, 1976.

_____. *Why Us? When Bad Things Happen to God's People*. Old Tappan, NJ: Fleming H. Revell, 1984.

Willard, Dallas. *The Spirit of the Disciplines*. New York: HarperOne, 1988.

Wood, Leon. *A Survey of Israel's History*. Grand Rapids: Zondervan, 1970.

Yost, Robert A. *The Layperson's Library: Essential Bible Study Tools for the Man and Woman in the Pew*. Eugene, OR: Wipf & Stock, 2021.

Also Available from
College&Clayton Press

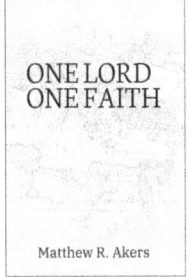

In *One Lord One Faith: Lessons on Racial Reconciliation from the New Testament Church*, Matthew Akers explores the deep racial divides that threatened the early church. Believers, who learned how to celebrate their unity by applying Christ's teachings to their lives, ultimately tore down the ethnocultural barriers that separated them. Their oneness astounded a world that had never seen this level of reconciliation. As a result of their commitment to love God and to love others, the Holy Spirit blessed their faithfulness, which convinced many that Jesus is Lord. The purpose of this book is to help twenty-first century American churches implement in their congregations the first century church's approach to racial reconciliation.

In *Bethlehem's Redeemer: Seeing Jesus in Ruth*, Daniel J. Palmer creates a Bible study for small groups or individual study that emphasizes the Messianic and salvific content contained in Ruth. Within the introduction, Daniel offers a practical, theologically-minded hermeneutic for his readers to trace and emulate his method as he deploys it through the text of Ruth.

The Great Commission is both a climactic promise and triumphant command of the victorious King to His subjects. As such, it is a mandate to follow for all churches as well as all individual Christians. However, the Great Commission is not a standalone proof text or isolated command. It is rooted within a grand biblical narrative that extends from its beginnings in Eden to its consummation in the New Heavens and New Earth. In *The King's Command*, Josh Howard explores the all-encompassing scope of the Great Commission and it's claim on our lives as Christians.

In *Worship of the Triune God: Finding Delight in a Life of Worship*, Nathan Skipper sets out to show that the whole of the Christian life is an act of worship. Skipper does this by exploring the major themes of systematic theology through a doxological lens, rooting our understanding of God, salvation, the church, and the age to come in this chief end—"to glorify God and enjoy him forever." Skipper's project finds its core in the Book of Ephesians, which is itself a letter of high praise to the Lord. The reader is left understanding that Christian worship is more than just a weekly act. Worship is the reason for which we exist and the only way to find true purpose and delight.

www.ingramcontent.com/pod-product-compliance
Lightning Source LLC
Chambersburg PA
CBHW061130120626
46546CB00005B/1723